CHINA RACE

John Dyson

CHINA RACE

C

CENTURY PUBLISHING
LONDON

Copyright © John Dyson 1984

All rights reserved

First published in Great Britain in 1984 by
Century Publishing Co. Ltd,
Portland House, 12–13 Greek Street,
London W1V 5LE

ISBN 0 7126 0304 2

Photoset by Rowland Phototypesetting Ltd
Bury St Edmunds, Suffolk
Printed in Great Britain by
St Edmundsbury Press, Bury St Edmunds, Suffolk

'Happy he who, like Ulysses, has made an adventurous voyage.'

Joseph Conrad
The Mirror of the Sea

For
Captain William Boyd
and all his descendants,
especially my Mother

CONTENTS

PROLOGUE:

Biscay

A CRACK SHIP in her day, the barque *Matilda* sailed from London on the first of March in 1834, carrying migrants for Sydney, New South Wales.

Among the passengers crowded below deck was a handsome young couple from Kent. Henry Ardent, a Medway shipwright intent on becoming his own master, had contrived to obtain for himself and his pretty wife one of the first assisted passages offered to attract skilled men half way round the world to a burgeoning colony only recently relieved of its status as a penal settlement.

Buffeted by strong head winds, the barque beat down the Channel. At once Mary Ardent was prostrated by violent and hysterical seasickness. Soon, weeks earlier than anticipated, her labour pains started. As the ship fought to weather The Lizard, a headland jutting out from Cornwall, the cries of a newborn child joined the moans of fear and wretchedness in the creaking, lurching cabins.

Later, rolling south in the trades, the young parents requested Captain Samuel Handyside to exercise his prerogative as Master under God and christen the infant. Beneath the hot sky a hymn was sung and a cup of sea-water blessed. The stout shipmaster took the baby in his arms and with a stubby thumb made a moist cross on the little forehead.

Then, in a lusty voice that swept the deck like a burst of spray, the captain proclaimed.

'My boy, I name you Henry Matilda Handyside Ardent. God bless you, and the ships you sail in. Trust in Him and mind your course. Amen.'

ONE:

Gravesend   1,460 *miles*

SEWN UP IN canvas and weighted with lumps of galley coal, the captain's body slid reluctantly from the tipped plank. Henry Ardent listened for the piddling splash then muttered 'Amen' and closed the prayer-book.

'Sail-l-l ho-o-o!'

The astonished cry ripped like a lightning bolt among the doleful men clustered at the lee bulwarks. Henry took the poop ladder at a bound, his fingers hardly touching the shiny handrails. So slowly was the *Partridge* ghosting in the balmy air that ripples of the splash still lapped the rudder. A thin stream of bubbles rising from air trapped in the dead shipmaster's clothing marked where the white bundle spiralled into the blue veils of oblivion.

The sun flamed on the young second mate's head and shoulders as he levelled the heavy glass. Charlie Meadows, who had spotted the distant white pyramid of sail over the port bow, scrambled into the rigging for a better look and stretched out an arm to show where it lay. In the vapoury blue Henry distinguished three raked masts and six tiers of snowy canvas.

'What do you make of her?' Henry asked.

Charlie Field's only concession to the blazing tropics had been to reverse his tarred sou'wester hat so that the long part of the brim shaded his face. Mindlessly shifting from one bare foot to the other on planks so hot that pitch oozed from the seams, he screwed up his eyes and stared at the distant ship. 'Some Yankee flyer, judging by the colour of her muslin.'

Henry agreed. Only canvas manufactured from American cotton could be so dazzlingly white. In October 1852 the sight of a Yankee clipper ship at this longitude in the middle of the Atlantic, and evidently bound for a British or European port, was sufficiently unusual to cause a stir of excitement. 'Put your helm down,' Henry told the man at the wheel. Then he moved to the poop rail from which he could see the length of the deck. 'Square the yards round and trim her full, Mr Meadows.'

Hopping on the scorched deck, the men moved reluctantly out of the bands of shade into which they had retreated. Listlessly they swung the yards and heavy sails to catch what remained of the fading breeze. Henry watched them at work, his anxiety mounting. It was easy for a mate to know when his men put their backs into a job. Or when, as in this ship, the men merely picked up the tail of the rope and leant on it.

Charlie Meadows swaggered aft, his thumbs in his belt. He had the curly black hair and swarthy complexion of a tinker, and the headstrong independence. As if to compound the image he wore a black waistcoat over a white collarless shirt that was less than dazzling. 'I s'pose yer askin' the Yankee for a pluck to London,' he jeered.

Henry glanced aloft at sails carrying barely enough wind to shape them into curves. 'We might catch her, if this puff holds.'

Meadows and Field exchanged amused glances behind his back. Both were Londoners and they had voyaged together for years. To the other men before the mast they were Oats and Barley, the farmers, and Field looked like one. He was a big and raw-boned man of prodigious strength and little beauty. His chunky features might have been whittled with a blunt knife. His few clothes, as Meadows was fond of pointing out, looked as if they had been thrown at him as he passed a slop-chest and had stuck on by accident.

Meadows was as talkative as his friend was silently stalwart, as lively and roguish as Field was strong and impassive. Now his scathing glance swept the worried young mate as he studied the other ship. 'Why don't yer ask 'im the way ter Charing Cross? I just fancy a touch o' fumble an' grunt dahn Lime'ouse.'

'You can fumble and grunt all you like on the end of an oar,' Henry told him. 'Swing out the gig and I want six strong pullers.'

For twenty-nine soul wracking days Henry Ardent, who had joined the ship in Sydney as a lowly second mate, had been in sole charge of the *Partridge*. His promotion was owed to a single man-killing wave that had crashed over the bulwarks as the ship slogged round Cape Horn. Henry had been below, lashing a line round his oilskin coat before struggling out into the screaming wind, when the ship staggered under the weight of a great blow. The wave had swept over the stern quarter, tumbled high across the poop, and avalanched the length of the maindeck. When Henry scrambled wide-eyed into the darkness he saw that the helmsman had vanished along with the chief mate. The wheel was a splintered wreck. The lee bulwarks had carried away. Hatchboards were displaced. And in the frantic race to effect repairs before another giant wave finished the job it was two hours before Captain John Plunkett was discovered, crumpled unconscious beneath the cast-iron machinery of the pumps where the rushing water had wedged him. It had taken him these many long days to die.

Finding himself acting master of a disabled ship, Henry Ardent had reacted instinctively. There had been little time to glory in his unexpected fate, or to worry about it. Although a greenhorn mate, he had spent an entire childhood crawling over the ships under repair in his father's boatyard on Cockatoo Island in Sydney Harbour and was not short on resourcefulness. In the space of a few minutes he had had an oar sawn in half and the two pieces lashed in the form of a cross over the remnants of the splintered wheel so the wildly plunging runaway ship could be dragged off the wind and brought under control. Then he had promoted Meadows and Field to act as his mates, for they were by far the most skilled seamen on board. In the bitter southern winter while the ship's survival hung by the thread of men's determination to put their backs into their work, the arrangement had worked well. Each man, in charge of a watch, was a tower of strength. But as the *Partridge* snored into a spring time of jousty tradewinds, and the grey-faced captain lapsed into increasingly prolonged periods of coma, things had changed.

Instead of backing up the authority of the inexperienced mate thrown unexpectedly into command, Meadows and Field took every opportunity to bate him. With the ship limping into the doldrums straddling the equator their mischief flowered into malice. At first Henry took it on the chin. It did the men good to laugh, he reasoned, and if he was really cut out to be Master before God of a British ship and her crew of sixteen 'Pommies' then he surely ought to be man enough to take the heat. But this was his undoing. The taunts and jeers became open. The hands became idle and slapdash. They had no confidence in him, and showed it, and Henry was losing confidence in himself. Now, with Captain Plunkett's body sinking slowly into the deep, Henry detected a new and dangerous edge in the nudges and sniggers behind his back.

Such friction was bound to come to a head now that the captain was gone but it was by no means the worst of Henry's worries. In the 120 days since the ship had sailed from Sydney and the dim profile of Barrenjoey Head had dropped from sight, there had been no reassuring glimpse of land. Though schooled in navigation Henry lacked experience. He had shot the angle of the sun when the weather permitted, and calculated the ship's latitude and longitude. The steady procession of pencilled crosses tracking northwards up the chart confirmed that his mathematics were at least consistent. But it was difficult for a lonely and untried shipmaster, bereft of advice, to have confidence in mere sums. Sometimes Henry would pace the deck, the loneliness of his situation a heavy weight on his shoulders, wondering if land really did exist. But now there was another ship in sight, first proof since the accident that he had not been condemned to voyage on for ever. Henry was excited, relieved, and anxious. If he could only come up with her the captain would give him a fix and end the navigational uncertainty that plagued him. Besides, there was an even chance of obtaining some fresh eggs.

Henry thrust the telescope into the waistband of his trousers and climbed to the foretop where he held the far ship in the glass. She was hull-up now, a slender black ship rolling in a field of heaving glass. The proud arch of her bow, sharp as a pike, proclaimed her to be a crack clipper – London-bound with her holds stuffed with China tea, Henry suspected.

Then his eye caught a second ship, becalmed as the Yankee was but a couple of miles ahead. Henry made out a chequerboard pattern of black squares painted to resemble gunports in a broad white stripe running the length of her stocky black hull. She'd be a Blackwall frigate, he thought, homeward bound from India or perhaps – like himself – from Australia.

As a boy who had hung on the lips of sailormen jawing the idle hours away while their ships were in port, Henry knew of the uncanny way in which calm conditions drew ships together. For so many days he had voyaged in lonely oceans, sighting not a scrap of sail. Suddenly, ten days out from the English Channel, he was becalmed in the middle of the Atlantic Ocean with two other ships in sight.

The gig was not yet hoisted. Henry made a trumpet with his hands and shouted, wishing he sounded more like a bull and less like a calf. 'Put some gunpowder in your pudding house,

Oatsy!' Then, as Meadows glowered at him with hands on hips, he added, 'You won't get to Charing Cross by sitting on it!'

Carrying her wind, the three-masted ship glided up on the clipper until, at hardly a mile, the wind deserted her and she was left rocking on her own reflection. Every block rattled, every rope slatted. The weather-faded sails, dark with patches and stains, shivered and flopped with shocks that sent vibrations jarring through every timber. Henry slid down a rope to the deck as the gig splashed into the water.

'Stay on board and take charge, Mr Meadows,' he ordered. The gleam in the Cockney's eye made him suspicious. Henry didn't want his ship sailing away without him. 'I want Mr Field to come with me in the boat,' he added.

Henry's tiny cabin which opened off the dim saloon had a bunk with drawers beneath, a settee just wide enough for a man to perch while pulling on his boots, and a fold-out flap for a water basin; above the wash-stand was a freckled mirror and beside it a brass lantern on gimbals.

Henry dragged a comb through his sun-bleached mop. Sticky with salt, it flopped over his eyes in front and made a turkey tail at the back where he had cut it short with a knife. He smoothed the wrinkles of his trousers with the flat of his hand and slapped uselessly at the ripple marks of salt that stained them after countless wettings. There was one fairly clean shirt in his drawer but when he spread it out he saw green mildew in the creases and a tear in one sleeve. He slit away both sleeves with his jack-knife then put it on.

The captain's cabin was as fusty as a sepulchre with the tarpaulin nailed over the stern windows to keep it dark. The smell of the dead man's sweat lingered. As Henry entered he was momentarily surprised that Captain Plunkett was not snoring softly between the grey sheets, as he had been for so many difficult days. Only that morning Henry had bathed his forehead. Now he took the cloth he had used from the tin basin, squeezed out the water, and made an ineffectual attempt at wiping the green mould from his sleeveless shirt. It did not help much. On impulse he knotted a faded red neckerchief at his throat, glanced at the chart to remind himself of the ship's position and climbed blinking into the sunshine.

The change in perspective as he slipped down a rope into the stern of the gig was startling. With his eyes hardly four feet above their sunslicked surface the ocean swells looked like trundling hills. 'Push off, out oars!' he ordered, fitting the rudder in its pintles and shipping the tiller.

To be outside the prison of the bulwarks, rowing away from the ship, was like a holiday. The six men pulled cheerfully. Charlie Field sat in the bow, his tarred sou'wester like a sinister bonnet.

The Yankee ship looked magnificent as she rose and fell on the swell, despite the lifeless droop and baffle of her dazzling canvas. Here was a ship to grapple with every element but fire. Everything about her – from the tip of her towering masts to the golden shine of her copper-sheathed underbody – evoked an impression of power and speed.

The black topsides, smooth and matt as velvet, showed off the beauty of her lines. A slender crimson stripe followed the elegant curve of her plank-sheer to a figurehead in the form of a golden hunting bird. Its wings, splayed in the hollows of the concave bow, were tipped with matching crimson. The masts, spars and thrusting bowsprit gleamed like shafts of amber.

Men were visible aboard her now. At least half a dozen figures were bunched at the end of the mainyard. What could they be doing? Over the heaving water Henry heard the crack of a gunshot followed by a sound of frenzied barking.

As the gig approached another noise was heard. The men bent over the yard which overhung the sea were singing out in a frightened way. At first Henry could not understand what they were chanting, then it came more clearly.

'Crow, you jungle monkeys, crow!' a voice cried. There was another gunshot. The men aloft chorused, 'Cock-a-doodle-doo!'

The gig lost way in a jumble of oars as the men looked over their shoulders. 'Christ!' said Charlie Field, 'That's Screech Gander, ain't it? Just our bleedin' luck.'

Henry was mystified. 'What do you mean?'

'If you ain't 'eard of Screech Gander you'll know soon enuff,' Field told him unhelpfully.

'He's a Blue Nose bucko – scalp yer for nothing,' a man grunted.

Among the gold scroll-work embellishing the bow Henry read the ship's name: *Musket*. So it was not a golden eagle that adorned her bow but a sparrowhawk, or musket. And she would fly like one, he suspected.

A sailor at the rail raised an arm and caught the painter. The port-side men boated oars then fended off as the black hull lurched towards them. The clipper rolled heavily with such high top-hamper, and the gear aloft made a constant clatter. Henry found a foothold on the channels as they dipped, reached higher for a grip on the lanyards, and hoisted himself up.

The dog sprang just as he was on the point of vaulting the rail. Henry jerked back from a blur of gnashing fangs and flying spit and nearly fell as he snatched his hands from the rail. Hanging outboard from the chainplates he saw the big brute was as grey as a rat, almost liver coloured, with tight curly hair, his eyes as yellow as brass. Lifting front paws to the rail, he snarled like a volcano and curled his lips. Henry gagged in the wave of meat-rot odour that gusted over him. 'Mind the dog, Cap'n,' Field said from the boat.

Aft, Henry saw a tall and imposing figure watching. 'Call in your hound!' Henry yelled.

'You coming aboard or something?' the man called, descending from the raised poop and strolling forward. Evidently he was the dreaded Captain Screech Gander.

'Thanks for the invitation,' Henry gasped.

'We don't sell no limejuice, pal. Better go to Liverpool.'

Henry edged his head above the level of the rail and the dog renewed its snarling. A shrill whistle cut the air. Quivering, the dog sank to the deck. Henry warily swung inboard, taking care to make no sudden movement, and lowered himself to the deck.

Shipmasters of the day were inclined to turn out in many a strange rig but Gander's was the oddest of all. His rangy and long-limbed frame with broad square shoulders filled a buckskin jacket stitched with sinew and decorated with tassles. His trousers were tucked into high leather boots. A revolver in a holster was slung low on one hip, a large skinning knife in a sheath on the other.

Henry made a conscious effort not to shrink from a formidable stare. The eyes, tawny and speckled with amber spots like bubbles in a glass of ale, were as deep as the Atlantic beneath his feet. And, like the ocean, they were calm for the moment but capable of violent furies. Bushy sideburns jutted along the line of the man's tight jaw, the tips curling upward like fish hooks. The hair, brown as bark, was drawn loosely to the back of his head and tied with whipping line. Gander stood well over six feet, taller than Henry and six or seven years older. He chewed on a match as he gazed incuriously at his visitor.

'The name's Henry Ardent, *Partridge* out of Sydney for London.'

'Is that so?'

'How long has it been calm around here?'

The rakish captain spat. Little splinters of wood tumbled in the air, floating down on the dog's shiny coat, and a gob landed at Henry's feet as if to remind him where he was. 'Can't say — haven't been around long enough to find out.'

Determined to crack the daunting stare, Henry said, 'I don't like your dog, I'd shoot him before he killed somebody.'

At the snap of Gander's fingers the dog crawled forward, smelling Henry's boots. He lurched to his feet and walked round him, thrusting his muzzle between Henry's legs and growling. 'Don't move a goddam inch,' Gander warned.

Henry's blood turned to ice and his heart made great slow thumps as if it would bound out of his chest. He concentrated on holding the Yankee Captain's dangerous and mocking eyes. The watching men — even the ship herself — seemed to hold their breaths.

Then something warm and wet sprayed his leg. Henry looked down and saw the dog pissing a yellowy-green jet on his trousers. He jumped away with an oath. The dog rounded on him instantly, snarling. Henry backed up to the rail. Gander doubled up with a guffaw. The crew laughed too, cautiously as if the joke might turn against them.

Henry knew enough about man-hunting dogs in New South Wales to avoid the creature's yellow eyes. And he knew, too, that every dog has its master. He took a deep breath, held it to make his face red while saying a quick mental prayer, then flung his arm out in the direction of Gander and bellowed with all his might, 'Siddown, shuddup, goddammit!'

The beast cringed. Henry followed up the initiative, stamping hard on the deck and roaring again. The dog slunk to Screech Gander's feet and flopped down, his dignity ruffled.

The laughter withered. Henry ran his fingers nervously through his hair and said calmly, 'If this floater were a ship instead of a convention of mountain men I'd ask the favour of a position.'

The dog started forward at sight of Charlie Field's head appearing at the rail but Henry stamped again, growling, 'Get on back, goddam!'

'Well I'm jiggered!' Gander was thunderstruck. 'Don't you know you could have been chewed to dishcloths?'

Henry thrust his hands into his pockets to show he was not impressed. 'If that mongrel moves one inch, I'll piss on it.'

Now the men shook with real laughter. Screech Gander shifted from one foot to the other, put a new match in the corner of his mouth, and asked, 'You want coffee?'

'Yes, and a bucket of water.' Gander made a slight movement of one hand. In a moment a bucket brimming with sea water was set at Henry's feet. He splashed the wet stain on his trousers. A grey-haired negro handed him a china mug of coffee. Not the boiled wood, painted, that passed for coffee in the *Partridge*, but real percolated coffee sweetened with molasses.

'More of your warmed-over bilge-water, Doc?' Gander asked as he took the second mug.

The old cook's eyes twinkled but he kept a straight face. 'Pumped it up m'self and spat in it, Captain, none better.'

Gander sipped and grimaced. 'The usual rat's piss,' he said. The cook went away, beaming. Gander nudged the dog with the tip of his boot and growled, 'In your bed, 'Gale.' Trailing a sticky paste of saliva, the dog crawled into the shade. 'What's your cargo?' he asked.

Henry noticed the captain's eyes were never still. Constantly they searched the horizon for shadows indicating cat's paw breezes. 'Wool, and copper in bags for ballast,' Henry told him as they ambled aft. 'You have a fine ship.'

'None better, none faster: eighty-six days out of Canton and sitting right here for two of 'em.' Gander led up the short ladder to the raised poop. 'Tell your captain, twenty-six degrees west and forty-two north, if you can remember.'

Henry was so relieved that his own calculations differed by hardly a degree, that he missed the opportunity to correct Gander's misapprehension. Sipping his coffee, he admired the sweeping sheer of the maindeck with its bone-white planks and brightly painted bulwarks. After the stumpy proportions of the *Partridge* the clipper seemed as long and slender as an arrow. But the magnificence of the Yankee clipper held an echo of horror, also. What thousands of aching man-hours at the holystones had achieved such a bleached satin finish? What hundreds of hours rubbing brass to bring up that lustrous golden sparkle of every metal fitting, from the speaking trumpet by the binnacle to the elegant caps of the knightheads in the bow? The deckhouse windows twinkled like crystal. Even the hog pen, its large pink incumbent snuffling, was as clean as a chapel.

The men, a typically mixed lot of twenty-six 'scandawegians', dutchies, negroes and pommies, had a hunted look about them. They did not glance aft except in a furtive way. None paused to ease an aching muscle without casting a quick look round to ensure he was far from the captain's tigerish eye. Their shoulders, arms and torsos bore ugly wounds, like bleeding or scabby bruises, the cause of which was a mystery. Henry looked at the *Partridge* dipping to the swells a mile off. The tubby merchantman might be bedraggled after her long fight around the Horn, and her company restless, but there was nothing like the smell of cruelty and fear that permeated the exquisite *Musket*.

Screech Gander went directly to the binnacle. The helmsman stiffened nervously as the captain checked the course, though the ship was not moving. Henry was wondering if he dared to ask for a couple of eggs when excited shouts and yells came from the fo'c's'le head. A grey blur like a cannon ball at knee height streaked along the deck. The dog crashed into a burly seaman who was carefully touching up the black paint on the pump near the mainmast. Man and paint-pot went flying.

Gander flicked the dregs of his coffee over the side. 'Smoke's got a shark, with a bit of luck it will stir up some wind.' As he strode forward with Henry following the captain did not notice the luckless seaman blotting the paint off the deck as if his life depended upon it.

The ten-foot shark was heaved over the rail on a watch tackle and went into a convulsive dance.

'Mind his tail!'

'Watch out fer 'is teeth!'

'Keep the dog away!'

The dog snapped at the shark's bulging eye, springing away each time it went into a spasm. 'Kill it, Smoke,' Gander ordered.

The man who picked up an iron belaying pin was a thin, foxy individual wearing trousers several times too large. Smoke Lapierre was the *Musket*'s chief mate. The shark shuddered as he rained blows on its nose. A plank of wood was slid under its scythe-like tail and the cook's chopper severed it with a meaty thud. The tail was carried away to be nailed on the bowsprit to bring a wind.

This was the signal for the men crowding around to draw

their knives and attack the carcass. Gander watched dispassionately, chewing a matchstick, as the shark was sliced to ribbons. When the belly was opened half a dozen embryos slithered out. The mate claimed them with a gleeful shout. He trimmed away the slimy tissues and dropped them in a tub of sea water. Henry watched amazed as the folded fins of the baby sharks came erect and they began slowly to swim round.

It was only when the men's passion was spent, and he turned away after telling them to clean up the heap of bloody guts and shark flesh on the deck, that Captain Gander took note of the black scar slashed like a powder burn across the silky deck. For a moment he appeared stunned, as if it was not paint but blood. With a growl of rage he sprang at the man who was on his hands and knees trying to blot up the mess with his shirt.

The sailor was a Polynesian, a stocky giant with heavily muscled shoulders and pale, almost golden colouring. Tattoed swirls patterning his cheeks converged at the corners of his lips. His straight hair, black as tar, was drawn up in a topknot with the grey and white feather of a seabird stuck through it. One-handed, Gander hauled him up by the scruff of his canvas jerkin and knocked him down with a brutish clout.

It was not fear that contorted the man's face but bewilderment as he backed away, crouching low and holding out his arms with fingers splayed. Henry read something in the expression that startled him: it was the look of a fighting man holding himself back. A shadow like the blink of an eye blurred in the sunshine. There was a crack, loud as a pistol shot. Like a slash of ripped cloth, six inches of the man's bicep sprang open and the gash filled with blood. As the victim winced, turning to glance at his wound, the captain took him from behind in a head-lock and heaved him off the ground by the rope holding up his ragged trousers. Then he swung the seaman around in a full circle and with a grunt tossed him clean over the rail.

A fountain of spray erupted from the sea. The dog leapt at the rail, barking. The mate coiled the long whip with which he had torn open the man's arm and rapidly scanned for signs of further trouble. As if nothing had happened, the captain strolled aft.

Henry jumped for the bulwark and began to free the coils of a halyard from the pin rail. 'Sharks, you fool, they'll get him!' he shouted. Gander did not look back.

The seaman surfaced with drops of water trapped like diamonds in his oily hair. He swam powerfully and grabbed the rope which Henry dropped in front of him. But already a tapered shadow circled swiftly upward from beneath the keel. Silent as a cloud it curved upward and inward. Little eddies flurried and slipstreamed along the shark's smooth grey flank as it broke the surface and tipped on its side to attack. Henry jumped.

The drop was about ten feet. With his legs and spine locked rigid, Henry plunged like a harpoon. His heels struck the shark's ribcage with all his weight behind them. The impact knocked the beast sideways. It whipped into the depths, the tip of its long tail slapping Henry's forehead as the water closed over him.

When Henry broke surface, with difficulty because his boots weighed him down, the seaman was hauling himself up. There was no other rope. Henry's toes tingled. He could sense the shark rounding on him. He shouted frantically for another line. Something blue-grey and slimy splashed in front of him and uncoiled in the water. He heard a laugh from the deck as the clear water turned cloudy red. Smoke Lapierre was bombarding him with offal.

Behind him came a swishing noise. Henry cried out as he tried desperately to swivel and meet the attack, but what he saw were the lapped planks of a ship's gig inches from his face. Two men reached down with brawny arms. Henry scissored his legs in a despairing kick to catapult himself upward, was jerked from the water, and flopped head first among the men in the boat.

It was a breathless few moments before Henry realised it was not his own gig in which he had landed. The men in the boat were strangers. When he struggled to sit upright on the thwart he found himself the bewildered scrutiny of a pair of bright blue eyes. The man facing him in the stern was the picture of a venerable sea dog. Thick white curls peeped from under the brim of a stovepipe hat and framed the round jaw of a sunburned face, but the chin and cheeks were clean shaven. Despite the pink and polished complexion, the grids of fine wrinkles round the eyes, as well as a barrel of a chest and a belly to be proud of, put him at around sixty, Henry estimated. The expression weighing him up from beneath shaggy white eyebrows was both stern and kindly, the voice a deep rumble. 'Why not put the bloody shark in a clinch and bring it aboard while you were about it, lad?'

'That was the idea,' Henry said, 'but it wouldn't stop wriggling.'

'Ha!' The man laughed explosively then shouted up at the *Musket*, 'Give us a ladder, you blue-nosed villain!'

Screech Gander propped his folded arms on the rail and looked down. 'Just you mind my paint, Sam, or Nightingale will take a piece out of your breeches.' A Jacob's ladder rattled down. The old man gripped it in powerful hands and climbed nimbly.

'Mind the dog,' Henry warned.

'You're quite safe, Sam,' Gander assured him. Even so, the new visitor took the last rungs cautiously and had a careful look before swinging his legs inboard. Nightingale was in the bow, feasting on heart of shark.

'What's the game, Screech, isn't ordinary shark bait good enough?'

'You know the old theory that sharks don't eat blacks? I was just testing it.'

'The lad's no more black than I am,' the old man expostulated as Henry reached the deck, his clothes streaming water.

'Well, he got a bit mixed up in the experiment, Sam. Anyway, he's no lad of mine. He's from the Botany Bay hulk over yonder. His old man got himself lost.'

'What! John Plunkett was never a man to confuse his navigation.' Henry's damp hand was taken in a strong grip and shaken heartily. 'Second mate, eh? Well, you can tell old John from Sam Handyside of the *Maid Marion* that I will pull over to help sort out his logarithms directly.'

'No, I can't do that, Sir,' Henry explained. 'Captain Plunkett has died. We buried him this morning. The mate's gone, too, overboard off the Horn. I'm in command.'

Captain Handyside stared hard at the young man, recognising lines of tension and anxiety at the corners of his mouth, the hollows of sleeplessness under his eyes. He clapped Henry on the back and said gruffly, 'Well I'm pleased to know you, lad, you're doing well.'

But Henry, his clothes steaming in the hot sun, stood in a daze of amazement. 'Handyside, did you say?'

'That I did, and what of it?'

Henry laughed delightedly but collected himself when he saw the squall gathering on the captain's brow. 'We've met before,' he explained.

'Can't say I recall.'

'Twenty years ago. You were master of the *Matilda*, bound

for New South Wales with migrants?' The captain reflected a
moment, then nodded.

'My name is Henry Ardent.'

It meant nothing. The captain looked nonplussed so Henry
hurried on. 'You must remember. I was born on board and you
christened me – Henry Matilda Handyside Ardent.'

Understanding dawned. With a bellow of surprise and
pleasure Handyside whipped off his hat – exposing to the fury
of the sun a gleaming pink pate – and beat his leg as he laughed.
'Blow me down, after all these years. How could I forget a
name like that? And now look at you, large as life and twice as
handsome, and still leaking water all over the deck like you did
before.' He turned a beaming smile on the mystified host.

'Does this prairie galleon have a glass to offer, Screech, or
does Yankee hospitality require every visiting captain to take
part in your damned experiments, eh?'

'Gentlemen,' Gander said, flourishing a bow, 'Luncheon is
served.'

Captain Handyside smacked his lips and beamed jocularly.
'Stand by to take aboard jerked bison, lad,' he warned.

In the wood-panelled saloon the men took seats at a heavy
rectangular table. A soft light diffused by canvas laced over the
glass fell from the skylight overhead. The panels were propped
open to catch the draught and bright laths of sunlight chased
over the crystal decanters on the mahogany sideboard as the
Musket rolled. Henry had left his boots and socks drying on
deck, and he rubbed the soles of his feet pleasurably over the
unaccustomed tickle of the carpet. Gander splashed dark rum
into three tumblers. 'None of your Newfoundland screech
from the bottom of the rum barrel, I trust,' Handyside said,
eyeing the liquor doubtfully.

'No, I gave up that rotgut when I was ten, this is good stuff.'
Gander skidded a glass across the polished table at Handyside,
but paused as he aimed one at Henry. 'Sorry pal, we don't have
any lemonade right now, will this do?'

Henry flushed. 'Only if you're not offering a decent claret,'
he said. The glass slid into his hand and he topped it up with
water from a cut-glass jug.

'Here's to a sou'wester before sundown,' Handyside
toasted, tipping his glass then drinking.

'I'll drink to that,' Gander exclaimed, and tossed off half the
undiluted rum in his glass. Smacking his lips, he went on, 'Six
pounds ten a ton, Sam, what do you think of that?'

Handyside whistled then scowled. 'Bad for the likes of me.'

'What's bad about making a fortune? The English merchants were climbing over each other to pay it, I tell you, and the best freight taken by any of your old India tea wagons, after waiting four months at Whampoa, was three pounds ten. Speed is the new commodity, Sam. The customers will pay for it and only we Americans can provide it.'

The negro cook brought in a serving dish heaped with dark rice and thick slices of white fish in a brown sauce. Nightingale, the dog, followed him in, peered around suspiciously, then flopped down and gulped the piece of bread roll which Gander gave him.

'Well if the Yankee clippers don't bring you out in a sweat, Sam, the sweet williams surely will. You Limeys have got your heads in the sand, you don't understand what is going on. We're reaching California by way of the Horn in less than ninety days! That's only three months from one end of the country to the other. A man will pay through the nose to cut fifty or sixty days off his passage. The people want to dig gold, Sam, not slop round in the ocean spewing their guts out. They're in a hurry.'

'A passing fancy,' Handyside protested. 'Ninety days or a hundred, what's the difference except you work harder and live more dangerously? There's no future in it.'

Captain Handyside shook his head doubtfully while helping himself to a liberal portion. 'Certainly, you have a crack ship here, Screech, a jewel.' He paused to wink across the table at Henry then went on, 'Well kept, too, except for a lot of paint on the deck, eh?'

Gander raised a sardonic eyebrow and passed the dish to Henry.

'But she won't last long,' Handyside continued, through a mouthful of rice and sauce. 'Softwood, isn't she? And hemp rigging? You keep driving her and pressing her and in five years she'll be sloppy and slaggy as a whore's drawers.'

Suddenly he stopped chewing. His blue eyes widened, watering. A red flush burned his cheeks. He gulped a mouthful of rum and dabbed with a napkin at the tears rolling into his whiskers. 'Phrorr!' he shuddered, fanning air into his open mouth. 'This is what I call curry.'

Gander took a taste from the dish as Henry passed it. 'Oh no, this is one of Doc's mild ones. But you forget one thing, Sam. Five years in a Yankee ship is ten for a Limey because we

cut passage times in half. Besides, who cares what happens
after five years? You Limeys don't think straight. Flour is
fetching fifty dollars a barrel in California and it stands to
reason you want to run a ship full of the stuff out there as often
as you can. And people are forming queues halfway round
London to get ships out to the diggings in Port Phillip. Let me
tell you something interesting. This is the *Musket*'s maiden
voyage. She's paid for herself already and will be fifty thousand
in front when we discharge in London.'

The rice was spiked with tiny chillis like red scimitars. The
sauce was fiendishly hot, hardly bearable. Henry washed it
down with glass after glass of water, ashamed of the tears and
sweat oozing down his face as he caught the glint of contempt
in Gander's eye. 'What's the fish?' he asked. 'I never heard of
sweet williams, we don't have them in Sydney.'

'I think you do,' Gander said.

'Baby shark, lad,' said Handyside, whose ruddy face was
turning the dark red of watery wine.

They were lunching on the shark embryo that not long
before had been swimming in the tub. Henry would have
preferred a fresh omelette but to taste anything new and
flavoursome after the monotony of weeks at sea was a delight,
and he concentrated on making the most of it while the
cocksure Yankee and the blustery Pommy sea-dog argued.

For well over a century navigation laws required all British
trade to be carried in British ships. The British fleet might have
been the lion of the seas but through lack of competition the
king of fleets was capable of no more than a majestic plod.
Passengers were concerned with travelling only in style and
safety. Cargo was in no hurry to go anywhere. Sail was
shortened at sundown to make all snug until dawn and it was
nothing to spend 150 days or more on a voyage home from
China.

With neither merit nor profit to be gained from speed, a
sturdy and capacious but sluggish type of vessel developed.
The tendency to unwieldiness was further encouraged by the
tonnage rules. Port charges, light dues, charter rates, valu-
ations, taxes – all were levied on a ship according to its
registered tonnage. This was found by measuring the length
and breadth, and multiplying it by the depth. The volume so
found – reckoning at one hundred cubic feet to a ton – was
termed the registered tonnage. The depth of the ship however,
was not actually measured. It was assessed at half the breadth.

Thus the cargo capacity of a ship was considerably increased, with no corresponding increase in registered tonnage, by building her deep and square. British merchantmen, chunky to beat the tonnage rules, were said to be built by the mile and cut off by the fathom.

In 1835 the old measuring system was revised to reflect more accurately a vessel's size. Most owners ignored the benefits of the new measurement and continued to build dumpy wall-sided vessels as before. A handful of the more enterprising found a longer and more slender ship carried nearly the same quantity of cargo, sailed better and registered less. Waterlines at bow and stern came to be tapered. Ships began to swim more like mackerel and less like bricks.

In Great Britain the pioneers of the new breed were the fine-lined schooners built in Aberdeen by Alexander Hall. The bows of his ships were so fine and rakishly angled they chopped through the waves like a battle-axe. When the first of the kind displayed a pretty turn of speed, cutting days off the passage between London and Aberdeen, others followed for the Royal Navy, the fruit trade, and the opium runners of the Orient.

American owners faced similar tonnage laws but worried about them less and concentrated on building the best and fastest ships for the trade. With the discovery of gold in California in 1848 fleet-footed 'clippers', capable of making the passage in half the time of an ordinary ship, could not be built fast enough. Between thirty and forty a year were launched in New York alone with a similar number in Boston. Public interest in the new ocean flyers was intense. With speed at such a premium it was hardly surprising that the names of the swiftest clippers were on everybody's lips – *Witch of the Wave, Staghound, Northern Light*, the little *Surprise* which had run out of 'Frisco in ninety-six days reefing topsails only twice in 16,000 miles. Only last year, in 1851, the magnificent *Flying Cloud* had reeled off 374 miles in a single day and had reduced the record time for the trip from 120 days to merely eighty-nine, unbelievable when some ships were taking 200 days on the passage.

Even in far-off Sydney the talk on the waterfront was of the passage records being set by the Yankee clippers and the informal but hotly contested races that often developed, like the bitter tussle between *Raven, Typhoon* and *Sea Witch* during the previous season. The ships had departed from New

England ports more or less together and sailed into 'Frisco on consecutive days.

The development of rakish and powerful American clippers was further boosted by two important events. Gold was discovered in the hills behind Port Phillip and suddenly people by the thousand and goods by the thousands of tons required immediate and speedy passage halfway round the world to the part of Australia soon to become known as Victoria, its capital the city of Melbourne. At the same time, Great Britain opted for free trade: the navigation laws that for a century and a half had protected her plodding merchant marine from competition were repealed.

Almost at once British shipowners were given an uncomfortably convincing demonstration of the new order. In December 1850 the clipper *Oriental* arrived in the Thames with her holds bung full of tea for the London market. The Stars and Stripes whipping in the breeze cocked a snook at the British mercantile empire, for she had run from China in ninety-seven days. Thousands turned out to see the Yankee wonder-ship enter the dock. In an editorial *The Times* raged at the insult and at the wretched state of Britain's own shipping.

But the *Oriental* was just one of half a dozen American ships to scoop sky-high freights for speeding cargoes of tea home from China. Though considerably smaller, a handful of Aberdeen ships like the *John Bunyan*, *Chrysolite* and *Stornoway* had made equally creditable passages of less than a hundred days but were yet to catch the public eye and command high freights.

The new breeze of competition had brought into play another factor. British shipmasters accustomed to jogging along under easy sail by night soon found passage times could be shortened by as much as a month if they broke a professional lifetime's habit and pressed on. With a favourable monsoon a number of apple-cheeked East Indiamen had voyaged from Canton to London in less than 110 days.

Now, as Henry forced down the last fiery mouthful of curried shark and rattled a cooling gulp of water between his teeth, it was hard to stiffen his features against the tide of excitement that surged up inside him. Four months ago he had prowled the Sydney waterfront in quest of a berth as an untried second mate. In fact he would have settled for any job, before or abaft the mast, that would transport him to the other side of the world where the talk about speed under sail was translated into decisions, appointments, action. At such a distance it had seemed useless even to hope against hope for a chance to sail one day in one of the new greyhounds. Yet here he was, wining and dining on board one of them and gamming on equal terms with her captain while his own ship lay half a mile off the quarter.

Born at sea, raised with one foot on a ship's plank, the other in the oggin and his fingers dipped in tar, Henry Ardent had grown up living for the day when he would begin his climb up the ladder to the command of a fine ship. In this ship, he had dreamt as a boy, he would shatter all records for the outward voyage to Sydney and have himself rowed over to Cockatoo Island where his father would greet him with that familiar horny handshake and a proud, 'Good morning, captain, finest ship I ever saw.'

The ambition had been a little set back when he had tried to hurry things along by running away to sea. He had found himself away from home for three years in a sealer that had first marooned him with a party of men on a remote island far to the south, near the Antarctic, and had then been wrecked on a reef in the Friendly Islands. The scar on the rim of his ear was a legacy of those cruel days. As he lay in an exhausted stupor in the dank fo'c's'le, a homesick and terrified lad of fourteen, two men had amused themselves by threading a twist of whipping twine through his ear and fixing it to a nail. Henry had stirred at the jab of the needle but did not awaken until a bucket of cold water was emptied over his head and a voice roared in his ear, 'Abandon ship, we're sinking!' As Henry lurched towards the ladder the thread ripped a jagged tear in his ear.

On his return home at nearly eighteen he had become his father's apprentice and took advantage of the opportunity to learn the crafts of shipwright, rigger and blacksmith. But his sights did not waver. More and more, nautical gossip focused on speed. Record passages and the tricks of hull design, rig and ship-handling that made one ship swifter than another were the talk of the saloons and mercantile counting houses where mariners gathered. The Cockatoo Island Shipyard in Sydney Harbour was no exception, nor was the cosy front parlour of the little house in which Mr Ardent entertained visiting captains. A new era was dawning and the new breed of ocean flyer would demand a new and dauntless class of captain. And if young Henry Ardent planned to be one of them, he could afford to kick his heels on the shipyard stocks on the wrong side of the world no longer. Curiously, although Henry had said nothing to his father about the feelers he was putting out, it was Mr Ardent who, out of the blue one evening, had said, 'I hear John Plunkett's second mate has lit out for the diggings . . .' Three days later, on Henry's twentieth birthday, the *Partridge* had weighed anchor and sailed out through the Heads.

Henry jerked himself back to the present as Captain Handyside, spluttering like a steam boiler, took another helping of curried shark. The Englishman was getting worked up about the great height and dangerous slenderness of the *Musket's* spars. 'It beats me,' he sighed, frustrated by Gander's assurance. 'It's got to stop somewhere, this compromise of safety for speed.'

Screech Gander, seemingly unaffected by the fury of the peppers, snorted his disagreement. 'Is that what you really think?' he demanded. 'You might find yourself astonished, Sam, but listen. This ship will astonish the world if not the great God Almighty. You haven't seen nothing yet. You and your slow-but-sure pals will lie rocking in my wake, safe and sure and stony broke.'

Henry knew the blustery Englishman was wrong and the rakish Yankee dead right but he couldn't bring himself to admit it aloud. 'What you say depends on whether men will sign on,' Henry reasoned. 'Men don't volunteer to be slaves. This lot on board will be off and away at the first sniff of land and won't wait to collect their pay. How can you bear to sleep nights, waiting for a jack-knife to slit your throat?'

'Sleep?' Gander scoffed, 'What's sleep?'

At that moment Nightingale sniffed Henry's bare toes under the table and he realised he had the answer to his question. 'Of course you have to keep your men hard at it, no room for soldiers in a crack ship, but I don't see how taking pot shots at men out on the yard and throwing the odd one to the sharks will improve your passage times.'

'Look at Bully Waterman in the *Challenge*, last year,' Handyside added, mopping his plate with a crust. 'Blood on the decks every day. Five men dead. One stitched up in a blanket and thrown overboard still groaning. And where did it get him? To 'Frisco in one hundred and ten days, which broke no records, and he had to sneak off the ship to avoid being lynched.'

Henry sneaked a red-hot chilli from his plate and offered it under the table. 'I hope they string him up,' he said. 'And the way you're going, Captain Gander, you will be dangling from the same gallows.'

'If a man's going to work he has to believe you're capable of killing him,' Gander said.

'You have to be prepared to hit out hard and quick,' Handyside admitted, 'but that doesn't mean you have to kill him. The first blow is half the battle.'

'That's where you're wrong, Sam, the first blow should *finish* the battle!'

A wet tongue slithered round Henry's fingers and there was a greedy gulping noise from under the table.

The dog let out a whimper. Demented, he crashed around the saloon rubbing his nose between his paws then bounded up the companion-way and raced round the poop, pausing every few moments to shake his head. 'How do you like that for speed?' Henry asked with a laugh.

Screech Gander jumped to his feet, blazing. 'By God I'll give you speed with a knife across your throat . . .'

As Handyside chortled and drained his glass the tension was broken by a crescendo of slatting and rattling from aloft which ended abruptly as the sails swelled to catch the weight of a breeze. The *Musket* gathered way at once, heeling slightly. Henry, nearest to the companion-way, led the race to the deck. Gone was the oily mirror, the hazy horizon. Instead a wind-ruffled blue and – piling up in the southern sky – a massive grey squall, the sea beneath it a sinister black.

Henry shouted at Charlie Field to hurry with the gig. He was pulling on his boots as Captain Handyside, with Screech Gander coming impatiently behind him, puffed to the deck. 'Thank you, Screech, I'll be standing on Blackwall pier to take your lines when you get in,' Handyside said jauntily.

'Ha! If you reach Blackwall before the *Musket* is discharged, loaded and away to sea again, Sam, I'll set up the finest bottle of claret The Artichoke can offer.'

Henry jumped to his feet. 'I'll let them know you're both coming!'

Handyside gripped his arm briefly in a friendly gesture. 'Good for you lad,' he chuckled, and made for his own gig, at the mainmast chains.

Determined to have the last word Screech Gander said stiffly, 'You will have something to celebrate, pal, if you make it past Ushant without going ashore.'

Henry vaulted the rail and dropped down the channels into the boat. 'Give way all. Put your backs into it. That's a real stinger coming out of the south.'

Though the wind was hardly yet a whisper, the *Musket* already made a couple of knots. A bow wave peeled from beneath her golden-winged figurehead. As the stern of the clipper slipped by, Henry raised an arm and shouted politely, 'Thank you for lunch!'

At that moment the Polynesian whom Henry had rescued from the shark ran to the rail and lobbed a package accurately towards the gig. Henry stood and caught it. Steering for the *Partridge* with the tiller in the crook of his arm, Henry sliced his knife through the tarred line binding up a square of old canvas. Within its folds he found a sealskin tobacco pouch containing something hard and weighty. He parted the drawstring and found himself looking into the large round eyes of a little green man.

The figure was fashioned from jade, highly polished. It was rectangular in outline, hardly two inches tall, half as wide, and no thicker than a book cover. The limbs were stumpy, legs in a crouching pose and arms meeting above a vast stomach. The head, tilted pertly on one side, was pierced at the point of balance and through the smooth hole was passed a length of plaited sennit, the ends meeting at a toggle worked from a splinter of bleached bone. Henry could only guess at the figure's significance, though he had seen similar objects in the South Seas, but in the deep lustre of the translucent green stone he recognised beauty beyond description.

Folding his palm over the stone Henry looked over his shoulder hoping there would be time to wave a meagre acknowledgement but the *Musket* was tramping away, the figures of her crew mere specks in the distance.

The squall struck as the gig was being swayed inboard. The sun was blotted out. The lazily billowing sails whacked into rigid curves. The running rigging racketed as every rope, sheet, strop and guy jerked tight in the blocks. As the ship heeled and the helmsman had to put all his weight on the spokes of the wheel to hold her steady, Henry sent a second man to assist. How foreshortened and squat the old *Partridge* seemed after the fine-lined clipper. Both were ship-rigged, with three masts carrying square sails, but there any resemblance between the two ended. If the *Musket* was an ocean greyhound the *Partridge* was something of a bull terrier, barrel-chested and stumpy. Every timber as strong as a tree, and as heavy, all her virtues lay in strength and doggedness rather than speed and daintiness. She had sailed the seas for twenty years and her decks were raddled with the scars of heavy usage but the old girl was probably good for another twenty.

The fierce wind brought a lashing rain. Henry gasped as the fresh water plastered down his hair, ran in rivers down his body, rinsed the clammy salt out of his clothes. He was joyful, too, for his confidence had been revived by the company of two captains, and the rum. The lively resonance of a hard-pressed rig standing up to the wind sent a surge of exultation through his veins. He took a proud turn round the poop as he had seen Captain Plunkett do. Every rope hummed, the iron-hard canvas murmured a steady booming note, the bows thrust deep into the back of a wave, cleaving a path with a bomb-burst of spray, and the old timbers shivered as the ship soared over every crest.

It was great sailing and the *Partridge* revelled in it. Her late captain had never been one for cracking on. But I can do what I like, Henry realised with a glow of excitement. Now the captain was gone, Henry was answerable to nobody. He was truly Master under God.

The wind lost its sting as the squall drove onward, trailing vapoury mists. The *Maid Marion* was revealed, hull down in the west, but there was no sign of the Yankee. Surely the *Musket* could not have sailed so far ahead in so short a time?

Henry peered ahead, feeling the steamy heat of the sun breaking from the dark cloud. Then he saw Charlie Field pointing to starboard. There she was, lying over to the wind with a bone in her teeth and her sails gleaming like porcelain as she cut straight for the *Partridge*. What madness was this?

It was Meadows who gave the answer. 'The bugger's sailing rahnd us,' he yelled, his shock and anger plain to see.

With sinking heart Henry knew it must be true. In the squall the Yankee had put in a board clear across his bow, worn round, and was heading back on a collision course. The *Musket* intended to deliver the most humiliating dressing down one ship could give another. She was making a complete circle of the *Partridge*. Indignant and glowering, the crew stared aft, blaming Henry. As the beautiful clipper bore down Henry felt nothing but desolation. Screech Gander might as well have publicly slapped his cheeks. But she was a spectacle! Tier after tier of trembling sail, faintly pink in the softening light, all swaying in unison as if riding the back of the golden bird gliding over the sunlit waves.

Henry was breathless. He could hear her muted thunder, the crashing tumult of water around the proudly arched bow. Gander was cutting it fine, shaving close to the *Partridge*'s square stern. One moment it seemed the great clipper would smash clean through his bulwarks. Then Henry found himself looking along the entire sweep of her deck as it tilted towards him.

Barely a ship's length distant, the *Musket* sliced through his wake. Her men mimed the act of passing a tow-rope and ribald cheers floated on the wind. Screech Gander, at the binnacle with his buckskin tassles flying and the big dog at his feet, lifted a long arm in a mocking salute.

Already the *Musket* was paying off, coming round to shape a north-easterly course. Under the lash of Smoke Lapierre's tongue her men rushed to ease sheets and brace her yards round. Then figures climbed smartly into the foremast rigging. Long thin booms were extended from the yards. From these flowered an acre of canvas. With stunsails drawing, the magnificent Yankee clipper danced swiftly ahead and vanished as rapidly in the north-east as did the sun in the west.

After two hours of baffling about the wind returned as a half gale piping out of the south-west, promising worse to come. At dusk Henry had ordered the royals to be furled. Now he was not so certain his caution had been wise. He tried to judge the weight of wind and match it with the creak and squeal and rumble of the gear aloft. Finally he reminded himself the old girl had taken a lot more off the Horn. Henry dropped down the ladder to rouse out Meadows and the watch.

There were sniggers in the lee of the deckhouse, where the watch huddled, and he heard Meadows say, 'Mind your worms, lads, here comes the blackbird.'

'Set the royals, Mr Meadows.'

'Royals is it?' Meadows folded his thick arms and jutted his chin. 'You'll 'av the sticks out of 'er, Cap'n bleedin' High and Mighty. If you think yer fit ter shit a seamen's turd you can 'oist the bleedin' royals yerself.'

Henry's first reaction was not fear but relief. A show-down had been long overdue and somehow, with the shadowy authority of the dying captain no longer at his back, it was easier to be decisive and stand up for himself. 'Call all hands!' he snapped.

The hands had already scented trouble and needed no calling. The other watch tumbled out of the fo'c's'le and clustered round, balancing on the pitching deck. Henry said, 'I'm ordering you men to set the royals. Now move!'

Wary faces glanced uncertainly at Meadows but no man moved. 'You can navigate the ship 'ome and fish fer glory, Mr h'Ardent, but we're gonna do the sailin', see, and we're not goin' out on the royal yards in this wind.'

'I see,' Henry said.

Meadows gloated as the young mate, wiping his palms on his trousers, stepped back from the crowd of men. But his grin faded when Henry, instead of retreating, jumped into the mainmast shrouds and ran lightly up the ratlines to the maintop. There he transferred to the topmast shrouds and climbed on, up into the wild darkness.

Gripping the lashed sail with a tight clench of his belly, Henry threw himself over the royal yard. His heels found the foot-ropes and he edged outwards, the sea a wilderness of peaks and troughs far below. The sail sprang free as he released the first gasket. The slender yard whipped frenziedly, threatening to throw him off. Henry tightened his belly muscles and worked his way to windward until the entire sail was free and clawing madly in the wind. Then he curled his legs around the halyard and slid swiftly to the deck.

The men watched stonily as he struggled to hoist the yard single-handed. Determinedly, Henry took a watch tackle, bent it to the halyard, and managed to hoist the royal yard a foot at a time. He belayed the halyard, crossed to the lee side, and as the sail filled with a crack he sheeted it home. The effect was immediate, the entire ship driving harder and heeling more.

The sudden increase in heel, though slight, caught Charlie Meadows unawares. He could not save himself from taking a shuffling step down the pitch of the deck. It was then Henry hit him, hard in the belly.

As Meadows folded with a grunt a ram-rodding left rose out of the dark and crunched the point of his descending chin. He fell over, sliding down the deck, but recovered quickly. Henry waited calmly. He stepped neatly outside the first wildly swinging fist, inside the second, and slammed a rapid one-two under the ribs. Meadows tottered, gasping, but Henry felt no pity. The frustrations of the last weeks, the loneliness and uncertainties, all peaked in a pile-driving upward jab of his knee. The force of it sprang Charlie Meadows twelve inches off the deck and landed him in a clucking heap in the scuppers.

Henry said nothing and did not look at the other men. Grimly he climbed the foremast. As he cast off the leeward gaskets of the fore-royal he felt a vibration in the spar as a man's weight was put on the windward side. In a moment the sail was cast off and thundering. Henry slid down with Charlie Field following close above him. By the time he reached the deck the crew had the yard hoisted, the sail sheeted home and drawing. Moments later the mizzen royal followed.

'Freshen your nips!' Henry bellowed. 'Let's get the old girl sailing.'

And he heard one of the men say, 'Poor old Oatsy, I reckon the Cap'n wrung his twist for 'im.'

Henry Ardent stamped numbly on the wet deck. The hour before dawn passed as miserably and reluctantly in the northern hemisphere as it ever did in the south. Silent and threatening, the waves ranged up astern like moving mountains. Each one seemed to pause at the taffrail to scowl and hunch its shoulders before rolling under the *Partridge* and hurling her forward in a smother of foam. Then the sweating helmsman would curse, heaving at the wheel to catch her before she broached, Henry leaping to assist. And as the ship was slung down the back of the racing wave, askew from her course, the helmsman would grumble, 'All over the place like a mad woman's shit.'

'Watch how you go,' Henry warned.

How the old girl sailed! She had seen nothing like it in Captain Plunkett's day. For seven days her stand-in master had driven her. The sea miles passed rapidly beneath her keel, but not without hard labour. The easy times were over. Henry had crammed upon her protesting spars every scrap of canvas for which there was space. The weedy beard on the hull had been scrubbed with a fothering mat, hauled back and forth along the bottom by ropes. The nips were freshened every hour, thus trimming the sails anew and ensuring the last half inch of slack was taken up.

At the same time the ship was spruced up for her arrival in port, requiring a thousand and one sailoring tasks. The greasy iron-hooped slush bucket was hauled up the mast and men rubbed galley fat on the timbers to prevent them drying out. They chipped rust off the anchors; swabbed the decks with short-handled brooms and holystones. Their lives were wretchedly hard but this discipline of work and more work was all too familiar. They knew where they stood and strangely *Partridge* had become a happy ship.

Henry drove himself no less hard. He was fatigued beyond belief. His eyes were bloodshot, pinched in deep folds of skin made red-raw from salt spray. His hair was a clotted wet mat and a week-old stubble roughened his jaw. As long ago as four days he had last glimpsed the sun and plotted a rough position on the chart. Ever since, the wild sailing through a succession of heavy showers and clammy drizzles had become increasingly nightmarish, for there had been a transformation in the sea itself, too. The glorious dark blue of the great depths out west had given way to a cloudy green. The *Partridge* was on soundings.

Henry was tinglingly aware that the surging lift of every wave hurried the ship into a giant funnel. Far off to port — though how far, he had no way of knowing — lay the coast of England. Somewhere to starboard lurked the shores of France. What would they see first, green fields and white cliffs, or a seething portcullis of granite poised to chew the bottom out of the ship?

All night he had wrestled with the decision of whether to reduce sail to slow the ship's headlong dash in case she should pile ashore in the dark but some instinct persuaded him to crack on. Henry blinked to clear his head and anxiously scanned the eastern sky, looking for the dawn.

Three bells. Men tumbled blearily out of the fo'c's'le, lashed by Charlie Meadows' blistering tongue. Hugging themselves against the wind and spray, they waited at the galley door for the cook to send out the so-called coffee. Whistling cheerfully, Meadows joined Henry on the poop. No jibes laced his tone now. 'That young h'Ardent's not 'arf bad,' he told the men, 'an' e's got more Newin'tons than the rest o' yer togevver.'

Now he rubbed his hands briskly and smiled. 'Day's a-dawning, Gawd 'elp us,' he said. 'Maybe we'll see a bit o' Blighty today, what d'you say?'

'Wind's going round to the north a bit.'

Meadows eyed the sudsy bubbles racing along the side, grey shreds fizzing on the heaving field of black. 'The old whip's fair lashin' along,' he muttered. He was gazing longingly at the galley, willing the coffee pot to appear, when his eye was caught by a bold and craggy shape standing far ahead. The land was near enough to discern the contours of the valleys dipping down to the shore. 'Well we've made it to Froggie land, at least,' he said.

Henry's heart turned over. Could his dead reckoning have been so inaccurate? The land could only be part of Brittany, the rocky peninsula reaching out into the Atlantic, and the ship was dashing headlong towards a lee shore. 'Stand by to wear, all hands!'

After a few hectic minutes the ship was settled on a new course, parallel with a forbidding shore of fisty headlands and knuckle cliffs lying seven or eight miles off to starboard. The overcast was breaking up. Patches of sunshine raced over shorter, steeper seas, tinting them a brilliant green where it touched, then flew on over brown cliffs and green farmland.

Then came a chilling shock as the cry of 'Land ho!' from the look-out in the foretop wavered on the wind. But this was land on the port bow, a broad and low-lying island blocking their escape. Henry knew at once what it must be, for he had stared at the chart so long that it seemed every detail was tattooed on his forehead. He said quietly to Meadows, 'Is that what I think it is?'

'That's 'er, I'm sorry to say, and no mistake,' he answered.

The crew stared anxiously at Henry then looked again at the land approaching at break-neck speed. To be embayed by Ushant was a homeward-bound sailor's worst dread. The island was surrounded by a multitude of out-lying rocks like gigantic up-ended cobblestones through which the currents seethed at a furious rate. No ship could make headway around them. Indeed, so swiftly do the tides wash around the island and the tip of Brittany, between the Bay of Biscay and the English Channel, that an old saying warns: when you see Ushant, it is already too late.

Again the look-out hailed, breaking into Henry's racing thoughts, with a voice pitched high to carry against the thrum and swash of sail and sea. 'Starboard-bow-vessel-in-trouble!'

Henry sprang into the shrouds and glimpsed a mastless hulk lurching over a crest. Some sort of coastal schooner swept clean by a wave she rode with her head to wind, on a sea anchor, a mile to leeward. He had an impression of figures huddled around the stump of a mast. They were at least alive, for one was waving, but for how much longer? The schooner was in the suck of the current, doomed to destruction. The *Partridge*, if Henry were to free sheets and run down on the wreck, would surely follow. It would be hard enough to claw to windward even now. Yet there was a passage between the island and the rocks reaching out from the mainland, and Henry knew from experience as a sealer on wild and desolate coasts that as long as a ship could float there was always a chance. He gave swift orders.

When the crippled schooner lay abeam, the ship lumbered into the wind. To be near enough for Field to hurl a rope was all that Henry hoped for, but he brought the two vessels so close that he found himself looking straight down upon the stricken schooner's deck. She was fine-lined and prettily kept, her silky decks showing none of the scars of hard usage associated with cargo carrying. A dozen bedraggled figures stared pitifully from the foot of the broken mainmast to which they were lashed. They watched in stark horror as the rope was braked by the wind and fell two feet short, into the sea.

Already the wind was driving the bigger ship away, widening the gap. Meadows had another heaving line coiled ready but Henry told him to wait. Swiftly he knotted the end of the line around his waist, kicked off his boots, and plunged head first into the smother.

The shock of cold drove the breath from his lungs. He surfaced with a splutter. This was no mild semi-tropical water but the North Atlantic and it chilled him to the marrow. When he struck out for the wreck a few powerful strokes brought him up to its stern quarter. He read the name *Arrow* and beneath it, Cowes.

Scrambling on all fours because the motion was so wild, two men dropped a rope over the side and hauled him roughly aboard. They unknotted the line from his waist while he caught his breath, then began to heave over the warp which Meadows had bent to the end of it. The merchantman was drifting down-wind swiftly. It was a race to get the warp aboard before the distance became too great.

The schooner was a shambles. Despite the splintered bulwarks, tangled rigging and smashed fittings, Henry caught a feeling of what a proud and beautiful craft she must have been. She floated low, half filled with water, a rich man's toy reduced to a wretched hulk.

Henry helped to drag the warp to the stump of the mast and found himself looking into a wan face. Not a young boy, as he had first thought, but a girl a couple of years younger than himself. Though she trembled with cold her expression was composed. 'I thought you were Frenchies,' Henry said.

The brown eyes smiled from a haggard face. 'I thought you were the Angel Gabriel.'

'Can you swim?'

'No, but I'm not frightened of getting a mouthful.'

The older of the two men was a stout, grizzled fellow, in middle age and wearing the clothes of a gentleman. 'George Chamberlayne and my niece Emma,' he said swiftly. 'What do you want us to do?'

When Henry explained what he wanted, Chamberlayne caught his drift at once and gave instructions to his crew. Henry made a bight in the line, large enough to pass over a man's shoulders, and knotted it to a small empty keg.

'I'll go first to try it out,' he said, smiling encouragingly at the girl who shuddered. From this level the heavily plunging ship looked vast. Men were out on her yards, furling the flogging canvas. He signalled to Meadows who watched from the bow then jumped into the cold sea, clutching the barrel to his chest.

The line dragged him over the raging water. Charlie Field reached out for him as he was thrown against the surging hull. A moment later he was jerked from the sea, much as the shark had been, and fell sprawling on the deck.

Knowing the ship would stand little more of this wild motion he ran aft, clawing at bulwarks and deckhouse for support. 'Hoist and back-wind the outer jib!' he cried.

The sail pushed the bows round and steadied the rolling. The first white-faced survivor was hauled aboard. The waves were growing steeper in the shallows and the features of the land were clear to the eye. He could see houses and a church spire. A veil of white mist rose like smoke from the breakers crashing into the reef of cobblestones.

The survivors were carried below, the girl tending her uncle whose head was covered with blood from a glancing blow against the hull. The instant the last man reached the deck Henry passed orders to let fall the reefed topsails. The yards were braced around. The ship came under control again with the land looming frighteningly close.

Pools of brilliant sunlight chased over the green landscape. The fields shimmered. The round white tower of a lighthouse gleamed like a pillar of ivory. 'Topgallants, Mr Meadows, quickly!'

Henry sensed the waters converging, speeding up, sucking the ship through the mile-wide gap. So swift was the current that every rock was half buried by its own bow wave and left a long wake of foam as if it were a steamer. The speed and power of the rushing water flattened the waves, and the ship's rate of progress gave the impression that the wind was dying. Henry had never imagined such a spectacle of peril.

Immense heaving circles of water like giant footprints a hundred feet in diameter whirled the ship round. Thanks to Henry's boldness in cramming on sail she had sufficient steerage way for the rudder to wrench her back on course.

The ship made six knots through the water but the water sluiced along at twelve: at something like twenty miles an hour the vessel hurtled through the passage, giving her crew and passengers the feeling of sliding off the edge of the world.

Suddenly it was all over. The current spat the *Partridge* into the English Channel. The wind piped up once more as the pull of the current faded. Henry became aware of the deep chill in his blue limbs. Charlie Field saw him stagger, ripped a blanket from the back of one of the yacht's crew who had come on deck, and draped it round Henry's shoulders.

Henry sank gratefully to the deck and leaned his back against the companion. The sun was bright enough to burn dry patches on the wet planks. A seaman passed up a mug of coffee but Henry was flaked out, dead to the world.

'Look at 'im, Oatsy,' Field called in amazement. 'The bleeder's sleepin' like a babe.'

'Shh!' Meadows whispered, tucking the blanket round Henry's legs, 'you can see he's pumped.'

It was mid-afternoon when Henry came abruptly awake and stared around wonderingly at the bellying sails and the sunlit water. 'All serene,' Meadows reported, pacing the deck with a worried frown. 'I must say yer lookin' h'exceptionably 'andsome, Cap'n.'

Henry rubbed his hands over his face. His hair had feathered in the drying wind, his cheeks were rough, his eyebrows powdered with salt. 'I need some tucker, my stomach's so slack I could wipe my eyes. What time is it?'

'Past kissin' time, near six bells.'

'I slept so long?'

'We've been tiptoin' like missionaries in a broffel, steerin' norf-east wiv a coasting schooner hull-down off the port bow.'

'Thanks Oatsy, you're doing great.'

Charlie Meadows shrugged as if to say he could run a ship any day of the week, but at heart he was relieved to turn his back on the poop and go for'ard to find the cook. He had made certain the rescued survivors were comfortable in the cabins aft, with rum bottles filled with hot water and wrapped in socks to keep them cosy. But his confidence had evaporated at first glance at the chart. The shape of the coast was clear enough, but how to take the elementary step from the map to the look of the land, with only a compass to aid him – that was a mystery.

Charlie Meadows was a victim of the system in which many a seafarer was trapped for life. It was the system of catch 'em young, treat 'em rough, tell 'em nothing. It made an expert though simple sailor of a man born for a life on the land. His father had been a drover, herding meat on the hoof from farms in East Anglia to the Caledonian Market in London. When the steam railway deprived him of this livelihood he became a butcher with a little shop at Limehouse, near the gates to the West India Dock. It was here young Charlie, who had spent his early years plodding the droving routes looking at the stern-ends of cattle, fell under the spell of swaggering and open-handed sailormen with their yarns of flying fish, dusky maidens and exotic adventure.

In a Boston cat house he had teamed up with Charlie Field, a river man raised on the Thames. His father's barges, too, were put out of business by the steam railway but Charlie's years of working the weirs explained the heritage of his strength: countryman's shoulders and boatman's grip.

Meadows had been negotiating with a comely red-head over a glass of forked lightning when a pimp suddenly sprawled backwards down the rickety stairs. Brandishing a jack-knife, wearing nothing but woolly drawers and a tarpaulin hat, Field had bounded after him bellowing loud threats to 'h'amputate the orchestras of the bleeder wot stole me cloves.' After springing to his defence in the mêlée that followed, Meadows dragged Field into the street. They recovered their wits next morning when the bucko mate of a ship bound for the Brazils dashed a bucket of freezing sea-water in their faces. Now they were nearing home for the first time in three years, or was it four? Neither had bothered to keep track.

Henry shaved, changed his socks, and after a feast of salt-beef and biscuit smothered in gravy felt a new man. In these constricting waters busy with shipping he was in for a hectic and nerve-wracking night but he was excited. Tomorrow, for the first time ever, he would see the white cliffs and green downs of Home. The only thing he had to be careful of was running into it in the dark.

Night had fallen and he had prudently reduced sail when George Chamberlayne came on the poop. By the light of a half moon dodging between the clouds he noticed Henry standing alertly by the binnacle. 'Hullo, young friend,' he said breezily. 'Your captain has been most hospitable but I have yet to have the pleasure of meeting him, I wonder if you would present my compliments?'

Nervous in the face of such dignity and assurance, and a booming voice accustomed to getting its own way, Henry shyly extended his hand. 'Henry Ardent, at your service, sir.'

Chamberlayne greeted him warmly but searched the poop with determined grey eyes for some other figure who, he felt sure, must be nearby. Then his brow wrinkled in surprise and he inspected Henry keenly. 'Well, I'm right glad to know you. My niece and I have much to thank you for. I never saw a man swim as if he was born with paddlewheels.'

'In New South Wales we swim a lot, I was raised there.'

'How unfortunate for you,' a new voice said lightly. It was the girl who stepped from the companion-way, her face pale in the moonlight. 'How ever did you fetch up in such a place?'

Chamberlayne took her arm. 'My niece, Emma,' he said. 'This is Captain Ardent, my dear.'

Emma Chamberlayne offered a hand negligently, as if she did not much care whether Henry kissed it or painted it. He took it and made a wary bow, unnerved by the girl's calm air of competence.

Dressed in an ill-fitting shirt, topcoat and trousers borrowed from the dead captain's wardrobe, none of which did anything for her tall and slender figure, Emma wasted no words apologising for her appearance or for the wrung-out state of her long dark hair. Her pale face tilted prettily in the moonlight as she cast a professional eye over the trim of the sails. Catching Henry's puzzled and surprised look she said with a smile, 'Just checking.'

'You're quite satisfied, I trust,' Henry said thinly.

'Oh yes, perfectly, but of course the poor old *Arrow* would have sailed rings round her.'

'There is one respect in which the *Partridge* has some technical advantage over the poor old *Arrow*,' Henry said drily.

'And what could it possibly be, captain? You're comparing

the most beautiful racing schooner with an ungainly old merchantman . . .'

'The *Partridge*, it seems, is still afloat.'

George Chamberlayne guffawed. 'Well said, young man. You can't argue with that, my dear. And our poor old *Arrow* would never have won a race in her life if she was forced to carry a few hundred tons of Australian wool in her hold, you have to admit.'

Emma sighed. 'What a pity she was lost, I did love her.'

'Won't you have some coffee?' Henry asked.

With frequent interruptions from his niece, George Chamberlayne told the story of their shipwreck. They had been sailing home from a wool-trade meeting in Bordeaux when the rudder snapped clean off. The schooner had broached under a full press of sail and the following sea had wiped her decks clean of mast, bulwarks, boat and four men. For two days the hulk drifted, washed by waves, until the Ushant shore threatened certain doom. 'I'm sure the rudder pintles must have been weakened when we grounded last year,' Chamberlayne concluded.

'That was in the race won by the schooner *America*,' Emma explained. 'We raced around the Isle of Wight and the upstart New Yorkers went off with the Cup.'

Chamberlayne was enraged by the memory of British yachting's humiliation. 'Mark my words, we'll get it back,' he glowered. 'Even if I have to sail across the Atlantic myself we'll have it back in the Squadron at Cowes inside five years. They're calling it the *America*'s Cup. If we hadn't hit the ledge off Shanklin it might have been the *Arrow*'s.'

When the visitors left him at his post, lonely but for the silent helmsman and racing moon, Henry was sorry. He had been heartened by George Chamberlayne's cheerful and blunt manner. And the girl was an interesting enigma. Normally, Henry had little time for frilly company. The world was far too interesting a place, he thought, to waste time on tittle-tattle. The colony had been full of so-called suitable young women whose horizons extended no further than the hems of their petticoats and not one of them had half the sparkle and self-assurance of Emma Chamberlayne.

Henry sighed and pulled a blanket round his shoulders. There was no point in lying down, he would never sleep. Not only had the civilised conversation with his guests unsettled him but he was nervous of what the day would bring. After so many years of hearing it discussed by his mother and father he would feast his own eyes on England, his homeland. How many times had ships' officers pulled out their charts to show the keen young son of the boatbuilder the landfall headlands of Cornwall, and the seamarks used by ships running up the Channel? And now he would be not only seeing familiar cliffs and headlands for the first time ever but navigating his own ship homeward by them.

'Land ho!'

The look-out's hail broke Henry from his doze in an instant. Through the glass he peered at a dense grey shadow lying beneath a filmy cloud. Half a dozen ships were revealed in the dawn but Henry's whole attention focused on the details of the shore, some ten miles distant and growing more distinct as the sun rose. He saw cliffs ending in spiky fragments, like pyramids and chimneys, with a lower run of land behind.

Charlie Meadows came on deck, took one look, and pronounced, 'That's yer Isle o' Wight, that is.' Then he swung the glass on a tall-masted ship off the port quarter, nearer the land, and his idle scrutiny ended in a startled grunt. 'Blimey, look there! We've done that Yankee scalper one in the eye.'

Henry could hardly believe the evidence of the long and lean black hull, the towers of snowy canvas, and the Stars and Stripes whipping from the spanker gaff. It was the *Musket* in all her glory, though she was missing her mizzen topmast and its yards.

Soon all the crew capered happily on deck. The noise brought out George Chamberlayne who was impressed when he learned the *Partridge* had made a swifter passage than the *Musket*. 'But then I don't suppose,' he began with a wink, 'the American skipper would reckon on your taking the short way round Ushant, eh?'

With the land slipping under their lee the two ships edged closer. Meadows, his head cocked up at the sails like an angry sparrow, went from mast to mast with a bunch of men freshening the nips and adjusting the trim. But their hopes of a bow-to-bow race up the Channel were dashed when Chamberlayne said he would be obliged if he and his niece could be put ashore at Portsmouth, whence they could take the steam railway and arrive in London before nightfall. It was a request that brooked no refusal. Henry gave orders to angle the ship for the land. The tracks of the two ships now converged on a collision course.

For twenty minutes it was impossible to predict which would pass ahead but it was the Yankee's obligation to give way and Henry firmly held his course. At last the three raked masts of the *Musket* came nearer in line and her silhouette narrowed as she altered course to steer across the stern of the *Partridge*. Only then did Henry suspect that perhaps Captain Screech Gander had not even recognised the identity of the ship to which he was offering priority.

As the clipper cut his wake a cable distant, Henry told Field to dip the ensign. The flag came rattling down in salute. Henry saw Gander languidly lift his glass and a moment later the Stars and Stripes fluttering from the spanker gaff above his head reciprocated. But when the Red Ensign climbed aloft again Charlie Field had bent a heavy rope to the halyard – the *Partridge* was offering a tow-rope to the *Musket*.

'Tit for bleedin' tat is what I say,' Meadows said smugly.

Henry said nothing, but even at this distance there was satisfaction in sensing his hair curling in the heat of Screech Gander's rage.

'Wind's all up an' dahn the mast again,' Meadows observed a few minutes later, as the stiffness fell out of the sails and the ship slowed. Small fishing boats danced along the shore. An outward bound steamer trailed a long plume of black smoke down the Solent. Another was inbound, coming up fast from the south. Naval gunboats, high-walled and sinister with squat funnels and low masts, were anchored at Spithead. Beyond them lay the roofs and spars of Portsmouth. A powerful cutter with PILOT painted large on her tan sail, beat up and surged alongside. A voice hailed, 'Be needing a Solent pilot, Cap'n?'

'London,' Henry called back through cupped hands.

'Can't help you.'

'Will you take a couple of us into Portsmouth, Skipper?' Chamberlayne called.

When the man at the tiller nodded, Henry had a sudden thought. 'Got any eggs there?'

The man's surprised laugh came clearly over the water. 'Wouldn't I be eating 'em, with bacon more likely? But if it's a pluck you're needing I see the *Napoleon*'s coming out and Sandy Goodwin will have a fair heap of coal in his stokehold.'

The steamer was a paddle tug, bearing down with a bone in her teeth and an umbrella of smoke making a canopy over the brass-railed platform on which a stout figure with ginger whiskers and a bowler hat was steering. The tug swung in with a spatter of paddles and stopped dead, right alongside. 'Morning Captain, Sandy Goodwin and the *Napoleon* at your service,' the man said, addressing George Chamberlayne.

'This here's Captain Ardent,' Chamberlayne replied, clapping a hand on Henry's shoulder.

'Wind's dropping away, Cap'n, and a warm sunny afternoon with not a breath of breeze, a dead muzzler she'll be before nightfall,' the tugmaster said. 'What do you say to eighty guineas to Gravesend?'

Henry waved him off determinedly. 'We don't want a tug, Mr Goodwin.'

'Sixty. I can stretch it to sixty but not a farthing less. Think of the coal, and it's a day and a half each way, mind.'

Then George Chamberlayne's deep voice rolled across the water. 'Forty pounds, Mr Goodwin, take it or leave it.'

Henry tugged at the older man's tailored coat. 'There's no money at all on board, Mr Chamberlayne. I can't contract a tow before the Downs.'

'Leave it to me, it'll be my pleasure to cover the cost from my own pocket.' Chamberlayne stared hard at the tugmaster who pulled his beard thoughtfully. 'You're wasting coal, Mr Goodwin,' Chamberlayne added.

The tugmaster was veteran enough to recognise a hard bargainer when he saw one. 'Pass your warp, Mister,' he growled.

'See to it, Mr Meadows,' Chamberlayne ordered, then beckoned the pilot boat alongside.

Emma thanked Henry warmly and simply, then scrambled expertly down to the cutter by way of the Jacob's ladder slung over the bulwarks. George Chamberlayne followed. 'Look us up in London, young man, you'll be needing friends,' he said with a cheerful wave as the cutter peeled away.

The tug sounded a shrill whistle and with a belch of smoke took the strain. There was a holiday spirit in the *Partridge* as she slipped along the coast, sails furled and deck squared away, parting the twin ribbons of beaten froth trailed by the tug. The gentle following wind matched her speed exactly. When Henry lit his pipe the blue smoke gathered round his head as did the black fumes around the tug.

The steep cliffs of Beachy Head – the fairly white cliffs, as Meadows described them – were passed at the end of the first dogwatch. Henry spent the afternoon glued to the telescope gazing at the cattle and church spires and fishermen and village roofs of England's bulwark shore. With evening the breeze died entirely and the sturdy *Napoleon* threshed onward over low and glassy swells. A speckle of lights marked the town of Hastings. Then came the mysterious and unlit shore of Romney Marsh, the smugglers' coast. Dover, a nest of lights beneath a towering cliff, passed in the early hours.

Dawn revealed, off to starboard, great expanses of sand bared by the tide. These were the dreaded Goodwin Sands, a graveyard of ships as feared by generations of sailors as the hungry rocks of Ushant. Between the sands and the small town of Deal, standing above a shingle shoreline, forty or fifty ships lay at anchor awaiting favourable winds to make sail down Channel or to the North Sea. Longshore boats pulled among them, delivering food, mail, messages and pilots. Henry was startled by the crack of a cannon and spurt of smoke from an anchored warship. As it rolled over the water every ship in unison ran up its ensign. It was eight o'clock precisely and many a master would be setting his chronometer for the long voyage ahead.

Now the flooding tide gave a lift. Around the North Foreland with its white lighthouse, the corner of Kent, they swept into the broad Thames estuary. The ocean was well astern now, for the water was shallow and muddy. Fleets of oyster dredgers crowded the water off Whitstable. Ungainly spritsail barges, inching down the coast, carried their way in a whisper of breeze. Some were stacked high with hay for the cab-horses of London. Through the long and exciting day the river became ever narrower and more crowded. The water was filthy, a city drain carrying all kinds of rubbish. In the mellow afternoon light it was almost black.

A stream of ships passed outward bound, their spars and timbers seeming to shiver at the taste of salt water and its promise of perils to come. For every vessel the great tidal gutter winding into the heart of the Empire marked the end – or the beginning – of an unimaginably hard and long road.

Gazing at the muddy banks, brick walls and distant smokestacks with hungry eyes, Charlie Meadows sighed as if he could hardly believe what he saw. 'What d'yer fink, Barley?'

'Beef pie an' onions and 'alf a gallon of gravy, that's what I'm gonna spread my gnashers round tonight,' Charlie Field answered.

'Wiv mustard?'

'And pickles, and cabbage, and parsnip ... Look, here's Gravesend already.'

A chill sprinkle of rain started as the ship passed between lines of ships moored to buoys in mid river. A small town lay on the left bank, on the outside of the river's sweeping curve. The tugmaster was looking back for instructions but Henry had no idea of what to do. He indicated they should keep going ahead. Among the small boats milling near the landing stages one of them, a double-oared pulling boat, was aiming resolutely for the *Partridge*. 'Cripes, I 'opes yer feelin' fireproof, Mister h'Ardent,' Meadows said, as he glimpsed the small figure hunched beneath a tall stovepipe hat in the stern-sheets. 'There's Monkey Winkworth hisself coming aboard. Better look lively wiv a gantline, Barley.'

Monkton Winkworth, shipbuilder and proprietor of the Arrow line, was a frail and withered bachelor who looked and behaved twenty years older than his sixty-six years. He sat stiffly, almost crouching on a green velvet cushion in a wide and upright wooden armchair. Underneath it were fixed four iron-spoked wheels while on top, in each corner, was a stout iron eyebolt. To each eyebolt was attached a rope and the four pieces met on a large iron cringle, or hoop, which the old man brandished in the air as his boat turned neatly alongside the slowly moving ship. The crew, two powerful young men in matching blue jackets, neatly boated their oars and threw a painter. 'Quickly, quickly, you fools,' Winkworth snapped. Amazed, Henry watched as Meadows and Field got busy. Fortunately they knew the drill. A gantline, passing through a block on the mainyard, was dropped into the boat and made fast to the iron ring.

'Haul away!' Winkworth ordered, and was snatched into the air. With his dark green suit, yellow waistcoat, beaky nose and thin, wide-eyed face, he dropped aboard squawking like a parrot. One of the oarsmen was already on deck to unbend the slings and push the chair aft. At the poop ladder he knelt in front of the chair. Winkworth pushed himself shakily to his feet then fell on the man's back and was carried up the ladder. 'Where's the damned mud pilot? Mr Brown, are you here?'

The fourth to come aboard was a beefy, taciturn man in a peaked cap and a double-breasted black coat who took up a position at the binnacle. 'Aye, Mr Winkworth, the docking tug is taking our hawser this minute.'

'Where's the mate? Bring me the mate!' Winkworth demanded. 'And Skitter, my legs are cold.'

As Henry stepped forward one of the servant boatmen, a surly youth with sallow cheeks and simpering mouth, tucked a blanket round the shipowner's thin legs. 'Here Sir,' Henry said.

'Where? Come closer. Oh there you are, and about time too. This ship came into my fleet two months ago. You're Master no more but Second Mate under my command, see? We're berthing at the London Docks. I want hatches open, yards cock-billed, jibboom run in, warps and fenders . . .' Winkworth switched his beady glance. 'Skitter, you can hoist my house flag.' Then, seeing Henry standing irresolute in front of his chair, he added blisteringly, 'Don't stand there looking as sloppy as a fathom of pump water, there's work to be done.'

Meadows shot Henry a sympathetic look as he hurried forward. 'Don't you worry, Mister h'Ardent,' he said consolingly. 'It's always the bleedin' same: after the Lord Mayor's Show comes the shit.'

The ship glided majestically up the winding river, following the tug on a short hawser. Sparks poured from its funnel and blew away into the dark. The bruised sky of smoke and cloud lying low over the roofs and chimneys of London glowed with the ghostly reflection of lights beneath. A yellow drizzle crawled clammily under Henry's clothes. He was depressed. Of all the triumphant or even cautiously warm welcomes he might have received from a grateful shipowner, this was the eventuality for which he was least prepared. He remained in the forward part of the ship, carrying out the pilot's orders, though his mouth watered when he looked aft and saw Skitter placing across the arms of Monkton Winkworth's wheelchair a silver tray. On it were set out a dish of warmed roast duck, a dozen oysters on the half shell, and a small decanter of port with a crystal glass.

The heavy gates to the dock swung open when the *Partridge* angled across the river as Mr Brown, the pilot, knew they would from frequent consultations with a large gold watch. A second tug took a warp on the port quarter. There was a conversation of toots and whistles and the ship glided into a limp pool. It was hedged with high spars and rigging and the black water was a mass of silver worms, wriggling reflections of the lights dotted around. The tugs gave the hull a sideways nudge into an empty space between silent ships. Men stepped out into the drizzle from the sheltering shadows and caught the heaving lines. In eerie silence they hauled the mooring warps across and dropped the bights over the bollards. 'Snub her there, snub her!' the pilot bellowed. There was a gentle jolt. The voyage had ended.

Whooping and shouting, the entire crew swarmed over the rail and vanished into the darkness along the dock. The pilot muttered 'Good night, Mister' and left the ship. The poop was deserted but a rosy glow filled the skylight. The saloon clock struck two bells — one o'clock in the morning — as Henry entered. Hatless, Monkton Winkworth sat at the head of the table, his bony little hands propping up his chin as he turned over the manifests and ship's papers removed from Captain Plunkett's desk. Henry saw he was bald but for a spriggy grey tuft over each ear. 'Ah, Mr Ardent,' he said, and Henry smiled, expecting at least the offer of a glass of port. But Winkworth gestured with a talon-like hand at the cabins opening off the saloon and said curtly, 'A new captain and two mates are joining at first light so you may as well clear out your dunnage and sleep for'ard unless you want to seek a hotel at this late hour.'

Henry fought down an urge to snap the twig of a man across his knee. 'I will not, sir!' he blazed.

The little man's eyebrows arched and he said crabbily, 'You will make a report in writing of the circumstances of the deaths on board, Mr Ardent. You will, of course be reporting to my office for the disbursements that are due. In view of your diligence I am prepared to offer you a berth in a vessel of my fleet, which is yet to be decided. So long as you are in my employ, therefore, you will of course follow my orders precisely.'

Winkworth raised an admonitory finger. 'You should realise I am not normally inclined to favour men in my fleet who are, let us say, of *colonial* background. Especially, I must admit, those from penal settlements. The wayward and unreliable characteristic of the felon is unquestionably a matter of bad blood which we in England are best rid of . . .'

White in the face and trembling, Henry drove his nails into his palms to control his temper. Dismissed with a wave of a bony hand he turned on his heel, went up the companion-way, and after taking a few angry turns of the silent and deserted maindeck stretched out in the sailmaker's berth in the midships deckhouse.

He would have enjoyed a steak and kidney pudding, with mustard, pickles, cabbage and parsnip.

Henry awoke suddenly to the thunderous din of stevedores stamping, hollering, and battering the deckboards with dunnage, cargo hooks, chains and hammers. Iron-shod wheels of wagons and drays racketed like stone-grinders on the quayside cobbles. Work-horses tossing their nosebags stomped iron-shod hooves with the mellow musicality of an ironworks. A silver sun burned through a low and misty sky. A burly young man, long black whiskers under a black cap, elbowed Henry aside and shouted to men rigging cargo derricks halfway up the mainmast. 'Who are you?' Henry asked, bemused.

'Second mate, John MacGregor, and who the hell are you?'

'Second mate, Henry Ardent, until yesterday.'

'Och, so you're the one!' the Scot said, pushing up the brim of his hat and taking Henry's hand in a powerful grip. 'I'm proud to shake your hand, mon.'

'What did I do?'

'You put that Blue Nose bastard in his place, didn't you? And hoisting your tow-rope with the ensign – a wee bit cheeky.'

'How did I beat the *Musket*? He went ahead off Portsmouth.' MacGregor, grinning and shaking his head, pointed upward with a finger.

Astride the main royal yard, Henry looked out over London. Nothing he had ever been told prepared him for the scale of the vista that sprawled at his feet – a wilderness of slate as corrugated as a heaving winter sea, the wavecrests parallel jags of smoking chimneys. Far away, like sea stacks and skerries, jutted domes and spires and turrets; the dome of St Paul's cathedral gleamed white as a bird rock caked with guano.

Twisting on his perch he saw the Thames: the Surrey Docks on the far bank, the serpentine loop it made around the Isle of Dogs, the forest of spars rising from what must be the West India Dock. Grey and wet as a road, the river was dense with traffic. There were coasters of all sorts, brigs, brigantines, topsail schooners, ketches, snows, spritsail barges, as well as fish carriers, eelboats and fishing smacks, pulling boats and lighters, passenger steamers and tugs, full-rigged ships and colliers . . . In a dense mass, all were drifting up on the flood, forming a procession that twisted far away out of sight to Greenwich and beyond. And lording it over the fleet, her raked

golden masts capped with white, the *Musket* rode to a buoy in
mid river awaiting her tide. The *Partridge* had overtaken her in
the dark as she lay becalmed somewhere off the Kent shore and
Screech Gander had evidently failed to find a tug until dawn,
off Dover.

With bad grace the surly servant-boatman called Skitter
gave him a mug of hot water in which to shave, and the address
of Monkton Winkworth's office in the City, but refused him
anything to eat though a panful of eggs and sausages sizzled on
the galley fire.

Henry waited until Skitter had gone aft with a pot of coffee
for his master. Then he nipped into the galley, shook the eggs
and two sausages on to a plate, snatched a fresh roll and some
butter, and climbed the ratlines to the maintop.

'Mon, that's fighting talk, you're taking a big risk,' Mac-
Gregor warned.

'If Monkey Winkworth wants his eggs,' Henry muttered, 'he
can come and get them.'

Later, as Henry left the ship with a kit bag over his shoulder,
a gang of stevedores cheered. 'Well done lad!'

'You showed the Yankee bucko!'

'Ain't 'e a young 'un!'

'Good going, chum!'

Henry did not look back and the jauntiness induced by the
princely breakfast soon faded as he wove between drays and
traction engines, squeezed between hugh casks of wine and
bales of silk, and found himself alone amid a bustling crowd of
strange and uninterested faces.

Dispirited, he paused outside the dock gate to look up and
down the busy street. The hand in his pocket touched the jade
figure in its sealskin pouch. Henry did not doubt that for many
years, perhaps centuries, the weird little green man had hung at
the throats of generations of South Sea warriors, even princes.
What luck had it brought them? More important, what would
it do for Henry Ardent, beached and alone in the great city of
London?

From a costermonger's barrow he spent a penny on three
oysters. They had been fried in batter at least three days before
and tasted of fishy rags, nothing like the fresh river oysters he
levered open with his jack-knife and sucked off the shell at
home. But it was the two-minute delay as he ate the oysters
with a grimace which sealed Henry's immediate fate. As he
crossed the road there was a shout and a clatter of hooves. A

cab-horse was reined in and he heard his name shouted. 'Hoy! Henry Matilda Handyside blooming Ardent, starboard your helm . . .!'

Captain Sam Handyside's head and shoulders jutted from a hansom cab, his white whiskers quivering on his jowls like a muffler of feathery question marks. 'Thank God! Monkey Winkworth's man Skitter told me you'd gone ashore. He had a lemon in his mouth about something, and I expect you shoved it there, eh? Throw your dunnage up, get in, don't stand there gawping. You've no money, no place to stay, so you'll come live with me and Meg. It's all settled. Drive on, driver!' With that, the captain rapped smartly on the roof of the cabin with the handle of his umbrella.

Dazed, Henry watched the shops, warehouses, wharfs and traffic as the cab rattled along at a good lick, the captain prattling jovially. His black suit showed neither a wrinkle nor a speck of dust, his white shirt was freshly starched. He had landed at Portsmouth late yesterday afternoon, just in time for the late train to London, and had spent the night at his home in Hammersmith. His chief mate was bringing the ship round and was due on tomorrow's morning tide. 'And where are you bound, lad? What are your orders? George Chamberlayne has spread the word and the whole town is talking about you.'

When Henry told the story of how he had rescued the merchant from the dismasted schooner, and described the surprised look on Screech Gander's face as their ships crossed tacks off Portsmouth, the captain laughed so uproariously the driver peered in to check that neither murder nor vandalism was being committed in his cab. Now Henry quite saw why Charlie Meadows had referred to him as 'Old Thundersides'.

Through open gateways and at the ends of alleys Henry glimpsed ships, docks, high warehouses honeycombed with mid-air caverns into which bales, crates and barrels of every description were swinging. His nostrils filled with the rich smells of molasses, jute, wine, hides, tar, fish, hemp . . . It was all strange and confusing, doubly so after months at sea.

After twenty-five minutes the hansom swung between high brick pillars and halted in a jam of carts, drays, carriages and steam engines. Henry saw scores of ships discharging in the West India Dock. The ribbon of black water, streaked with rainbows from lumps of tar and spotted with floating rubbish, stretched away into the distance. Just this one dock seemed larger than Sydney Cove. And parallel to it, behind a line of brick warehouses, was the Export Dock where ships loaded. Beyond lay a third stretch of water, the South West Dock. Enormous though it was, the complex was just one small corner of the great trading enterprise, the Port of London.

Progress along the milling quays was slow but the far corner of the South West Dock was quieter. Sam told the driver to make for three white masts jutting high above the warehouse slates. Henry slung his bag on his shoulder and they picked their way through baulks of timber, coils of manilla and tins of paint to the dockside. There Sam stopped, thrust his hands deeply into his pockets with the umbrella hooked on one arm and said with a sigh: 'Feast your eyes, lad, you will never see a finer beauty in all your days.'

It was true. The dainty clipper was a vision. The tall masts were bone-white against the grey sky. The gloriously sweeping sheer of the bottle-green hull was set off by a gold stripe just below the line of her scuppers. Her bow was powerfully flared but the stem and underwater section were slender as a blade for cutting into the wind's eye. Amid the fancy scroll-work decorating her elliptical counter, curved and tapered like a champagne glass, the name of the exquisite vessel was picked out elegantly in gold: *Quiver*. Below, in more squat letters, was her home port: London.

Although the dock was dead still the delicate ship swayed lightly as riggers worked among her spars, setting up the halyards, buntlines, clew-garnets, sheets and the thousand-and-one running parts that would make of her tangle of ropes, timber and canvas a highly tuned sailing machine. Like a wild deer surprised in the forest, the ship lived up to her name: she seemed a-flutter with suppressed excitement. As he gazed upon her with open admiration Henry felt he need only blink and she would be startled into fleet-footed flight.

'A wild one, and wet,' Sam exclaimed. 'She'll dive as much as she swims, but ain't she a honey?'

'Your next ship?' Henry asked.

'Lord no, Monkey wouldn't waste a galloper like the *Quiver* on an old fogie with bricks in his breeches, I'm sorry to say.' Sam paused, looking wistfully at the proud thrust of the bowsprit and the luridly painted winged cherub beneath, Eros with bow drawn and an arrow aimed across the dock. 'Anyway, I've made my last trip. Meg made me promise to retire and here I am, on the beach for the rest of my days.' Sam fell silent. He, too, recognised the dawn of a new era. The world was going mad for speed and the new breed of ship demanded a new breed of seafarer. If Britain were to rise to the American challenge she needed daring, tough, wilful youngsters, not veterans like himself who furled topgallants at night. What wouldn't he give to be young again!

Standing tall and straight at the chubby shipmaster's shoulder Henry felt a pang of remorse. Monkey Winkworth could not be rotten all the way through if he was capable of building masterpieces like the *Quiver* for his fleet, the Arrow Line. If Henry had remotely suspected the irascible old man might have been choosing mates for such a dashing and dazzlingly beautiful ship he might have thought twice before stealing his breakfast.

Swinging his furled umbrella like a cane, Sam set off at a brisk pace. 'Come on lad,' he urged, 'no use mooning over might-have-beens.'

Vessels bound for the West India Dock entered through a lock which was operated only when the tide was high. This lifted them above the level of the river and they were warped out into a basin. Roughly oval in shape, Blackwall Basin formed a junction between the lock and the three docks with which it was connected by narrow brick-lined channels.

A barque lay in the basin, outward bound, waiting her turn to be locked out. Crowds of well-wishers and relatives made pathetic farewells. Perhaps from this very spot Henry's own parents, voyaging to an uncertain future on the other side of the world, had bidden England goodbye.

Crowds of small boys and dock wallopers loitered along the lockside and the basin quays. They hung on the rails of the swing bridge that cut the busy road where shuffling horses and swearing draymen queued impatiently. A ship was gliding out of the lock. Henry was startled to see it was the *Musket*.

Sam shouldered powerfully to the quayside as the gold and crimson figurehead cut by, near enough to touch. 'Perfect timing,' he said.

The shark's tail was still nailed to the bowsprit but the clipper's decks were already stained with soot, smoke, stevedores' boots and filthy river water trickling from wet ropes and muddy chains. Henry saw the negro cook grinning at the onlookers. Directing the crew handling the towing warp at the bitts was Smoke Lapierre, the wicked hunting knife sheathed on the rope which held up his trousers.

Captain Screech Gander, standing beside the mud pilot on

the poop, cut an imposing figure. He was dressed from head to foot in pearly silk with a black ribbon tied at his throat. His boots were highly polished and his dark features had the same leathery tan.

He raised a silver-topped stick made from the vertebrae of a shark and proclaimed so all could hear, 'Ninety-eight days from Canton, gentlemen!'

There was such a din of yells and whistles that the *Musket* had gone past Sam and Henry before they could catch Screech Gander's eye. The crowd surged along the quay, following the ship as she entered the basin. As the bridge swung across her stern the traffic moved off with a clatter of hooves, whip-cracks and curses.

Sam took Henry's arm and led him across the bridge. Then they darted across the road, cut through an alley, and came out on the river. A few yards downstream of the lock, with low windows looking out on the ships shaping up for the entrance, was a weather-boarded house. Sam opened a wicket gate and pushed through the front door into a crowded smoky room. As Henry ducked his head to follow he saw the name Artichoke Tavern in faded letters over the door.

Sam handed his umbrella to a pale young man wearing a floor-length apron. 'Take care of the young gent's dunnage, there's a good fellow.' The waiter looked askance at Henry's salt-stained trousers, wrinkled shirt and damp-smelling reefer jacket as he stowed the kitbag beneath the coat-rack. The room was packed with thirty or forty men, all drinking, smoking, playing cribbage and talking loudly on red plush settees. The sturdy mahogany furniture, Henry learned later, was salvaged from the cabins of East Indiamen. A coal fire flickered smokily under a mantelpiece on which a stuffed albatross with spread wings appeared to be making a shaky landing. The walls were covered with scores of company houseflags and ensigns faded by countless tropical suns and frayed by trades and squalls.

At a small table by a window overlooking the river, three men greeted Sam jovially as he wove through the crowded room, Henry following shyly in tow. 'Henry Ardent – here's Captain Alfred Joy, Captain John Tidewater, Captain Nick Mangles . . . '

'And this young man here, gentlemen, is second in the *Partridge*, who brought his ship home and gave Screech Gander one in the eye.'

All three shipmasters were tough, self-assured men in their forties. They inspected Henry with quick, discerning glances and pushed back their chairs to make room. 'You did well,' Captain Mangles said, pulling at a ginger moustache. 'I never suspected the old *Partridge* had it in her. Maybe the Monkey did right in buying her up, eh?'

'It proves what I've always said, speedy passages owe as much to determination as to new-fangled designs,' asserted Captain Joy as the waiter brought a tray of tankards. 'The *Musket* sprang her mizzen topmast, I gather. These Yankees are over-hatted, too easily damaged aloft.'

The third captain, John Tidewater, had a bushy grey beard and a bullet-shaped bald head. 'What I don't understand, young man,' he said, 'is how you happened to be so close to Ushant you could pluck that man Chamberlayne out of the sea.'

This was getting near the knuckle and Henry was reluctant to air his shortcomings in professional company but Sam leapt to his defence. 'Let's just say it was a calculated risk, eh John, and don't tell me you haven't taken a few of 'em in your time.'

'It was a lucky one for Chamberlayne,' Captain Tidewater said drily. Then he lifted his tankard and said, 'Well, here's looking at you, boy – down the red lane!'

Henry almost gagged on the tepid and bitter ale but it was a small penalty to pay for the thrill of being welcomed into the privileged circle at the Artichoke, for decades the exclusive drinking hole of shipmasters while in port.

'You wouldn't have heard, Sam ...' Captain Joy was saying, 'The American Navigation Club has put up a challenge.'

'Ten thousand quid!' Captain Mangles interjected.

'To do what?' Sam asked.

'An American ship with American crew to race a British ship with a British crew from London to China and back.'

'Bloody nerve.'

'Shameful.'

'Don't tell me we're not going for it,' Sam asked.

The three captains shook their heads in unison. Captain Joy wiped the beery foam off his moustache and added, 'We all hoped Monkey Winkworth would throw in that *Quiver* of his but he won't, the wretch.'

There was loud jeering from the drinkers near the door and every head turned as Captain Screech Gander entered. He doffed his wide-brimmed straw hat at the captains whom he recognised. 'Sam! Where did you come ashore, Plymouth? I didn't expect to find you here. Hoist my flag for me, there's a pal.'

As Screech Gander joined the group he handed over a rolled-up flag. Sam let it unfold beneath his chin, showing the jagged yellow lightning bolt on a scarlet background that was the houseflag of Joseph O'Cain, of Boston, owner of the *Musket*. It had long been a tradition at the Artichoke that newly arrived captains hoisted their flags to a beam in the centre of the room. Smiling, Gander took a thin cheroot from a silver case and looked around. 'The drinks are on me, I guess. Six pounds ten a ton, what do you think of that for a freight gentlemen? A man has to be careful, or he could get rich in this business.' He lit the cigar and was shaking out the match when his eye fell on Henry. 'Well, well,' he said, 'the boy from Botany Bay who rides side-saddle on sharks. You came up by train with Sam, I guess.'

Henry shook his head. 'No, we docked up the river soon after midnight, a tide before you. What will you drink?'

Screech Gander's surprise showed only in the prolonged spurt of smoke expelled steadily from his nostrils. 'Champagne,' he said.

'Champagne and six glasses,' Henry told the waiter. Then he added more loudly, 'Captain Gander is celebrating that a Yankee sailor can make a landfall in England without losing more than a mizzen topmast.'

In the centre of the smoke-filled saloon Sam was bending the flag to the line threaded through a little pulley on the black oak beam. 'Watch out for Gander, lad, he bites.'

'Yellow dogs don't frighten me,' Henry murmured. As Sam shot him an anxious look Henry had a more pressing problem on his mind. 'Monkey hasn't paid me and I've only half a quid in my pocket, will you help me out?'

'Of course, but I don't grubstake dead men.' To his dismay, Sam saw Henry unpinning the Arrow Line flag that had been hung on the wall by some previous returning captain. It was the flag which Henry had seen Skitter hoisting in the *Partridge*: square, with a broad green border and the silhouette of a drawn bow and arrow in black on a white ground. Henry took the line from Sam's hands. 'Let's get this right,' he said, knotting swiftly. A moment later boos and whistles carried on a gale of jeering laughter as the two flags were hoisted to the ceiling of the tavern, the Arrow above the Lightning.

As Henry returned to his seat Screech Gander smiled, his mouth a thin line between the points of his sideburns, and his dark eyes glinting with malice. 'The old Artichoke isn't half the place it used to be,' Gander said conversationally to the other captains, 'not with all this colonial riff-raff drinking in here nowadays.' Suddenly he leaned forward and pulled up the edge of Henry's salt-stained trouser leg. 'Look at those shackle marks, healing mighty well wouldn't you say, gentlemen?'

Henry flushed as the older men laughed at his discomfiture but he was saved from the need to reply by the waiter who arrived with the champagne. When he had gone, Henry emptied one glass into a large ashtray which he put in front of Gander. 'Give the Yankee dog a bowl,' he said.

The captains chuckled again, warily wondering how it would end. Such sport hadn't been seen in the Artichoke for many a day. Not a man in the crowded room was unaware of Captain Screech Gander's fearsome reputation. Nobody could say for certain how many sailors he had actually picked off the yards with the six-shooter he was supposed to wear on his belt, but the stories about him that circulated among the fo'c's'les and waterfront dives of the world lent him an aura of almost wholly black-hearted infamy that he wore with the same easy and rakish assurance as his crisp white suit. What made his fame as slave driver and crew killer acceptable and even enviable among distinguished nautical company was the fact that as a seaman and shipmaster, Screech Gander was second to none. All sins could be forgiven a captain who made a passage from Canton to the Thames in anything less than a hundred days. But if you had to admire his professional accomplishment you also had to wonder how long it would be before the Blue Nose got what was coming to him. This was the compelling mystery of the man, and explained why the clamour in the tavern was suddenly hushed as Gander spurted smoke from his nostrils and held Henry in a gaze of calculated contempt.

Taking advantage of the quiet, Gander prodded the stub of his cheroot into Henry's glass then took another glass for himself and rose to his feet. 'Gentlemen, an invitation to you all . . . Supper aboard my ship the *Musket* in the West India Dock tomorrow evening at six o'clock . . . It will be a great occasion and my pleasure . . . '

Silencing the buzz of chatter with a lordly wave, he went on,

'Now I want to propose a toast. Let's drink to the merchant navy of the United States of America, finest ships to sail the seas!' Gander tossed off his drink to a burst of jeering laughter and catcalls then resumed his seat with a satisfied smile. 'You're not drinking?' he asked, cocking an eyebrow at Henry.

'I'll drink to the Red Ensign.'

'I see you're a man with an eye for lost causes,' Gander scoffed. 'Never mind, drink up and we'll have another.'

It was the first time Henry had drunk champagne. He was surprised by the mildness of the taste, little but fragrant water. He had another glass. When the bottle was finished Gander ordered another and when that was empty Gander proposed it was time they had a proper drink: brandy. The mood of prickly hostility became blunted by alcohol. Whatever sort of a lion he was at sea, Screech Gander was evidently a warm host ashore. The liquor never stopped flowing and the Blue Nose watched with sardonic and satisfied amusement as the circle of men round him became increasingly red in the face and loud in their laughter. It was in the middle of Sam Handyside's story about the piano that Henry's head first started to spin. 'You must have known Tod Campbell, had a face like a farmer's arse on a frosty night,' Sam recounted. As the others nodded knowingly, guffawing, he went on: 'You never saw such a man for a deal as Tod, and he could never resist a bargain. One trip in the old *Star of Dorset* a few years back he finds himself standing at the back of an auction and bidding for something that costs a couple of pounds. It's a piano, and when he gets it on board the carpenter has to take half the companion-way to pieces to get it down into the saloon though of course the old boy never played a note in his life. After a while he gets fed up with the thing lashed down with ropes in the middle of his saloon so he decides to raffle it before the mast. Of course every man-jack buys a ticket, which at five bob each brings in three pounds. The cook wins it and is mighty proud of his new piano but he can't get it out of the saloon and even if he did there's nowhere to put it so Tod charges him two bob a week storage. Finally the poor old cook goes down with an axe and it takes him all day to break the thing up and get it over the side, piece by piece.'

Only as the three captains roared with laughter, and Gander smiled thinly, did Sam notice that Henry's head was rocking as if it might fall off his shoulders. Sam had taken a few on board himself and had trouble getting to his feet. 'Time to cast off, gentlemen,' he said, making a brisk attempt to pull Henry to his feet.

'He's scammered, Sam,' Captain Joy observed.

'Come on lad,' Sam urged, a whip in his voice. 'Up she rises!'

Henry managed to hold himself erect but only for five seconds. The rocking and pitching of the hot and smoke-filled room was worse that any Cape Horn storm. He turned up his eyes, folded in the middle and fetched up under the table with his legs sticking out.

Screech Gander stood up with the calm air of a man who has completed some tedious but necessary business. With one hand he dragged Henry effortlessly into the centre of the room. Dumbfounded, Sam and the other captains in the tavern watched as the Yankee shipmaster busied himself with the flags.

In a few moments Henry's legs dangled from the centre beam, the flag of the Lightning Line flying above them and the Arrow flag shrouding his face.

Dusting his hands in a composed way, Gander picked up his wide-brimmed straw hat and dropped two gold sovereigns ringingly on the table. Then he said to the astonished assembly, 'I look forward to meeting you gentlemen again tomorrow.' Without so much as a sideways glance he sauntered out.

Rigged in his comfortable old green and threadbare smoking jacket and scuffed slippers, Captain Samuel Handyside was contentedly reading the *Morning Post* with a magnifying glass, catching up on the details of the forthcoming funeral of the Duke of Wellington which was evidently going to be a national pageant on a grand scale, when his wife Meg bustled in with the boiled eggs. She spread a napkin of embroidered nankeen on her knee and efficiently beheaded her own egg and passed the inverted cap to her husband. Sam closed his paper with nervous swiftness and spooned out the soft white, not quite runny, 'Perfect, my dear,' he mumbled appreciatively. Mrs Handyside passed over the dish bearing his own egg in a silver cup. It was a treat to be mollycoddled by his dear wife, who sacrificed her own egg in order that his could be returned to the hot water for a few moments longer if it were not quite to his satisfaction. For the rest of his life, Sam realised, he would experience this morning ceremony. It gave him a jolt and a shadow of concern settled round the usually merry blue eyes. 'Eat up your egg, Captain,' Mrs Handyside told him.

'Yes dear, it's quite delicious.'

'I've another one put by for your young man, when he comes down.'

'He may not feel like eating too much, the Yankee drank him under the table.'

'The poor boy.' Meg Handyside was a trim little woman whose managing and abrupt manner was born of long years of solitary living. She had devoted her life to keeping what she called 'the captain's little house and dusting his little treasures' which filled the room. Delicate fans of silk and bamboo lay on the walls like giant moths. Shelves groaned under the weight of carved ivories, gorgeous arrays of mother-of-peal and trochus, and rainbow swirls of abalone shell. There were models of sailing ships worked in bone by French prisoners in the wars half a century before and a box which Sam assured her was constructed of salt beef so hard and weathered it had the texture and beauty of solid mahogany, though to this day she only half believed him. On the dresser, like a row of giant snails, were beautiful cowrie shells; they had been buried for weeks in the sands of some tropical beach for the ants to remove the meat then they had been placed within the trunk of a banana tree for the sap to give them their brilliant sheen. In one corner of the room, on top of a small wooden barrel that had once saved Sam's life after a shipwreck in the Bristol Channel, stood a gaunt tree of white coral that Meg always thought of as the bleached antlers of some strange under-sea monster.

Sam Handyside had sailed with men who had sailed with Captain Cook, the great navigator who had put half the world on the map. As a youth of fourteen serving in a fleet transport, he had heard the guns at the Battle of Trafalgar and seen the wreckage left afloat in its aftermath. Then, progressing rapidly through an apprenticeship in the Honourable East India Company, he had been promoted master at a young age. Long before the company's 300-year monopoly in the eastern trades came to an abrupt end the shipmaster read the portents and joined an Australia-bound ship called the *Matilda*. In three decades as a shipmaster Sam had made judicious use of the freight space allotted for his personal trade and made himself moderately well off. He had purchased the riverside house at Hammersmith, put by a handsome little nest-egg for the future, and with no children to support Meg and Sam developed a fascination with ornamental jade from the East.

While the parlour where they ate breakfast was filled with souvenirs of the captain's voyages, the drawing room was equally cluttered with their prized pieces of jade. On shelf after shelf lustrous dragons, flowers, oriental gods and other beautiful carvings fashioned in translucent green stone caught the soft light stealing between the curtains. Sam had obtained the best of it through his contacts with the Hong merchants in Canton during the three-month enforced wait for the monsoon winds which for years had been the pattern of his life. Today's new clippers did not bother to wait, for not only were they capable of miraculous speeds down wind but their lean and powerful lines allowed them to beat up into the wind. They were intended to defy the contrary monsoon, to struggle the length of the China Sea into the very teeth of it.

Sam sighed suddenly and shook his head as if to clear it. Never again would he drop his hook in the turbid Pearl River or hear the ribald shouts of the washee-washee women as they sculled their sampans alongside, nor would he see the hooded look come over Fowqua's eyes as they bargained over a piece of jade. 'I'm an old shellback from now on, my dear, I hope you grow accustomed to the idea.'

Mrs Handyside cast her husband a shrewd look. It was always the same. Two days at home and already he was impatient to cast off his moorings. But this time the captain had nowhere to go. 'You're sixty-two years old, it's time to drop your anchor, you deserve a long run ashore . . . you promised me.'

'I know, I know,' Sam admitted hastily. 'Fact is, if I were half my age I would have trouble keeping up. The new generation is all huff and puff, and I don't have much puff left in me, Meg dear. Can't see to read without a glass, rheumatism in my knees . . .'

'What nonsense!' Mrs Handyside interrupted. 'The fact is, you try to pretend you're a gruff old fogy who doesn't understand what these new ships are all about while every moment you're aching for a chance to show these young men how good you are. Go on, admit it!'

Sam's laugh thundered through the house. He walked round the table and hugged his wife fondly. 'No, you're wrong, this old shellback isn't made for scorching round the ocean in cranky, over-hatted ships . . .'

'Good morning.' The shy voice startled them both. Freshly shaven, Henry waited nervously in the doorway. He was doubly embarrassed. Not only did he have to explain his behaviour last night but he had stumbled upon the Handysides embracing at the breakfast table.

'Come in lad, come in,' Sam boomed warmly. His wife went out and returned after a moment to say his egg was on the boil and please sit down. Henry mumbled some heartsick apologies. 'Let's face it,' Sam agreed forthrightly, 'you have a lot to learn about holding your liquor. But no harm done, today's another day. What's your plan?'

Henry gazed wonderingly at the curios lining the walls of the cosy parlour. A low fire burned in the grate. There was a glimpse of honeysuckle trailing around the outside edge of the window, and an ash tree with yellowing leaves. Sam returned to his place and reached over with the coffee pot from which he filled Henry's cup. Fleetingly, Sam felt a sharp stab of envy. This youngster was one of the new breed of shipmaster, Sam could see it in every inch of him though he could not have explained it. Instead, he laughed and brandished the coffee pot. 'You'll never guess where this came from,' he said.

Henry peered closely at the inscription, so worn from use as to be nearly illegible. He read the words aloud as he deciphered them: 'To Captain Sam Handyside, with gratitude, Mary and Henry Ardent.'

'That's right, who'd have thought the lad I christened on my own deck would be sitting here with me enjoying a cup from the pot presented by his parents, eh?'

Later in the morning, Henry climbed the grassy slope of Greenwich Park. He paused often to look at the prospect of London sprawling at his feet in a pall of smoke, and to shudder at the memory of the previous day's shame. What a fool he had been. Since leaving the Handyside's home Henry had been unable to control the shame that raged within him like recurring waves of nausea. In ports around the world shipmasters would tell the story. Did you hear about young Henry Ardent, son of the Cockatoo Island boatbuilder? That devil Screech Gander drank him under the table and left him hoisted feet-first in the Artichoke. How long would it be before the story, embroidered in the telling, reached Sydney Cove? No longer than it took the first ship to arrive there, no doubt about it.

Following Sam's instructions he had taken a steamer from Hammersmith Pier to Westminster. Near the new Houses of Parliament under construction he had changed after a short wait to another steamer which bore him rapidly down river and landed him at Greenwich. In Limehouse Reach they had passed the beautiful *Quiver* towing slowly up to load at the London Dock and Henry had sighed in aching admiration. What a ship she was! But after making such a nancy of himself before the assembled captains of London he thought he would be lucky to be judged worthy of a berth as cook's skivvy in a collier brig.

His leg muscles protesting at the unaccustomed steepness of the slope, Henry breasted the rise. The very air, though wet and smoky, hummed with a vitality unknown in far-off and sleepy Sydney. Again admiring the view he saw a tall ship, well down in the pickle, inching out of Blackwall Basin. Where was she bound? Melbourne? 'Frisco? Calcutta? Henry's heart beat faster as he saw the men busy in her rigging. He knew the risks they ran, the hardships they would endure, the man-killing labour of driving a sailing ship along the trade routes of the world. Nevertheless, he wished he were one of them.

Though the humming city was new and strange and exciting Henry already felt restless for the sparkle of sun on wave, the headlong dash of flying fish whirring low over the lifting swells, the prickle of salt turning to dust on his back. With an intuitive flash that gave a new spring to his stride, Henry suddenly caught a glimpse of his own destiny. He was not a castaway in London for he could see his escape. London, in every sense, lay at his feet. London had laughed at him, but soon – somehow – London would change her tune. And then he would leave.

Captain Plunkett's widow greeted Henry at the door of a small white house that gave an impression of bowing under the weight of pink roses which hung in tangled clusters from wires and trellises. Dressed in black, she was plump with double chins and calm grey eyes that had a twinkle despite her bereavement. Ducking his head beneath low black beams, Henry entered a cheerful parlour. A painting of the captain in a silver frame on a table by the fire was draped with a black ribbon. Beside it was a picture of another man also draped with black, the Duke of Wellington. Over the mantel was a picture of the *Partridge* creaming along under full sail with a mass of signal flags trailing from her mizzen. Henry's attention was so absorbed in the painting that for a few moments he failed to notice the third person in the room, a young woman of about his own age, also in black, who set her embroidery aside and rose to greet him with a shy smile. 'I am Louise, the captain's daughter, how kind of you to come, Mr Ardent.'

Sheepishly Henry took the delicate, finely boned hand in his own tarry and sea-calloused fingers. He brushed the pale knuckles to within a discreet three inches of his lips. She was like a China doll, he thought, but for the bright and lively eyes that regarded him solemnly.

Henry sat awkwardly on the edge of a small chair by the fire, ill at ease amid the clutter of furniture and ornaments. The room was filled with Chinese lacquerware, fans, carved ivories, a screen and other oriental paraphernalia that the captain had brought home from his voyages.

The widow and her daughter listened gravely, without so much as a quivering lip, as Henry described the giant wave that swept over the poop of the *Partridge* and carried away the chief mate and the helmsman. He told how they had thought the captain was missing, too, until he was found under the pump with a broken head.

With a solemn air of ceremony, Mrs Plunkett set out the tea. The delicate porcelain — cups, saucers, plates, sugar bowl, cream jug — was patterned with an oriental motif. The tea was brewed in a silver pot. Everything was placed just so, on a lacquer tray standing upon a lacquer table.

'Sugar?' Louise asked, offering the bowl. Flustered, Henry struggled with the dainty teaspoon. What madman had invented these solid bricks of sugar? He was on the point of using his fingers when the girl suggested helpfully, 'You may use the tongs if you wish.' Henry operated the tiny silver tongs and dropped eight cubes of sugar into his cup.

At once he could tell from their ill-disguised horror that he had blundered but did not know how. He plunged into an account of how he had nursed the captain for three weeks until he had passed away peacefully in his sleep and been buried at sea just north of the Equator.

'But that's not the end of the story, Mr Ardent,' Louise said, leaning forward with shining eyes. 'Do tell us how you raced the *Musket* home. How pleased and proud Father would have been!' Henry was not so certain Captain Plunkett would be cheering from his grave, but he told the story with modesty and relaxed in the glow of the women's admiration.

'How exciting it must be to dig for gold,' Louise said, refilling Henry's cup and watching with eyes as round as saucers as one sugar cube after another was again dropped into the cup. 'Only last week,' she went on determinedly, 'we read of a prospector who dug an ingot from a hole, wheeled it to the bank in his barrow, and pocketed four and a half thousand pounds for his morning's work. Just fancy!'

Henry smiled. 'It's not always as easy as that, I'm sorry to say.'

'They tell us to expect a shortage of wool because the gold fever has stripped the farms of labour,' Mrs Plunkett observed, passing Henry a scone.

'Well I can bring you good news on that point, Ma'am, because the holds of the *Partridge* were stuffed with it.'

'But I fear the supply must diminish. So many want to try their fortune in the diggings. Even the convicts at Woolwich have rioted. They are insisting on their right to be transported instead of working at the dockyard. At this minute a hundred of them have mutinied in the *Warrior* and are holding the officers hostage with knives, it's a terrible business.'

As the small talk ground on, Henry could barely contain his impatience. His head ached abominably and he could sense his courteous smile beginning to wilt. When Mrs Plunkett suggested Louise show him the catalogues of the Great Exhibition it was all he could do to restrain himself from running away. 'Such a pity you arrived just too late to see it,' Mrs Plunkett went on. 'The Crystal Palace is being removed to Sydenham piece by piece, you know. What engineers can do in this great day and age!'

'Thank you, I'd be greatly interested,' Henry responded woodenly. And when he realised Louise and her mother were laughing at him in a quiet and fond sort of way, Henry found he did not mind a bit. He smiled and shrugged. 'I'm sorry, I had a busy night last night . . .'

'I'm sure, you don't have to tell me anything about shipmasters,' Mrs Plunkett said. 'Don't worry, no more Chinese torture with talk of Great Exhibitions. You're dying to get off, back to your precious ships, and quite right too. But Louise and I have something we would like to give you.'

Wonderingly, Henry followed them into an adjoining room, the late captain's study. Henry glimpsed a small, leather-covered writing desk with a crystal inkwell in a mahogany frame, shelves of books, pictures of ships, and a comfortably upholstered leather armchair. In the centre of the room was a large wooden chest with heavy brass clasps and cornerplates. An inset plate was inscribed with the name Captain John

Plunkett. It was the old man's sea chest which Henry had seen often enough in the *Partridge*. Now his widow opened it to reveal the captain's sextant in its wooden box, the chronometer, and the telescope with which Henry had first inspected the *Musket*. The instruments rested on top of a pile of clothes; neatly folded reefer jackets of thick pilot-cloth, cap, scarves, a tailored top-coat, oilskins, leather boots that had never been worn. Henry found himself the scrutiny of a pair of wise eyes. 'You strike me as a young man who will go far, Mr Ardent,' Mrs Plunkett told him. 'I'm sure my husband, the late captain, would have wanted to help you on your way.'

Overwhelmed, Henry could only nod and smile. The sea chest was a treasure-trove beyond imagining for the instruments would allow him to navigate the oceans of the world to the end of his days.

It was with a jauntier stride that Henry retraced his steps down the steep slope of Greenwich Park, the heavy chest to follow later by cart. Now for the *Musket*.

In darkness Sam Handyside and Henry paid off their hansom and walked the last few yards along the cobbled alley between gloomy warehouses to the dockside. The American clipper was transformed. Lanterns glowed like brilliant stars from the tip of every yard and at every masthead. Flares lit the red-carpeted gangway. The entire maindeck was covered with a tautly laced awning of snow-white canvas and all the way round it were more lanterns. Sam and Henry were greeted by a liveried footman who offered glasses of champagne from a silver tray as they stepped wonderingly aboard. Sam took one. As Henry reached out, a shark-bone cane was laid firmly across his forearm and a voice commanded, 'Fetch the boy from Botany Bay a lemonade.'

'Good evening to you Captain, I'm impressed,' Sam said.

Gander's dark eyes swept the elegantly dressed guests conversing in groups on the holystoned decks. He smiled. 'We Yankees don't do things by halves, you know.' With a half-length coat of fine blue cloth, white trousers, and a diamond pin winking amid the froth of light silk at his throat, the captain cut a handsome figure.

Swallowing his pride, Henry took the tall glass of lemonade that appeared at his side on a tray. 'I hope your man-eating dog is chained up for the evening.'

'Oh yes, I wouldn't want to upset his constitution by feeding him convict flesh,' Gander acknowledged. 'I'm saving that treat for later.'

As the tall American turned to greet other guests Henry and Sam peered incredulously down the mainhatch. The red carpet on a temporary staircase led down to the 'tweendeck which had become an opulent buffet. Tables draped with white linen were heaped with game pies, cold joints, barrel of oysters, stiltons and bottles of wine. On every table stood tall candelabra. The round timbers of the masts, dropping through the deckhead like stout leaning pillars, were decorated with ribbons of red, white and blue. On a platform for'ard a string quartet sawed at a polka.

Bowing his head beneath the beams, Henry followed Sam through the elegant crowd. Sam waved at his friend, Captain Tidewater. 'What a spectacle, eh John? When did you ever see anything like it?'

'Not since I was last at Kensington Palace,' the bewhiskered shipmaster replied drily. Then he tapped with an ebony cane on the canvas covering the rough floorboards of the hold and eyed Henry distrustfully. 'You're staying with the lemonade, I trust, Mr Ardent?'

'Damn right,' Sam interjected, frowning a warning at Henry. 'What do you make of all this, John? It's more than the usual Yankee show-off, surely?'

'Everybody that matters is here. Look, there's Dicky Green. His *Challenger* is at the Nore, ninety-six days out, did you know? Apparently she fell in with the *Challenge* at Anjer and the Yankee hasn't been signalled yet.'

Sam whistled. 'Is that so?' A Blackwall shipowner, Richard Green had taken the lines off the American ship *Oriental*, when she caused a sensation by arriving at London with tea in December 1850. He had built his own smaller version, named her *Challenger*, and sent her out to China. On the way home she had fallen in with the crack clipper *Challenge* – in which Bully Waterman had reputedly killed five men on the outward voyage to San Francisco – and now it looked as if the little British ship was first home. Captain Tidewater took another glass as a footman passed with a loaded tray. 'Have you heard what they're doing in Boston? The shipowners are trying to bring back flogging.'

'Not before time.'

'Perhaps, but it seems a funny way to encourage real men into the fo'c's'le instead of the usual pack of dockside rats.'

'Some hope. There's only one thing worse than a rat, and that's a frightened and bleeding rat.'

'And the *Typhoon* is in Liverpool, did you hear? Thirteen days and ten hours across the big ditch.'

'Down-wind all the way, of course.'

'Not a steam kettle afloat could beat that,' Sam concluded happily.

With so many candles burning it was stifling in the 'tween-decks so the group moved up to the maindeck. A strange procession was crossing the gangplank. It was led by Skitter with Monkton Winkworth riding on his back. Two men followed, carrying between them a heavy wooden wheelchair. This one was a different model. There was a seat of thickly padded horsehair, and the upright back was carved with the drawn bow and arrow of the Arrow Line flag. At the front of each arm was a horizontal wheel with a winding handle on its rim for driving the chair along. It looked fun and Henry itched to have a try, but he wanted to keep his distance from Winkworth until his own recent escapade had been forgotten.

The shipowner's darting eyes absorbed the opulent scene. At the foot of the stairs Skitter knelt, Winkworth slid off his back and tottered as the wheelchair was pushed into position behind him, then slumped into it with a shrill protest. A moment later a cushion embroidered with the Arrow Line motif was handed down the stairs. Skitter levered it behind the scrawny rump.

The talk resumed its headlong dash. The orchestra struck up Yankee-doodle-dandy. As some of the guests raised their glasses to him Screech Gander danced a few steps of a horn-pipe. Then he held his glass high and called out in a ringing voice that cut the music and hubbub dead: 'Your glasses, gentlemen!'

Gander jumped on a chair and the guests shuffled back to give him the floor. Winkworth stared up from his chair with a look of a rumpled fowl. 'It's my pleasure to welcome you all aboard the *Musket*,' Gander went on. 'You will have seen for yourselves that she is the finest vessel afloat. And . . .' The dark eyes swept the company sardonically as cries of 'Hear, hear!' mingled with mocking jeers and whistles. 'And, gentlemen, the fastest.'

Gander waited patiently for the outcry to quieten. 'My toast, gentlemen, is to you, the London mercantile community. Let us drink to British trade, to our mutual prosperity, and to the Yankee keels that made it all possible. Gentlemen, your health!'

Sam growled 'To trade!' and tossed off his glass. Captain Tidewater looked doubtful then followed Sam's example. Henry sipped his lemonade as he tried to understand how these English merchants, insurers, shipowners and builders could bring themselves, under the circumstances, to partake of the taunting Yankee's hospitality. These smug and self-satisfied merchants and mariners were surely not the tooth and claw of the famous British Lion. What would Lord Nelson have had to say, or for that matter the late Duke of Wellington, in memory of whom many of the guests wore black armbands? Would the Iron Duke have suffered the sneering insults of Napoleon for the sake of drinking his champagne? His mouth a thin line of frustration and disappointment, Henry craned forward to hear what Screech Gander was saying as he bent over the wheelchair. 'You're not drinking, Mr Winkworth?'

'You take a lot on yourself, Captain Gander,' the shipowner replied coldly, turning the iron handles to swing his chair round. 'If your seamanship were matched by your bravado I would drink to you, but I fear it is not.'

'How so, Mr Winkworth? You can't deny that ninety-eight days out of Canton is notable, to say the least.'

'It seems quite ordinary, Captain.' Winkworth's thin voice carried easily in the sudden hush. 'The *Challenger* has taken a pilot at Dungeness, ninety-six days out, and there is no sign yet of the *Challenge*. I see nothing to crow about.'

'Then why are you so reluctant to accept the challenge of the American Navigation Club? The stake is now doubled to twenty thousand pounds. And I will give any British contender a head start of fourteen days.'

'Bah!' Winkworth's contempt silenced the sudden hush of surprise that swept the company. 'Are we talking of racing pretty yachts, or of seamanship, Captain Gander? I'm sure we would all compliment your winsome little vessel on her fine appearance. But remember it was my own ship the *Partridge* – navigated as we all know by a mere boy – that docked in London a tide ahead of the *Musket*.'

Henry felt all eyes turned on him. Many hands clapped him on the back. Despite all his efforts to remain out of the limelight, he found himself propelled to the front. Screech Gander flicked back his coat tails and stood with his fists on his hips, his gleaming boots placed wide on the deck. His expression was scornful. Hardly knowing what devil was guiding his tongue, Henry said loudly, 'I don't suppose he feels so brave without his dog to protect him.'

The collective gasp of the crowd made a noise like a squall gathering breath before the strike. Gander's expression switched abruptly from anger to relish. 'You heard it, on my own deck, gentlemen. This jerk of Botany Bay bilge is accusing me of being a coward.'

'Not exactly.' Henry's crisp denial brought another sigh, this time of disappointment.

'What then?' Gander demanded.

Henry shook his head gravely. 'I don't think a coward would throw his men to the sharks, or take pot-shots at them with a gun as they work aloft. I think it's more in the line of a murdering son-of-a-bitch who would do that. A murdering villain unfit to walk the deck of any ship – even a Yankee.'

Screech Gander broke the thunderstruck silence with a knowing laugh. His eyes fixed steadily on Henry, he removed and with deliberate care, pocketed the diamond pin and unknotted his cravat. Then he took off his coat and passed it behind him. 'Nobody . . . ' he said at length, pausing only to sweep the astonished and silent audience with grimly determined eyes. 'Nobody stands on my own deck and talks to me like that – nobody.'

Henry laughed lightly and removed his own coat. 'Anything a Blue Nose can do an Australian can do better,' he said.

Somebody shouted, 'Hooray, a masthead chase!' and the crowd took up the cry. Screech Gander looked startled, angry at losing the initiative. Henry was silent and determined. He had come to London to make his mark and now he was making it. Whether it came to pistols, fisticuffs or a race through the ship's rigging did not make a lot of difference.

A blade sliced the lashings and the awning over the deck was rolled back. A man was despatched to the main royal yard from where he could check that each competitor touched all three masthead caps without cheating. Many of the guests took the opportunity to dive down the red-carpeted stairs and load their plates with meat, cheese and oysters. Handfuls of guineas exchanged hands as wagers were made. The waiting coachmen and carriagemen pressed along the dockside as the clamour reached fever pitch. Henry heard one of them say, 'I'll put a shilling on Botany Bay.' At the same time, a stout merchant with a red face sealed a bet of ten guineas on the Yankee.

Henry removed his coat and shoes and tensely flexed his shoulder muscles. 'Which way is the betting going?' he asked Sam.

'About evens, I'd say,' Sam replied worriedly. 'You've stuck your neck out, lad, I hope it doesn't get chopped off.'

Henry shrugged. 'Do or die, eh Sam!'

'Look out for the dirty tricks department aloft, and remember it's a long way to fall.'

Henry glanced up at the gaunt threads of wire and rope silhouetted against the glowing cloud, and shivered. The contenders measured up at the binnacle as a florid man in a bowler hat waved a red handkerchief and shouted, 'Starter's orders, ge'men!' Henry stretched out his hand for a gentlemanly shake. Gander slapped it away. His long, whippy limbs were relaxed and his silk shirt fluttered open at the throat. Henry, with jutting chin and baleful stare, fought a mental battle to resist the daunting effect of the Yankee's formidable self-confidence. 'Ready gentlemen? Set?' The red handkerchief fluttered down. 'Go!'

It had been agreed that Henry would take the port-side rigging and Gander the starboard. As Henry sprang for the shrouds he crashed flat on the deck. Screech Gander had tripped him from behind. Winded and grazed, he started his climb when Gander was already spider-walking up the futtock shrouds.

The three masts of a sailing ship are supported on each side by heavy shrouds which have smaller ropes called ratlines placed horizontally, like the rungs of a ladder, to help men climb aloft. The masts are also braced one to the other by stays. From the foremast the stays angle downwards to the bowsprit. The stays spanning the fifty-foot gulf of blackness between each of the masts offered an almost direct route between the mast-heads – as long as a man has the agility of an acrobat, the strength of an ape, and courage unimaginable.

The noise as Henry ran up the ratlines into the darkness was deafening. The mass of upturned white faces in white shirt-fronts put him in mind of the craggy rock covered with shrieking gannets he once passed under sail in Bass Strait.

Henry had forgotten the *Musket*'s mizzen royal mast had been damaged. Much of the running gear and other fittings were yet to be attached to the new spar. It towered above his head, smooth as a flagpole, shaking under Gander's weight as he hauled himself up with explosive gasps. There was no way up until the Yankee came down, and then he would have an unassailable lead. Unless something could be done to slow him.

Plenty of slack rope dangled around the doubling, left by the riggers. Henry worked fast. Screech Gander touched the cap with a triumphant shout and at once began to descend, braking his slide where the mizzen royal stay branched off. At a downward angle of about forty-five degrees it slanted across the gap to join the mainmast halfway up. Clinging to the spar just below, Henry waited for Gander to transfer to the stay. Then he looped a noose over the Yankee's foot and pulled it tight. The other end of the rope was made fast somewhere in the darkness below.

Henry neared the top of the mizzenmast, his biceps and forearms shrieking with strain, as Gander's swift slither down the mizzen royal stay was arrested by the rope. The arm-wrenching jerk came close to shaking him off the wire. Now he had to haul himself a few feet up to obtain some slack, then work the noose off his ankle while clinging to the wire with one hand.

The breathing space gave Henry a chance. He spotted one rope that crossed to the mainmast at a higher level. It was the main royal brace, angling upward and outward to the top of the royal yard where the umpire was sitting next to a lantern. But the rope was by no means taut and climbing up it for such a great distance would be difficult. Henry did not hesitate.

Gander untangled his foot and pounded up the maintop-mast shrouds. Then Henry, dangling in space midway between the masts, sensed his rope beginning to move. For a stomach-churning moment he thought he would fall. Then he realised somebody below was slackening off the brace so it would swing him forward on to the topgallant yard. God bless Sam! As his body jarred into the yard he clambered along it to the mainmast and found himself a bare ten feet ahead of Gander.

Reaching the smooth part of the mast where it jutted above the royal yard, Henry threw his arms and legs around it and climbed. He touched the cap, transferred to the stay cutting across to the foremast, and worked his way steadily across, hand over hand with his legs hooked over it. It was easy going because the stay sloped downwards at a shallow angle and he could almost slide. He was halfway across, feeling the wire shudder as Gander put his weight on it, when he heard a laugh. An image flashed into his mind of a belaying pin smashing down on the nose of the shark and he recalled where he had last heard that dry cackle. It was Smoke Lapierre awaiting his arrival in the shadows ahead.

Henry realised he was trapped. The man would lash out with a knife or kick him off the spar as he transferred his weight. Already the stay was bouncing heavily as Gander slid down the wire towards him.

A gasp rose from below as Henry let his legs drop from the stay. With a convulsive heave and a twist he launched himself into space. It was only six or seven feet to fly but it seemed as many hundred. It landed him on the stiffly furled canvas of the fore-royal yard and drove the breath from his body. But Lapierre was on the other side of the mast. 'Smash him, Smoke!' Gander hissed.

Henry jumped to his feet and ran along the spar. He leaped for the topmast shrouds and climbed frenziedly. As Smoke reached up with his knife Henry lashed out and the blade went spinning out into the darkness. The splash went unobserved in the tumult of cheers and boos as Henry's fingers touched the cap. But now he was in trouble. How to descend with Gander and Lapierre waiting just fifteen feet below him?

There was only one way, by the forestay that angled out to the tip of the bowsprit which was almost as far away from the deck as the masthead. To reach the deck Henry would have to cover two sides of a triangle.

Hardly had he started on his long route downward when he realised Screech Gander had touched the top and was taking the more direct way down. Crying out at the burning in his hands Henry braked his descent, transferred to the royal stay and from there to the flying jib stay. Then he heard Sam's bellow from the deck, 'Halyards, lad!'

Henry wrapped aching fingers around the flying jib halyards and let his feet swing. The halyards sagged heavily, nearly tearing his arms out of their sockets. Then he found himself dropping rapidly as the halyard was paid out. It stoppped with a jerk as Sam came to the tail end. The sudden shock was too much. Henry fell ten or twelve feet, landing jarringly on the fo'c's'le head face to face with Nightingale.

Covering his face, Henry rolled away. There was a ripping sound and a slashing pain in his leg. He took a flying leap to the maindeck.

As he landed, Henry's ankle twisted and he tumbled over and over. From twenty feet up, Screech Gander saw Henry jump. He let go the rope and dropped. His feet were knocked from under him by Henry's headlong sprawl.

Dozens of hats flew in the air to a thunder of cheering as the two men, battered and gasping for air, fetched up in a tangled heap at the foot of the foremast. Willing hands helped them up. Henry winced from pain in his ankle and Captain Tidewater loaned him his ebony cane as a prop. Blood flowed from the bite on Henry's leg and there was a long rent in his trousers. Screech Gander dusted himself down casually, his silk shirt ruined by tarry rope marks burnt into the weave. A grinning footman offered a tray on which golden whisky danced in a crystal decanter. Gander filled two glasses, gave one to Henry, and tipped his own in a salute. 'Dead heat, wouldn't you say, gentlemen?'

Henry stared round, appalled. Was not one man game enough to stand forward and say it was Henry who had obviously reached the deck first? Else how could Gander have dropped on top of him? As the whisky blazed down his throat he blinked the smarts out of his eyes. 'Give me half a chance, I'd whip you with no dead heat about it,' Henry said, glowering.

Gander rounded on him, incredulous. 'You'd whip me, you say? Ha, that's rich! With what would you whip me, my petal?'

'With a ship,' Henry continued doggedly. 'Give me a ship to sail I'll make you Yankee slave-drivers look so small the American Navigation Club won't know which end of the telescope it's looking through.'

Some of the spectators sniggered as Gander looked round wearing a nonplussed expression. 'But you don't have a ship, my heroic friend. Last I heard you were second mate, newly appointed. Indeed, I'd eat my hat if anybody in this distinguished company were silly enough to sign you on as ordinary seaman. And you're talking of a race round the world, God help us . . .'

'You might have to do just that, Captain Gander!' The voice boomed from the back of the crowd which parted to let a man through. It was George Chamberlayne, a lantern in his hand, who climbed up on the pump machinery to address the crowd. 'Most of you know my name. I'm George Chamberlayne from Manchester, and I'm in textiles. The Chinks, as you know, are shivering. What they need is woollens so I'm sending a ship full of the stuff to sell 'em. And she'll come home with best tea. Now let me tell you something . . . '

Chamberlayne jabbed a determined finger at the crowd. 'Speaking as a Manchester man I'm amazed at you fellows leaving the American challenge lying on the table. What is the great British fighting spirit coming to? To survive, gentlemen, we need new blood. Men of fire, like this young fellow who saved me from a certain grave in the English Channel only this week. I will tell you what I plan to do.

'My ship will sail with this young man her master and if Captain Henry Ardent wants to challenge the famous Screech Gander to a little race it's all right by me, on one condition . . . '

Chamberlayne glowered into the excited roar of surprise. 'On one condition,' he repeated, his forefinger making its point as clearly as any lighthouse. 'The lad had better bloody win . . . eh?'

Dizzily Henry bowed his head. Every muscle ached. His palms were blood-raw. Blood pulsed wetly down his leg from the dog bite. The ankle was agony. Everything else was a mystifying dream.

He heard somebody call from the back, 'What ship? You're not expecting him to poke the Yankee in the eye with the old *Partridge*, I hope?'

George Chamberlayne thrust out his burly arms, commanding silence. 'You all know my dear wife's father, Monkton Winkworth. The ship I have chartered from the Arrow Line will sail any Yankee off the face of the ocean if she is driven with the courage and determination this young man has already displayed . . . '

'Tell us what ship?'

Henry felt his arm being raised into the air as George Chamberlayne said, 'Top up your glasses, gentlemen, and let us toast Captain Henry Ardent and a crack British clipper.

'Gentlemen, drink to the *Quiver*, and God speed her.'

The British clipper ship *Quiver* lay in Blackwall Basin with mooring lines singled up. In a few minutes she would glide forward into the lock then be released into the Thames outward bound for New York, San Francisco and China. It was a quarter past ten o'clock on the morning of Wednesday, 20th October 1852.

Huge crowds lining the quays waved their hats as the ship's young captain, Henry Ardent, limped up the companionway and took a worried look aloft. Grey clouds were chasing out of the north-west, nothing but the answer to a prayer. Tensely Henry greeted the mud pilot as he came aboard. 'Ah, Mr Brown again, is it not?'

'That's right Cap'n,' the pilot replied, beaming.

'We will cast off at five bells precisely, if that is convenient.'

'Aye it'll do well enough, Cap'n.'

The beautiful *Quiver* was dressed overall, every flag from her locker flying in a fluttering line from taffrail to bowsprit by way of her three white-painted mastheads. A new Red Ensign crackled from the spanker gaff. Her miles of manilla rope, yet to be tested by the wind's strength, were the golden colour of fresh straw. Her brasswork was bright enough but yet to acquire the deeply burnished lustre of hours of elbow-work. Her deck was smooth and clean but had still to achieve the pale and silky smoothness that hours of back-breaking labour with holystones would bring. The new canvas was furled in tight rolls on the white spars. Henry knew that like any ship embarking on a maiden voyage, the first few days – if not weeks – would bring nothing but endless problems while the rigging was tuned into a powerful wind-driven machine. But this was not the only reason he shivered with suppressed tension, grateful for the heavy blue brass-buttoned coat, altered by a tailor, which not only kept him warm but concealed the trembling of his limbs.

The five days since he had found himself propelled into command of Great Britain's most beautiful and famous ship had passed in a blur.

It had been half past two in the morning before Henry had at last been able to leave the party in the *Musket*. Without consultation Sam directed the cab to drive them to the London Dock where the *Quiver* lay. The black water of the dock was restlessly still, as if some invisible pulse pounded beneath the skim of reflections. Or was it just the beating of Henry's own heart as he stepped aboard a ship sleeping with every nerve poised for flight, like an eagle in its eyrie?

Sam had followed him over the bulwarks with a grunt. 'I'm getting old and stiff for this lark, but you'll light a fire under her stern, see if you don't.'

Henry hardly heard him as he limped along the deck, wonderingly reaching out with sore hands to touch the painted timbers and assure himself he was not in a dream. A watchman stepped out on deck, a white-haired old man more frightened than threatening, who shook his fist and brandished a stick. 'Who are you? Go away you young devil, I know your game.'

'I'm the new captain.'

'You don't look like no captain to me,' the old man said, squinting at Henry's torn trousers, the bandaged calf, the young and bruised face. 'You're some scallywag from another ship bent on mischief, that's what you are. Push off!'

At that moment another cab rattled on to the dock and George Chamberlayne walked over to the ship. 'I thought I might find you here,' he said warmly.

The watchman sprang to attention and touched his forelock. 'I'm chasing the bleeder off sir, he's just some bugger bent on mischief, that's all.'

Chamberlayne's loud laughter echoed round the Dock. 'You can say that again!' he said delightedly. Henry and Sam walked with him to the cab. 'There are two important things to remember,' Chamberlayne told them. 'First, the wager is between Gander and myself. You can put up money if you want though I don't suppose you've got a lot to your name. Not twenty thousand pounds, at any rate.'

'My God, one hundred thousand dollars!' Sam gasped.

'That's the first thing you have to remember,' Chamberlayne said. 'There's a lot at stake in this affair and I'm not the only one throwing in a fortune. This might be a sporting challenge but it's winning that counts. I want you to win.'

Henry nodded numbly.

'Second important point is the route,' Chamberlayne went on. 'The details agreed are these. It will be a race around the world by way of New York, 'Frisco, and any port in China. The winner is the first ship to discharge fifty chests of new season's tea at the West India Dock. This is to forestall any brainwaves you might have of leaving your ship and racing up from the South Coast by train. We don't want to see your pretty face, we want your cargo. Is that clear?'

Henry's senses were in a whirl, 'Do we have to start together, like a horse race?'

'Not at all, get away when you're ready. Three or four days will see the *Quiver* loaded, the *Musket* about the same.'

Henry noticed a second man waiting in the shadows of the cab. It was Monkton Winkworth. 'Chamberlayne tells me you're just the man to pull this off, Mr Ardent,' he said, leaning forward to speak through the open window. 'You ought to know my feelings in the matter. I think he's wrong.'

George Chamberlayne was preparing to swing up into the cab when Henry's words rooted him to the spot. 'Just a moment, Mr Chamberlayne, I have one condition of my own.'

The textile merchant's eyebrows arched. 'Have you indeed?'

'I must have Captain Handyside in my ship.'

'Oh no, I couldn't, I promised Meg to come ashore . . .' Sam's protests withered on the vine. He sucked in his lips, tugged at his short whiskers, and tried unsuccessfully to conceal his delight. 'My God, do you really mean it? But it's a young man's game, we all know it.'

Henry spoke up firmly. 'I need a chief mate and a second to sail the ship. I can whip that Yankee's hide off him in a straight sailing match but there's more to it than speed. This race could be won or lost in port. You know I have never been to China. I don't know the ropes as Sam does. We can call him the pilot. At sea he can check out my navigation.'

As Chamberlayne nodded his agreement Winkworth leant forward into the open space of the window once more. 'Excellent,' he muttered. 'What Mr Chamberlayne sees fit to put in my ship is his affair. What he does with her is his business, also. Mine is to see the ship comes home again. I am counting on you, Mr Handyside.' Winkworth banged on the roof of the cab which immediately rattled away with Chamberlayne swinging himself in through the door.

Two men stepped suddenly from the shadows. For a moment Henry did not recognise them. Charlie Meadows was threading the brim of a bowler hat through nervous fingers and Charlie Field, tall as a church door, was for once without his tarred sou'wester. 'Cap'n h'Ardent? We 'eard yer was lookin' for good 'ands,' Meadows said, 'And Barley and me was thinkin', like, that . . .'

'Oatsy!' Henry exclaimed. Then he turned to Sam. 'What do you think? These two farmers reckon they've got salt water in their veins but I've an idea it's ditch water . . .'

'No,' Sam said, 'what do *you* say, Captain?'

Henry stopped laughing abruptly as the realisation dawned. He tugged at his jaw. 'I need a bosun and a bosun's mate, if you think you're up to it?'

'Up to it? Blimey, when can we sign articles?'

Henry jerked his thumb at the ship. 'The main topgallant lift wants reeving and there's a power of squaring away to be done. You'd best get started at dawn, but don't kill the night watchman, he's only doing his job.'

With the two most important decisions in a year-long race around the globe taken within the first five minutes, Henry felt the first stirrings of a new-found confidence.

Later, exploring the potential of his new power, he discovered it was absolute – and frightening. A ship at sea, like the *Partridge*, was a going concern. Henry's job when he took over as master was merely to keep her wound up, like a watch. With the *Quiver* he faced a different challenge because the ship was an empty shell. All the cogs had to be installed in just the right place, and when the whole machinery was set in motion it had to operate perfectly. And a sailing clipper had many more finely balanced cogwheels and springs than an ordinary watch. The detail was endless. Chief mate and second mate to be selected. Twenty-six sailors to be signed on, plus sailmaker, cook and steward. Navigation charts and almanacks to be ordered. Rowlocks and sea anchors for the ship's boats. Paint, tar and spare canvas to be purchased and stowed. Fresh water loaded, tested and tasted. The cargo of 228 tons of baled woollen goods from Chamberlayne's factories to be stowed, along with 312 tons of general cargo for New York. Every minute of the day brought a fresh problem. Meadows wanted more shackles and cash to buy carpenters' tools. And could he and Field partition off the aft end of the deckhouse for their exclusive use? The sailmaker wanted thread and eyelets, and two spare palms on board were not enough. The insurers required details of the cargo in triplicate. The mates made a long list of chandlery such as oil and paint and deck-scrubbers. George Chamberlayne wanted him to meet representatives of the press and tell his story, for the sailing of the *Quiver* and the *Musket* were second in the public consciousness only to the grand state funeral of the Duke of Wellington which was to take place in a few days. Even when the ship returned to the West India Dock to complete her loading, the quay alongside swarmed with sightseers. With all his heart Henry yearned for the relief of sailing day and his escape into the boundless horizons of the open ocean.

Now that the moment had come he could feel his courage ebbing away with the passing of every interminable minute. For some, this noisy farewell to a glamorous clipper on her thrilling challenge race round the globe might be a gay and festive occasion. For him, he thought dourly, it was more a public hanging with himself the victim. This morbid impression was heightened by the black armbands many people wore in mourning for the Iron Duke, and the black crepes, ribbons and banners that decorated doorways, lamp posts and even the nosebands of cab horses. Though he would not have changed places with anybody in the world at this moment, remaining calm and indifferent to the storm of excitement around him was torture. Soon, like a gallows trap, the lock gates would swing open and the drop would spill him out into the tideway.

The young captain, standing aloof and silent at the poop-rail, his wind-tanned features stiff and stern, was by no means the only man on board wondering what fate awaited them on the voyage ahead.

Sam Handyside, his beefy hands locked firmly behind his black coat, prowled the poop as restlessly as a bull in a yard. After thirty-two years as master of his own ship he would find it hard enough keeping his mouth shut now that he was stripped of authority. What madness had impelled him to agree to sail as Henry Ardent's so-called pilot he would never understand, but he couldn't help being excited. How strange it all was. The christening at sea so long ago, which had stuck in his mind only because the Ardent couple had made an odd choice of names. And now the babe he had held in his arms was to be his captain. A good judge of men, Sam was confident Henry Matilda Handyside Ardent would live up to the name, but he could only grow into the job by making mistakes. That he would get the ship round the world in creditable time was unquestionable, in Sam's opinion. Only one thing had him wondering. Did the lad also have that inborn streak of witch-craft necessary in crack captains? He would need it to beat Screech Gander.

From the corner of his eye Sam observed Henry sneaking an impatient look at poor John Plunkett's gold watch. Would he betray his nerves by harassing the mud pilot with a question? The watch-case shut with an over-loud snap but the captain merely hitched a foot up on the rail and casually leant forward to rest his folded arms on his knee. Good lad, Sam thought, as he waved a farewell to his dear Meg on the quay.

At the other end of the ship, on the fo'c's'le head, Will Lamshire kept an eye on the tall and calm figure of the captain. He was not dwelling on what sort of a hell might be made of his life by the demands of this unknown and untried master, for the *Quiver*'s chief mate was a taciturn and phlegmatic man. He was only watching for the signal to begin hauling the ship forward on the head warp.

Though Will Lamshire might never rise to a higher station in life, no more dependable or skilful mate sailed on a British keel. Raised in a hard school of brigs trading out of Cardiff, he had been a mate in Arrow ships for years and Monkton Winkworth himself had selected him for this job. When Old Lampshades – as he had been known by all his shipmates through thirty-six years at sea – first reported aboard Henry had taken him for the new cook. He was a small and thin figure of a man, slightly warped as if by the sun, but he was as tough as a branch of driftwood and took no nonsense from any man who breathed, be he ship's boy or captain. As chief mate of such an exalted vessel he had considered himself worthy of a badge of office and bought a bowler hat which was too big. It tilted forward on his beak of a nose when he looked down and was in danger of flying off when he glanced aloft. He shoved his thumbs nonchalantly into the pockets of his waistcoat – red silk brocade squirming with gold dragons, bought from a tailor's sampan in Whampoa – and concentrated on keeping his head as still as possible, at least until the ship got out into the river.

The second mate, Martin Peake, stood at the taffrail aft ready to order his men to pay out slack on the stern warp. He made full use of the delay by feasting his eyes on the prettiest girls in the crowd and trading heroic waves for blown kisses. He was a square-built Hampshire lad with dark curly hair and a moustache that he was prone to finger in the hope it could be provoked into taking on a new lease of life. He had just completed four years' apprenticeship in a Blackwall frigate of the Arrow Line and could hardly believe his good fortune to be posted to such a ship as the *Quiver*. He was the same age as the captain and regarded him with undisguised awe.

A swell of noise in the crowd, cries of 'Make way there!' and 'Mind your backs!', brought a small carriage into view. George Chamberlayne alighted then handed down his niece. Never before had Henry seen Emma Chamberlayne as any-thing but a shipwrecked waif and he caught his breath. For the first time in five days all thoughts of the *Quiver* and the anxiety and excitement of commissioning her were driven from his mind. The tall girl smiled as Henry vaulted the bulwarks and bowed awkwardly over her hand. She wore a dark blue suit with a small jacket piped with white. A dazzling diamond brooch in the form of a galleon sailed on one lapel. Her dark hair was shot with chestnut lights and lifted prettily in the breeze but she paid it no attention. 'No, I won't come aboard but I do want to wish you God speed,' Emma said. Then she added in a whisper, 'Make certain you whip that Yankee right out of his boots.'

Chamberlayne shook the captain's hand curtly. 'On your way, my boy, and no slacking.'

'What news of the *Musket* this morning?'

'You've got the edge of a tide on her, maybe more. She's still loading cargo.'

'It's a long way to China,' Henry muttered, and turned away. 'You may take the con and cast off when it is convenient, Mr Brown,' he told the pilot.

'Aye aye, Cap'n. Heave away for'ard, handsomely . . .'

Even Will Lamshire was surprised at the readiness with which the ship seemed to spring forward at the slightest heave on the warp, so light and fine was her hull in the water.

''Vast heaving there!' he told his men after their first strong heave had started her gliding forward. The bowler hat tipped maddeningly over his weather-lined forehead and bushy eyebrows. As he tugged the hat from his head his eye fell on the sailmaker who was sitting on a bucket sewing. First things first, he was making a cushion to keep him comfortable through the long hours of patient stitching that would be his lot during the voyage round the world. 'Hey Manfred, want something to keep your needles in?' Will shouted, and spun the bowler at him.

An old man with a face that looked as if it was already dead and had been pickled in brine, Manfred Longhandle was a native of Schleswig-Holstein. His real name was so difficult and unpronounceable that in some British ship long ago he had been called Longhandle and the name had stuck. Nobody knew for certain whether he spoke English for he said so little. Will Lamshire winced as the sailmaker scooped up the hat, punched in the crown to make it flat, then set it on the deck beside him.

In a few moments the ship was in the lock. At the taffrail, Martin Peake directed his men to take a turn on the bitts. The ship slowed and stopped. The gates closed behind her. Suddenly Emma Chamberlayne let out a cry of alarm, and waved frantically at her carriage driver who came along the quay bearing a wooden box. 'I nearly forgot, I brought you a present,' she told Henry.

'For me?' Henry asked, mystified. As the ship began to drop in the lock he reached over the rail and lifted inboard a heavy wooden crate. It was tied with green and golden ribbons, the ship's colours. He lifted the lid but there seemed to be nothing inside but straw.

'Tip it out, but gently,' Emma advised from the quayside which was now above the level of Henry's head.

As Henry carefully tipped the box on its side there was a rustle, an agitated sound of squeaking, and a little pink piglet ran out on deck. The crowd roared its laughter. Standing at the galley door with a ladle in his one and only hand, the cook's eyes gleamed. That little sow would fatten up nicely and provide a feast for all hands, thought Nix Barlow with a gummy smile.

The far gates were opening. Henry waved his thanks and caught the eye of another well-wisher. Louise Plunkett smiled and threw a pink rose to the deck. Martin Peake saw it land, sniffed it appreciatively, and scanned the crowd to see who had thrown it. 'Mine, I think, Mr Peake,' Henry said firmly and put it in his button-hole.

'Take the bow warp to the knuckle there!' Mr Brown roared. The ship edged out into the river. The tug manoeuvred under the bow to take the line which Will Lamshire and his men had made ready. With a brave whoop-whoop on her whistle she took the strain. The last warp was let go from shore and fell with a splash into the river. To a frenzy of shouts and cheers the ship came clear of the lock and turned her bowsprit downstream.

With their chins propped on their elbows, Charlie Meadows and Charlie Field watched the dirty banks of the river begin to slide by. ''Ere we goes again, hey-ho fer bleedin' China,' Meadows said with a heavy sigh.

'Why didn't we buy a bleedin' farm while we 'ad the chance?' Field muttered, his grin as wide as his friend's.

Will Lamshire gave orders to square away the fo'c's'le head and came aft; there was much to do before the tug cast the ship adrift in The Downs. Martin Peake told his men to stow the stern warp, it was unlikely to be needed before they reached New York. Sam Handyside made a conscious effort to stay in the background and gave one last wave to the shore. Mr Brown walked to the helmsman's side to relay quiet instructions. A spurt of smoke from the galley chimney signalled the cook was getting to work. The sailmaker hooked wire-framed spectacles over his hair-tufted ears.

Captain Henry Ardent was a man in a daze. He took four brisk turns of the poop to bring the thudding of his heart under control. Then, as his eye fell on the foot-long piglet backed up nervously against the skylight, he gave the first order of his sea-going command. 'Mr Meadows! Bring your farming friend and catch the pig, then build a pen for her under the break of the fo'c's'le. And wipe that hungry look off your face, she's personal property – mine.'

TWO:

Sandy Hook   3,320 *miles*
Golden Gate   16,240 *miles*

WESTBOUND CROSSINGS OF the Atlantic were for sailing ships a long and arduous struggle into the teeth of prevailing westerly winds. Voyages were uncomfortable because sailing ships had to slant across head seas, pitching violently and throwing up spray that constantly swept the deck, and long because the zig-zag route of a ship beating into the weather covered many more miles. The new-fangled steam packets carrying mail across the Atlantic, however, could plug into the eye of the wind. By this means news of the China Race was carried to New York long before either of the contenders was sighted.

When he sailed in through the Narrows, the entrance to New York harbour, Screech Gander was astounded by the size of the fleet of steamers, each listing beneath a heavy load of sightseers and sounding long whoops of greeting on its whistle, which escorted the *Musket* up the East River. Big crowds had cheered and waved their hats from the piers, and mobbed the black clipper as she came alongside her berth.

Now Captain Gander squinted hard at the distant white masts and spars cross-hatching the sky off Battery Point. The lofty ship slanting into the river was undoubtedly the *Quiver*. And the welcome for Henry Ardent, he noted wryly, would be every bit as spectacular as his own.

But it was neither his first glimpse of his rival, nor jealousy at the interest she was raising in the city, that had Gander grinding his teeth in helpless fury as he walked with the crowd down South Street and listened to the ranting of King O'Cain. Only by thrusting his clenched fists deeply into his pocket did he resist the burning temptation to throw the owner of the Lightning Line into the tide.

'To hell with the British!' O'Cain was raging. 'Let them starve, feed them rat poison but even that is too good for 'em!' The old man carried a whippy Malacca cane with which he emphasised each point by rapping the Captain's shin. The cuts

were hurting. 'The English let my people starve in the famine.'
(*Crack!*) 'A blockade of their ports that gave them the feel of
their bellies rubbing their backbones is what they need – not,
Captain Gander, the chance to get their thieving hands'
(*Crack!*) 'on my dollars.' (*Crack!*)

Screech Gander snatched the cane from the shipowner and
shook the silver eagle that formed its knob under his nose.
'Three days astern of the Limey we sail from London and three
days ahead we arrive in New York, ain't that good enough?
British freights on American keels is what makes your fortune
and when I hand it to you on a silver platter all you can do is
stand there jabbering.' Gander made a whistling slice with the
cane, causing the curiously watching crowd to take a hasty
step backwards. 'Don't give me any more of your chicken shit,
Mr O'Cain.'

Joseph 'King' O'Cain was the only man whom Screech
Gander never failed to address as Mister, even when he was
angry. There was nothing imposing about the round shoulders, the flabby jowls that went pink when his blood was up,
the wispy grey hair. Nor was it a question of strength, for
Gander could have picked up the shipowner with one arm and
hung him by his broad velvet collar on a coat peg. Many a time
he might have succumbed to an overpowering temptation to
do so had it not been for the eyes. O'Cain's grey-blue eyes
could stop a strong man in his tracks. They had the pitiless
staring brilliance of the raptors after which he named his fleet
of ships. Just to feel the steely gaze of them lock on your face
was to sense the caress of razor-tipped talons seeking the soft
spot. Screech Gander was one of the few men in the world not
frightened by King O'Cain, but he was wary enough to watch
his step. Gander depended on him, and knew that no man ever
crossed O'Cain without shedding blood.

A gust of wind off the river swirled mixed aromas of vanilla
and pepper with the dust round the two men as they glared at
each other like fighting cocks in a circle of onlookers. The
nearby hoot of the Wall Street ferry made some people jump
but Gander and O'Cain did not blink. Abruptly King O'Cain
snatched his cane and set off at a brisk pace, the crowd melting
before his mercilessly slashing Malacca. Longshoremen,
urchins, dogs and sea captains scattered. In the great port the
word was out: mind your back, the King's as savage as a meat
axe.

The merchant king had not been so deliberately thwarted

since an eddy of the flood tide had deposited his schooner laden with otter pelts on a reef in Alaska, half a century before. On that occasion he had built a new ship from the wreckage and sailed her home. Now it was not God who had wrecked his plans and put a hundred thousand of his own precious dollars on the line but the infernal Screech Gander.

Brought to Boston by his Irish parents at a tender age, Joseph O'Cain had been sent away to sea on a kill or cure programme. He had sailed as a sickly lad with little hope of a robust and active life and had returned a captain. On his second voyage, instead of flogging homeward around the Horn, the canny young Irishman took his cargo of glossy sea otter pelts direct to Canton, in China, where he traded them for a rich cargo of silks and tea. It established his fortune. By the time he was twenty-two he owned three schooners. At twenty-four he built his first full-rigged ship. The *Falcon* was the genesis of the Lightning Line which had grown into one of the most powerful of Yankee mercantile companies.

Six years ago, in 1846, news had filtered across the Atlantic of a disastrous failure of the potato crop in Ireland. King O'Cain was one of the prime movers in a massive charity drive that collected hundreds of tons of provisions to relieve the starving. The two sloops of war provided by the US Congress to speed relief supplies to Ireland were hardly sufficient for the great mass of cargo. Four additional merchantmen were required and O'Cain had donated the services of one of his own fleet, the *Sea Eagle*. It was when the ship's captain refused on principle to volunteer his services and make the voyage without payment, and O'Cain fired him, that the ship's chief mate stepped up to command.

The mate was a man of Nova Scotia, nursery of the toughest and hardiest breed of sailors on the coast – a Blue Nose. O'Cain had heard tell he was born the son of a sailmaker serving the schooners fishing for cod on the banks. His name was James Gander, though he had always been known as Screech because, as an infant, he liked to dip his finger into the thick, sticky rum of that name which fishermen traded for their salt cod in the West Indies. Gander had run away to sea as a lad and gravitated to Boston after leaping aboard the barquentine that had loomed out of the fog and cut his schooner in two. He had come into O'Cain's fleet as an ordinary seaman, persuaded an older mate to tutor him in navigation, and risen rapidly. As third mate in the *Osprey* trading to Calcutta he had put down a mutiny with his flying fists. Then second mate in the *Hawk*, he had taken command of a hulk found drifting in mid-Atlantic and sailed her home to New York with half a dozen men.

Though untried, unpaid and twenty-two years old, Screech Gander had made a mark for himself on the voyage to Ireland. He had driven the *Sea Eagle* to Limerick in fifteen days three hours, a record for the down-hill passage at that time. Further, on the return voyage he had filled the empty holds with ninety-eight young men who, in exchange for the free passage to the New World, pledged to work for five years at fixed low wages on O'Cain's ice ponds and in his warehouses.

Again, as master of the *Harrier* which happened to be in New York when news of the California gold strike filtered back east, Gander had pulled off another coup. Without reference to the owner who was away in Boston he filled the ship with eager gold-diggers, put together a ballast of shovels and bags of flour, and departed for San Francisco where he arrived in the record time of 109 days. That year more than 760 ships sailed for California, compared with hardly forty the year before, and Gander's time was soon eclipsed. But the young captain had proved his mettle. It was always said of a Blue Nose that you only had to show him wet grass and with a log and a jack-knife he would build a ship to sail on it, and Captain Screech Gander was the living proof.

When King O'Cain built the *Musket* as a flyer for the California trade there was no doubt in his mind which of his hot-shot captains most deserved the prestigious command. The pride of his fleet had sailed nearly a year before but instead of returning directly to New York, as ordered, Captain Gander had taken advantage of the amazingly high freights that Yankee ships were commanding in Canton and had carried a cargo of tea to London. The new ship had paid for herself and brought in a profit of some fifty thousand dollars, all in a single voyage.

If the Blue Nose had let the success of the voyage rest on these results King O'Cain would have been well pleased. He would have rewarded Gander with command of his new clipper, the *Saker*, being launched tomorrow from William Webb's shipyard higher up the East River. But the mails hurried to New York by steamer had brought worse and worse news. First, Screech Gander had committed the *Musket* to a race around the world. Then he had staked one hundred thousand dollars on it.

And now, as the two of them strolled down South Street beneath the thrusting bowsprits of ships loading or discharging at the piers which formed a vault of rigging across the sky, Gander had casually announced that he didn't have ten cents to scratch his arse with — the money left on the polished mahogany table in Hoare's Bank, London, was not his own but King O'Cain's.

For a few moments Screech Gander had known how it felt to be a defenceless rabbit in the shadow of a falcon scything out of the sunlight with talons bared. All the way across the Atlantic he had dreaded telling him. He knew O'Cain was trapped by the simple fact that he could not dismiss his captain without also losing the wager and therefore the money. But Gander also knew O'Cain would not let him escape without a mauling. Trailing the angry shipowner through the crowd he was uneasily aware that by one means or another his fur would fly.

'This new clipper of the Monkey's, what's she like?' O'Cain demanded.

Gander shrugged contemptuously. 'Her captain's a slimsy young sucker, green as a cabbage . . .'

O'Cain stopped abruptly and turned on Gander. 'Just a greenhorn who beat you in from the Atlantic in a hulk trailing weed a yard long on her bottom?'

Gander gave a sneering laugh. 'And all but wrecked himself on Ushant, remember. He should be dead.'

'Too bad for you he's alive and kicking and sailing his ship into New York this very minute and likely to cost me a hundred thousand dollars, Captain, what do you say to that?'

The whip-crack of the cane on Gander's leg brought water to his eyes. He tore it out of O'Cain's hands. 'Don't tell me you won't make damned sure the American Navigation Club underwrites the wager! Ain't you treasurer of the bloody outfit?'

'Let's hope they will, for your sake,' O'Cain said.

'And you know as well as I do the race itself will bring in the highest freights ever. Win or lose, you'll make a fortune out of it or your name's not King O'Cain . . .'

With a loud report the cane snapped in half. Screech Gander looked at the two pieces sheepishly then tried to fit them together and handed them back with a small shrug of apology. 'It will make your fortune, Mr O'Cain.'

To Gander's amazement the shipowner chortled. It was a cooing sound, more like a dove than a hawk. Gander had never heard O'Cain sound more dangerous. 'I must admit, I admire your nerve Captain Gander. Fact is, you think yourself sharp enough to take off a pig's ear so slick he won't know it's gone till he scratches it . . .'

Gander waited as the old man's voice faded away. O'Cain was staring at the *Quiver* as she presented her dark green profile to the spectators on the pier before turning in from mid-river. Suddenly the blue-grey discs swivelled. 'I'm sixty-five years old,' O'Cain announced. 'Since you have been so free already with my company's earnings, Captain Gander, you won't have any objection to accepting my offer of a partnership in the Lightning Line. What do you say?'

'How could I say no?' Gander replied cautiously.

'Exactly,' O'Cain acknowledged, beaming. He tapped Gander's shoulder with the silver eagle as if knocking at a front door. 'I will be honoured to welcome you at my residence for dinner tomorrow evening, Captain Gander, after the launching of the *Saker*. My daughter Flora will be happy to meet you, knowing how long you have admired her beauty and talents.'

Brilliant pain flamed in Gander's breast. His gasp of surprise quickly became a cough. Flora O'Cain was a prim spinster whose beauty amounted to a downy ginger moustache and a freckled nose. She amused herself with a stable of horses that she trained for the track and her personal charm and beauty was respected throughout the Lightning Line as a model of the kind of reception a shipwrecked sailor might expect from a cannibal chief.

Every nerve thrumming tautly as a windward shroud in a gale, Gander staged a discreetly submissive bow. But even for a partnership in the Lightning Line he was damned if he would be palmed off with O'Cain's dreadful daughter. He would go to hell in a steamship before he let Flora O'Cain into his bed.

The two men watched in silent and critical assessment as the *Quiver*'s warps were passed to capstans on the pier and she was winched into her berth. 'I wish I had your confidence, Captain Gander,' O'Cain said at last.

'You forget I whipped him by six days already.'

'Around the world is a long way.'

'For both of us.'

Suddenly a voice in the crowd cried, 'Look at the flag!' Hundreds of pairs of eyes along the pier were lifted to the large house flag of the Arrow Line fluttering stiffly at the head of the mainmast. On the shaft of the arrow, impaled by the neck, was a limp form of a hawk-like bird – a musket. O'Cain observed it in the same instant. Ripping every syllable as if it were flesh in his beak O'Cain said, 'The insult! What are you going to do about that, Captain?'

'Sink the bastard,' Gander replied.

O'Cain stared at him briefly with flaring eyes then stormed away, using the upper half of his cane like a truncheon to beat a way through the crowd.

Screech Gander did not follow, but climbed up on a hogshead for a better view of the ship. He saw Henry Ardent pacing the poop like a restless gundog too long on the leash. Gander knew just how he would feel: nervous of so many eyes and confused by the hustle and bustle that always descended round a captain after a long voyage. But any sneaking sympathy Screech Gander might have felt for the plight of a fellow captain went no further. With glowering eyes and jaw clamped shut, he watched and calculated. King O'Cain and his daughter did not worry him. The King would sing a different tune when the *Musket* sailed up the Thames to win the unbounded admiration of the mercantile world. But somehow, Gander realised, he had to put the seal on it. As the rival clipper's bottle-green hull squeaked against the wicker fenders and the boarding house runners swarmed over her bulwarks to win her crew with wild promises of liquor and women he remained brooding on the barrel. The sightseers on the pier saw him and whispered and stayed clear. The famous captain looked as if he was planning murder. Which he was, of a kind.

With a start that jerked him back to reality, Gander realised he had been staring sightlessly at Sam Handyside who boomed at him from the bulwarks. 'What ho, Screech Gander! Come to see what a proper ship looks like?'

Gander jumped down from the barrel as Sam came ashore. The tall and dark-faced captain took the weather-burned, white-haired head in a light armlock and danced with him around the pier. 'You thundering old rogue, how did you find America? There's me thinking I had the drop on you and what happens? Here comes old Thundersides following me round like a bad smell.'

'Let me free you Blue Nose devil,' Sam panted, his dignity as ruffled as his whiskers.

He jerked himself free then, shrugging his rumpled reefer jacket back into order on his shoulders, glared mistrustfully at Gander who had a more than usually zestful gleam of madness in his eye. 'And what's opened the door to heaven on your behalf this fine day? Wouldn't have thought you could find that much to smile about.'

'Hallelujah!' Gander said with exaggerated fervour. 'Some days God looks down from his heaven and puts the darndest ideas in a man's head, ain't that the truth!' Changing his manner abruptly, he cast a professional eye over the white masts. 'You've done a good job of setting her up, but your stopper knot's working itself out on one of your foremast lanyards . . . see?'

'Not me, I'm supercargo,' Sam explained loyally. 'Captain Ardent knows his stuff, you'll get a good run for your money.'

'Huh, you don't think it's my money do you?' Gander sneered. 'Look here, King O'Cain's launching his new ship at William Webb's tomorrow, the *Saker*. He's hosing the red-eye around. You and the Botany Bay brat can stand there with your mouths open, suck in a bit of whisky as it droppeth down from Heaven . . . I'll send a coach alongside at noon, you're very welcome.'

'Maybe, but there's a lot to do,' Sam agreed guardedly.

'Sure, and don't I know it. The poor young sucker's been awake for a week and now he's got his head down on his arms among the bottles on the table, dreaming of a world without God-damned quill-pushers, form-fillers and agents.'

'You've got the strength of it. Head-winds all the way west from The Lizard and fog as thick as wet socks on the banks, all the usual crud.'

'Figure I'll catch you tomorrow, old pal,' Gander said, and drifted away in the crowd leaving the old shipmaster gazing after him suspiciously.

On board *Quiver* Sam found the mates grumpily adjusting warps, setting up springs and positioning fenders to protect the hull when the ship surged in the wakes of passing ferryboats and tugs. Most of the crew had lit out for the shore – 'Off to see the Mother Judge,' Will Lamshire muttered darkly, meaning the brothel madam, mother judge of pricks. Lured away by crimpers and boarding house runners, most of the vanished crew would never return to collect their wages or resume their

positions; by dawn they would be dead drunk, fleeced, and
ultimately shanghai'd aboard an outward bounder.

With the ship settled comfortably at her berth there was still
much to do. The main and fore-yards were cock-billed for use
as derricks to swing out the cargo. The hatch boards were
knocked away and the tarpaulins that had covered them
spread out to protect the decks from longshoremen's boots.
Will Lamshire stooped as if carrying a heavy burden of
problems. He disliked ports. His whole world lay inboard of
the bulwarks and as usual he would not be going ashore.
Martin Peake could hardly contain his impatience to be liber-
ated. 'You wanna steer clear o' The 'Ole In The Wall,' Charlie
Meadows told him in a fatherly way. 'It's a drinkin' 'ole run by
One-armed Monell and 'is bouncer is Gallus Meg. She's
dangerous.'

'The bouncer's a lady?'

'Not a lady, 'xactly,' Meadows laughed. 'Woman like a
sewer barge, heavy an' wide an' stinks. Some fighter! Throws
you down on the sawdust and bites yer ear orf!'

'That's right,' Charlie Field affirmed. 'Then she puts it in a
jar o' pickle behind the bar. She's got jars full of 'em, all these
ears like – you know – fried oysters.'

And Gallus Meg wouldn't be the worst young Peake would
find down Cherry Street, Sam thought as he went below. The
smoke-filled saloon was just as Screech Gander had painted.
Agents, port officers and other officials crowded round the
table and Tom Withers, the aft-cabin steward, was kept on the
hop plying the rum. Hardly had Henry joined them, and taken
a nip, than exhaustion overwhelmed him. His head lolled
forward, his arms swept a smother of papers beneath his
forehead, and he dropped into a deep sleep. The visitors saw
nothing unusual. Most captains arrived bone weary after the
long and difficult approach to Sandy Hook in usually miserable weather. Nimbly they saved their glasses first and their
papers second, then switched their attention to Sam. Arrangements for discharging the cargo, assembling the cargo to be
loaded, taking on victuals, topping up the water tanks, buying
a new crew from the shipping masters who worked hand-in-
glove with the boarding houses – this was the other side of a
shipmaster's function and Sam knew his own long experience
of it was the real reason Monkton Winkworth had wanted him
to come.

Head-winds, lashing rain, bad visibility and a tense landfall

had made the thirty-eight day crossing a difficult apprenticeship for the young captain and Sam had been given many
an anxious moment. On any maiden voyage teething problems
could be expected. Yards would stick halfway when hoisted
because halyards or lifts were wrongly rove. A sail would be let
fall without a clew rope or a sheet. The new ropes were
constantly stretching so the rigging needed continual adjust-
ment. But Will Lamshire had an instinct for this kind of work,
and with the help of Meadows and Field the ship was soon all
a-taunto aloft and in workable trim. But the ship did not
handle like any other in which Sam had sailed. When knocked
down by a squall it was conventional wisdom to turn a ship
away from the wind and run before it. Henry had made that
mistake only once, and the fine-lined *Quiver* had come perilously near to driving herself right under the waves. Instead,
Henry was refining the art of luffing up to the wind, pointing
her up until the sails shivered as the strain came out of them.
The tactic required a deft touch on the wheel and continuous
concentration, for if the ship came too high into the wind she
would be caught aback and in such a sea the sticks would whip
out of her. The courage and imagination Henry applied to
developing the new technique, and the speedy ease with which
he mastered it, were impressive. Sam's confidence in him was
boosted, but he remained worried for the ship and, he had to
admit, a little scared. Cracking on under full sail in weather
that reduced most ships to nothing but reefed topsails went
against all Sam's instincts. 'Anybody can make a horse gallop
but it takes a genius to make it stop,' he would mutter, eyeing
the masts and spars arched in creaking, springy curves by the
weight of wind in the sails. But he did not interfere and nobody
would ever know what effort the silence had cost him. Only
once, when thick and clammy fog had wrapped around the
ship as she shaped up for a landfall on the unlit and dangerous
Nova Scotia coast, did Sam offer unsolicited advice. For Henry
Ardent the fog was a new and horrifying experience. Such a
phenomenon was rare in his part of the Pacific. Now his
instinct was to heave to and wait but Sam urged him to press
on. 'Don't let it scare you, lad, the ocean's a big place and ships
are small.'

'Perhaps, but North America's big enough and we're likely
to hit it.'

Sam had noisily sniffed up a long draft of fog. 'But can you
smell land? Can you feel the nearness of it in your bones?

When your heart pumps does a little part of your backbone rattle, like beach pebbles in the backwash?'

'Can't say it does, these are deep-water waves, feel the pitch.'

'So clap on sail. It's a fair risk. Judgement is what command is all about, not only the driving force but knowing when to stop and when to crack on. Captain Cook never got anywhere by dickering, not like the Dutch. If they had pressed on boldly like Cook instead of turning tail at first sight of land, you Australians would be gabbling Dutch.'

When the last of the official guests had been pumped full of rum it was evening. Henry awoke suddenly, looked around in a startled sort of way at the clutter of bottles and glasses around him, then stumbled into his cabin and dropped on his bunk. Sam took a turn round the deck. Discharging would not begin until dawn and for the moment all was quiet. A lantern glowing in the bosun's locker under the fo'c's'le head showed Will Lamshire making an inventory of the paint and gear to be ordered from chandlers ashore. In the deckhouse the seamen's bunks – wooden shelves with thin straw mattresses – were deserted. A crescent of dark shadow in the sailmaker's hutch showed Manfred Longhandle had taken to his hammock. Next door, in the galley, Nix Barlow sat in the warm glow of his cooking range, smoking a clay pipe and humming. The farmers' two-bunk cuddy was also empty. Meadows and Field had gone ashore with Martin Peake in tow, determined to put a curl in the young mate's moustache. The pink pig, christened Neptunia, snuffled in her pen. She was fattening nicely on galley scraps.

Ashore, a knot of dock-wallopers gazed at the British clipper from the quay and discussed her in low tones. Wagons, drays and carriages rumbled noisily on the cobbles of South Street. It was the last day of November with a smell of snow about but it was not just the bite in the wind that brought a shiver to Sam's backbone. It was a familiar warning. Often enough, on the many ocean passages he had made, this touch of shivers had him tucking in a precautionary reef and doubling the look-outs. Alongside pier 22 on New York's East River there was no call for such measures but Sam was troubled. It was that smile on Screech Gander's face that haunted him. Hallelujah indeed!

On impulse Sam Handyside crossed the gangway and set off up South Street beneath the arcade of jibbooms reaching almost to the second and third-floor windows of the counting houses, lodging houses and warehouses opposite. At street level each shop was an emporium of delight and Sam strolled slowly, lingering in front of every window. The neighbourhood was crammed with a variety of trades: bakeries and flour-millers, printers, tinsmiths, silk stores, provision merchants. The shops that held Sam's interest were the nautical specialists, the church-like calm of the navigational instrument makers, the noisy sidewalk stalls selling sailors' traps like tarred trousers and tarpaulin hats, like the big one, almost an umbrella, that was Charlie Field's badge of office. Hawkers offered coffee, and strange round cakes with holes in the centre, for five cents. Clam chowder and buckwheat cakes were ten cents. Sam bought a cob of corn with hot butter and gnawed as he strolled with the good-natured crowd hearing snatches of conversation about the *Musket* and *Quiver*. 'The Limey? I wouldn't stake half a dollar on his chances . . .'

'Who'd sign articles in that Yankee blood boat, only a crazy man . . . ?'

'If that Gander gets beat I'll eat my hat . . .'

'It's time his throat was cut, the murderin' swine . . .'

Sandwiched between the shops and business premises the sailors' dives were doing a roaring trade. Swinging signboards embellished with sexy mermaids, crossed harpoons, and turbaned niggers' heads bore names like Eddystone Light, Bucket of Blood, False Love and The Cable Locker. Harpies gave the stout old shipmaster the eye and sang out invitations. 'Never too old to love, Captain!'

'Short-time, Grandpa?'

'Old wine in a young bottle, eh Skipper!'

Sam turned a deaf ear and sauntered on with a twinkle in his eye. He found the *Musket* at O'Cain's private pier near the drydocks at the foot of Clinton Street and for a few minutes he watched her from the other side of the street. Screech Gander had stevedores working late. Cargo was still being swung aboard. To judge by her marks she was about half loaded. The usual knot of sightseers was gawping from the quay. Sam was turning to go when he saw a horse-cab rattle up to the gangway and jerk to a stop. Screech Gander's leggy and long-limbed figure strode aboard shadowed by the dog. He seemed in the devil of a hurry about something. Sam tossed the corn-cob in the gutter, wiped the butter from his chin-whiskers with a handkerchief, and was suddenly aware of weariness stealing over him. Time enough to worry about Screech Gander in the clear light of dawn, he thought.

In the *Musket* the mood was very different from the shadowy calm Sam found when he returned aboard the *Quiver* and went to bed. In the Yankee clipper two oil lamps lit the cabin brilliantly and spilled bright beams of light through the skylight and scuttles. Gander dropped into his mahogany swivel armchair at the head of the table, sat forward tensely, and shouted for coffee which Doc brought at once. Smoke Lapierre slipped into his seat on Gander's right, his foxy features alert with excitement. Gander turned down the corners of his mouth as he saw the mate's black-rimmed fingernails raise a storm of dandruff from his thin black hair, some of which drifted over the table. The captain removed his coffee and sat back in his chair. 'What about the tug, all fixed?'

'Sure, but they want to know what the mystery's all about.'

'They'll find out.'

Ben Whipple, the new second mate whom Screech had appointed on the strength of his powerful frame and broken nose, took his place on the settle. He was a tough young New Englander, son of a Salem sea captain, who admired Screech Gander's reputation as a man-driver and had signed on to learn from him. He was clean shaven and his fair hair was cut short to provide no handhold in a fight. After running from The Hole In The Wall he was puffing and he made his report in gasps.

'Monell's got the men for us . . . Twenty good 'uns, he reckons . . . Alongside one o'clock.'

'Not enough, half of 'em will be junk, get ten more,' Gander snapped. 'How's loading?'

'Slow, we haven't got half of it.'

'Too bad, it can stay on the dock. What about your runners, will they keep their mouths shut?'

'Midnight,' Ben Whipple confirmed, answering the last with a shrug as he got to his feet. 'I'm on my way, I'll try Ma Kettle's place for the other ten.'

Screech Gander nodded his approval as the second mate left, then turned to Smoke Lapierre. The French Canadian leered a scummy tobacco smile and his ferret eyes, the whites permanently bloodshot, glittered. 'Now for the fine and famous Botany bastard, how are you gonna do him?'

'Very carefully,' Gander said. 'Where's the cannibal? We need him.'

The sailor whom Gander had thrown to the sharks was a Maori called Big Tree who crouched on an upturned bucket in the galley, as close as he could get to the stoked-up cooking range. His legs were pressed together to catch the shavings his jack-knife peeled from a whale's tooth as he sculpted the streamlined form of a shark circling as if to attack. His mind was far away, dreaming of home as he scraped and rubbed. He was at the steering oar of his canoe, flying towards Tapeka after his great voyage to the south to collect boulders of the precious jade-like greenstone. He was standing awe-struck at his father's side as the towering kauri tree toppled with a whispering roar into the ferns. He was on his hands and knees in the wet black sand, surf and wind cracking round his ears, as he dug with his finger for delicious *toheroa* shellfish.

Big Tree sighed bleakly. How long would it be before he saw the green islands and blue bays of Kororareka again? He took out his precious greenstone *patu* and reverently caressed its smooth, hard surface. The *patu* was a short-handled war club, twelve inches high. It was oval in outline but slender in profile, its polished green sides meeting in a sharp edge like the cutwater of a ship. It had been given him by Takiri Titore Nui, his father, and Big Tree kept it constantly to hand, stuck inside the waistband of his trousers in the small of his back.

So much had changed. Kororareka had been given a *pakeha* name and the little town that had sprung up on the curving shore was now called Russell. The land, too, had a new name; it was called New Zealand. Even his own name had changed, though this was unusual for a Maori of the Ngapuhi people.

From his birth some twenty-five years ago they had called him Totara, after the hardest and heaviest of the timbers culled from the forests for constructing voyaging canoes. His father had been an expert in woodmanship and it was he who had been first to supply spars of fine, straight-grained timber to the *pakeha* sailing ships. His father's constant shadow, the lad gained from the visiting sailors a knowledge of English and a desire to see the world from which they came. As a tall and robust youth, his family had dubbed him Totara Totika – the straight totara. For years he had devoted all his spare time to building a voyaging canoe in which he had made an expedition of 1,500 miles to the south end of the country to obtain precious greenstone for his tribe. This earned him the name Totara Taniwha – the Totara from a great distance. Encouraged, he decided to voyage even further and at the age of twenty became a harpooner aboard an American whaling ship that put in the port of Russell, in New Zealand's Bay of Islands, for firewood and water.

With no ear for the mellifluent Maori tongue his first ship-mates had struggled to pronounce his name until Totara Taniwha finally thumped his chest and told them, 'My name — Tree.' And the sailors, out of respect for his strength and stature, dubbed the young Maori, Big Tree.

Overwhelmed by the milling streets and immense buildings of London and New York, Big Tree — along with Doc, the cook — had been one of the few among the *Musket*'s crew not to cut and run. Though he was desperate to escape the merciless lick of the mate's blacksnake, Big Tree feared the cities more. But this was not the only reason he stayed. For five years he had bounced from one fo'c's'le to another, fetching up in many ports of the world but coming nowhere near New Zealand. But at last he had found a ship that would take him there. It would be the *Musket*'s next port of call: Captain Gander had promised it.

Doc came into the galley with the empty coffee pot from the saloon. 'Cap'n wants you, boy,' he said.

An hour later, comically burly in the many layers of ragged clothing he had piled on to keep out the chill of the northern winter, Big Tree found himself travelling for the first time in his life in a carriage. He could see nothing because the blinds were lowered.

As it stopped on South Street across from the pier where the *Quiver* lay, Smoke Lapierre alighted and spoke to a youth propping up a lamp post nearby. 'What have you seen, son?'

The boy jerked to attention. 'Nothin' much, Sir. The captain is still on board, and the old 'un with the face lace.'

'Nobody else?'

'I figure the cook's in the caboose, you can see the light, an' the one with the big conk. There wasn't no comin' nor goin' these two hours . . .'

Lapierre pressed a quarter into the boy's hand and dismissed him with a jerk of his thumb then climbed into the dark carriage and reported to Gander.

Screech Gander jetted smoke from his nostrils in a satisfied way then weighed the Maori with a long stare. 'Now then, you cannibal,' he said at last. 'You want to go home, to New Zealand?'

'Plurry right, me go home,' Big Tree grinned eagerly.

'So I thought, but the *Musket* is sailing to 'Frisco, then China.' The Maori's face fell but Gander leaned forward and emphasised each point with a prod of Big Tree's knee. 'Listen good. Do this right, and I will show you a ship departing for New Zealand, understand? Here, take this letter. You know Henry Ardent, he jump in sea with shark? All right, you go find him in the cabin of the ship, probably asleep. Give him the letter, no talk. When he come, you bring him here.'

Big Tree took the white envelope. 'Why you do this thing?' he asked, his black brows knitting.

Gander smiled. 'I want to talk to Mr Ardent, very important. Tomorrow, we find ship for New Zealand.'

Satisfied, Big Tree sprang down to the cobbles, lightly for such a big man. He shivered and tucked the ragged woolly muffler more closely under his throat. A slender shaft of greenstone dangled from one of his ears and a jagged shark's tooth set in sealing wax adorned the other. As he emerged suddenly from behind a pile of barrels and hogsheads across the street a couple of men who were passing by gave him a startled glance. Swallowing a cough that rattled in his throat he crossed the gangway. The ship seemed deserted but for a dim glow lighting the skylight panes from below. His bare feet padded silently on the damp tarpaulins and boards. He slipped down the companion. All the cabin doors opening off the saloon were shut except one. Big Tree entered and found himself in a small sitting room. In the light looming faintly through the door he saw a writing bureau, an armchair and settee, a mock fireplace and fender, and another door from which came the soft breathing of a man asleep. Henry Ardent awoke at once – one of the skills of sailoring – and blinked with surprise at the dark and tattooed face peering over him. He swung upright, took the envelope thrust into his hands, and opened it beneath the dimmed lamp in the saloon.

I hear you have met this cannibal already. I am with Screech Gander. There is an important change of plan. Can you come at once? We have sent a carriage.
Emma Chamberlayne

Henry read the note a second time. When he looked up, the messenger had gone. Puzzled, he pushed his feet into his boots and hurried on deck. The Polynesian was waiting on the dock, across the gangway. He saw a carriage standing across the street.

Big Tree smiled as he passed the stack of barrels. He liked the young captain who had saved his life. Perhaps there would be a chance to talk with him. And tomorrow he would find a ship to take him home. Before crossing the quiet street Big Tree paused to wait for Henry to catch up and looked back.

Henry saw the bulky figure waiting for him and hurried on. A split second before it struck, Henry felt the wind of the blow descending towards his skull. There was no time to react. Pole-axed, he crumpled on the cobbles.

In the first flash of consciousness Henry Ardent registered a shrieking pain somewhere in the far deeps of his eyes. In the second he realised he was wet. Cold water cascaded over his face and weighed heavily in his clothes. As he opened his mouth to gasp, it filled with salt water.

Spitting and blinking, he rolled over on the wet deck and opened his eyes. Agony gave way to bewilderment as he realised he was on board a ship. Another jet of cold sea water hosed his face. He tried to dodge, spluttering and cursing. Somehow his wrists had become locked together. He lay motionless, willing unconsciousness to release him from this living nightmare. All he got was another reviving bath of freezing water.

With difficulty he crawled to the bulwarks and hauled himself dizzily erect. He was at sea. In the horny light of dawn he distinguished the Narrows through which he had entered his own ship only a few hours before. Men aloft were shaking out topgallants. Topsails, jib and flying jib were set to the brisk wind. The ship dipped her bows heavily, flinging up a high rain of spray. For'ard, the tug was letting go the towing warp.

Henry focussed on the tall, sombre figure in a tassled buckskin jacket who regarded him stonily. Beside him was a large rat-coloured dog with curling lip, its ears pricked and its yellow eyes as remorselessly unforgiving as those of its master. Then realisation dawned. Dear God!

Stunned by the gross enormity of his fate, Henry let his head sink into his hands. In a daze he heard Gander tell Smoke Lapierre to rig the deck pump. 'We'll rouse these shuckless wonders with a cold bath of what's coming to 'em, then the Lord God help us.'

The rest of the men of whom the *Musket* could boast for a

crew were laid out in varying stages of stupor. Some were woozily sitting upright, groaning and holding their heads. Some hung dizzily over the rail, vomiting. A small number who had walked aboard under their own steam loitered near the fo'c's'le door, nervously awaiting the orders that would commence their sentence of slavery.

The crew had been bought from two different lodging houses for the price of a month's wages that would be deducted from their earnings on the voyage. As crews who joined ships in this manner were invariably too scammed to stand upright, let alone haul on a rope and do useful work, a special team was hired to work the ship out of harbour, hang some sail on her, and get her pointed in the desired direction. These 'runners' would be taken off by the tug then it would be up to the captain and his mates — and their flying fists and knuckledusters — to whip the men into shape as seamen. The system served nobody well except the crimps, who reaped the profits. A seaman returning from a long voyage could find himself shanghai'd and dumped aboard an outward bounder with never a sight of the money due for his unremitting labour on the previous voyage. And shipmasters had to take what they were given. The crimps were none too choosy about a man's nautical ability. If he had two legs and two arms and was breathing he was sailor enough for the tally as the drunken or unconscious bodies were slung inboard over the rail.

His long legs planted wide on the tilting deck, Captain Screech Gander surveyed the motley collection of men upon whom he depended to work his ship around Cape Horn and sail her sixteen thousand miles to San Francisco. Recoiling from the jet of the deck hose, they milled blearily around the main hatch abaft the foremast. 'Jesus wept!' Gander exclaimed as his eyes went from one pair of hands to the next, looking for the tar-blackened splits in the nails and the horny callouses on the palms that were the trademark of the useful sailor. Hardly a dozen in the whole bunch passed muster. The rest were an assortment of riff-raff swept off the streets, men who had the misfortune to accept a free drink from the wrong man in the wrong place at the wrong time. One who did measure up was a stocky individual with reddish hair and a brilliant black eye. A turn of his head revealed a large gap missing from his ear, blood caked thickly around the crescent-shaped wound. 'Another for the pickle bottle,' Gander observed drily.

Then his eye returned to Henry. 'Amazing the class of

person you find in a goosing slum, eh Smoke?' he sneered.

The first mate, wiping the coils of the long blacksnake whip through his hands, grinned. 'Yer didn't 'alf paralyse 'im.'

'I've a notion he won't feel like the big dog with the brass colour no more,' Gander said.

Parading imperiously among them, duffing up one with a fist here, kicking the ankles of another there, deliberately daring any of them to take a swing at him, the Yankee captain addressed them in a hectoring way. 'Ha! As likely a bunch of plough-pushers and hog-minders as ever set foot in farmyard muck! Your hay-making days are over, my braves. I'm the bull-whacker around here, and it's blood for breakfast every day of the week . . .'

Next he separated the dull-eyed men into two groups. 'You with the ivy, that side,' he said, pushing a bewhiskered man to the port bulwarks. 'And you, Sambo,' he went on, shoving a grey-faced negro to starboard, 'dat side, boy.'

The wind hummed in the cordage. The ship was beginning to drive ahead and the flying spray barrelled in fusilades along the deck. Automatically the men huddled closer and hunched their backs to it. Ben Whipple, the new second mate, had the topsails and topgallants set to his satisfaction and called the runners down from aloft then signalled the tug to swing alongside. A heavy knotted length of rope was thrust into his back pocket, his starter.

Gander pointed first to one group then to the other. 'All right, this be port watch and this be starboard. Now mark my words. This ship is the *Musket*. We're a crack ship and we have a reputation to improve upon . . .' Gander let a satisfied smirk pass fleetingly over his grim features as he met Henry's eye. 'We don't carry no passengers. No room for barrel-boarders or scrimshankers. You're here to work, and that means work your hearts out. When I say walk I want you to run and when I say run I want you to fly. You can rest when you're dead.'

Henry found himself on the starboard side, in the mate's watch. In the other watch he recognised at least two men who had sailed with him across the Atlantic as seamen in the *Quiver*. Sickly they held their heads in their hands and massaged their throbbing temples, yet to notice their recent captain. Also on the port watch was the big Polynesian with the tattooed face who turned away, shamefaced and miserable, as he caught Henry's look.

A dim memory stirred in Henry's brain. The messenger in the middle of the night . . . The carriage waiting in the shadows . . . He could remember no more but when he put his fingers to the tender lump on the back of his skull it was not hard to figure out what had happened.

Smoke Lapierre inspected the hands of the heavy man with the torn ear and a bruise as round and black as a cannonball over one eye. 'You, what's your name?'

'Evans, Able Seaman.'

'Take the wheel.'

Besides Evans another heavy-set man, balding with a florid moon of a face, lurched on the heaving deck and nudged Lapierre who sprang away fearfully. In two strides Gander reached the man and cracked him a double blow across the cheeks. The knuckleduster broke a jagged crevasse in the flesh of either cheek. 'Is it a fight you want, Dutchie?' he snarled.

The man staggered backwards, tripped and fell. Ben Whipple was on him in an instant, lashing his ribs with the rope starter. The Dutchman got to his feet, murder in his eyes. Gander saw it and confronted him at once, jutting his jaw and thrusting his blazing eyes to within an inch of the Dutchman's. Nightingale followed and stopped a pace behind, growling softly. 'You got something to say, Dutchie?'

The big man could not hold the baleful stare. He hung his head and shuffled backwards. 'Nay, nay, nuttin' to say.'

Gander swaggered to the quarterdeck. He cupped a match in his hands and lit a cheroot then faced them once more, a picture of confidence and mastery. 'All right, men, keep your daylights open and your potato traps shut and don't get to leeward. That way you'll keep out of trouble and catch a free ride to California . . . Smoke, get the main backed.'

The runners lined the rail, ready to jump aboard the tug as it circled in. Lapierre drove the men to the braces. With the wind on the beam, as it was, the *Musket* could be stopped nearly dead in the water by reversing the sails.

Henry eyed the tug, only yards away now, but even as his fogged mind wrestled with the problem of how he could get aboard, a thin black cord of plaited leather coiled round and round his body, pinning his arms to his sides. Smoke Lapierre gave the blacksnake a strong jerk and Henry staggered along the deck. 'I know what you're thinking, my fancy friend — don't!' the mate warned. He chuckled as Henry fixed him in a stony, determined gaze. As the tug sheered away with a farewell toot on its whistle, Smoke twitched the whip and the supple leather coils fell away.

Grey-faced, wet, pathetic, the men stood about uncertainly. Ben Whipple waded among then, laying on the starter and driving the men back to the braces. At the same time the port watch was chased aloft to set the royals. Henry took a stinging cut across the shoulders. He whirled round as Whipple raised his knotted rope for another blow. This was the way ships were run Down East. A man learned by taking punishment then he was promoted and meted out the same form of instruction. He learned by doing, it was the Yankee way, and if he couldn't swallow the medicine it was his own look-out. But Henry was having none of that. Yankee education was for Yankees, not the likes of him. All the weight and fury of his pent-up rage went into the two-handed rammer that caught Whipple in the midriff and folded him like a jack-knife. Henry jerked the rope starter from Whipple's nerveless hands as he lay gasping on the planks and hurled it overboard. 'Don't ever touch me with that thing!' he growled. The satisfaction of dropping the mate gave him a charge. One down, two to go. He could take over the ship and sail her back into the river.

It was only his sudden decision to make for the poop that saved him. The full weight of the iron belaying pin wielded by Smoke Lapierre missed his skull by a fraction. It grazed the side of his head and smashed down on his shoulder. Groggily Henry got to his feet and started aft. His vision blurred. He could see three, five Screech Ganders at the top of the ladder, contempt in every inch of them.

Henry's feet were kicked from under him and again he fetched up in an untidy sprawl. Heavy blows from the whip handle rained across his ribs. He stood up and staggered on, glaring at the mocking captain. Again Smoke Lapierre tripped him and this time it was Ben Whipple who thudded revengeful kicks into his kidneys. Doubled up and lurching, Henry managed only a few more steps before the blacksnake wrapped around him and jerked him flat. Barely conscious, Henry lay in a ball of fiery pain and blinked up at Gander who ran a hand through the pointed jags of his sideburns and spoke with affected patience. 'You're in a Yankee flyer now, Mr Ardent, it's no use sitting on your hind legs howling.'

The two mates standing on either side of Henry jeered and Lapierre pointedly wiped the soles of his boots on Henry's ribs. 'We got him tamed, Cap'n,' he said.

Henry climbed shakily to his feet once more and reached his shackled hands towards the ladder handrail but Lapierre slapped them away with the whip handle. 'You're captain no more, get for'ard,' Gander growled.

Henry tried to speak but his voice failed him. He caught his breath and tried again. 'What's it worth?' he gasped huskily. 'Put me ashore. Must be worth something to you.'

Gander chuckled mirthlessly. 'No chance, pal. Let's face it, you came a gutser. You're not the first man to be bunkoed and you won't be the last. Might as well knuckle down.'

Henry cried out through his shame, 'You're a cheat and a villain, you bastard, God help you!'

For the space of two steady breaths the Yankee captain stared contemptuously at the wet, battered, hunched man looking up at him with pleading, angry eyes. 'You forget, *I'm* God around here, till 'Frisco,' Gander said, and signalled with a nod at the mates. With whip, fists, boots and a rope's end the two men hammered Henry to the deck. He sagged to his knees, trying to protect his head beneath his arms. The beating continued until there was no movement in his huddled form. The mates turned on the crew who had been watching the drama with expressions of dread. Gander pointed aloft. 'Set the royals, I said.'

As the mates advanced along the deck the men scattered, scrambling into the shrouds. The blacksnake snicked invisibly through the air and raised a stinging welt on the shoulderblade of the limping negro, who whimpered and hurried on. As the men climbed the ratlines Gander shouted, 'Faster, this ain't no Sunday School picnic!' The crew's mournful progress became a race for their lives as Screech Gander fired six rapid shots at their feet. The rounds plunked harmlessly into the grey waves but served their purpose. Well satisfied, Gander reloaded his revolver from a stock of bullets in his pocket and went to the binnacle. Nightingale read this as the 'all's well' signal and flopped in the wedge formed by the tilting horizontal of the deck and the leaning vertical of the companion-way.

The sound of shots registered in Henry's brain. Though his bruised and intolerably aching body did not stir, his wits revived. Despite the battering he found his mind could remove itself to a different plane, a level of bitter resolve. Left for dead on the wet deck, Henry began to think. What was it Charlie Meadows had said as they sailed up the Thames? After the Lord Mayor's Show comes the shit. And he was in it, up to his ankles and head down. The gut-wrenching humiliation of it was already fading in the blaze of his determination to save himself.

But he had learnt his first lesson early in the game. The Yankee way was to tame and drive men by fear and brute force, and an essential part of the programme was to make an example of the roughest and toughest customer on board. And Henry had walked right into it. It had been pointless trying to fight Screech Gander and his henchmen at the moment when spirited resistance was what they were waiting and praying for. He must learn subtlety. And that was a joke for a man wet through, pierced by cold, immobilised by aches and pains, and lying face down on a spray-washed deck. Henry's bleak laugh came out as a groan.

Preoccupied with the difficult task of setting and trimming sail with a numbed and largely ignorant and incapable crew, the mates paid no attention to Henry as he crawled away. Testing his strength he hauled himself up on the lee bulwarks then, half crouching, inched his way slowly for'ard. When he thickly asked the negro cook for some coffee, Doc at first sympathetically shook his head. But he changed his mind when he saw the defiant look in Henry's eye, recognising this was a man of whom it would pay to keep on the friendly side. Hidden from the poop, Henry splayed his legs against the ship's increasingly lively movement and cradled the hot mug gratefully in his hands. The steam warmed his bruised face and the strong, sweet brew steadied him. No point in appealing to Gander's finer instincts, the Blue Nose bastard had none. Impossible to take over the ship single-handed; he would need help but for the moment the men were stoned with despair. By the time he drained the last of his coffee Henry had made up his mind. He knew where his future lay, at least in the short term. It was goodbye to New York, goodbye to the beautiful *Quiver* and goodbye to Chamberlayne and his fanciable niece and his new friends like Sam and the farmers. Henry handed the mug to Doc and went aft. He must submit, there was no point in being a packet rat.

Nightingale growled the moment Henry's hand touched the ladder rail. 'No man comes on the poop unless he's invited,' Gander said.

'You're short-handed.'

'What do you want me to do, burst into flame?'

'You need all the seamen you can get, not clod hoppers.'

'Don't worry pal, I'll make a sailor out of you.'

'I want mattress, boots, duds . . .' Henry was interrupted by a dismissive laugh. But then Gander regarded him more thoughtfully. 'And a blanket and knife and 'skins,' Henry added.

'All right, if you agree to work and give no trouble I'll fit you out.'

'None of your slop chest rubbish, I want good stuff.'

Gander bit off an angry retort and ordered Henry for'ard. 'Smoke's got the key to your shackles.'

For four days the *Musket* beat determinedly back and forth, struggling to make her southing against a rattling nose-ender. The head wind showed little sign of changing its ways and drove Captain Gander to a high pitch of frustration and bad temper. From the first, after Lapierre unlocked his handcuffs and the aft-cabin steward shook out a mattress for him as well as a pair of dungarees, a jersey and a tarpaulin jacket, Henry not only co-operated with the mates but made a show of it. They treated him guardedly but left him alone. For him there was no indiscriminate lash of a rope's end or blood-letting lick of the blacksnake. The initial hours of forcing his pain-wracked limbs to heave on ropes had hurt like hell, but the agony had been a salve for his humiliated pride. After two days of torture the pain in his battered muscles was reduced to a dull stiffness. His head cleared and his appetite returned. The routine was little different from that on the old *Partridge* when he had been a lowly second mate – an exalted rank compared with his situation before the mast in the *Musket* – and the work was second nature. Action got his blood going and he shivered less, unlike many of the other poor wretches who were hazed to a high pitch of nervous and physical exhaustion.

In his haste to escape New York, Screech Gander had been saddled with the doziest, dirtiest bunch of no-hopers Henry had ever seen tailing on a rope. Hardly a dozen had the basic skills of sailoring and could hand, reef and steer. Most were tramps, destitutes and drunkards – shrinkers and slinkers and men fit only to keep bread from mouldering, Gander told them.

With Henry under Smoke Lapierre's command in the starboard watch only six of the twelve could call themselves sailors. Most skilled of them was the red-haired Albert Evans of Liverpool, minus the best part of an ear, whose fate in the *Musket* was little different from the lifelong pattern of knocks

and bruises he had suffered in twenty years of sailoring. As he
had been through it all before he adapted readily and did his
job with a sturdy indifference to the frenzied hazing of the
mates. Though something of a simpleton, the moon-faced
Dutchman also knew his business and worked stolidly. Every
time Lapierre shouted an order Dutchie answered under his
breath, 'I kill de leetle bokker'. And the others, when they had
energy to spare, would dig him in the ribs and urge him on,
'That's the style, Dutchie, wring the bugger's dirty neck'. The
negro with the white beard went by the name Snowball and
had been a cook in Down Easters; he was aghast at finding
himself before the mast and feared going aloft but feared the
blacksnake more. There were two blue noses, hard men raised
in the three f's of Nova Scotia – farming, forestry and fishing –
and although neither had experience of voyaging in any vessel
larger than a coasting schooner carrying local produce,
Richards and Claridge derived a certain grudging satisfaction
from seeing how the powerful clipper could fly.

For the rest, Henry was stuck with a wan young lad wrung
out by seasickness, a commercial gent of fragile constitution
who was decidedly less chipper without his sales patter and
travelling bag, a dull-witted young thug of a farm boy who
never learnt port from starboard though whip and starter beat
him black and blue, and two slip-eyed men with greasy,
tangled hair, horse-thieves or worse, so unmanned by seasickness and exhaustion that neither was capable of the simplest
act of self-preservation.

The port watch was no better off. The two who had sailed
from London in the *Quiver* kept their distance from Henry, as
if he had a contagious disease. In the fo'c's'le it was every man
for himself. On the first night at sea, when they had at last been
released to drag themselves exhausted into their bunks, Henry
had selected the best one – near the door for fresh air but
protected from the water that would wash in – and found it
occupied by the farm boy. Henry threw him out and took over
the bunk. When supper was brought and Henry wordlessly
slung a bad-smelling Dago from the seat he wanted, the man
whipped out a knife. The nearest weapon to Henry's hand was
the man's dinner, hot meat and gravy on a heap of potatoes.
He thrust it into the man's face and he collapsed with a howl
then crawled to a seat at the other end of the table. In the same
rough manner Evans, Dutchie and the two Nova Scotiamen
claimed seats near Henry.

With every passing day the plight of the dead-beats at the other end of the table grew more wretched. The youngster looked near to death and when dragged out of his bunk simply crumpled, eyes purple in a white sheet of a face, and Henry persuaded Doc to get some gruel down his throat. The farm boy collected a pulpy wound on the jaw from the lash of the whip and moaned himself to sleep. Henry could bring himself to pity the captain and his mates faced with the task of whipping these dead-beats into seamen before their mettle was tested by the Horn. He had seen some cruelty in his time and had the scar on the edge of his ear to prove it, but in the sealing ship sailing the lonely byways of the Great Southern Ocean the depravity had been of the sneaking and illicit sort, perpetrated by crew and stamped on by the afterguard, but nothing had prepared Henry for the sickening barbarity that ruled the *Musket*.

The most bestial treatment was reserved not for the incapable in the crew, but the coloured men. Snowball in the starboard watch, and two other negroes in the port watch, as well as Big Tree, inhabited a world of holy terror. The cause of it was the dog. Nightingale loathed the sight of a dark skin. The big dog would stalk them along the deck, creeping low along the bulwarks while the men were busy hauling a rope, then ambush them with a bound. Woe betide the man who slackened his pull, despite the beast snapping at his limbs and drawing blood. One day Henry saw why. Mounting the ladder to take over the wheel, just before dawn, he came upon Smoke Lapierre worrying the dog with a golliwog. The doll was made of tanned canvas, with strands of tarred hemp for his hair and eyes of large buttons. When Nightingale was playfully pulling at the golliwog, Lapierre suddenly snatched it away and struck him across the muzzle. The dog yelped and cowered away, licking its chops. Later, when Lapierre went for'ard to check the watch and left the golliwog on the skylight, Henry picked it up to see what had caused the dog such pain. The head of the golliwog was filled with spiny sea urchins. Henry tossed it into the ship's wake.

Where depravity and brutality ruled perhaps the ship earned the men she deserved. Yet the *Musket* was herself a living beauty and Henry was compelled to admire the deft and dashing seamanship with which her captain handled her. Indeed, Screech Gander would never know how much his rival learnt from observing him at work – the technique of putting the helm down to get away on the ship before driving her through the eye of the wind on to the other tack; the trick of luff-and-touch to shake the wind out of her in a squall, which he had tried to master for himself; playing the spanker, the big fore-and-aft sail hoisted on a gaff abaft the mizzen, to achieve the right touch of weather helm so the ship was always in balance and not dragging her rudder. Henry salted it all away.

And life was not unremittingly bad. As a willing and industrious hand, Henry earned a certain respect from the mates and immunity from their curses and ill-treatment. Compared with any other ship he knew, living conditions were tolerable. Food and coffee were plentiful and tasty, the meat came in large hunks with lashings of gravy. When the supply of fresh vegetables ended there were pickles, onions and spices. Doc's pots gleamed like mirrors and Captain Gander inspected them daily. The fo'c's'le was clean and airy, only the men smelled like skunks and behaved like rats. But there was sweat in plenty, too. Henry and the elite group at his end of the mess table had to do the work of two men apiece. In this Yankee flier the men enjoyed everything on board but status, unlike British ships in which there was fierce pride and a strict code of honourable behaviour towards one another but living conditions and food were dreadful. In the *Musket* no such code existed. It was every man for himself, especially aloft. Even in the old *Partridge* there was a spirit of teamwork and mutual protection: when a seaman found a frayed ratline that could break and send a shipmate plunging to his death he cut it through or repaired it at once. In the *Musket* a man waited until he was told to do it.

For Henry there was satisfaction at least in seeing the ship make little headway against the weather. On the fifth day his luck changed. The clammy Liverpool weather gave way to bright sunshine. A brisk wind on the beam charged the clipper with energy and sent her creaming southwards, the Virginia coast in her lee. Though he welcomed the warm and frisky sailing, the new slant of breeze was dispiriting. It carried Henry relentlessly further from his own ship in New York and out into the reaches of the open ocean.

Every minute of every day Henry wrestled with plans of escape but all seemed hopeless. An uprising on the part of the crew was out of the question: the few able-bodied among them, like Evans, accepted their lot with the fatalism of sailors. This roving life was what they were born for. Only Dutchie continued to bear any sort of single-minded grudge, the scars of the knuckle-duster blows still fresh on his cheeks, but he was not a man on whom to pin any faith. Sabotage was equally unthinkable. No man alone could cripple a sailing ship at one blow unless he was at the wheel in a gale of wind, but if he let her broach and put the masts over the side it would imperil the lives of all on board. Gander was alive to the possibility of someone tampering with the compass and periodically inspected the binnacle in case Henry somehow slipped in a magnet, but Henry had no inkling of the ship's position and any action of that kind would have been a blind risk with unpredictable results.

Henry's only chance was another ship, but every time a sail was sighted on the horizon Screech Gander kept well clear. As the *Musket* pounded south-eastwards into warmer weather, heading for the rump of Brazil, Henry grew increasingly reconciled to his lot.

The good weather brought a change of another kind. The greenhorns discovered their sea legs and regained their wits. The farm boy, Tom, was put in charge of the livestock – a dozen hens, two pigs and a calf – and recovered his spirit. The seasick lad emerged hollow-cheeked and shaky out on deck one day, and the next was clambering happily up to the royal yard. The horse-thieves, as Henry called them, recovered their nerve. With a jolt Henry realised the *Musket* could boast a half-decent crew.

Although the mates could at last afford to relax their discipline, having whipped their men into shape, the cruelty persisted. Smoke Lapierre had spent some time searching for his dog-bating golliwog. Though he must have suspected that one of the crew had thrown it over the side, he neither said anything about it nor gave up his sport. When Big Tree or a darky came too close to Nightingale's curling lip, and she sprang at them, the mate fondled the dog's ears and told him he was a good boy. And every man knew that to take a poke at the dog was suicide, for Gander would never forgive.

It nearly happened when Nightingale's fangs sank into Big Tree's bare feet. The Maori let out a ferocious cry and jumped away. The other men dropped the rope. The sail thundered chaotically. Furious, Lapierre sikked the dog on Big Tree who, with a despairing glance at Henry, took to the rigging. By evening he was still hunched on the mainyard staring miserably at the dog waiting for him below. Having pity for the man, Henry climbed up with his supper and handed it over without a word. He was beginning his descent when Big Tree said, 'Captain, please . . .'

It seemed a lifetime since Henry last heard the rank addressed to himself and he paused, smiling faintly at the irony of it.

'Captain,' Big Tree went on earnestly. 'I am your brother. I did not know the captain would slug you.'

The Maori's dejection and loneliness struck a chord of sympathy in Henry. He threw his leg over the yard and for half an hour they talked. He heard how Big Tree had joined a Nantucket whaler in New Zealand and had wandered the world for five years, never finding a berth that would take him home, until Screech Gander had lured him aboard the *Musket* with a promise that the ship was bound for New South Wales.

Such tales were familiar enough in the fo'c's'les of ships plying the trade routes of the world. As he listened, Henry found himself liking the quiet Maori. His softly rumbling voice betrayed no self pity but the dark eyes in the high-cheeked and strong face curled up at the corners with a hint of gentle self-mockery. 'Tell me something,' Henry urged. 'Why are you so frightened of the dog? You must be the boss – kick it in the mouth.'

Big Tree flexed his hands. 'At Kororareka we eat dogs, plurry good,' he said flatly. 'Dogs don't scare me – when I touch that dog it dies.'

'Then Gander will kill you?'

Big Tree's sudden grin lit up his face. The tattoo lines coiled like springs being tightened, accentuating his smile. 'Maybe a tree will fall on him first,' he said. 'A big totara – plurry good!' He smacked Henry's shoulder and laughed silently, his wide shoulders shaking up and down.

Henry took the pouch from his pocket and removed the jade figure. Big Tree took it from his hand and reverently rubbed it between finger and thumb, as if drawing upon a reservoir of strength. 'Nobody ever gave me anything like this, tell me what it is,' Henry urged.

Abruptly Big Tree leant forward and hung the figure on its rough cord around Henry's neck. His fingers pushed it under the collar and held it flat against the skin of his chest. 'The stone is *pounamu*. See the colour, like a river pool? We call it *kahurangi*.' Big Tree ran the tip of his finger over the smooth indentations of its pattern. 'This is a man, a *tiki*.' The Maori almost whispered the word, as if in awe.

'Why should I wear it, is it supposed to be magic?'

Big Tree shook his head firmly. 'Not magic, not good luck, not bad luck. Many of my ancestors have worn this *tiki*. They have worn it in battle, on long voyages, at councils. When you wear it they go with you, at your shoulder ...' Big Tree floundered for words but Henry knew what he was trying to say. The wearer gained the prestige, bravery and wisdom of those who had worn it before him. Some called it *mana*.

Henry buttoned up his shirt and smiled his thanks. 'You're not staying up here all night?'

The Maori looked far away into the dark night but said nothing and Henry descended to the thin straw mattress in his wooden bunk.

The chiefly ancestors seemed to be exerting little influence on his behalf next day. Dawn found the *Musket* snoring through a sunlit blue sea with white water hissing beneath the golden wings of her figurehead. Big Tree had been bailed up the mainmast by Nightingale all though the night. Henry climbed up with a biscuit in his pocket and a mug of coffee in his hand, then slipped down by way of a halyard. The dog growled but kept his chin on the deck and only rolled his eyes. Henry paid it no attention and collected his own breakfast. Screech Gander took a turn of the poop, his shirt open to the wind and his long hair streaming. With a piercing whistle he called the dog then looked up at Big Tree. 'Get down from there, you big ape,' he ordered.

At that same moment Smoke Lapierre, a mug of coffee in each hand for himself and the captain, carefully mounted the steep ladder to the poop. He had just reached the top step when Nightingale bounded straight up the ladder and darted between his legs. The mate overbalanced, tried to save himself as well as the coffee but failed on both counts and fell sprawling.

It was the moon-faced Dutchman, eating his breakfast in a sunny spot at the starboard bulwarks, who laughed.

Smoke Lapierre was up in a flash. The blacksnake whistled. Dutchie screamed with pain and clutched his breast as the lash circled his torso. But he was quick for such a big man. He grabbed the lash as the mate drew it back for another blow and jerked the handle from his hands. In a second Dutchie had the stock in his grip and the lash was singing over the deckboards as he made a testing stroke in the direction of the horrified mate.

In that moment, quicker than anything Henry had ever imagined, Screech Gander took three giant strides the length of the poop and with a flying leap smashed his shoulder into the Dutchman's ample belly. The impact flung him twenty feet along the deck. Lapierre regained possession of the whip and cracked it over his head, a blood-thirsty grin lighting his red eyes. Then a dark shadow fell over him as Big Tree dropped from the shrouds, wrested the blacksnake from his grip, and threw it over the rail. Nightingale sprang at the Maori. Henry stepped in front of Big Tree and, half crouching as if he would wrestle with him, stopped the dog with a glare and a shout. Henry's yell froze not only the dog but officers and crew alike. In the silence, Ben Whipple ran up the companion-way and fired a revolver into the air.

Screech Gander laughed and imperiously reached out for the gun which Whipple handed over. Lapierre had wasted no time in picking up the belaying pin with which he was advancing on Big Tree but Henry stopped him with the same curt command that had halted the dog. 'Quit that!' Then he added, 'You won't get to 'Frisco by killing us all.'

Gander blew on the barrel of the revolver and eyed Henry narrowly. 'Any more trouble, you'll get first bullet.'

Henry said nothing but edged away, pushing Big Tree ahead of him. Screech Gander tipped his head at his mates and they followed him to the binnacle where he buckled the gunbelt around his waist. Dutchie climbed painfully to his feet. 'I'll kill the dirty bokker,' he gasped thickly.

'That's it, Dutchie,' the Nova Scotian called Claridge urged in fun, 'wring the bastard's neck while you've got him cornered on the poop.'

Near noon, Henry was working astride the mizzen top-gallant yard more than eighty feet above the poop. This was the kind of sailoring every man enjoyed, working at nautical crafts high in the wind as the ship rolled easily across the bright blue sea. For a while Henry's pleasure in the simple and routine job of splicing a new lift allowed him to forget the humiliation and disappointment of his lot. Far below, a stunted figure on the holystoned planks, Screech Gander prepared for the noon sight. A broad-brimmed straw hat shielded his face from the brilliant sky and the brass sextant in his hand glittered as if it were made of gold. As he looked down Henry noticed something odd about Dutchie working twenty feet below him on the topsail yard. There was a cat-like tension about him as he balanced easily on the swaying yard, his ankles locked around the spar and a marline spike dangling from a lanyard that he held in his fingers. Gander glanced up at the sun and walked to the rail. He was directly below the yard. The seaman holding the foot-long steel spike in his fingers only had to wait for the roll of the ship to swing him vertical and the captain would be directly in his sights. When he released the lanyard the spike would plummet like a spear from the hands of God.

It all happened so quickly that Henry did not pause to think. He reacted instinctively, as would any man seeing murder about to be committed. He shouted and threw a ball of whipping twine at Dutchie's head. The spike fell from his fingers. In the same moment Gander looked up and took a single sideways step. The spike drove into the deck a yard from his boots. In a blur of action he scooped the revolver from its holster, cocked it with the heel of his other hand, crouched, fired.

Dutchie cried out and clutched his shoulder, then pitched forward and fell from the yard. His gurgling cry ended abruptly as his skull smashed into the rail with a thud that trembled through every timber. The body slithered over the bulwark and splashed into the sea.

Screech Gander casually holstered his gun. His grunt as he heaved the spike out of the deck was loud in the silence. Tossing it end over end in his hand he walked the full length of the deck to the fo'c's'le, where he replaced the spike in the store. In the same stony silence he returned aft, settled himself at the rail, and carried on with his navigation.

Nothing was said about the killing, neither by the mates nor the shocked crew. Soon after eight bells sounded in the tense air, Doc leaned out of the galley and gave his customary ringing salute with a ladle beaten on a pan lid. Henry took his dinner but had no appetite. He stared gloomily at the radiantly blue water sluicing along the black side. He felt sick – sick with himself for spoiling Dutchie's effort to kill Screech Gander, sick at the callous and cold-blooded murder he had witnessed.

'Sail ho . . . !' Young Tom's cry from the foretop prompted a ripple of interest. The sight of a ship beating up from the south was a welcome diversion and Henry joined many of the others in swinging himself into the shrouds. A barque by the look of her, making heavy weather against the wind. Her masts lifted quickly over the horizon as the *Musket* ran down on her, but Gander told the helmsman to run her off a couple of points: he did not wish to pass closer than a couple of miles.

Four flags climbed to the barque's yard as she hoisted her numbers, the universally recognised signal for a desire to speak. 'No numbers, hold your course,' Gander growled to his mates.

Henry jumped down to the deck and weighed his chances. His heart pumped wildly in his breast and his mouth was dry. He knew this was the time for action, his last opportunity to escape the *Musket*, but the memory of Gander's swift and ruthless reactions was vivid.

The wind had come almost on the beam. The *Musket*'s gentle and rhythmic rolling had given way to a steepish heel. The other ship would pass to leeward. While Gander remained at the binnacle, Smoke Lapierre went to the lee rail and was balancing on the tilted deck with his arms folded while he watched the far sail approach.

Grasping all his courage, Henry glided smoothly up the ladder. The mate had eyes in the back of his head and turned round sharply, as Henry knew he would. But Henry was ready. He directed his eyes at the water rushing along the side and pointed, shouting, 'Hey Smoke! Look at the size of that bloody shark!'

The mate might have been the devil incarnate but he had a human side. He stepped down the deck and peered over the rail. Henry had his scrawny arm up the middle of his back in a blink of time. For a desperate moment, as the mate swayed over the rail on the point of balance, Henry thought he would lose him. Then he managed to grab a wildly kicking foot and catch it in the noose he had prepared. Ignoring a thudding kick from the mate's other foot, he lowered Smoke Lapierre head first over the side.

The speed of it all took even Screech Gander by surprise. As the captain reached for his gun Henry waved a stiff finger in the air. 'Touch that gun, I'll drop this bastard into the drink before the slug finds its mark.'

Gander smiled. 'Jesus Christ, there's a temptation! But why all the circus? I'm damned if I know.'

'Hoist your numbers and speak to that ship.'

'You should have let the Dutchman do his worst. Why did you stop him?'

'I saved you for myself,' Henry said. 'If anybody kills you it will be me! Hoist the bloody numbers.'

The mate let out an anguished cry as a tip of the ship caused his face to drag in the water. It brought Nightingale to the poop in a bound. Henry diverted him by shaking the other end of the rope. The dog snatched it in his jaws and heaved backwards, growling.

Screech Gander tipped his hat to the back of his head and laughed as if he couldn't believe his eyes. Henry was not fooled. Those eyes were as good as a double-barrelled shotgun trained on him, and he was uneasily aware of the initiative slipping through his fingers. If Gander fired and Henry let go the rope, Nightingale could hold it long enough for a man to save the mate. And Gander knew it.

The belaying pin hurled like a spear from the maindeck caught Screech Gander on the chin and wiped the smile from his face. He stumbled backwards, the gun falling from his fingers and sliding into the scuppers. Almost as swiftly came a larger projectile. Big Tree flung himself up the ladder and with a mighty heave on the rope lifted the dog off its feet. His other hand grabbed the dog by its heavy studded collar and the momentum of the swing carried the animal clean over the rail where Big Tree held him, whining and pawing at the ship's black paint as he hung helplessly in his collar.

Screech Gander groggily wiped the wound on his chin with the back of his hand and saw blood. He glanced at the gun in the scuppers but did not go for it. 'Mr Whipple,' he muttered, 'hoist our numbers and put the helm down.'

The sails thundered as the ship altered course. 'Trim the bloody yards!' Henry yelled at the crew gazing horrified from the deck.

The helmsman was the seaman from Liverpool, who knew his stuff. 'Box her off, Evans, and get me as close to windward of that ship as you can.'

Evans covered himself by looking to Gander for confirmation of the order. Henry lowered the mate an inch and drew a scream of terror. Gander nodded.

As leeward vessel it was the other ship's job to heave to so the *Musket* could run down on her. Henry watched her swing away and back her mainsail until she lay athwart the wind, dead in the water.

Ben Whipple moved menacingly towards Big Tree. 'We can take 'em from each side, Cap'n.'

'Move one inch and you've got a dead dog!' Henry warned.

'Stand back!' Gander snapped.

The barque was close now. Long tresses of glistening green weed trailed from her hull as she rolled. Henry removed a hand

from the rope long enough to loosen his boot-laces then he
toed them off his feet. 'Closer, damn it, Evans!'

The ship fell off the wind a point. Henry saw men on the
other vessel staring at the *Musket* through telescopes, no doubt
trying to see what strange bundles she had slung over her rail
just abaft the mizzen channels.

Suddenly she was abeam. Henry stooped and threw two
turns of the rope round the bitt. At the same time Big Tree's
muscular arm swung like a branch in a gale. Henry sprang over
the rail and hit the water in a clean dive. Nightingale flew
inboard and crashed tail-first into Gander's legs. The dog
scrabbled frantically for a grip on the smooth planks as Big
Tree rolled over the rail and dropped into the *Musket*'s wake
while the ship surged quickly out of range of Gander's gun.

Henry trod water as a mop of black curls and a brown face
split by a happy grin surfaced as few feet away. Then both
struck out strongly for the barque hove to not a cable distant.

No man could sleep through the racket of a ship being
unloaded by a gang of nail-booted swearing longshoremen.
Sam Handyside breakfasted early and took his coffee up to the
poop. The pier was crowded with drays, heavy horses tossing
nosebags and rattling harnesses. The bales and cases of general
cargo the *Quiver* had brought across the Atlantic were lifted
out of the hold in a sling. The sling was hoisted on a two-inch
manilla that passed through a block high on the cock-billed
mainyard and down to another block on the deck. From there
it was pulled horizontally along the deck by half a dozen men
who stamped their boots as they walked and made the deck
ring like a drum.

The morning was grey and wretched. Snow had not ma-
terialised though it was cold and dank enough. Sam saw that
Lampshades had matters in hand. Manfred Longhandle was
making use of the uncluttered poop to lay out bolts of canvas
and cut a ringtail, an extension to the spanker which might
come in useful in the trades. For'ard, Barlow scraped out his
iron pot into the pig trough. Young Peake was lending
Meadows and Field a hand in screwing and bolting the
hardware to a shaped sprucepole, a new fore-royal yard to be
swayed up the mast later in the day to replace the other which
had split due to some fault in the timber. There was no sign of
the captain but Sam was not surprised. He knew from rich
experience how many hours a shipmaster could waste in

agents' offices, fruitlessly discussing such weighty matters as manifests, bills of lading, rates of exchange, and the eccentric behaviour of other captains. Having slipped ashore earlier in the morning Henry would now be jawing in some dark-panelled office nursing a coffee laced with rum. Sam winced at a wintry ache of rheumatism in his joints and came to a decision. He was not needed here. He would stroll up Fulton Street to the bath-house behind the market and indulge himself. A long soak in a piping hot bath and a cigar would set him up for the hooley that Screech Gander had promised at the launching of the *Saker*.

It was late in the morning when Sam returned to the ship. He felt a new man. His grey whiskers, washed and brushed, fluffed up in the wind. His round face was pink and shiny and his poor old joints, knotted up by a lifetime spent keeping his feet on heaving decks, felt better than they had for days. He wore a new shirt under his heavy pilot coat and had left the old one at a laundry in Water Street to be delivered later. Humming contentedly and keeping a weather eye on the cargo sling lifting above his head, Sam crossed the gangway and was hailed by Martin Peake. 'Mr Handyside, Sir, did you hear the news?'

'Should I sit down before you tell me?'

'The *Musket* sailed during the night, she's gone.'

Sam's first thought was not for the race but his invitation to the launching. What should he do? As he stood nonplussed the clock on the ferry pier struck twelve and a carriage drew up under the *Quiver*'s bowsprit. While a boy held the leading horse the driver came along the pier. 'Captain Gander's carriage for the launching party,' he said.

Sam turned uncertainly on the mate. 'Are you sure?'

Peake nodded emphatically. 'Everybody's talking about it. Screech has left half his cargo sitting on the pier.'

'We must have frightened him,' Sam said. He decided that as Henry was not yet back from his travels he would go on alone. Through the thirty-minute drive to the shipyard Sam puzzled over the abrupt departure of the *Musket*. It seemed to make no sense, especially as Gander had implied he would himself be attending the launch. When the carriage drew up at the shipyard gates where flags were flying, brass bands played and tables groaned under mountains of clams, oysters and cold joints, Sam found the same question on every lip. Why the mysterious departure of the *Musket* in the early hours, leaving behind all her premium passengers and much of her cargo? Yet every face in the excited crowd bore a triumphant smirk. Captain Gander had stolen a march on the Limey, that much was certain. Power to his elbow. The *Quiver* would have trouble catching the *Musket* now.

Black and sheer as a rock of wave-washed basalt, the hull of the new clipper loomed high above the crowd. Excited faces of those who would ride her down the ways peered over the rail as from the brim of a cliff. Only the thick lower sections of her masts were raised. Bunting and signal flags flew from bow to stern. A vast Stars and Stripes flapped heavily from a temporary jack on the taffrail and an equally large house-flag bearing the jagged lightning bolt of O'Cain's shipping line flew from the top of the stumpy mainmast. The yellow metal of her copper sheathing, hundreds of overlapping rectangles rimmed with tiny tacks, gleamed as if the entire underbody of the beautiful ship were constructed of gold bricks.

Sam, escorted to the enclosure directly beneath her forefoot, gazed up at the concave bow. Like a gigantic thunderhead, its anvil point merging into the mystical form of a great bird, it filled half the sky. He had an uncomfortable feeling the golden-winged saker was diving down, talons bared, its eagle eye fixed on his bald head.

Oddly, the same feeling came over him when he was greeted by a man of his own vintage, mild-looking but for an intensely unblinking gaze. 'Ah, Mr Handyside of the good ship *Quiver*, is it not? Good morning to you.' Joseph O'Cain's welcome was courteous but his handshake was cold and curt.

'What's this I hear about the *Musket* sailing ahead of schedule?' Sam demanded.

'Captain Gander chose to sail in the early hours,' O'Cain said thinly. 'I trust you won't be too many days behind him.'

'Obviously we've got him worried,' Sam said jocularly. 'Else it's a rum way to run a shipping line.'

O'Cain did not smile. 'I was looking forward to meeting your own young captain.'

'Caught up somewhere on business, I'm afraid. No doubt he'll be here presently.'

'Hmm.' The Irishman held Sam in a piercing stare then presented the plumed and feathered creature at his side. 'My daughter, Miss Flora O'Cain, Mr Handyside.'

The shipowner's daughter was a small, coarsely featured woman in her middle thirties. Her pale skin and lank gingery

hair had the garish, sun-dried look of a ship's figurehead in
need of a coat of paint. Across her upper lip, as if the ship's boy
had amused himself with a paintbrush, grew the reddish fluff
of an incipient moustache. 'Charmed,' Sam muttered, sensing
as he brushed rough-skinned fingers to his lips that he was
being nailed down by iron-sharp penetrating eyes.

'You must come to the race meeting during your stay in New
York and see my horses run,' Miss O'Cain said.

'Thank you kindly ma'am, perhaps I will.'

Sam drifted into the crowd. He accepted a glass of mulled
wine and sipped it, facing the gate so he would see Henry
arrive. Screech Gander must be rattled to have sailed at such
short notice, he reasoned. But Henry Ardent would have to
look slippy if he was to get after him. What could have kept the
lad?

The first chill of apprehension shivered Sam's bones when he
saw two fellows, shipping men by the look of them, doubled
up and slapping their knees with laughter.

'Shanghai'd him, by God!'

'Cooked the Limey's goose, I'd say!'

In a cold sweat, Sam stood through the speeches. Flora
O'Cain cut the ribbon with silver scissors. The bottle of
champagne, carefully grooved with a file to ensure the glass
would shatter on impact, smashed into the lean forefoot.
Slowly at first, as the blocks and wedges were knocked away,
the great black hull began to move. With the dignity of a
cathedral astonished at finding itself gliding unstoppably
down a slippery slope, the ship gathered speed. There was a
crescendo of rousing cheers, a barrage of flying hats, a fanfare
of trumpets. The slender rudder, braced to withstand the
shock, parted the muddy waters. A high wall of lava-brown
water and spray avalanched away from her stern. With a
thunderous roar of tallow-greased timbers, breaking surf and
dragging chains, the *Saker* burst into the tideway and bobbed
to her warps, proud as a duck in mid canal.

Sam had no eyes for her beauty, no appetite for the admiration of her lines, no heart for the celebrations that followed.
The buzz he heard in the crowd was loud and clear, its
implications appalling. Sam found a cab and returned directly
to the *Quiver*. With faces as long as seaboots, Meadows and
Field greeted him at the gangway. When they saw him arrive,
Will Lamshire and Martin Peake also came ashore. 'Is the
captain on board?' Sam demanded sharply, and the silence of

the four men as they studied the planks of the pier and sucked their teeth confirmed his worst fears.

Charlie Meadows took the arm of a man waiting nearby and pushed him forward. 'This turkey's a runner, Barley and me 'eard 'im lording it all 'igh and bleedin' mighty dahn Ma Kettle's.' The man took off his cap and faced up to Sam, hanging his head. He was a shabby nondescript individual with hungry, frightened eyes. Meadows poked him roughly in the ribs and said, 'Go on, flap the red rag 'fore I stir yer puddin'. Tell the captain wot yer seen . . .'

'Ain't no duff, Cap'n, swear it!' the man squealed, dodging away from Meadows' prodding finger.

'Leave him alone,' Sam said sharply, and with a calming smile urged the runner to tell his story. It was conclusive enough. His name was Bill Adams. He was a bean-eater, a man of Boston, and he had been a deep-sea man all his life until lately. One-arm Monell had fixed him the job to run the *Musket* out to The Narrows. It was a midnight job and they had to keep their traps shut. Come daylight the old man and his mates had roused up the crew. One of them was a big bug, Adams could tell that by his duds. That's right, a coat of dark blue serge and grey trousers, dressed like a gent. Hair yellow like new rope, blue eyes, knacky sort of crittur . . . Yes, and a rip in his ear. Lord, you should have seen how the mates hammered him into the deck . . . Hell no, he didn't cash his checks, plenty of fight left in the bugger. Tried to jump the tug, though he was in irons, but the mate wrapped him in his blacksnake and that were a sight, Christ!

'That will do,' Sam ordered, and pushed half a dollar into Adam's fist.

Meadows tipped his head and growled, 'Scat!'

Sam sighed and gazed at the anxious faces around him. 'Now we know where we stand, anyhow.'

'Yer feelin' strong by any chance, Mr Peake?' Meadows asked, his black brows crumpled in a deep frown.

'No more than usual,' Peake replied. 'Why?'

''Cos if you think yer man enuff to shit a miracle, now's yer big chance.'

In the three days it took Sam Handyside to come to terms with the disaster there were no miracles. In fact the reverse. The pier alongside *Quiver* milled with sightseers gloating over the fate of her master. Shippers cancelled the cargo space they had reserved. Passengers willing to pay a premium rate for a swift voyage to California transferred their bookings to other ships. The crew vanished as if into thin air, only a handful returning to the agent's office to collect wages due to them. The ship became the butt of music hall jokes and newspaper cartoons. Some wag doctored the notice hanging from the bowsprit to read 'Broken Arrow Line'. Flora O'Cain renamed her slowest and ugliest stallion Captain Ardent and at the Saturday race meeting it trailed in last by miles, becoming the sensation of the day.

Sam Handyside had not suffered this kind of scoffing and insolence since he was a ship's boy, half a century ago. Not knowing how to deal with it he brooded and became grumpily indecisive. Martin Peake hated to go ashore because of the sneers and remarks poked at him. Will Lamshire, conversely, set out on a number of expeditions because he was looking for a ship to take him home. Meadows and Field drowned their sorrows in red-eye and returned from drinking bouts with bloodied knuckles and bruised faces.

The young second mate was all for setting off in pursuit. They could fall in with the *Musket* off the Horn, he argued, for it could take only a small trick of the weather to delay her there. Sam urged caution. What if Henry were put ashore? What if he came back to New York the day after *Quiver* sailed? 'If that Blue Nose villain lets young h'Ardent wipe 'is boots on dry land it will be the coast of Brazil,' Meadows said miserably.

'If not the bleedin' Falkland Islands,' Field agreed.

Three days after Henry Ardent's disappearance Sam Handyside made his decision. The *Quiver* would sail for San Francisco on 14th December, allowing her master two weeks' grace. It would be Sam himself, not Mr Lamshire, who would take command and he was advising Monkton Winkworth of that fact. He said nothing about the race. In his heart he knew it was over. It was within his skill to get the ship around the world by way of 'Frisco and Canton as planned and he might even turn a pretty profit, who could tell? But then he would retire, as he ought to have done two months back. Sam donned his tall hat and best coat and called upon the agent of the Arrow Line to announce his plans. The ship's departure date was advertised. Arrangements for victuals, navigation charts, water and other requirements were put in hand. The *Quiver* might no longer be a crack clipper involved in a round-the-world challenge race but she was nevertheless a fast-sailing merchant vessel under a reputable flag and she had a long passage to make. Acting captain, mates, bosuns, cook and sailmaker fell with relief into their accustomed roles.

Sam was relentless in his efforts to drum up freights but as the schedule departure neared he had to admit the truth. 'Sailing is postponed a week,' he told the others. 'There is no point in carrying an empty hold round the world, we don't have a single piece of cargo to put in it.'

'What about crew, can we get men?' Lamshire asked.

'Reckon King O'Cain's pointed the bone at us,' Meadows said. 'None of the shipping masters an' boarding 'ouse men want to know us, we're lepers.'

'We won't find a tug to touch us when we want to sail,' Sam went on. 'And when we cast off I won't be surprised to find half of New York on the pier hanging on to our bulwarks to prevent us sailing.'

'Can we fight our way out?' Peake suggested hopefully.

'Wiv wot?' Meadows sneered. 'The only weapon we got is on our flag, and that's only a bow and bleedin' arrer.'

When Sam's planned departure date drew near it seemed the *Quiver* could be stuck in New York past Christmas. The enforced delay and uncertain future was too much for Will, who told a gloomy group over breakfast he would be shipping out as third mate in a Liverpool packet. Sam tried to change his mind. He was confident things would change in the new year, when the *Musket* would be so far ahead that New Yorkers would soften their hearts and let the *Quiver* go. The mate was in the act of shaking his head, at the same time wiping gravy from his plate with a piece of bread because he could not meet Sam's mortified gaze, when footsteps were heard ringing on the deckhead.

A pair of unfamiliar boots descended the companion ladder, followed by a familiar grin beaming from within a shock of tangled blond hair and a new beard.

The stress of the past two weeks was charted in dark contours under Sam's eyes but his round face glowed as Henry, pinkly scrubbed, clean shaven and dressed in his own togs, appeared once more on the poop of the *Quiver*. 'Take the slack out of those halyards, Oatsy, we're flying a flag not a snot-rag,' he said briskly. 'When you've done that I want a new harbour stow on the fore-royal and fore-topgallant, they're drooping like a whore's drawers. Put Big Tree to cleaning the poultry cages, we'll be taking some livestock on board for the voyage.

Tell him he drops just one spot on my deck I'll have him back in the *Musket* before he knows he's quivering or shivering. And you, Barley, get your daisy-beaters up here, I want to speak with you.'

Grinning, Charlie Field came aft at a run and bounded up the ladder. 'Strewth, where did you get the shiner?' Henry asked. The big man looked embarrassed and fingered his bruised eye. 'Some geezer in a grog-shop tried to hang one on me.'

'I bet!' Henry said admiringly. 'After you told him *Quiver* could show a bare backside to any Yankee afloat, I suppose.'

'Nah, nuffink like that, I only told 'im the *Musket* wasn't fit ter carry stinkin' fish ter Billingsgate an' 'e tried ter tell me my brains was so full o' shackles they rattled like skeletons shaggin' on a tin roof . . .'

'So you knocked it out of him?'

'We 'ad six Yankee blighters on our backs, didn't we Barley!' Meadows interjected proudly. 'They was 'eaped on us like flies on a turd, but we sorted 'em.'

Henry laughed. 'All right, now you two can show 'em how a ship's 'tweendecks can be squared away in double quick time. We will have an army of Yankee carpenters banging away down the hold before noon, and it's not the kind of banging skeletons do on a roof.'

Henry turned on the mates. 'What's this about finding a crew? Men ought to be falling over themselves to sail for the diggings in a crack ship like this.'

When Sam explained the problem Henry took a turn of the deck and whistled. The long drag north had given him plenty of time to think and he had anticipated trouble of this kind. 'Go and tip Manfred off his bucket and get him up here,' he ordered.

The sailmaker came blinking into the weak sunlight, showing no surprise at the captain's return to the fold. 'What for you want?' he demanded. 'No goes anywhere, no sails, maybe you want shroud to bury in?'

Henry explained in detail. Manfred nodded, though it was evident from his side-slant glance as he left the deck that he thought the captain had gone mad.

'How's cargo?' Henry asked Sam.

The old man shrugged tiredly. 'You want the long answer or the short? We ain't got none, that's the strength of it, apart from Mr Chamberlayne's bales in the lower hold, of course.'

As Sam started to explain the hours of labour he had exerted in a fruitless bid to find cargo Henry silenced him with a friendly grip on his sloping shoulder. 'No matter, Sam, we don't need no Yankee ballast. We're filling the 'tweendecks with temporary bunks and carrying two-legged livestock. How many can we cram in – a hundred? So we need drinking water for a hundred passengers, some kind of galley where they can cook, provisions to last them three months . . . No, make it three and a half, we don't want 'em eating each other. See what you can do, Sam.'

'Lord, you don't want much, lad. It's going to take a few days to put all this together. When are we sailing?'

Henry took a quick look at Captain Plunkett's gold watch then dropped it back into his waistcoat pocket and fixed his blue eyes levelly upon Sam. 'Tomorrow morning, eight sharp.'

By the time the early dusk of a wintry evening darkened the sky, the *Quiver* was transformed. Lanterns glimmered on the ends of every foremast yard, like candles on a fir tree. An immense banner that Manfred made from a tarpaulin was hoisted between foremast and mainmast, at the level of the topsail yards, where it could be read from afar by every soul passing up or down South Street. The words, painted large in letters of green and yellow and illuminated by a string of oil lamps, proclaimed:

FASTEST TO S.FRISCO GOLD!!

A second banner, smaller than the first, was stretched between the topgallant and topsail yards on the foremast so it could be read from the street. The words read:

BERTHS FOR 100 ADVENTURERS
$300 PER HEAD
Ninety Days (Or Less) To Frisco
Or Passage Money Refunded In Full

'That ought to fetch 'em,' Henry said, dusting his hands as he stepped back to admire his handiwork. Already crowds of people swarmed along South Street, attracted by the extraordinary scene.

Henry felt a hand plucking importantly at his sleeve. 'Oi, Captain! Do you mean what you say? Ninety days to Frisco or the whole three hundred dollars refunded? Is that the deal?'

'Sure is,' Henry replied. 'I'll take the first one hundred men standing at the gangway with their money in their hands, six o'clock in the morning.'

A steady thunder of hammering came from the hold where hired carpenters were busy building bunks. Already more than twenty bunks had been constructed in double tiers and the rest would be ready by sun-up. Extra hogsheads of water were lashed along the bulwarks. Sam had purchased an entire deckhouse, or caboose, ready fitted with cooking stove and pots and pans, which was craned aboard and lashed to the hatch cover to serve as cookhouse for the passengers. But Sam was unhappy and he confronted Henry as he strode confidently up the gangway. 'All this is wasted effort without a crew, lad, and the shipping masters have frozen us out – we tried it before.'

'There's more than one way to slice a cabbage, Sam,' Henry said and barged past him calling for Meadows. 'Oatsy, bring me the board I asked you to paint black this morning, it should be dry by now. And I need a pot of white paint and a small brush.'

A few minutes later Henry finished painting white letters on the black board, four feet by three, and handed the wet brush to Meadows. 'This ought to curdle their milk,' he muttered smugly.

'Gawd, they'll murder us,' said Meadows as he read the words.

'Pikes and cutlasses, Oatsy!' Henry told him encouragingly. 'Hang it high on the bowsprit, where they can't drag it down and stamp on it, and don't do anything silly.'

With a lantern hung on each side of it the notice was lowered on two ropes beneath the jibboom which jutted over the cobbled street. As they secured the ropes Meadows and Field heard the crowd laughing and pointing, as they read:

CREW WANTED
Frisco Bound
Top Rates Paid
NIGGERS AND IRISHMEN
NEED NOT APPLY

The first bottle hit the deck not long before midnight. A barrage of cobblestones, loose ends of timber and other dockside refuse followed. Henry, dozing fully dressed in his bunk, was out in a moment and saw Meadows running aft, picking his way through the broken glass littering the deck. 'Get Barley and let's go,' Henry called.

Wearing a silk topper borrowed from Sam to lend him dignity, Henry strode down the gangway and marched with measured tread towards the shadowy mob firing missiles at the offending notice. Meadows and Field, looking worried and scared, followed a few paces behind. Sam and the mates lurked near the gangway with belaying pins to hand, ready to pitch in if necessity demanded.

As the angry men caught sight of the little procession advancing resolutely along the pier they fell quiet and stepped back to form an arena lit by the lamps which illuminated the offending notice above. Half were blacks, big and well-muscled men. The rest, judging by their readiness to brawl and the red flush of liquor in their cheeks, were Irish.

Henry mounted a bollard and spoke out. 'What's up, men? Why are you attacking the finest ship that ever floated?'

'You the skunk wot put up this notice?'

'Of course, Captain Henry Ardent of the *Quiver* is my name and I'll put up any notice I please – want to make something of it?'

'If it's a fight you're pickin', Cap'n, I can soon set one up for you. D'you carry a shooter?'

'No,' Henry replied, 'but I can spit.' The men laughed. Henry composed his features into a picture of honest puzzlement. 'Just tell me what's troubling you, I don't have all night.'

The man facing him, big in the bones and pink in the face, was evidently leader of at least part of the bunch. His big hands were blotched with yellow stains of tar and the fingernails were split from wrestling with sails. He was every inch a sailor and every ounce an ugly customer. 'I'm an Irishman and I want my rights and so do my mates,' he growled.

'What's your name?'

'Tom Dingle, that's my name, and it will take a better man than you to stop me putting it down on any crew muster I please.'

A black fist was shaken under Henry's nose. 'You's insultin' me an' all nigrahs ever'where, we's better men than white trash!'

Dingle shouldered him aside. 'Out of my way, you black rat.'

'You don' call Adam Robinson a black rat and live, spuddy . . . !' The Negro was bigger than Dingle, a firebrand embodying all the merits of the clipper ship: strength and driving power aloft, speed and agility below.

'Gentlemen!' Henry cried. He smiled indulgently, indicating the angry faces of Dingle and Robinson. 'Here's proof, if you want. Niggers and Irishmen go together like sparks and gunpowder. Would you want me to mix 'em on board my ship?'

A howl of protest answered him. Something heavy flew overhead, bounced off the notice, and struck Henry's shoulder a glancing blow. It was a dead cat.

Henry extended both arms, commanding silence. 'It's not right to bend the rules but let me see, how many men here can hand, reef and steer? How many of you are man enough to handle an English clipper, fifteen dollars a month, Yankee rations and no dead horse?'

Fifty pairs of arms, brown and white, waved in the lamplight. 'Line up and let me look at you, I'm not taking no hog-minders and plough-pushers,' Henry said, recalling Screech Gander's withering phrase. 'Paddies behind Dingle here, darkies behind Robinson. I'll take fourteen of each.'

Henry moved along both lines, selecting men by their strength and the callouses of their fingers and palms. Those he touched on the shoulder went to the gangway, whooping joyfully and hanging on each other's shoulders.

There were angry murmurs as the other men were dismissed. Martin Peake was already bringing the notice inboard. Henry turned on Meadows and Field. 'You two have a big job till daylight – stay with the men in the fo'c's'le and keep 'em lubricated, one bottle at a time. We don't want trouble and we don't want second thoughts.'

Meadows took the dead cat by the tail and held it at arm's length. 'Wot about our furry friend?'

'Find some brown paper and make it into a parcel then we'll arrange a messenger before we cast off in the morning.'

'Eh! Where in Gawd's name will a messenger take a dead cat?'

Henry ran a satisfied eye over his ship. 'We will address it to King O'Cain,' he said.

The deck became a battlefield from the first day out. Hardly had the *Quiver* been cast adrift outside the harbour heads than a pair of Irishmen suddenly released their hold on the mizzen topgallant halyard and lammed into the two West Indians who had been helping them. The topgallant yard dropped, parting one of the lifts. The spar was left drooping like a lame wing. The end of the halyard flew away in the wind while the four men rolled over and over in the scuppers, hammering each other with fists and boots. Henry Ardent waded in, kicking them apart. With bleeding faces and heaving chests the men glowered at each other, two against two. 'No nigger tells me what to do,' muttered the young seaman called Pat Flynn, his temper as hot as his bright orange hair. O'Casey, his partner, spat blood on deck and nodded his support.

The West Indian called Bunce folded his muscular arms and stared at Flynn. 'You gonna pull on a rope then you gotta *pull*, man!'

'You tellin' me I wasn't pullin', is that it?'

'I ain't pullin' de same rope as no whitey, it ain't fit.'

The rain storm that had blotted out the land now smoked around the ship. All the fight went out of the men as they turned their backs to the stinging pellets whirring in the wind. Henry pushed them back to their jobs and returned to the poop. 'They'll settle down after a bit,' he told Sam breezily.

But the men did not settle down. After several days of constant flare-ups Henry had to face up to the facts. This was not the usual bad-tempered squabbling that occurred when a crew of strangers was shaking down in difficult circumstances. It became evident that Irishman and Negro were incapable of pulling on the same rope. They could not climb rigging on the same mast without trying to shake each other off, nor was it possible for them to sit at the same table without brawling, or to share the same living quarters without murdering each other.

As long as the ship slugged into wintry gales, the air filled with freezing spray and the lee decks swilling waist deep in icy water, the need to work the ship and fight for survival kept a damper on men's tempers. But the hatred smouldered, growing hotter by the day.

Henry knew an explosion was inevitable and did not know how to avoid it. What a fool he had been, signing articles with Niggers and Irishmen. He had walked into it with his eyes open, had even boasted of the risks. He had found himself a crew, certainly, but had given no thought to how they could be made to work. He had learned the hard way it was not good enough to fill the ship with men. They had to be drilled and schooled. The men had to be driven or they had to be led. Anything but give them a free hand to rampage as the mood took them, and this was becoming the alarming state of things. The authority of the mates was eroded because William Lamshire and Martin Peake were not cut out for bucko tactics. They had the nerve but not the ruthlessness. On the third day out young Peake bravely faced up to Dingle as the hulking Irishman turned on him with a belaying pin. 'This ain't no hell ship 'less you make it one,' Martin said, calmly taking the iron bar from the Irishman's hands. 'But the devil himself will be right up your arse if you don't move it . . .' Dingle got on with his job but Peake did not smack him over the head with the pin as a Yankee mate would have done. This was a mistake, and all the crew knew it. Observing his mates clinging to the remnants of their authority, Henry could spare a sneaking sympathy for Screech Gander and his methods. What wouldn't he give for a blacksnake, and the guts to use it?

After five days of thrashing into relentlessly grey weather, the ship broke into thin wintry sunlight. Henry saw the six Negro members of the port watch huddled along the windward rail, seeking what shelter they could from the biting breeze. 'You men are off watch, why aren't you in your bunks?' he asked Bunce.

'We's not goin' in dere, we get killed,' the West Indian replied.

Henry found the seven Irishmen of the watch sitting around the scrubbed table in the cosy warmth of the fo'c's'le, a pot of hot coffee between them. He was getting to know their names now; O'Grady, O'Mara, Maguire, Gabb, O'Dwyer – the Paddy O'Blimeys was what Meadows called them. Grudgingly they let the captain persuade them into sharing coffee and dry bunks with the Negroes but Henry knew the peace wouldn't last.

In the port watch the hostility was at least as bad but it was the darkies who lorded it, and would have thrown the Irishmen out of the fo'c's'le had it not been for Dingle. There was a man called Greenland, more Dago than Nigger, whose throwing knife could skewer a man's hand to the deck at twenty paces: Peter O'Mahoney had made the mistake of telling Greenland he was so black that charcoal would make a white mark on him, and had an ugly wound through his hand to show for it.

'What am I going to do, Sam?' Henry asked, as he watched Meadows and Field – armed like Peelers with truncheons of iron – patrolling the deck on the lookout for trouble.

'Two things to think on, lad,' Sam replied, scanning the brightening sky. 'First, you'll not beat round Cape Horn with this pack of rats. Second, it will get a lot worse before it gets better.'

Soon afterwards, on the evening of the eighth day out, the *Quiver* struck the welcome pull of the trades. During the balmy tropical night Henry walked back and forth across the poop, whistling the same flat tune as if – like a blacksmith's bellows – the draught would somehow heat up his brain and spark a few ideas. The possibility of having to put back, or to divert to another port, was too appalling to admit. After ninety days the passengers would be demanding their money back, and it was money he did not have because he had spent the best part of it settling up with the agents in New York. He thrust the problem to the back of his mind. San Francisco was half a world away. At this rate – if she arrived at all – the *Quiver* would sail through the Golden Gate with her passengers dragooned into acting as crew and her real crew a heap of corpses. Already the score was four to two in favour of the Negroes. Sam Handyside had splinted a broken arm while Manfred Longhandle had stitched up two black cheeks and one pink neck; one was groggy after a blow on the head with a shackle and another was coughing blood after falling – or being pushed – from the foremast shrouds. All six men occupied bunks at the after end of the fo'c's'le where they were nursed by Big Tree when he was not busy looking after the livestock.

But as the sun rose into a clear blue sky on the ninth day out, and the *Quiver* ran large before the trades Henry could persuade himself that things would settle down with the good weather.

The sun intensified its heat by the minute, flooding warmth into tired, chilled bones. Charlie Field stood at the wheel, his leathery palms massaging a dull polish into the teak spokes as he kept her on a heading of south-west-by-south. He could see light steam rising from every seam and stitch of her, and feathering away in the dazzling morning light. The sails were baking a pale, crisp, golden brown as they dried out. Even the ropes were smoking and Field could almost see the slack working into them as they dried. As if wearing comfortable creases into a set of new clothes, the lady seemed to go all the better for it. The water speckling the compass was drying, leaving a crust of salt which clouded Field's view. As he dampened his fingers with a lick and wiped the crystals away, a lift of the quartering swell twisted the ship askew. 'Watch her!' Henry growled, sensing the ship's breakaway bid as he planted his legs wide apart and gazed forward, momentarily content with his lot.

Of the eager adventurers travelling in the 'tweendecks there was no sign. Henry had instructed the mates to allow them on deck in hour-long shifts, twenty-five at a time, so each man could enjoy a good breather every watch. But the passengers had learnt to keep below at this time of day. The crew, roused from their bunks by Charlie Meadows' merciless, 'On your feet, darlin's, sun's scorchin' yer eyeballs out!', had rigged the pump and were setting about 'morning prayers'. They were down on hands and knees in the sloshing water, wielding deck scrubbers and holystones. Smoke curling from the passengers' cookhouse chimney signalled the first of the day's stew ration on the bubble: every passenger received one hot meal a day and for the rest had to make do with coffee and dry biscuits. The ship's own galley fire also smoked its long-awaited promise of coffee at eight bells. Under the break of the fo'c's'le head Big Tree sluiced out the pig pen. The six black hens cackled their protests as a tongue of water slopped through the bars.

It was Charlie Field who noticed it first. As Henry became aware of the way the big man's head was cocked, a frown cutting a gulley between his doorstep brows, he too listened. It was eerie. On such a pleasant morning the deck would normally be alight with ribald jokes and splashing. Today there was not a whistle or a jesting remark to be heard, only silence. Tom Dingle moved his scrubber across the planks without putting weight on it, his hard eyes never wavering from the baleful stare of Adam Robinson who knelt over a holystone a dozen yards along the deck. The other men locked stares in the same way, black with white. A vivid memory of seeing a pack of prison dogs being fed, when he was a boy, flashed into Henry's mind. Every dog had taken the raw meat thrown at it while keeping its eyes fixed on all the others but the instant one took a snap at another all had leapt at each other's throats. Now, despite the warming sun and dazzling sky and the satisfying stride of the ship across a brilliant sea, there was the same tension on the deck of the *Quiver*. At any moment the men would dive at each other's throats and when it happened, Henry knew, he would be powerless to prevent murder.

Humming cheerfully Sam Handyside climbed out on deck.

The woolly tea-cosy hat he had worn through the bad weather had given way to a crumpled and torn straw affair, bought from a bumboat in Madeira on some voyage years back. It gave a comic look to the ruddy face with its even, inch-long trim of beard and bushy white eyebrows. But the old man's gnome-like smile faded when his nostrils caught the whiff of gunpowder in the air. 'In all my sea days I never saw a bunch of seamen so silent,' he rumbled in a grave tone. 'I don't like it, it's not natural.'

Henry spoke quietly from the side of his mouth. 'Sam, take the wheel, will you?'

'What, me . . .?' Sam's initial surprise turned quickly to understanding. Charlie Field relinquished the wheel and needed no telling what to do. He caught the attention of Meadows who was walking slowly aft, aware that sudden movement would trigger the explosion. Idly swinging a be-laying pin apiece, they took up stations near the port and starboard ladders to the poop. Then Big Tree came aft, proudly bearing two newly laid brown eggs in his big hands. The Maori was a new man since joining the *Quiver*. His grey pallor had disappeared, taking the cough with it. He had shed his skid row outfit for a pair of duck trousers that Manfred Longhandle had cut and stitched for him. Charlie Field, the only man on board as wide across the shoulders, had given him a tar-stained dungaree jacket. But not a boot existed that would fit Big Tree's horny splayed feet.

It was bad luck, only a small lurch of the ship as Sam got the feel of the helm, that caused Big Tree to stumble. Intent on saving the precious eggs he let his bare foot tangle with Dingle's long-handled scrubber. The ugly Irishman cursed and raised the scrubber as if to strike him. Big Tree smashed the side of his hand across the bridge of Dingle's nose. The seaman dropped, his red face a pulpy mass of yolk, slime and shell. Three Irishmen at once leaped on Big Tree and half a dozen blacks tried to head them off. In a moment the deck was a riot.

Henry watched Big Tree fight his way to the bulwarks then swing himself up into the shrouds, the greenstone *patu* dangling from a lanyard on his wrist. Lamshire and Peake retreated hastily to the fo'c's'le head and stared aft, waiting to see what the captain would do. But Henry had decided to do nothing. With calculated indifference he strolled back and forth, his hands clasped at his back and a tuneless whistle coming from his lips. Sam bleated a protest from the wheel but Henry silenced him with an angry gesture. He did not want to be distracted by arguments. His decision was made and it was too late to go back.

The battle swept up and down the deck. Passengers peered out in alarm, the sound of it rumbling like thunder on the deckhead, but dodged back as four men wrestling in a tangled heap crashed into the hatch. Three Paddies chased a Negro up the fore-rigging, intent on throwing him into the sea. Two Negroes swung an Irishman between them, on the point of catapulting him over the rail. Dingle's raw-boned frame struggled beneath the weight of Bunce and Greenland; Henry saw the latter's knife glint in the sunlight, an inch over Dingle's eyes. Adam Robinson had Flynn's orange hair locked in his fingers and was hammering the head again and again into the deck while another climbed on his back and tried to drag him off.

Henry judged it was time. From the binnacle locker he removed the heavy brass air pump with its flared trumpet. He fitted the two pieces together then raised the handle of the plunger and pushed it down, all his weight behind it.

Enormously loud, the thunderous boom of the foghorn stopped the brawl dead.

Hands in pockets, Henry descended slowly to the maindeck and strolled among the crew. The instant two of them moved to resume their struggle he stopped them with a curt and certain command, as he had when controlling Nightingale. Forcing a slight and mocking smile to his dry lips, he went from one group of men to the next and swept them with derisive stern blue eyes. The groups of fighters slowly dispersed. When the captain's circuit was complete he found the Irish had moved to the starboard side and the Negroes to port.

And there, with a wild leap of hope that brought a tight grin to his face, Henry recognised the solution to his difficulties.

The men read the smile and glanced at each other uncertainly, a shaky alliance forming momentarily among them as they faced the calm young captain whose unholy confidence was more unnerving than any bucko threat or whip-crack.

'You men want war? You can have it!' Henry did not shout but his clear and precise tone carried above the slap and roar of the bow wave and was plainly heard on every part of the deck. 'Don't say I'm not a fair captain. The welfare of my crew is always dear to my heart. You don't want to work this ship like any other bunch of seamen, you want to fight. All right, you can fight. But we're going to make it official.'

Meadows and Field replaced their belaying pins in the racks. Field returned to the wheel. Lamshire and Peake descended slowly from the fo'c's'le head. The ship was beginning to breathe again.

Henry dusted his hands purposefully, a signal that a new era was dawning. 'It's obvious Niggers and Paddies can't work together, so Niggers and Paddies will have to work separate. We will change the watch system. One watch of blacks and one of whites. The Paddies will work together in the starboard watch and the Niggers in the port watch. The farmers will divide the fo'c's'le with a bulkhead so you can sleep and eat separately . . .'

Pausing while eight bells were struck by Sam, Henry scrutinised the men and saw the tension flowing out of them. But this was no time for his own grip to relax. Hands on hips, he compelled their attention with a joke. 'General Lamshire is appointed officer in command of the starboard watch and Colonel Peake will lead the port watch fusiliers . . .' A weak joke goes a long way at sea and the men laughed. 'Fact is,' Henry went on, 'I reckoned on shipping a crew of seamen but I find myself stuck with a bunch of soldiers.' The grins faded; to be called a soldier was the worst insult. 'And here is my promise. Any man who knifes, punches, kicks or interferes with another will be flogged. By me.'

Henry paused to let the point sink in. 'Now get your coffee and be quick, the war begins at one bell and you soldiers will wish you'd never been born.'

While the men breakfasted Henry called the mates and the farmers to the poop and gave them detailed instructions. As one bell struck the men came aft, curious to see what was in store. They soon found out. 'It's a straight fight,' Henry announced, choosing his words with care. 'We have to change the canvas, strip everything off the yards and bend the light weather sails. Port watch will take the foremast, starboard watch the main. We'll soon see which of you are sailors and which are soldiers. Ready? Go!'

Channelled into competition, the bloody animosity evaporated. As the *Quiver* barrelled southwards beneath a steady procession of fleecy clouds, contest followed contest. Every aspect of ship-handling became a race governed by Captain Plunkett's gold timepiece which the duty mate wore from his neck on a cord. The times were noted in a special logbook kept in the saloon. When a record was broken the watch received a small but significant reward, such as a nip of rum or an extra ration of sultanas in their Sunday duff. But more important than the prize was the honour and glory of beating the other watch. Rivalry was intense. The mates became involved in the spirit of it, and bent their minds to improving and streamlining the method of handling sails. Once the fine-weather canvas was bent to the yards the steady trades did not demand a lot of sail handling but Henry did not let this stop him. If there was no work he made it. In the middle of the afternoon when the hands were employed in painting and sanding and other maintenance chores he would suddenly announce a race: 'Double reef fore and main topmasts the watches, the clock's on you!' The sport infected the entire ship. The passengers dubbed the watches Murphies and Macaroons, and ran books on which would be the first to form up at the poop rail, their sail reefed and properly set. When both watches, panting and jeering at each other, had reached the deck Henry would order them to do the whole thing in reverse, 'All right you soldiers, the clock's running, shake out the reefs!'

As the rivalry intensified, Henry and the mates had to devise more ways of giving it an outlet. While the ship lay becalmed in the doldrums the boats were launched and pulling races organised. Planks were slung over the side and it was a race for each watch to paint its own side of the hull – 'And don't leave no holidays,' Lamshire warned as he searched for unpainted areas. After a week of baffling breezes the *Quiver* found the south-east trades and struck out for the Cape. Fortunately the two watches were more or less evenly matched, and by judicious rationing of prizes Henry helped them to improve their comfort. When the port watch knocked ten seconds off the time for setting the royals, Henry awarded them a square of canvas with which to make cushions for the benches in their fo'c's'le; next thing he knew the scuttle of the Macaroons' quarters sported a pair of curtains made from a faded red bandana. Not to be out-classed, the Murphies clipped half a minute off the time for furling the maincourse, begged some paint for a prize, and decorated their door with strange Celtic symbols and emblems. 'Are we sailin' a ship or a bleedin' tinker's cart?' Meadows grumbled.

'Who cares Oatsy, long as it keeps 'em quiet,' Field replied.

The *Quiver* became a happy ship. More, she could boast a

smart and eager crew. Though her captain never permitted himself the least glow of satisfaction, and always one watch or the other had to make do with second place in the scale of tributes, taken as a whole the crew's sail-handling and seamanship would have knocked spots off any ship afloat.

Every day soon after sun-up Henry climbed through the towering, tilting edifice of sail. Methodically he worked his way out to the end of every one of the twelve yards bowing under the weight of wind. It was a private conversation with his ship, a way of escaping the prison bars of command and familiarising himself with every stitch and seam of her. In the grain of the golden spars trembling against his stomach muscles as he lay across them, his heels hooked into the foot-ropes, he could sense how much further they might bend before they snapped. With fingers pressing lightly into the bulge of stiff flaxen canvas he could gauge the weight in the wind, strong and clean aloft compared with the buffeting turbulence lower down, and assess the trim of every individual sail. The best moment of his day came when, balancing precariously on the soaring spar, he worked his way out to the furthest end of the jibboom. There, clutching the stay for support, he gazed aft at his ship scattering flying fish as she cleaved her proudly flared bow into the hump-backed swells. It was a wild ride, like clinging to some winged chariot plunging through the heavens. This was the kind of sailing a man was born for. It was hard to rein in his dignity as captain and restrain himself from whooping an exultant *Ya-hoo!* and dancing a jig of sheer happiness.

Fortified by these few moments of private joy he returned to the maindeck and shouted for Big Tree. Swinging the heavy mahogany bucket with its brass hoops, the Maori scooped it brimming from the sea and emptied it over Henry's head. When the water had dried to a white powder on his tanned shoulders, Henry donned the comfortable tropical garb of the common sailor – sleeveless tunic open at the throat, light duck trousers cut off at the knee, bare feet. Then, after he passed his orders for the day to the mates, came the ceremony of the cock-a-doodle broth. Sam Handyside, perspiring in a formal shipmaster's coat and disapproving of Henry's casual dress, could hardly bring himself to watch as Tom Withers, the steward, brought a fresh egg and a glass of cold tea to the poop. Henry broke the raw egg into the glass, stirred it briskly, then gulped the frothy mixture down in one.

Only one hostile element continued to fester among the

crew, and on the fortieth day it erupted. After his morning
inspection of the rig Henry decided the watches should pit
their skills against each other at stripping the light canvas from
the yards and hoisting aloft the heavy-duty flax with which the
ship would fight around the Horn. It would be a bitter contest
and the whole job would take the best part of two days. The
passengers were delighted at the promise of action and made
their bets; the Macaroons rated five to four on.

During the few minutes before the single ding of the bell
signalled hours of back-breaking labour, Adam Robinson
made the most of the respite. His whippy, athletic frame lay
flat on the deck, his legs crossed and propped up on a bollard, his hands clasped behind his head and his eyes closed
against the sunlight. A skilled seaman in his mid-twenties, he
day-dreamed of the whales he had harpooned and the island
maidens he had pleasured on his previous voyages, four
years in the South Seas. Suddenly the contented smile was
wiped off his face. His ankle was caught in a fierce grip. As if
shot from a cannon his body was propelled almost the entire
length of the maindeck.

Hearing the drawn out wail of shock and agony, Henry
thought a man had fallen from a high yard. His keen glance
searched the waves but saw no splash. Then he saw Robinson
wedged in a scupper on the starboard side, his feet hanging
outboard and only the breadth of his torso preventing him
from being pulled through. The rope on his ankle was pulling
the heavy bucket which acted like a drogue, near to jerking the
luckless Negro's leg clean out of his body. At once Henry
realised what had happened. The whole trick had been set up
in advance. A long rope had been threaded outboard through
the scupper. A noose was tied in one end of it and the handle of
the bucket bent to the other. As the red-headed Flynn dropped
the noose over the dozing Negro's ankle Dingle had tossed the
bucket over the side. The drag of it had given Robinson a
sledge-ride to remember.

In a moment Big Tree had swung outside the bulwarks and
taken the strain of the bucket. Others rushed to grip Robinson
by the shoulders and help him wriggle inboard. Henry's glance
fell on the sunburned figure of Tom Dingle, smirking among
his compatriots who rolled on the deck, helpless with laughter.

Nobody liked Dingle and even the Irishmen were wary of
him. With his uneven scummy teeth, narrow face and wild
hair, Dingle's was an ugliness that impressed even Meadows

and Field. 'I seen a prettier sight on the sarf end of a cow headin' norf,' Meadows said. Now the brute was going to get what his victims had been promising him for a long time.

With a leap like a breaching whale Robinson launched himself at Dingle. Bare steel twinkled in the sunlight. Dingle struck out with a snarl. Robinson staggered back, a scarlet slash efflorescing beneath his breast bone.

Henry vaulted the poop rail and tore into the crowd as the Negro sank down with blood pumping through his fingers. The Irishman was suddenly uncertain, his fingers opening and closing on the handle of the knife. Henry, jabbing him hard in the chest, backed him up to the shrouds. He disarmed the man easily and tossed the knife overboard. 'You remember what I said, Dingle?'

The Irishman's lips curled. 'Niggers is apes,' he growled.

Henry spoke with ringing authority. 'There is to be no murder in this ship. Mr Meadows, put this man in irons. Then make me a cat. Twenty lashes.'

In stunned silence, crew and passengers watched Dingle pinioned with rope. It was the best Meadows could do because the *Quiver* carried no man-shackles. Robinson was flat on his back with Sam trying to stem the flow of blood. 'I imagine he'll live if Longhandle puts a seam in him,' he pronounced. 'It was more of a slice than a thrust, thank God.'

Henry nodded curtly and returned to the poop, his anxious whistle reduced to an angry hiss.

After a few minutes Meadows approached. 'I never made a cat-o'-nine-tails in my life, never clapped eyes on one, never saw a man flogged . . .'

'Use your imagination,' Henry snapped. 'Get Longhandle to help you, but be quick. I want it over and done with. Ten minutes is all.'

A silence charged with whispers took hold of the ship. News of the imminent flogging spread like a fire in the 'tweendecks. The sunlight shift of passengers stared aft, eager that the entertainment should begin before their time was up. At last Meadows mounted the ladder bearing a sinister coil in his hand. Henry took a grip on the handle and let the tails unravel. The handle was a length of stiff manilla hawser, two feet long. Whipped to the end of it was a bundle of nine cords, each one three feet long and knotted at four-inch intervals. The tails whistled mournfully as Henry made a testing stroke. His face was set and pale. He was sick with himself for what he had started, angry that he had let the competition between the watches reach such a pitch. But he had to go through with it. 'This will do,' he said grimly. 'Muster all hands and string the man up.'

Dingle kicked his feet wildly and Meadows beckoned a pair of Negroes to assist him. Henry waved them back and pointed at two of Dingle's compatriots. 'Let them do it.'

Running the tails of the cat through his fingers, Henry approached Dingle. He was spreadeagled at the mainmast shrouds, port side, his face twisted in a silent snarl like that of a cornered animal. Sam Handyside had been long enough at sea to have seen men flogged and was old-fashioned enough to approve, but the abruptness with which it all happened had shaken him. He moved to a strategic position between the pin-rail and the ladder to the poop. No telling how the rest of the crew would react. Will Lamshire took up station beside him, Martin Peake at the other ladder.

Henry slashed the empty air with the cat. Its tails sang. Dingle winced and a couple of passengers, young men with a lust for blood, hooted derisively.

Suddenly, as if dazed, Henry shook his head. He tossed the cat over the side, took a jack-knife from his pocket, opened it, and cut Dingle's lashings. The man sprang away, crouching behind bunched fists.

With slow deliberation Henry closed the knife, replaced it in his pocket, and unbuttoned his faded blue shirt. 'Flogging is a savage practice, Dingle,' he said calmly, letting his shirt fall to the deck. 'But I reckon it's too soft for the likes of you. I shall thrash you myself.'

A frisson of relief and renewed excitement trembled in the crowd. Sam betrayed his anxiety with a muttered curse; it was all very well for the lad to play the hero, but what if he lost the fight?

Henry had served a hard apprenticeship in the school of sneaky fighting. You did not run with waterfront larrikins of a penal colony, and share a fo'c's'le with tough and rough Antarctic seal hunters, without graduating with honours in the art of self preservation. From the instant he squared up to Dingle, Henry was alert for the feint followed by the murderous swipe intended to finish him off in a single blow. It came at once. Dingle stepped to one side, snatched a belaying pin from its slot in the rail, and raised it high above his head. For an instant, as the iron bar touched the fore-brace, Dingle was off balance. His arms were above his head and his pinkly burned belly offered the perfect target. Henry struck a bull's-eye with a two-footed kick. Dingle collapsed with an explosive grunt. Henry rolled clear of the pin as it fell and scrambled to his feet. Dingle came in like a bull, head-down and roaring. Henry grabbed the head in an armlock. Running with the charge he steered it straight into the rail. Dingle's head met the timber with a meaty thud and the man dropped.

Ignoring the awed cheers Henry picked up his shirt. Meadows asked, 'Shall I tie him up?'

'What for? The man's got a job to do, like all of us . . .'

But the fight was not yet over. One moment Dingle was on his hands and knees, shaking his head dazedly, then he seemed to fill half the sky like a great pink, dirty-smelling cloud. Henry crashed to the deck with the big man on top of him. He felt his throat taken in a horny-handed grip. The thumbs were squeezing, squeezing. No matter which way he struggled he could not get free. His scrabbling fingers found Dingle's nose. He jabbed two fingers up the nostrils and pushed. His vision was blurring, the pain in his throat unbearable. Dingle's own head arched far backwards from the pressure in his nose. Henry bunched his fist, took aim, and with all the muscle he could muster rammed a killing blow into the taut windpipe.

It was all over. With a gurgle of pain Dingle subsided, gasping. Henry levered the hands from his throat, shrugged off all help, and resumed his familiar station by the binnacle. He felt he should order the men to work but his voice box felt crushed and he did not trust himself to speak. Gratefully he heard the mates taking control and he turned away, massaging his bruised throat. Big Tree appeared at his side, hot coffee stiff with rum. Sam came on deck with the sextant and looked him over with concern. 'You all right, lad?'

'I should have stayed in the *Musket*,' Henry replied huskily, 'It was a pleasure cruise compared with this.'

'You won't have to do it again,' Sam assured him. 'If you have any more trouble with men for as long as you command at sea, well – I'll be taken for a chinaman.'

Later, Henry lay flat in the wedge formed by the deck and skylight, just as Nightingale did in the *Musket*. He could have napped in his cabin, but he found it a restless place. The orchestrated music of a full-rigged ship pounding through the ocean under every kite she could fly sounded below deck like a volcanic eruption. The rattle of spray like small-shot ambushing the deck; the whining hum of the taut shrouds and stays; the thunder of holystones scraping the deck and the gush of water in tune with the clank of the pump; the surge and suck of water creaming along the hull; the groans and creaks and cries of beams, ribs and timbers. Out on deck the music was hardly audible. It was felt rather than heard, and Henry preferred to make a pillow from a scrap of canvas and sleep where he could escape the greatly magnified and irregular noises that kept him on the edge of nervous alertness. On deck, instead of puzzling over what might be happening, he only had to open his eyes. As he dozed fitfully, his throat on fire, a conversation drifted to his ears. 'How are yer makin' out Barley?'

'All serene, Oatsy, all serene.'

'Reckon the ugly bug o' the bog had the stuffink knocked out of 'im?'

'Let's 'ope, the old man did a good job on 'im.'

'Wot d'yer fink of our chances?'

'Ninety days ter Frisco?' Charlie Field gnawed at his thumb-nail, considering. 'Not a snowball's.'

'Don't you be too sure, mate,' Meadows chided him. 'The ol' man will pull somefink out of 'is 'at, see if 'e don't.'

Henry stirred. To be called the 'old man' was something. He was the youngest on board, except for Martin Peake, younger by six months. But living up to Meadows' faith in him would be a different matter, he thought glumly, as he went below and unrolled the chart. Ninety days! He had put his head on the block and now it would be chopped off. To reach San Francisco within the time he had rashly guaranteed would now be an impossibility, he realised, as he measured distances with the span of his fingers. And so it proved.

The *Quiver* was let off lightly by the Horn. Henry put in a long tack to the south, picked up a fair slant of wind, and weathered the cape by such a wide margin that the gaunt cliffs were never sighted. Then luck deserted again. The winds blew from the right quarters but were hardly man enough to raise a ripple on a saucer of tea.

Seventy days out, Sam worked his morning figures. He found the ship had sailed precisely 12,000 miles since leaving New York. And she had not only crossed the Equator heading north, but had drifted back in the baffling calms and had crossed the line a second time. This was encouraging for the passengers who were becoming excited at the prospect of seeing their passage money refunded, but cold comfort for Captain Ardent. So far the ship had put an average 170 nautical miles under her keel every day. Now, if she was to achieve her target, she had to make 200 miles a day.

At dinner Sam blamed the lack of wind on the invention of the steam engine. With eyes twinkling beneath his snowy brows he looked round the table and said, 'When I was a lad, you know, we got dead-muzzlers six weeks on the trot, and that was only in March.'

The others chuckled but Martin said earnestly, 'You can't blame steam engines for head winds.'

'No, it's the calms I'm talking about,' Sam explained. 'It's logical enough when you think of all that smoke and steam and soot boiling out of smokestacks, funnels, factory chimneys and the like. It's got to make the air heavier and stop it blowing around so much. No wonder we get these long calms. The equatorial zone is first to be affected. Soon the tradewinds will dry up. Mark my words, lad, the sailing ships of the world will be out of business.'

'It's a vicious circle, I suppose,' Henry put in. 'The more steamships we get, the less wind. So the more we need them . . .'

'That will be disastrous,' Martin exclaimed, flushing as the others laughed and he realised he had been gulled. 'Well, I wish I was in a steamship now, I don't mind admitting,' he sighed.

Seldom had Henry seen the ocean so lifeless. When Will Lamshire gingerly removed a red-hot coal from the galley fire and dropped it over the side, to gauge the direction of ghosting air currents too soft to sense on a dampened cheek, the steam rose in a perfectly vertical plume.

So useless were the sails hanging slackly in their running gear that all the passengers were permitted on deck at the same time. Soon the maindeck was the scene of a carnival. In the deepening purple twilight men with shirts open and sleeves rolled up perched along the bulwarks clapping to the foo-foo band that started up on the deckhouse roof. One man beat a large black kettle with a wooden spoon, one had a tin whistle, several beat foot-long steel marline spikes with metal tools so they chimed like bells and half a dozen hummed into combs covered in tissue paper. A biscuit box and sundry soup dishes beaten with forks and spoons added to the clamour, along with a weirdly fluttering wail from a knife wedged between two planks and twanged so it vibrated back and forth. To

Henry, smoking his pipe at the taffrail, it all sounded like a lot
of plates being cleared away. But the people were happily
shouting out words about some Johnny coming marching
home, and at every 'Hurrah!' Martin let loose a bellow on the
fog horn.

Meadows and Field, sitting on the bollards by the boat
skids, starboard side, leaned over the rail with fishing lines in
their fingers. 'This lot will go bonkers if the ol' man don't come
up wiv the lolly after ninety days,' Field said. 'Fink 'e can do it,
Oatsy?'

'No chance.'

'Wot's 'e gonna do in 'Frisco, sell the ship to pay 'em orff?'

'Cap'n h'Ardent will fink o' somefink, you wait. Gawd, wot
a racket!'

As the foo-foo band rounded off the last discordant bars
of *Yankee-doodle* and the listeners cheered with gusto, the
carrot-haired Irishman called Flynn jumped up on the capstan.
His clear, strong voice lifted in *Danny Boy* brought a hush,
complete but for the slatting of the idle gear aloft. Then the
Macaroons, sprawled around the harness cask, lifted their
bass voices in a haunting, melodic chorus that earned its own
field of silence.

In the little pantry opening off the saloon Tom Withers
rolled pastry. He was a shrivelled and pale figure who looked
as if he had spent the last twenty years living underground, but
his spatula thumbs were to flour and water what Manfred
Longhandle's muscular fingers were to twine and canvas: the
pies he made were hymns to beauty, like the sailmaker's sails.
In the galley for'ard Nix Barlow sucked his gums in his curious
way and with the stump of his forearm beat time to the music.
The old man had lost his hand in the battle of Trafalgar and a
few years later his teeth had fallen out from scurvy when, as a
cook in a timber-drogher out of Quebec, the masts had gone
over the side and they had been three and a half months
making port with no fresh food. In the shadows of the fo'c's'le
head, Big Tree propped himself against the windlass and
whittled a wooden figure of Tangaroa. The black shadow of
Bunce creeping towards the hen coops had not passed him
unnoticed, though Big Tree gave no sign. Only as the West
Indian's fingers sneaked through the bars of the coop did the
Maori move. The wooden figure he was carving flew like a
bullet through the air. His aim was true. Bunce howled with
pain and fled, the egg not clutched in his hand as he had hoped

but growing on the side of his head where the missile had hit him.

Near the starboard water closet the Murphies sprawled in the soft darkness. 'There'll be trouble right enough in Frisco,' John Gabb said, shifting a quid of tobacco from one side of his mouth to the other.

'I won't be dere to see none of it,' Flynn said.

'Where'll you be then, Pat?'

'Off in dem hills scoopin' up de gold bricks, dat's what I come for.'

'What about your wages?'

'Ha! I won't be waitin' on t'irty measly dollars when the gold's just waitin' to be dug out o' the dirt. Anyways, what good is t'irty dollars, you could hardly buy a glass o'red-eye wiv it out west, what I hear.'

'You gotta buy a shovel, Pat.'

'To be sure, I got one o' dose already.'

Dingle scowled up at the luminous sky. 'I don't need no shovel. The bastard captain will dig his own grave wid bare hands then I'll break his neck an' t'row him in.'

'That I'd like to see! You and who else, Dingle?'

The big Irishman sourly eyed Adam Robinson, who had overheard his remark. The tall Negro's ugly scar caught the lamplight as he swayed to the rhythm of his compatriots' song. Dingle growled, 'On me own I'll do it, in Frisco, and the cap'n will see de broit red colour of his blood, the Lord God help him.'

Twenty days, four thousand miles, and not enough wind to stir the smoke from his pipe. Henry mooched for'ard towards the rail and encountered a group of passengers. 'What's this? You men are not allowed on this deck, go for'ard!'

The men stood their ground. Squinting in the darkness, Henry recognised the leader, the so-called Colonel George Brewer. A pompous little man in his mid forties who claimed to have experience in the law, Brewer had a hectoring voice, a hooked nose and grey side-whiskers. Since the voyage had begun his demands – on behalf of all the men in the 'tween-decks, he claimed self-importantly – had been insistent. He wanted better food, more water, more time on deck, comfier beds, smoother seas, cooler sunshine, drier rain. Henry had stonewalled all requests. 'Good evening, Colonel, you have something to say?'

'I do indeed, Captain,' Brewer said. 'It's quite clear to us all that the ship won't make Frisco in ninety days, not unless she sprouts wings. We want to see the colour of your money, sir. We demand to be paid immediately.'

'Is that so?' Henry replied with exaggerated courtesy. 'I am willing to pay you, Colonel Brewer, if you are ready to take the money?'

'What do you mean, sir? Of course I am ready to take the money, and I speak for all my colleagues of course.'

'Then I hope you are able to walk on water, Colonel,' Henry told him calmly. 'I will pay the money at the end of the voyage. The voyage will end the moment you disembark. If you are ready to disembark immediately, I can, of course, arrange matters to suit your convenience.'

The colonel and his friends vanished hastily down the ladder and Henry heard Sam sigh heavily. 'Joking apart, lad, what are you going to do?'

Henry walked away, pausing in his whistling only long enough to say, 'That's a good question, Sam.'

The ninetieth dawn found the *Quiver* running large before a brisk south-westerly, every stitch hoisted. Henry felt many eyes watching him speculatively as he gulped down his cock-a-doodle juice. When the colonel and a delegation accosted him at noon and made the same demand for a pay-out Henry made the same reply. He maintained an air of breezy confidence but still had no idea of how he was going to avoid being lynched from his own yard-arm.

Nine days later the Yankee clipper *Eclipse*, outward bound for the east, was sighted and spoken briefly. In a few words exchanged as the ship sped by, Henry learned the *Musket* had made a passage of ninety-six days. This depressing news meant she was nearly three weeks ahead but might well still be in San Francisco. Henry had no doubt the gang of plug-uglies whom Screech Gander called a crew would skin out for the hills the instant the anchor touched bottom, and it would be tough for the Yankee captain to find replacements. Not that this was much consolation, for the *Quiver* would face exactly the same problem when she sailed between the bold headlands guarding the mouth of San Francisco Bay – the famous Golden Gate.

The bay was reputed to be filled with ships awaiting cargoes and crews, some for more than a year. Others had been sailed straight up the beach and abandoned by crew, mates and captain alike. A number of the hulks grounded on the shoreline had been converted into lodging houses and drinking dens. Would the beautiful *Quiver* suffer the same fate?

No matter how swift the passage, nothing dragged like the last few hours. One hundred and one days out, the dark green ship came in sight of the coast. On a crisp, sunlit February morning the high rounded hills of California lay back-lit by the rising sun, a blank wall of blue capped here and there with feathers of white cloud. The sunshine shift of passengers, eager to head for the diggings, hung over the starboard bulwarks gazing at the land. The ship snowed along under full sail, shafts of rainbows dancing in the halo of spray smoking from her bow.

Four bells. The watch turned out but had no heart for washing the decks. Sam and the mates were as edgy as the rest and Henry could hardly blame them. In a few hours the ship could be stranded, crewless. And one hundred angry men would demand their money, three hundred dollars a head. Henry had no need to count the cash in the padlocked compartment concealed beneath his bunk. It contained the grand sum of eleven thousand dollars and a few cents. The helm was relieved, Adam Robinson handing over to Bunce and telling him to steer east by north, but Henry paid them no attention. Sam came over and tried to cheer him up. 'Even so, lad, a hundred and one days is a creditable passage, the Monkey will be pleased enough.' But both knew in their hearts that Monkton Winkworth would be far from pleased and George Chamberlayne would be devastated. The unvarnished truth was that the *Musket* had given the *Quiver* a hiding.

Henry stared with glum hopelessness at the galley chimney, willing Barlow to reach his good arm out of the door and bang on the deckhouse bulkhead with his ladle to signal that coffee was ready. Henry frowned. Funny how the ribbon of smoke bent sharply in mid-air as it was sucked into the windflow of the powerful fore-course. It made you realise what a powerful engine a sail could be, its influence on the air currents reaching far beyond the tautly curved fabric. Smoke?

The captain stared at the smoke. Though his breathing had virtually ceased he whistled like a demon and his brain was busy as the devil in a gale of wind. Sam had been with him long enough by now to read the signs. He shot Henry a suspicious glance, wondering what he was thinking.

After a few moments Henry summoned Meadows to the poop and they conferred near the taffrail. The swarthy Cockney had trouble disguising the broad smile that lit his face. He ventured a suggestion or two then composed his features in an unnatural frown and went for'ard.

Henry ignored Sam's unspoken questions and went below to his cabin. He returned on deck after a few moments. Bulging in the side pocket of his reefer jacket was the one item he had purchased for himself in New York. A revolver.

'Mr Peake!' Henry called. 'Send word below that the diggers may come on deck and take a look at the land of their dreams, all of them.'

Sam was startled. 'Is that wise? If I was you I'd batten 'em down else you'll have a riot on your hands.'

Henry remained stubbornly silent and inspected the distant coastline with the long glass. Sam went away, shaking his head. The coffee which Big Tree delivered aft was a welcome diversion, a way of stiffening his self control. Henry clasped his hands round the steaming mug to prevent them from revealing the taut stretch of his nerves.

One bell of the forenoon watch, eight-thirty. The hands were spinning out their breakfast, all eyes were on the land where valleys, ridges and headlands gradually took form and substance as the sun rose higher. Half a dozen vessels were in sight, porcelain chips scattered on the broad blue carpet of the Pacific. The nearest, Henry noted with satisfaction, was a coasting schooner of sorts, a mile off to starboard and running parellel with the *Quiver*, probably loaded with hides from little beach ports to the south. The schooner was being rapidly overhauled. Even better.

It was Henry who saw the smoke first, a wisp curling from the open mainhatch and feathering away in the breeze. He set down his coffee mug, curled a fist round the butt of the revolver in his pocket. His heart hammered like thunder. He did not have long to wait. The cry of alarm struck terror in all who heard it. 'Fire! Fire! The ship's afire!'

Sam ran to the poop and stared with undisguised horror at the thickening smoke boiling out of the hatch. Martin Peake dashed to the ship's bell and commenced a strident, sustained ringing. Will Lamshire, lingering over his breakfast in the saloon, was on deck in an instant, his laces flapping and shirt unbuttoned. 'Fire in the 'tweendecks, Mister, rig the deck hose and see what you make of it,' Henry snapped.

The mate might never have made a shipmaster but he was resourceful and quick in a crisis. With surprising agility he vaulted the poop rail, shouted at Peake to quit ringing the bloody bell and bear a hand, and pushed his way through the frightened men to the pump at the foot of the mainmast. As the first spurt of water splashed from the nozzle he soaked a cloth, squeezed it out, then clamped it over his nose and mouth and dived down the mainhatch into the smoke.

It was the trouble-making Colonel Brewer who first gave vent to his feelings and started the panic. 'Hoist out the boats or we'll fry!' he shouted.

Others took up the cry. 'Away the boats, quick for our lives!'

'She'll explode any minute, remember the blasting powder.'

'We can pull for the coast!'

This was the danger signal for which Henry had been waiting. He slipped along the starboard bulwarks and climbed a few feet up into the shrouds where he commanded a view of the entire deck as well as the gig and lifeboat inverted on the skids that arched across the deck and the larger longboat upside down in its chocks atop the deckhouse.

The mob seethed uncertainly beneath the skids. Infected by the panic, Negroes and Irishmen fought each other to release the lashings and free the hoists. Henry fired two shots in the air. The struggling men froze and turned to stare at the captain, whose calm and certain tone demanded obedience. 'I'll plug the first man to move!' he threatened.

His face red and streaming with tears, Will Lamshire staggered out on deck in a swirl of smoke. 'The 'tweendecks are filling but it's only smoke, the seat of the fire is lower, in the main hold,' he reported. 'It's the cargo smouldering, I reckon. God knows how far it's gone. The fore lower hatch is hot to touch, maybe nearly burned through.'

An outbreak of panicky shouting was silenced by another shot. Henry calmly gave his orders as he reloaded. 'You want to save your skins, men? Then do exactly as I tell you. There will be no panic. The passengers will move to the port side and sit down on deck . . .'

Henry cut short Colonel Brewer's panic-stricken argument by sighting the revolver directly at the man's frightened eyes. The colonel sat down and the others followed his example. 'Good,' Henry said firmly. 'Now, Mr Peake, the port watch will furl main and fore courses, the sooner we get way off her the better . . . Mr Lamshire, you will please hoist out the boats.'

The wind was dying. Henry could distinguish the headlands

of the Golden Gate, a tongue of water reaching between them and broadening out beneath the circle of ridges beyond. A smudge of black indicated a steam tug scouting for work.

The smoke spurting from the hatch trailed away in a plume as high as the topgallant yards. As soon as the big sails of the lower yards were clewed up and roughly furled with a speed that broke all records, and the royals and topgallants were taken off her, the ship slowed and the smoke began to fog the deck. Only now did Henry give orders for the hatch to be closed. The three boats splatted into the water and towed alongside, a man in each to fend off as the ship sailed under topsails alone. 'The boats won't carry all of us, who's going to drown, not me!' The cry sparked another inflamed burst of panic but Charlie Meadows, his face blackened by smoke, pushed through the crowd and knocked the man flying.

'See for yourselves,' Henry assured them. 'We're making enough smoke for other ships to notice. The schooner is already putting her helm up. She'll take you off.'

Henry caught Meadows' eye and raised his eyebrows. The bosun wiped the back of his hand over his stinging eyes and said in a low voice that only Henry understood, 'All serene, Cap'n.'

At the point of the gun an orderly evacuation was commenced. Gig and lifeboat carried twenty men apiece, the heavier longboat a few more though there was precious little room for wielding the oars. The men left on deck looked worried as the last places were filled. Henry shouted for Dingle. The Irishman gloated as he heard his orders. 'You're a good man with a tiller, Dingle, you can go in charge of the longboat.'

It was only then, as the troublesome seaman scrambled eagerly to his post, that a suspicion dawned in Sam's brain. A man called plaintively from the rail as he swung his leg over, 'Captain, what about my gear, I can't afford to lose it?'

'First thing is to save your life,' Henry told him. 'Once we get the ship inside the bay we can open her up and deal with the fire, and you can stand on the pier and take our warps, eh!'

Will Lamshire shot his captain a troubled glance. What mad talk was this? If the hold were opened up the inrush of air would feed the fire and the ship would be instantly engulfed in a sheet of flame. Then he caught Sam's eye and was visibly startled. The old man had winked at him.

The schooner ran alongside and hove to. The men trans-

ferred to her from the boats which returned for the next load.
The tug had seen the clipper's plight and bore down fast but
the cursed wind had died to nothing and the blue sky was
becoming skimmed with thin white cloud. A gale was on its
way, but there was no telling from which point of the compass
it would blow.

With the last of the passengers over the side it was now the
crew who were in a panic to get off the ship. But their flight was
arrested by the sight of Pat Flynn. A few moments before,
Charlie Meadows had thrust a bottle of rum into one of his
hands, a gold sovereign into the other, and had hissed brief
instructions into his ear. Flynn had not stopped to reason the
why of it. Drink and play drunk were his orders, and he
followed them to the letter. His hair flaming brilliantly in the
smoke-hazed light, he reeled along the deck gulping deep
draughts of rum from the bottle, letting rivulets of liquor
overflow his mouth and run down his chin.

The bottle was snatched from his hand as others fought for a
share. The knot of Irishmen, joined by a bunch of Negroes,
rushed the poop. His face like thunder, Sam tried to stop them
but Henry pulled him aside. Tom Withers cowered in his
pantry as the men poured down the companion-way, mad
with the lust for liquor. But the steward, too, had his secret
instructions. He shouted, 'In the day-room is where he keeps it,
look in the locker under the settee!'

With a crazed yell the men crowded into the captain's
day-room and found half a dozen bottles, as Withers had
promised. Hardly had the door shut behind them than Charlie
Field emerged from his hiding place in Sam Handyside's cabin.
With planks, hammer and nails he firmly barricaded the door
so the men could not smash their way out.

Meanwhile the tug had wheeled alongside. 'You're on fire,
Skipper,' the grizzled tugmaster shouted.

'Is that right, sir?' Henry replied. 'Tell me the worst.'

'Five thousand dollars now or salvage later, either way suits
me just dandy.'

'Not likely! One thousand on arrival is the best I can do.'

The tugmaster pushed back the brim of his cap and laughed
heartily. 'I'm a busy man and I don't like the look of the sky.
What do you say? Take it or leave it.'

Henry capitulated. 'All right, five thousand if you get us in to
the shore where I can scuttle her in the shallows, it's our only
chance. We'll have the warp for you on the starboard bow.'

Those of the crew still remaining on deck looked about them uncertainly. Had their mates abandoned ship already? 'Put us aboard the tug, for mercy's sake!' a man called.

'You heard the tugmaster,' Henry replied. 'We'll be inside the Golden Gate in three or four hours. We can save this ship if we stay together. There's a fifty dollar bonus and a bottle of rum for every man. But if you want to swim for it, now's your chance.'

None did. The topsails were furled, the warp was passed. As the *Quiver* steadied in the track of the tug Meadows put half a dozen bottles of rum on deck.

Like conspirators the afterguard gathered round the binnacle, Charlie Field on the wheel. Tears and sweat cut wriggling pink channels in Meadow's smoky face. Sam and Will had long since guessed the mischief Meadows had wrought in the lower hold and Martin's red-rimmed eyes nearly popped from his head as he realised how passengers and crew had been tricked. 'It was 'arder than I fort, gettin' the stuff started,' Meadows related. 'Had to break open one o' them bales o' woollen things. Dropped a few of 'em in a big iron cooking pot, 'long wiv some oil and tar. Gawd, it didn't 'alf spout some smoke. Fort I'd run out o' breff before I got clear . . .'

'It was well done, Oatsy, you did a good job,' Henry said. 'You had me worried for a while, I thought the whole ship was alight. How many seamen did we lose?'

'Only Dingle, and he's no loss.'

'Good, keep the rest fired up on liquor.' A gust of wind came off the land bearing a powerful tang of pine, herbs and dust. The naked top-hamper shivered. The wind came again, stronger. 'She's going to blow scissors and thumbscrews,' Will said, cocking an eye at the sky.

With the entrance to the bay hardly two miles ahead, Henry saw the broad sweep of the harbour opening out, the buildings of the burgeoning town and the forest of masts and spars where the ships lay. Was *Musket* one of them? If Screech Gander were watching at this minute Henry thought with satisfaction, he was in for the surprise of his life.

Henry mustered his team around him and gave his orders. Mr Handyside on the wheel. Withers and Big Tree to hoist jib and jib-staysail. Mr Peake to let fall the fore-topsail and Meadows the main-topsail. Henry himself would slip to the deck and bear a hand on the braces. 'Wot abaht me?' Charlie Field asked woefully, scared of being left out.

Henry eyed his beefy shoulders and massive forearms. 'Your business is the towing warp, Barley.'

'Wot do I do wiv it?'

'Chop it – when I give the word.'

The tug took a blast of wind on the chin and visibly slowed. Sheltering from the stinging spray and mentally disposing of the small fortune he was earning by towing in the burning ship, her master saw movement from the corner of his eye and glanced aft. The spectacle froze his blood.

Canvas billowed from the Limey's topsail yards. All sign of smoke had disappeared. Even as he watched, aghast, an axe sliced through the towing warp. Her bow fell off and one by one her sails were sheeted home. The tug swung round, though not so sharply that she over-ran the trailing warp, but soon gave up the chase.

With sail flowering from every spar, the *Quiver* tramped away to the west.

THREE:

Pearl River   8,360 *miles*
Min River   570 *miles*

THE RUM DANCED in Captain John Tidewater's glass as he banged it down on the wicker table and glared at Henry Ardent, his peppery complexion oozing sweat and contempt. 'I agree it was a mighty fancy trick you pulled in 'Frisco but here's one bit of advice you'll get for nothing. It won't wash in the Pearl River and I'll give you two reasons why not . . .'

The six other captains slumped in a circle of cane chairs under the awning on the *Quiver*'s poop, nursing drinks with legs spread wide for coolness, grimaced or nodded agreement. Despite the shade there was no escaping the steamy air that boiled off the slick river and collected in seeping beads of oily sweat as if every pore in the skin were a greasetrap.

It was eleven days since the ship had dropped her hook in the fleet waiting at Whampoa Anchorage, fourteen miles downstream from the city of Canton. The visiting shipmasters, hitting the bottle after a long luncheon on board, had demanded why the elegant green clipper was alone among the fifty or sixty other ships in failing to strike her topgallant masts and upper yards, a normally routine and seamanlike precaution to reduce windage and weight aloft in the event of a dreaded *tai-fun*, or iron wind. Henry's innocently matter-of-fact reply – that he had not sailed all the way to Canton to lay up but intended to load tea for England – did more than raise a few eyebrows. It revealed the depths of resentment and bitter suspicion with which the other British masters regarded the high-flying young upstart who, in any of their own ships, would have been judged hardly fit to fill the shoes of a raw second mate. The captain of the *Reindeer*, whose cane Henry had borrowed after the masthead gallop against the Yankee in London, was on the point of exploding.

'First . . . !' Tidewater hunched furiously on the edge of his chair and jabbed a thick forefinger at Henry. 'First, this is the heavenly sodding kingdom, not your Circular Quay with ships running fat on sweet Botany Bay contracts. Perhaps you haven't inspected these celestial yellow apes. They don't even look like human beings, let alone think like them. See for yourself . . . '

The broad reach of the river indicated with an angry flourish of the shipmaster's arm seethed with strange oriental craft. Henry was reminded of picking up a log overgrown by long grass and exposing to the light an alien world of scurrying insects. Like hordes of ants, hundreds of sampans wobbled back and forth on urgent mysterious errands. Great junks with bat-wing sails hanging flat in the limp air drifted in like ponderous snails. Tiny one-man skiffs sledded slug-like through the ooze in the shallows, filtering the slime for worm meat. The ornately lacquered boats of the patrolling mandarins lorded it like grand earwigs while the many-oared 'smug boats', cutting along like orange centipedes, steered well clear of them.

Henry expressed his contempt with a grunt and strolled to the taffrail. Everyone was a little drunk, himself included, and he had no wish to start a fight on his own poop. He noticed the shite-hawks wheeling hungrily across the sky and felt the eyes of the other captains boring disapprovingly into his back, then his glance fell on a headless corpse spinning slowly in the current eddying abaft the rudder.

There was a cry of triumph from a nearby sampan as the Tanka girl working the long sculling sweep spied the trophy and drove alongside it. A hag dressed in black leant outboard and deftly debagged the bloated corpse. The younger woman snatched the trousers, wrung out the water, then measured them against her own bowed legs. Catching sight of the tall and tousled Foreign Devil staring down from the green ship she pinched her tiny nipples and called in a sing-song voice, 'Me sew-sew velly good, maybe jig-jig?'

Henry stepped back with a shiver of disgust and faced the fiery little captain. 'What do you want me to do, burst into tears or lie down and kick my legs in the air?'

Tidewater carried on as if Henry had not spoken and with two fingers hacked at the invisible blankets weighing down the air. 'Second, all of China is going up in smoke. The rebels have flattened Shanghai and are hammering on the gates of Canton, thousands of 'em, and harvesting Manchu heads like they was cabbages. Right here in the anchorage foreign ships have been raided for powder and arms. I guarantee you wish you were in a position to put a broadside up John Chinaman's arse, *Captain* Ardent . . .'

The angry shipmaster mouthed the rank with withering contempt. Henry blinked but did not rise to the insult and Tidewater banged on. 'Meanwhile, our venerated Royal Navy feels obliged to defend the welfare of a handful of frigging missionaries and to hell with trade. Sir George Bonham leaves Hong Kong to look after itself and runs off on some goose-chase to the north. And what do you do, my friend?

'You sit here calm as Queen Victoria, God bless her, saying you're not housing t'gallant masts like the rest of us, you're not scared of the iron wind like the rest of us, you're just going to fill your hold with tea and scoot off home. Ha! Who do you think you're drinking with, Her Majesty's bloody Marines?'

Facing the hostile gaze of the other shipmasters, Henry felt himself the accused in some underhand court martial. Even Sam, supposed to be the prisoner's friend, sagely nodded his head. But this was only to be expected, Henry realised, for these were Sam's old cronies from years back.

Hardly a year ago Henry would have been awed to shake any one of these crack passage-makers by the hand. Like Anthony Enright, a tall and handsome figure of a man who sat bolt upright and fixed Henry with a vinegary scowl. This Enright was hardly as pure as the driven snow, Henry knew. Two years ago, master of the famous *Chrysolite*, one of the first British clippers to challenge Yankee supremacy, he had overhauled the American ship *Memnon* in the approaches to the Macclesfield Channel in the South China Sea. When the other captain hailed to ask if he intended to beat through the reef-infested channel by night, Enright replied in the affirmative. Unable to ignore the challenge the American sailed on, hit a reef, and made a lucky escape as pirates swarmed aboard. Enright himself prudently anchored until dawn and reached Liverpool in a record 103 days. Now Enright made a pistol with his fingers and aimed it between Henry's eyes. 'Some of us have been in the game a long time, young man, and we know the ropes. You will keep your place in the queue, at the tail end where you belong.'

'Don't come the gum game with me, Captain Enright,' Henry snapped. 'Since when was there a priority list at Whampoa? I'll bid for freights on equal terms with all of you, and frankly I don't fancy your chances.'

The tall captain had the grace to raise an eyebrow in mock

salute but Thomson of the *John Bunyan* and Robertson of the *Stornoway* shook their heads with small condescending smiles while Findlay of the *Foam* blew a contemptuous spurt of smoke from his curled pipe.

'The rest of us have sweltered here months and months and you will serve your time,' George Brook of the *Abergeldie* stated emphatically. 'When the tea comes down we'll take our turns – and pray God let it be tomorrow.'

'What tea?' Tidewater demanded. He jumped up and walked back and forth with jerky strides. 'You gentlemen are missing the point. If your compradores haven't driven the message home, surely your agents have drummed it into your thick heads – there ain't no bloody tea!'

'So why is the *Reindeer* sitting here, besides growing a pretty garden on her bilges?' Henry demanded, and Tidewater threw himself into his chair and downed the rest of his drink at a single gulp.

Despite his cynical response Henry knew Tidewater's summary had put their dilemma in a nutshell. There was no bloody tea in China, but who would believe it? Rumours abounded, especially at a social carouse like this. The visiting captains had indulged their professional curiosity in eagerly inspecting the *Quiver*'s lean and racy lines but their first drink was hardly an inch down in the glass before the hottest news from up-river and down was being aired. The Grand Hoppo had fled . . . America had despatched a war-steamer . . . Pirates had got the *Challenge* in Banca Strait . . . The tea godowns in Canton had been fired by rebels . . . No, the rebels were not yet in the city but all routes inland were cut off so the tea could not get through . . . A Vice-Consul at a treaty port up the coast had made concubines of six Chinese girls in an Anglican orphanage and the Bishop of Hong Kong had sent a Royal Navy gunboat to deal with him . . . The head man of Russells had been sick for weeks after using a new lacquered chair which, though dry, had been insufficiently cured and continued to give off poisonous fumes . . .

Nothing was the subject of greater speculation than the Americans. The Flowery Flag Nation, as America was known to the Chinese, was up to something. Her clippers were clustered together at the head of the reach – *Witch of the Wave*, *Nightingale*, *Fiery Cross*, and others – and their captains were cagily stand-offish. The United States had not participated in the 'opium war' of 1842, when Britain had

forced China to open up to foreign trade five more treaty ports
along the coast, but had benefited greatly from the result.
What worried Sam and his British colleagues was the unusu-
ally closed-mouth attitude of Russell and Company, the long-
established American agency at Canton. Although the British
and Americans were rivals they usually guarded each other's
backs but this season there had been none of the usual
camaraderie.

So far, at least, the Yankee ships were growing as much
weed on their keels as the British. There was no tea for the
Flowery Flag Devils either. So far.

For Henry Ardent the continued absence of the *Musket* was
a gnawing anxiety. A hundred times a day he stared down the
river hoping for a sight of her distinctive masts beyond the rice
paddies. As if reading Henry's thoughts Captain Enright
asked, 'What about your blood-sucking Yankee friend, who's
to say he didn't get into Shanghai and load up before the rebels
hit the place?'

Sam shook his head knowledgeably. 'The whole coast is
locked solid, you know that. And anyhow, it's only the green
tea that goes out of Shanghai. The Americans might like the
stuff but the British market demands black tea, and that comes
out of Canton.'

'Black or green, it comes off the same bush,' Thomson
muttered lazily.

Seeing the alarm cross Henry's face, Enright taunted him
further. 'Bet you a *lac* of silver dollars to a penny the *Musket*
is down to her marks and barrelling for the Cape, eh?'

As the captains sniggered and nodded their heads, Henry
drained his glass and said glumly, 'Well, thank you for the
moral support, gentlemen.' Then he looked across at Sam who
winked broadly, and he felt a little encouraged.

For Sam Handyside the Whampoa Anchorage was a second
home. He had spent more hours of his life couched in a rattan
chair under a deck awning while swinging round an anchor in
the Pearl River than in his own armchair by the fireside with his
dear Meg. During the seven-week crossing of the North
Pacific, following immediately upon the long voyage around
Cape Horn from New York to the Golden Gate, Sam had
bitterly regretted allowing himself to ship as supernumerary in
this mad enterprise. There was little for him to do on board, for
he had neither responsibility nor authority, and the young
captain, gaining confidence and experience by the day, had

grown into the job thrust so unexpectedly on his shoulders.

Only when the bald and jagged peaks of the China coast lifted over the bow and Henry Ardent's wide-eyed innocence of the Orient revealed itself, did Sam realise he was not entirely redundant. Guiding his uneasy and stiff-backed protégé through the complex protocols and etiquette of the Celestial Empire, Sam relived the wonder and awe he had experienced in his own young days as the fifth mate of an East India Company tea wagon.

The Pearl River spilled from the heartland of the Celestial Kingdom and divided into numerous marshy channels as it wound across a wide plain towards the bare-knuckle ranges fringing the coast. The principal strand of the river passed the ancient walled city of Canton, for nearly two centuries the only port through which trade with foreigners had been permitted. Downstream of the city the creeks and channels, now parting, now merging, created a maze of low and muddy-shored islands before uniting in a broad stream infested with shoals that pinched through a rock-walled canyon into a funnel-shaped bay. Nestling among the islands at the western side of the bay's wide mouth was the old Portugese settlement of Macao. Forty miles across the bay, established as a trading base by the British after the recent war, lay Hong Kong.

With a sense of brimming joy Sam had conned the *Quiver* close into Macao so a boat could be sent in to obtain the *chop*, a letter of permission to proceed up the river. A pilot in the usual baggy blue pyjamas had come aboard. The ship made her approach close by the high island of Lintin, known as the Solitary Nail, with its closely guarded hulks stocked with opium for distribution by 'smug boats' into creeks and inlets, out of the eye of patrolling mandarins. The outer pilot, paid off with cash, salt beef, and some wine glasses, handed over to the inner pilot who guided the ship through the six-mile gorge known as The Bogue. Henry had dubiously eyed the cannon in the three forts but Sam reassured him. 'Not as dangerous as they look, lad: the barrels are not on carriages but set in mortar so their aim can't follow you down the river.'

With the flood tide sweeping her through The Bogue and over the first sandbars where the river widened, the *Quiver* emerged in what seemed like the rural heart of China. On every side lay a shimmering sea of brilliant green, for the rice was in blade. Against a distant range of variegated mountains the villages of mossy stone houses with curving eaves, surrounded by fruit orchards, bamboo groves and fields of sugar cane, were set like tropical islands. Where the land rose in a mound it was capped with a pagoda, serene as a lighthouse. The bunds between the paddy fields were crowded highways and because the earthen dykes were higher than the level of the paddy fields the eye was fooled by a mirage of processions of peasants in conical hats – with ducks, water buffalo and pigs – walking in the sky.

The winding silver-grey waterway, like the Thames a river of life, was thick was floating traffic. The muddy banks were lined with houseboats, stranded hulks, stilt houses and fish traps. Narrow channels through the marshes, filled only at high tide, were choked with craft. Where a crook of the shore formed a breakwater, sampans congregated by the thousand in floating cities. Each small boat, shaped like a shoe and knitted to its neighbours with grass hawsers, was home for a whole family living with poultry, cage-birds, dogs, cats, children and old people, none of whom set foot on dry land from one year to the next.

The anchorage was a broad reach three miles long and a mile broad where several river channels converged. Though it lay thirty miles up from the sea it was still fourteen miles short of the Provincial City; even in former days the ships of the Outer Barbarians had never been permitted to proceed further. On one bank lay Danes Island. Its untidy rock crag draped with the black nets of fishermen was the highest point of land for miles around and the foreshore was cluttered with docks, chandleries, agencies, custom house and cemetery. Opposite was the straggling and wretched village of Whampoa whose name had become as famous through the trading world as those of other great ports such as Bombay, Liverpool and Boston.

Long before the anchor plunked into the turbid water the sew-sew and washee-washee boats had hooked on, women and young girls stridently touting for the ship's business. Then came a procession of officials who crashed alongside in elaborately ornamented junks and swept aboard in flowing robes or baggy pyjamas of richly embroidered silk. Sam knew most of them of old and greeted them in his best going-to-meeting suit and stovepipe hat. With growing dismay Henry saw their small stock of eleven thousand dollars disbursed as *cumshaw*. The Chinese might have invented the compass, the lug rig and the wheelbarrow but they knew nothing about soap, he thought, as Sam gravely kow-towed before a wizened, monkey-like figure in a gown of peacock blue. Henry was idly scrutinising the fancy needlework embellishing the visitor's wide sleeves when he realised with a nauseous shudder he was admiring scrolled threads of dried snot. This official was the 'Jack Hoppo', or revenue inspector, who chained his large and comfortable junk fifty feet off *Quiver*'s stern to ensure no articles of commerce crossed the ship's side without proper dues being paid. In fact he remained out of sight, a shadowy figure behind his window screens, because the amount of revenue was agreed directly between the Hong merchant who acted for the ship and the Grand Hoppo who was the Emperor's chief financial official in Canton.

The thirteen Hong merchants, Sam had explained, acted as security agents for all foreign ships. When a ship arrived, her selected agent put up a bond to indemnify the Celestial Kingdom against loss or damage, however it might be caused, by vessel, captain or crew. The Hong merchant was intermediary in all matters, cargo operations and supply of provisions included, and on every transaction raked off a handsome percentage. Most Hong merchants accumulated enormous wealth but they lived dangerously. It was treason to fraternise with foreigners or become too friendly with them, though one who did so – the peacock feather in his cap betokening the Emperor's special esteem – was the rich and powerful Fowqua.

It was through Fowqua that Sam collected the many pieces of jade and oriental porcelain with which he had delighted his beloved Meg. Over the years a discreet but warm friendship developed between the merchant shipmaster and the powerful mandarin. In Sam's experience, Fowqua was unique in being openly curious about the world beyond China. He was fascinated by machinery and scientific instruments and Sam never made a voyage to the orient without a sample of British industrial craftsmanship with which to impress Fowqua during a cordial meeting at his palatial residence. On this voyage, however, no word had come from Fowqua. Even when Fowqua's compradore came on board with the customary gifts of fresh vegetables, fruit, and sides of buffalo beef that were hoisted in the rigging out of reach of the flies, there was no message. It was a sign of how bad things must be up in Canton, and Sam grew increasingly alarmed.

Sam threw himself into a busy round of visits, dragging Henry to meet every British and American agent, merchant, tea-taster, shipwright and clerk. 'You might think yourself a red-hot sailor, my lad, but getting your ship from one port to the other is only half your job,' Sam instructed his reluctant apprentice. 'Only one man keeps you going as shipmaster – your owner. And only one thing keeps the owner happy – your cargo. Owners don't make money with an empty ship and it's the master's job to keep it full and on the go. That's why you have to show your face. Shippers and merchants and agents have to know you, so bear up and for God's sake make some conversation or they'll begin to think there's truth in the rumour that Botany Bay folk only talk Abbo.'

There was more to Sam's wisdom than simple profit, Henry learnt on the day when he was dragged down a stench-filled alley on Danes Island and led into a tea-house as dark as a cave where Sam mysteriously handed a fistful of silver dollars to a living skeleton hunched at a corner table playing cards. Through an intermediary he was paying off the guild of beggars, and the *Quiver* was never bothered by hordes of pilferers who were known to float down-river by night, their heads concealed under driftwood, to pick the very copper sheathing off her bottom.

While Sam fretted about Fowqua, and Henry made his official calls with a bored and distracted air, the mates fought a running battle with the heat and humidity of the south-west monsoon. Shady awnings might prevent the deck planks from splitting in the sky's bleaching glare but little could be done to protect the hulls and masts. Paint blistered and flaked away. Manilla and hemp ropes rotted into mouldy tangles. Moisture was sucked from the grain of the masts and spars. Without persistent efforts to keep the ship fresh, by rigging wind funnels to catch and circulate the air, mushrooms sprouted in every dark corner and dry rot would steal like a dark and deadly ivy through her timbers.

The captain's blunt refusal to strike topgallant masts and send down the canvas was another frustration, because sails saturated in the daily downpours had to be dried. Will Lamshire and Martin Peake listened to Henry's justification with the same wooden ears as did Sam. 'The fact is, once the ship is immobilised we're here until Christmas,' he warned them. 'As long as we're ready to move we can keep our options open. If the iron wind scares you so much, put the squeeze on your yellow friends to find us some tea then we can get the hell out from under his Celestial Majesty's imperial arsehole.'

The Murphies and Macaroons who sailed before the mast in

the *Quiver*, once they had sobered up and observed the coast of California dropping over the horizon astern, accepted their lot. The sour prospects of yet more long weeks at sea were sweetened by the promise of exotic oriental delights awaiting them in Whampoa.

By Imperial edict a Foreign Devil sailor was not permitted to go ashore during his stay at Whampoa Anchorage for more than one day, but from the constant procession of boats hawking wares through the fleet he could buy anything his heart, belly or flesh desired. He could have a haircut and a shampoo, and have his ears cleaned, by the barber who paddled his skiff ringing a bell. He could be attended by a doctor who advertised his services with a drum, or have his fortune told by a sage clanging a cymbal. Herb sellers cried the benefits of queer twisted roots, dried snakes and frogs in jars. Book sellers drew attention to flimsy volumes pegged on bamboo frames, although it was treason for Foreign Devils to be taught the language. From passing boats which signalled their wares with a bunch of sugar cane tied to the mast, Nix Barlow had bought fresh vegetables. From other hawkers came trussed-up pigs and white ducks for the saloon table, and a potent liquor called *samshu* – brewed from rice wine, tobacco juice, garlic, licorice, and God-knew what other brain-rot – for the fo'c's'le. From a floating tailor Martin Peake fitted himself with a waistcoat that for sumptuous glory outshone even Will Lamshire's golden dragons squirming on a background of scarlet silk. Manfred Longhandle purchased a shiny umbrella of oiled paper. The seamen bargained for tortoiseshell combs, fans, ivories and other knick-knacks.

Nothing moved on the river without noise and the bombardment of cymbals, gongs, firecrackers and bells was unceasing. 'There's a good reason for all this din, yer know, Barley,' Charlie Meadows expounded philosophically as he leant over the rail gazing at a washee-washee girl who tantalisingly refused to catch his eye.

'Yeah?' Charlie Field grunted.

'Yer averidge John Chinaman can't fart without bangin' a drum so when he squats he 'as to let orf a string o' firecrackers, see, and it scares the shit out of 'im.'

Field cuffed him on the arm with a laugh. The girl looked up suddenly, just as Big Tree put his head over the rail to see what the farmers were admiring. At sight of the Maori's swirling tattoos the girl screamed and, like a tortoise retreating into its shell, crouched beneath her wide straw hat with her hands over her eyes.

Meadows clicked his tongue as Big Tree withdrew sadly inboard. 'You've only one chance, yer cannibal, and that's wait till dark and don't put the light on.'

After dark Meadows and Field lowered themselves quietly down a rope to a waiting sampan that sculled them up the reach to the flower boats rafted together and joined by little gangways. Each vessel was a houseboat, a golden dolphin standing enchantingly on each corner of its curved roof and rows of potted flowers lining its side-decks. Behind the col- oured windows that beckoned like jewels in a fabulous cave a Foreign Devil could drink *samshu*, smoke opium, or sport with oriental maidens who regarded their most maidenly virtue to be the warped joints of their pathetically clubbed feet.

The lure of Joy City had for weeks been the talk of the ship but the reality proved sadly lacking in joy. Three mornings in succession, Meadows and Field returned on board exhausted and disappointed. The girls' resigned and listless responses to their ardours was too much for them. 'I like a bit o' grunt, myself,' Meadows reported sourly, 'but these yellow birds are as lively as hens plucked and gutted for the stewpot – there's more fun in shaggin' a rolled-up 'ammock.'

With the wilting humidity, worry over events at Canton and the lack of cargo, and the blighted delights of the flower girls, the ship was in a glum and dissatisfied frame of mind from stem to stern. And to judge by the moody and resigned manner of the visiting captains, the *Quiver* by no means suffered and sweated alone.

Henry put his head out from under the poop awning and looked up at the darkening sky. 'What will it be, gentlemen, another drink or do you want to get away before the rain? There's a real slammer brewing.'

Muttering thanks for the hospitality, the visitors eased themselves blearily out of their chairs. Tidewater glimpsed the mountain of vermilion cloud piling overhead. 'My God, will you look at that!' he exclaimed.

Seeing movement on the poop, the waiting sampans started a noisy race for the gangway. But the captains were too late. The heavens opened and rain fell like a cart-load of bricks. Drops as big as silver dollars bounced on the river, raising a blurred carpet of bubbles and froth. Water cascaded in solid curtains off the awnings, streamed in flood-waves across the deck and jetted in tangled spouts from the belly of every rope and line aloft. 'Nothing for it but stand still and breathe shallow,' Enright observed gloomily, shaking his head at the offer of another drink. The roar of rain on the awning killed conversation. Thunder rolled and crashed overhead. The boat people out in the rain moved like misty figures in a dream, the impact of rain making a halo of spray around every wide straw hat.

Listlessly the assembly of captains watched an ornate junk thread its way through the fleet. The windowed house with curved eaves occupying its waist was crusted with gold. Brilliant banners and streamers hung limply in the rain. Propelled by half a dozen sweeps a side, the junk approached at a fast clip and rounded up on the *Quiver*'s port side.

'That's Fowqua's barge,' Tidewater said, shooting Sam a sharp look.

'He's coming on board!' Enright warned.

Sam discreetly nudged Henry who let out a resigned groan then plunged into the torrent. His whites were instantly drenched and his shoes filled. He stood at the gangway as the junk crashed alongside with the usual oriental delicacy. Henry roared an order for'ard and it was Big Tree, his large brown frame stripped to a short canvas skirt, who ran to help with the lines.

A young man stepped aboard and stood rigidly to attention as if the stinging rain did not exist. He wore a linen tunic blackened by water which was held at the waist by a belt with an elaborate gold buckle. Voluminous matching trousers were thrust into high leather boots. A wide-bladed sword was slung at his hip and a helmet of finely plaited straw, like an inverted fruit basket, adorned his head. He bowed stiffly three times from the waist, his arms at his sides, then offered a large package tied with heavy seals. Once more he bowed three times and without meeting Henry's eye returned to his craft. His boatman indicated that Big Tree should throw back the lines.

Henry took the package to the shelter of the poop awning and the other captains, burning with curiosity, looked over Sam's shoulders as he cut away the seals and folded back the waterproof oil-cloth coverings. Inside was a chop-letter, a large crimson paper hung with gold tassels and illuminated with black Chinese characters. Sam peered at the few words written small in English. Swiftly so as to keep his mystified friends guessing, Sam hid the paper in its wrapping. 'Just a letter,' he explained enigmatically, with a deliberately obvious wink at Henry who did not have the faintest idea what it could be all about. He soon discovered.

Even with the tide lifting the gig along it was a pull of nearly three hours up to the city of Canton. Perspiring in their tidiest formal suits, Henry and Sam sat stiffly erect in the sternsheets. Henry was in a rage of frustration. As always, first light had brought no sign of the *Musket*'s golden spars lifting above the paddy fields down river; where could the Blue Nose scoundrel be? And Sam, nursing a canvas-wrapped package that he had brought from London, was infuriatingly close-lipped about why Fowqua might have bidden them to attend a meeting at his residence. 'Fowqua's a wily old bird, devious as hell, but I've know him twenty years and if there's one thing I've learned it is that we need him on our side,' he told Henry, and refused to be drawn into further speculation.

The curved tiller locked under his arm, Henry steered the slender white gig a few yards out from the goggle-eyed junks ranged along the banks. In the fishing junks the eyes painted on the bows squinted downwards, looking for fish, while the trading junks stared ahead with a far-away look. Hong-sha, their compradore, had answered Henry's questions in the strange 'pidgin' English that was the lingo of the port: 'No have eye, no can see, no can savvy.' Henry had seen aboriginal huts that looked more seaworthy than these strange craft; their hulls seemed to be constructed of firewood while gaping holes showed between the planks and in the straw mats stiffened with strips of bamboo which formed their sails. It seemed incredible they could float, never mind make long voyages. Henry's wondering eye caught a tiny boy staring down at the gig as it passed. His lower half was naked and a watertight bladder painted with coloured hoops was fitted to a harness between his shoulder blades. As he saw the white-suited Foreign Devil staring at him the child solemnly gripped a tuft of his own hair and with his free hand made a slow slicing movement across his throat.

The men, put off their stroke by the abrupt sheer of the gig to the centre of the river, grumbled low curses. Meadows and Field at the for'ard oars had wanted to come for the ride but there was no room unless they took their turn. Now, heaving with set and streaming faces, their eyes glazed from the effects of the night's *samshu*, they were regretting it. Though it had healed well enough, the vivid scar slashing Adam Robinson's sweat-glossed breast flamed brilliantly. Beside him, the West Indian called Bunce grunted like a beam engine as he tugged at the smooth shaft of his oar. Amidships, John Gabb and Pat Flynn pulled stolidly with their eyes fixed on the rippling muscles of the Macaroons in front of them, intent on matching them stroke for stroke. Tall and straight as a totem pole, Big Tree took a breather in the bow. As the gig jerked forward the shark figure he had carved from a whale's tooth bounced lightly on his broad chest and the shaft of greenstone hanging from his left ear danced in the sunlight.

The low marshy countryside was dotted with the sails of craft ghosting ponderously along other channels of the river, their hulls concealed. The rice paddies were a little lower than the high-water mark, and connected to each other by the treadmills with which water was pumped to flood the fields. Among the clutter of fishing weirs along the banks people with rolled up trousers rambled in the ooze, pausing occasionally to bag the prawns and shrimps trapped between their toes. Where green sward came down to the waterside strange craft top-heavy with tiers of cages lowered ramps down which scores of white ducks paraded on shore leave. Big Tree scooped a tail feather from the water and thrust it at a jaunty angle into his top-knot.

At last the nine-storey tower of the Great Halfway Pagoda drew abeam and Sam produced the bottle of rum with which gig crews were traditionally rewarded. The men rested panting on their oars and the bottle passed from one thirsty pair of lips to another was soon emptied. Meadows hurled it towards the moored junks and before it splashed down a dozen children were swimming madly to grab it.

'Give way before we're mobbed,' Henry growled as sampans converged on the gig like seabirds on a dead whale. The nearest was sculled by a girl with a pert round face under a conical hat who cried, 'You wan-shee orangee, velly good!' As the gig pulled away she determinedly gave chase but the moment she rested on her long sweep Henry told his men to stop rowing and beckoned her on. Grinning broadly at the prospect of selling oranges to Foreign Devils, she came up at a smart lick until, at twenty yards, the gig darted ahead. The gig ate up the miles and the men were kept in a good humour as the trick was repeated over and over. The girl's smile soon became an angry scowl and her face darkened with effort until the jeering men took pity. Every mouth in the gig watered at the prospect of sucking a juicy orange as the panting rowers rested on their oars and waited for the sampan to come up.

Henry stood in the sternsheets and called with a friendly smile, 'All rightee, we buy muchee orangee . . . '

But the girl spun her sampan round and folded her arms belligerently. 'No can!' she blazed.

Sheepishly Henry resumed his seat and the gig plugged on into the morass of traffic seething off the city like an ant's nest poked with a stick. Huge junks with bubbling bow-waves bore down from every side. Among them, sampans and all kinds of tiny, curious craft darted willy-nilly with a groaning and creaking of timbers, bursts of firecrackers, shrill curses, and clashing cymbals. Leaves of crimson paper on fire suddenly wafted about the men's shoulders as the gig was caught up in some propitiation of gods, and there was a mad scramble as they beat at the red-hot ashes dropping on their bare skin. Sam indicated the row of buildings fronting the river, their European roofs jutting above a dense mass of vessels moored in ranks ten or twelve deep along the right bank. Henry had imagined they would bring up at a nice little pier flying the Union flag, nothing like this desperate struggle to squeeze the gig through a maze of twisting alleys between the high splintered walls of this creaking, shifting city.

The oars were boated and exchanged for paddles. Sam donned an old oil-cloth coat and told Henry to do the same. Meadows and Field took up positions on either side of the bow, where they could lean out to pull the gig along by any hawser or handhold that offered. A rain of missiles came down from the crowded decks on either side. Rotten vegetable stalks, fish guts and every kind of filth bombarded the gig. A rainbow flashed vividly through an arc of piss emptied over it. As the men yelled with bunched fists, all set to pile aboard the nearest junk to take revenge, Henry growled at them to shut up.

A brick thudded into the boat, narrowly missing Big Tree's head, and there was a smell of burning paint. The Maori howled with sudden pain and sucked his seared fingers, because the brick he had tried to throw over the side, torn from a cooking hearth in a junk, was red hot. Meadows tugged Field's tarred hat from his head, filled it with water, and emptied it over the brick which sizzled steam into the air.

Sam shuddered and tore frantically at his collar as a hot and slimy boiled noodle wrapped around the back of his neck. 'I've never seen it this bad,' he said tightly.

It was no better when at last the *Quiver*'s gig had been elbowed through the smaller boats packing the landing stairs near the gates of the compound where the European agency buildings, known as factories, lined the water front. For nearly two centuries, foreign merchants in China had been restricted to this row of factories and their small gardens in Canton. Moreover, they could come only at certain times of year and women were prohibited. Sam had dined at the Honourable East India Company's establishment, now the British factory, on previous voyages but he had never felt as unsafe as he did now. Hundreds of scowling dark eyes bored into him, setting his nerves jumping like fireworks. With relief he recognised the sword-wearing young man, deliverer of the letter, who bowed stiffly and introduced himself as Fowqua's captain, Chin-ta. 'Pliss, you come.'

Henry's skin crawled as he felt his arm nudged and he looked into porcelain-white eyes staring from a beggar's ravaged face. He quickly gave his orders to the men. 'Whatever happens, guard the boat and mind you stay out of trouble.'

Meadows grinned confidently. 'Don't worry, nuffink will bovver us dahn 'Og Lane.'

Henry shot him a doubtful look then hurried after Sam as the crowd fell back in front of the impassive messenger. After a few moments, sensing he was being followed, Henry was startled to see Big Tree a few paces behind. If nip came to tuck the Maori would wield a handy pair of fists.

At once they were swallowed up in a rat's nest of cobbled alleys. There were neither carriages nor beasts of burden in Canton so the streets could afford to be narrow. Bulky goods were transported by pairs of coolies who elbowed aside any pedestrian who blocked their passage as they jogged along with a shuffling gait, a bamboo pole between their shoulders bowing from the weight of the load slung in baskets beneath it.

So dense was the human mill-race that anybody who did not watch himself was knocked down, but if he stepped aside it was difficult to find a gap in the stream. As he hurried along, keeping a tab on Sam's stovepipe hat which bobbed through the crowd like the funnel of a steam engine, Henry felt sweat break out on his forehead, not only from the sultry heat and press of the crowd in the airless alleyways. He felt a tingling awareness of being swept away in a powerful torrent, like being washed down a drainpipe.

On every side strange new sights and sounds intensified his prickly unease: cripples and half-starved children scrambled in his wake, the racks of skinned rats which were sold for the pot, a man at a small table methodically decapitating and skinning frogs that continued to leap against the smooth sides of the porcelain pot at his feet, the pigs' heads and jars of coiled snakes among varnished ducks hanging like giant-sized bats over shop doorways, fluffy white puppies trussed in rattan baskets ... He swallowed and wondered how the chinks would take to a fillet of fried Nightingale; the mad dog was unlikely to be tougher than their buffalo meat.

Henry's nostrils withered in the sweet smoke of burning joss and his throat gagged as a coolie pushed by, bent double beneath a vast stone jar filled with human excrement. He saw luckless individuals crawling in the gutters wearing heavy wooden collars in which one hand was locked, the collar too large in diameter for a wearer to feed himself and covered with written notices proclaiming the nature of his crime. In an open space between buildings Henry witnessed another demonstration of Celestial justice. Supervised by a magisterial mandarin sitting beside a clerk at a small desk, a citizen was being chastised. Stripped to the waist with hands bound, the victim lay face down in the dirt before them. A strong and sinewy official wrapped the victim's queue two or three times around his hand, put a foot on the back of his head, and flailed him with a stout bamboo.

At last their guide turned down a broader and quieter street and stopped at a tall gateway, spanned by a tiled roof, where he rang a little bell. The gate was opened at once by kow-towing servants and the harassed visitors stepped out of one world into another.

The courtyard was a mass of pink and white flowers and small shrubs, their pots covering much of the granite paving and crowding on stone tables. Small dark trees stood in the corners. Creepers festooned the high walls and crawled over the gate which was silently closed.

A tiny skeleton clothed in gorgeous silks appeared behind the flower-lined parapet of a low terrace. Like a pair of starved ferrets emerging from twin burrows, pinkish-yellow claw hands appeared from opposite sleeves then embraced and did a little dance up to the height of the black cap with its smooth gold button. Bloodless lips parted in a fractional smile and a thin voice cried, 'Werry fine day, I chin-chin you.'

Sam set down the package he had brought from the ship, then bowed and made the same gesture of clasped hands, which Henry copied. 'And I chin-chin you, Fowqua, my friend,' Sam replied gladly.

After the stench and clamour of the alleys the tranquillity of the little garden numbed the senses. Henry fancied he could even hear the buzzing of bees. He bowed as Sam introduced him to Fowqua, whose bright little eyes moved past him to dwell with curiosity and amazement upon Big Tree. Fowqua led them into a cool, tall-ceilinged reception room hung with square glass lanterns painted with flowers. The walls were festooned with water-colours of peacefully flowing rivers, reflecting lakes, boys playing flutes while squatting on the backs of water buffalo, and other scenes typical of rustic oriental charm. Henry wondered sourly if a Chinese artist was ever known to look out of a window.

Servants brought steaming perfumed towels with which Sam and Henry wiped their hands and faces while Big Tree made his station evident by sitting cross-legged inside the door, his arms folded across his chest. Fowqua and Sam politely disputed the place of honour, on the left of the three straight-backed chairs placed at a small table, until Sam reluctantly allowed himself to be persuaded to accept. Pale amber tea was brought in tiny bowls so fragile that Henry could see daylight through the egg-shell porcelain. Its subtle flavour satisfied his thirst like nothing he had ever tasted. Dishes of chopped walnuts and small squares of apple were placed on the table.

'Vellee solly much trub, more-proper you stay Whampoa-side,' Fowqua said accusingly, as if they ought not to have come. Henry sensed hard little black eyes shrewdly weighing him up. It was impossible to gauge the man's age. The sallow skin drawn tightly over the skull was speckled with liver spots, and half a dozen white hairs, all of eight inches long, sprouted from a mole on the edge of his jaw. The bearing of the feeble-seeming frame was taut and springy: Fowqua could swagger while sitting still, so imperiously conceited was his manner.

'We stay Whampoa too-long-time,' Sam replied. 'Barbarian captains all talkee Canton much trub.'

Fowqua inclined his head in grave agreement. 'Bandits makee die, number one chow-chow, too bad.'

Henry stirred restlessly. What sort of conversation was this? The strange manner of speech called 'pidgin' – the name itself derived from the awkward Chinese pronunciation of the word 'business' – was mystifyingly comic. A *chop* could define anything from a cargo lighter to a letter or permit, and a chop stick was the oriental answer to a fork. Chow-chow, too, seemed to mean anything under the sun, from a jar of mixed pickles to appetising puppies; chow-chow cargo was an assorted one, a chow-chow shop sold a bit of everything. While a first-chop man was to be respected, a number one chow-chow sort of person was worthless. Then there was the chow-chow chop, the little boat that in pleasanter days carried the captain's baggage down-river to his ship when he embarked for his voyage home, and in which he packed his personal illicit exports like bolts of silk and carved ivories. Impatiently, Henry tried to turn the conversation to the small matter which, like a fire smouldering deep in the hold of a ship, had for days been burning a cave in his brain. He asked bluntly, 'We wanshee muchee tea-cargo, you have got, no have got?'

The button eyes enfolded in slanting lids of parchment regarded him coolly. 'Lat cargo no can walkee just now.'

'Talkee-me when will lat cargo go walkee?' Henry demanded, feeling like a court jester.

Fowqua's thin shoulders lifted fractionally. 'Not tomollow, oh no! Too bad. You must wait, all-o same 'Melican. Maybe bandits bling tea for you, eh?'

Even in Canton the challenge between the British and American clippers was known, Henry realised, and Fowqua evidently thought it was all a good joke. Henry was framing a barbed comment when the rumble of a distant explosion sent the lanterns swaying on the ceiling. Fowqua paid it no attention but touched the palms of his hands together. Instantly Chin-ta appeared at his side. Compared with his master's brilliant peacock-hued robes, Chin-ta's uniform was unostentatiously drab but when Henry looked more closely he saw the hems and collar of the dark blue silk were richly embroidered with black. The unlined face beneath the fruit basket gave nothing away but the resemblance to Fowqua was striking.

As Fowqua rapped brief instructions to Chin-ta, who was also his son, Sam cut the coverings from the package he had brought to reveal two wooden boxes which he reverently laid on the table beside Fowqua's chair. The Hong merchant let an excited smile hover for a brief second on his thin mouth. He opened the first in a manner that suggested he knew what to expect and Henry was astonished to find it filled with tea. 'What, you brought all that stuff from England! Why do you bring tea to China, we're trying to get the bloody stuff back?' Henry said.

Sam waved at him to be quiet. 'No, it's his own tea, the voyage to England is supposed to give it special qualities.'

Fowqua frowned as he lifted the lid of the second box, larger and heavier than the first. He peered inside uncomprehendingly. Sam reached into the box and set on the table a miniature steam engine. Its pipes and tubes were made of polished copper and brass that glinted in the soft light; the boiler was green enamel, the smokestack black, and the spokes of the flywheel were bright red. 'The old boy's fascinated with machinery, and China's still in the age of the ox cart,' he muttered from the corner of his mouth. Then he spun the flywheel with the tip of his finger and said more slowly. 'It's the same as the engine in a paddle steamer.' When Fowqua continued to look blank Sam translated into pidgin, 'Allo same fire-ship walkim-outside, savvy?'

Sam had primed the little engine with water and prepared a few crumbs of coal before leaving the ship, and now he only had to apply a flame to start the fire. He closed the firebox trap with a click. More tea was brought until at last the boiler began to hiss and spit steam. Fowqua regarded it dubiously, and jerked backwards as Sam flicked a polished lever with his stubby finger, sending the pistons rattling up and down in their cylinders, revolving the connecting rods which turned the flywheel. Fowqua cried his astonishment aloud. 'Ai-yah, firebox number one chop, vellee fine!' Soon Henry heard a scuffle and he saw round-eyed faces of women and children peeping from behind a hanging bamboo screen in a doorway.

Sam demonstrated how to drive the engine. The old man delightedly stopped and started it, flicking the controls and burning his talon-like fingers in the process, but showed no understanding of the need to keep the tank topped up with water and the boiler stoked.

Remembering his duties as host Fowqua stood and with a bow suggested Sam and Henry should follow him. Now it was Sam's turn to be gratified as Fowqua led them through room after room in which porcelain vases, urns, intricate ivories, and beautiful jades were displayed on carved and lacquered tables. One room contained nothing but tall and slender jars patterned with glorious blues, the like of which Henry had seen only in the deep shadows cast by a ship while sailing in mid-ocean. The tour took them across another courtyard to an outbuilding where a strong and acrid tang brought juices spurting into Henry's mouth so he had to swallow and swallow. It was filled with raw tea.

At one end of the barn-like building, between bulkheads forming a space as large as a stable, mountains of tea were being mixed with heaps of fresh flowers, jasmine in one, orange blossoms and roses in others. The scent was overwhelming. For twenty-four hours, Sam explained, the dust-dry tea would soak up the juices of the flowers. Tomorrow an army of workers would painstakingly pick over the tea to remove the flowers then they would be sold to the poor who would make tea from the few tea-leaves caught amid the petals.

Henry stopped Fowqua with a discourteous hand on the sleeve. 'Everyone says there is no tea in Canton,' he exclaimed, excited by a vision of the *Quiver* creaming to London with her holds stuffed. 'Why can't you send some of this down the river for us . . . ?'

The intensity of Fowqua's stony and stubborn glare stopped him dead. 'No can!' the merchant whispered balefully, and for the second time that day Henry was stymied by the same pair of simple words.

As he fell into step behind, Sam told him, 'This stuff is all top of the crop, you won't find it exported except in a few caddies shipped privately by captains.'

'At least it shows there's tea in Canton,' Henry argued.

'True, but hardly enough to fill a twentieth part of one ship.'

A sound of loud cries and shouting carried over the adjacent rooftops as they crossed the open courtyard, returning to the house. A veil of black smoke from a fire some distance away drifted across part of the sky but Fowqua paid it no attention.

Henry, anxious to see an end to this socialising which was getting them nowhere, worried about his men minding the gig. He prayed they were being led to the front gate, but in vain. Fowqua ushered them into yet another room where a round table was set for a banquet. Again there was an elaborate argument about who was to sit where. Sam had schooled Henry in the use of chopsticks but nothing had prepared him for the lavishness of the feast as dish after dish of exotic flavours was placed before him. Henry set his mind against thoughts of the puppies he had seen, and such things as gorilla lips, creamed cicada and lung of hare that were supposed to be the finest of delicacies.

Sam watched approvingly as Henry fastidiously tested one morsel from every dish. The lad was learning. But Fowqua's air of distraction worried him. Even within the confines of the merchant's grand house Sam sensed the tension that wracked the city. It showed in the quick shuffling step of the servants, the buzz of alarmed chatter that could be heard every time the door to the kitchens opened, and the icy aplomb with which Fowqua ignored the general air of uneasiness. If there was nothing wrong, Sam reflected, Fowqua would long ago have calmed the noise. Sam consoled himself with the one lesson of his long experience: in the East, nothing is what it seems.

Henry was setting his silver-tipped chopsticks down with a sigh when the door flew open and Big Tree appeared. 'Plenty noise outside, Cap'n,' he reported. 'Better you come and see.'

Learning from Fowqua's calm demeanour, Henry stopped himself from crashing his chair backwards. Their host took a sip of tea then rose and made a slow inspection of Big Tree who stood stiff and still, his eyes fixed anxiously on the far wall. Interestedly, Fowqua reached up and ran the tip of a long fingernail along the swirls patterning the Maori's cheeks, then he tapped the greenstone shaft in his ear which rang like a chime.

Big Tree removed it from his ear and handed it to Fowqua, who held it admiringly up to the light and smiled. 'Velly fine piece, I like.'

Henry fumbled for the jade *tiki* on his neck and showed it through a gap in his shirt-front. Fowqua peered at the figure's fat belly and with a sideways look at Sam said, 'Allo same my flend, savvy?' His thin shoulders shook with silent laughter then Chin-ta appeared at his side. 'More better you go, maybe much trub,' Fowqua told Sam, making a small bow. 'I chin-chin you werry fine voyage, ol' flend.' In a few moments Henry, Sam and Big Tree found themselves following Chin-ta into the other world. People were fleeing with panicky screams. Flames erupted from a roof just yards away. An explosion made the ground leap under their feet. Hurrying with the crowd in the smoky twilight, it was not easy to keep Chin-ta's black basket hat in sight. 'What's going on?' Henry demanded.

'The rebels must have breached the gates,' Sam puffed, his breath coming in laboured gasps. At a cross-street they glimpsed men uniformed in loose blue suits and scarlet sashes hacking with swords at prostrate figures. Suddenly Chin-ta was no longer in sight. To avoid a bottleneck Henry diverted along a passage which came out on a broader alley. They stepped out into the path of a dozen blood-crazed men running straight at them, brandishing naked swords. Big Tree halted and faced the attackers, his greenstone *patu* snatched from his waistband. Legs planted wide apart, fists on hips and elbows jutting forwards, he rolled his eyes horribly and stuck out his tongue, then beat his chest powerfully and let out a blood-curdling whoop. The rebels skidded to a halt and fled.

With Sam's unathletic bulk unable to go faster than a lumbering trot, Henry decided that more haste would make for less speed. With many twists and turns, keeping their direction by the glow in the sky where the north part of the city was afire, they made their way by slow degrees towards the river. Where the streets were clogged with panic-stricken people Big Tree took the lead. The crowd melted before the huge and terrible figure with its lolling tongue, staring eyes and engraved cheeks. Henry could almost believe he was seeing his *tiki* springing suddenly to life.

At the rear of the compound of foreign factories they worked left and arrived at the landing where Meadows and Field had stayed behind with the four seamen to guard the gig. In the light of the many lanterns wriggling across the water from the tiers of junks blocking the stages they saw the gig, swamped and turned on its side amid the press of sampans and small boats. There was no sign of the men.

'Bloody farmers, I might have guessed,' Henry muttered.

Breathing hard, his face red, Sam said, 'There's only one place to look.'

Hog Lane was a passageway, parallel with the wall of the British factory, striking back from the waterfront. So narrow and cluttered was it that until Sam plunged inside Henry thought its entrance was the doorway of a shop. This world was as insulated from the panic in the streets as Fowqua's flower garden but a greater contrast could not be imagined. Henry glimpsed rooms like dark and mouldy burrows where dim lanternlight showed withered Chinese lying smoking on hard beds. Tattooists and hawkers peddled cheap knick-knacks with imploring cries. Bar-keepers emerged like nocturnal rodents and tugged at Henry's sleeves hissing, 'Hello Johnny, come along-a-me, velly fine *samshu*, pretty girl makee jig-jig.'

After the first few paces Sam paused. 'They're bound to be in this warren somewhere but how do we find 'em?' he asked.

'They don't call you Old Thundersides for nothing,' Henry reminded him.

Sam's first bellow brought a fearful jabber, like a flock of startled starlings. But this was only a testing stroke. He made a trumpet of his hands, filled his lungs, and the word '*Quiver*' rolled like a gigantic cannonball the length of Hog Lane. As the awe-struck crowd of hawkers and touts peeled away before him, Sam advanced deeper into the lane letting rip the ship's name in broadside after broadside until suddenly there was an answer. 'Giss a lift up!' a familiar voice cried. 'Over 'ere!'

The gig's crew lay in an untidy heap in the doorway of a drinking dive. Only Meadows was upright, his shirt open at the front. Then the mound of bodies seemed to erupt and Charlie Field staggered to his feet with the red-headed Flynn draped like a muffler over his shoulders. With the weight of the Irishman off his back, Adam Robinson staggered woozily to his feet then slumped against Meadows who propped him up. Big Tree scooped up Bunce. Henry tried to bring Gabb to his senses with a stinging blow on the cheeks but failed and hoisted him on to his back. Led by Sam, the sorry procession stumbled out of Hog Lane. The sight of the Foreign Devils seemed to inflame the people who began to shout angrily. 'Head for the British factory, we'll lie up until daylight,' Sam puffed.

'No, back to the ship!' Henry countermanded. His muscles cracked and bulged with the strain as he staggered to the landing and dropped his burden into the water. Gabb came up coughing. Henry held his chin clear of the surface so he didn't drown and after a few moments roughly hauled him out. Leaving Gabb vomiting on his hands and knees Henry scrambled across the sampans to the gig. When Big Tree and the farmers followed, having meted out the same treatment to the others, the gig was righted and Field's hat employed as a bailer. Cobblestones and bits of timber started to rain down on them as the crowd advanced along the pier, yellow faces lit by lanterns prettily painted with flowers and Chinese characters. Though a foot of water still covered the bottom boards, the men splashed to their seats and laboriously worked the wallowing and half-submerged gig out of range. With cupped hands and boots they emptied out what remained of the water then pushed through the moored junks and emerged in open water. A great explosion cracked overhead. As he slotted the tiller into the rudder-stock Henry looked back at the city, expecting to see half of it erupt into the sky. For an instant he thought his upturned face had been struck by a brick but it was only water, sheets of it as the heavens opened and the thunder rolled.

Rowing only four oars – the farmers for'ard, Big Tree and Henry aft, Sam steering – the gig crabbed out into the middle of the river and the tumultuous city seemed to dissolve away in the downpour. After half an hour Flynn and Robinson began to stir and the rowers paused long enough for the two seamen to take their places amidships; Bunce and Gabb sprawled in the wet slime that washed down into the bottom of the boat.

Sam could see nothing at all but guided by some sixth sense he headed blindly downstream. He didn't care to admit, even to himself, that he had been scared when running from the yellow devils and his heart still tripped from the effort. Never had he seen Canton in such a frantic state. The trouble was worse than the captains at Whampoa had feared. Not only had their own expedition proved to be a sorry disaster, but Sam himself had wasted an expensive gift. It was unlike the old dog to behave so discourteously and Sam could not understand why. He shivered as a chill cut through his sodden clothes. The rain was letting up, thank God. He moved the tiller a fraction to avoid the looming shadow of a sailing junk.

Steam rose from the heat of Henry's body as he slaved at the oar, wincing as the wooden shaft opened new blisters on palms grown unaccustomed to this kind of toil. His hair was plastered in rats' tails over his forehead, his clothes were heavy with water, his shoes had filled, but the exercise was a vent for his fury. It had all been so futile. What had Sam expected to achieve besides a lump of jade for his precious collection? He had failed even in that. The sky lightened as the thunderstorm rolled back, silhouetting the craft along the banks and other sails on the river; they looked like hayricks gliding magically through the darkness. Henry pondered what they should do now. Obviously no tea would be sent down through Canton for a long while, and there was no other source of it. He ground his teeth in helpless rage. If only he knew what the devil Screech Gander was up to.

As Sam reported he could see the pillar of the Great Halfway House Pagoda a couple of miles away Henry, facing aft as he pulled on his oar, realised the gig was being paced by two large craft crawling like dim shadows along the north bank. It was the sound he heard first: the creak of twenty or thirty oars in each vessel, their strokes not quite synchronised and carrying loudly across the water as a weird *tick-tock . . . tick-tock . . .*

Moments later the night sky behind Sam's shoulder was filled, as if by a vast vampire bat sweeping down to prey on the little gig: the mat-and-bamboo sails of a pair of junks that peeled out of a tributary. Henry watched them narrowly. Both vessels were silent but for the basket-like scratch and rasp of tattered sails vibrating in the breeze, the squeal of a rudder, the bubbles frothing from their low bows. Though he saw no movement on board, Henry's skin prickled at the sensation of being watched by scores of hostile eyes.

'Don't . . . look round . . . Sam,' he said between strokes. 'Go starboard . . . near the bank . . . D'you hear me, Oatsy?' Meadows' grunt echoed his own dread. 'Kick those . . . dead buggers . . . back to life . . . we need 'em.'

Sam peered over their heads at the shadows along the crowded banks. 'Easy all!'

With relief the men rested on their oars. Henry slid his blade inboard then hauled the bleary Gabb and Bunce on to the thwart and signalled Big Tree to go for'ard into the bow. For ten minutes they lay doggo, listening to the muttered conversations, children's cries, and domestic sounds within the barn-like junks towering above them. Suddenly there was an excited shout as the gig was spotted. Standing in the sternsheets for a better view, Henry growled to the men to give way. The gig glided away, keeping to the shadows. The tall pagoda was passed and none of the crew thought to ask for the traditional rum ration. Now came a relatively deserted stretch of river and they cracked on speed. Henry guided the gig close along the shore. They passed a duck boat, its gangways drawn up, and sped through a fleet of one-man canoes from which eels were being fished by lanternlight. There was no sign of the fast-sailing junks that had come upon them so suddenly and the haunting *tick-tock* of the more distant oared vessels disappeared. Henry had made up his mind that it was all a mistake of his jittery nerves when Big Tree suddenly turned and shouted in alarm. Too late. A rough hawser stretched tautly above the river took Henry under the chin. The gig shot from under his feet and with a loud splash he fell backwards into the water. A moment later the gig crashed into something solid which tore at its bottom. The men tumbled backwards, head over heels. For a moment Henry struggled in panic as strong twine entangled his legs and arms. Then he realised what had happened. He had steered the gig into a fishing trap.

The noise raised a buzz of chatter from the raft of junks a few yards away. Henry swam quietly after the gig, using breaststroke so as not to get a mouthful, and hauled himself over the gunwale. 'Next time you men want to get rid of me just ask and I'll go quietly,' he whispered and it raised a weak laugh. The men untangled themselves and poled the gig clear of the underwater stakes and nets. 'I figure those fellows must have been after somebody else, we seem to have lost them,' Henry said. 'All right, give way!'

Henry steered a wider course out into the river and after another mile was slowly regaining his confidence when it came again, the relentless *tick-tock* as, in each boat hidden against the far bank the oars were swung forward for the next stroke.

With dry mouth he squinted into the darkness astern and saw two large sailing junks converging. 'God almighty! How far is it to the anchorage, Sam?'

'A long way, lad. Several miles. Four or five.'

The eerie noise grew louder as two shadows detached themselves from the shore and angled towards them. The oared boats had high poops, with platforms jutting from their broad transoms. Their three masts, bare of sails, were tilted at the usual crazy angles. They might have been mandarin boats but Henry could make out the long rows of bamboo pikes jutting upright along their bulwarks. 'Smugglers,' Sam said, after a long scrutiny. 'The Chinks call 'em scrambling dragons, or smug boats. They run opium and other contraband into the creeks and inlets along the coast.'

'What are they doing here then?' Henry wondered aloud.

'We'll soon find out,' Sam replied.

The gig plugged onward down the centre of the river, sweat streaming down the faces of the anxious and fatigued seamen at its oars. The two sailing junks came directly up its wake until their spoon bows lay hardly a dozen yards astern. But they did not attack. In unison, their sails spilled the wind to slow down. Without a break in their stride the smug boats took up positions on either beam, thirty yards away, then their rhythm slowed to match the slower pace of the gig. 'If they're gonna do us, what are they waitin' for?' Meadows asked, echoing all their thoughts.

'It's a bleedin' escort, more likely,' Field said.

'I don't like the look o' them pikes.'

His heart hammering in his ribs, Henry ordered the men to stop rowing. The gig ghosted on, slowing. At once the tempo of the smug boats changed. The sailing junks split away to either side, spars rattling as their sheets were over-hauled to spill wind. The convoy stopped in the water, waiting. The gig rowed on and the shadowy junks gathered way again.

Riding lights gleamed in the darkness ahead and spidery lattices of ships' rigging grew taller in the sky. The gig ran swiftly along the line of slumbering vessels until the tall masts of their own *Quiver* were spotted. Field said, 'Blimey, them Chinks 'ave 'opped it.' It was true. The silent escort had vanished into the darkness.

Relieved to see the last of them, whoever they were, Henry put the tiller over and the gig lost way as it came up on the Jacob's ladder which Martin Peake and a couple of men dropped over the rail.

Aching with cold and weariness, Sam was first on the ladder. His head was just level with the deck when the shadow of a large sail gliding up to the opposite bulwark froze his blood. There was no time to shout a warning before the junk crashed into the *Quiver* with a force that shook every timber. In the flash of a cannon firing he saw a human tide swarm over the rail then it was concealed behind a wall of drifting smoke. The cannon fired again but it was Henry, stunned by the appalling horror of the spectacle confronting him as he swung inboard, who first realised the attack was not what it seemed.

The cannon were not firing into the ship but away from it. The boarders did not scream war cries but were completely silent. They were not even armed.

Big Tree was beginning his war dance when Henry stepped forward and quickly grabbed the arm wielding the vicious *patu*. As the smoke cleared a familiar figure wearing a fruit-basket hat was revealed standing still and erect in the centre of the deck.

Meadows and Field ran to calm down the rest of the crew who tumbled out of the fo'c's'le ready to fight for their lives. A bunch of Chin-ta's men leant over the taffrail hacking at the ropes by which the Revenue Inspector's junk and the mass of wash-boats and sew-sew sampans were attached, and they drifted away on the tide.

Henry quietened the thudding of his heart with an effort as Chin-ta bowed. 'So sollee, much trub. No makee die, no hurtee. Pliss, you wait.'

In the faint glow radiated by the riding light Henry saw a smug boat manoeuvring alongside. It made a neat job for once, the fifteen oars disappearing inboard a moment before it touched. At least sixty men crouched in the low waist made no move except to throw up ropes.

The poop of the smug boat, level with the *Quiver*'s main-deck, was stacked with coffins. In the space of two or three minutes these were manhandled over the side and laid in a row of twelve abaft the mainmast. The smug boat cast off and disappeared into the dark. Henry's breathless questions were stonewalled. 'Pliss, you wait.'

With fifty Chinese on the deck, armed or not, Henry and his men were in no position to argue.

When the second smug boat came alongside only one coffin was passed across and lowered with great delicacy to the clipper's deck. The boarders disappeared over the rail and the vessel fired a cannon to seaward as she moved away, leaving only Chin-ta and half a dozen of his henchmen.

Henry beckoned Meadows and Field who helped him lift the lid of one of the twelve coffins. Whatever it contained bore no resemblance to a corpse. A lantern was brought and Henry reached into the coffin. Hard, round, sharp-edged . . . something clinked at the touch of his nervous fingers. The coffin was filled with silver.

Weighing a handful of coins in his palm Henry turned on Chin-ta who muttered an order. Two of his men stooped over the last of the caskets to come aboard. It was more elaborate than the rest, with gold scroll-work on its corners and a rampant dragon adorning its lacquered lid. Inside lay a thin body couched on silk pillows. Chin-ta marched forward and extended a hand. The occupant of the coffin grasped the hand and pulled himself upright then stepped out on small, black-slippered feet.

'I chin-chin you, werry fine day,' beamed Fowqua. He bowed before Sam and offered with both hands a package he had withdrawn from the folds of his robe. Then he kow-towed to Henry. 'Werry excellent three-piecy bamboo, captain, but more better we makee go chop-chop fashion, savvy?'

The captain of the *Quiver* breathed deeply refreshing draughts of clean salt air. A pearly dawn light bathed the white-sailed clipper as she ghosted seawards over smooth water on wings so limp it seemed that nothing but the smell of the ocean could be drawing her forward. Glancing up at the flag sails Henry saw two sides of red meat dangling from the fore-topgallant yard. 'You can take a reef in the buffalo-beef, Mr Lamshire,' he said sarcastically, and the shame-faced mate hurried for'ard to deal with it.

The land breeze and a favourable tide had wafted the ship out of Whampoa Anchorage and down the river into the gorge, Fowqua's pilot ensuring they did not run their keel up on a shoal. The forts in The Bogue showed no sign of alarm though the ship passed without stopping to present the necessary chops to prove she had official clearance. Fowqua himself had remained in Henry's day cabin drinking tea.

There was still no sign of the *Musket* and he was on the point of replacing the telescope in its rack by the binnacle when his eye was caught by war junks gliding like floating fortresses from behind an island.

Here was a sight to ruffle an imperial feather or two, Henry thought grimly. Six war junks were closing on the *Quiver*, three on each bow. The white ports painted along their black sides suggested heavy armament. Rows of tall bamboo pikes stood erect along their bulwarks and shields of woven cane were hung in Viking style over their gunwales. Burning papers fluttered in their wake as the Gods were solicited for their blessings on the enterprise. A plume of smoke burst from the poop of the nearest junk and moments later a fusillade of firecrackers carried over the water.

The trap was sprung and the *Quiver* was helpless. What could she fight with? A revolver, an axe, a greenstone *patu* and a number of iron belaying pins? A ripple of fear spread through the ship. 'Blimey, now we're in a clinch.' Meadows muttered. He put his head into the galley where the cook was preparing dumplings. 'Put yer water on the boil, Nix, maybe we can scald a few yeller heads before they cut us in little pieces.'

Chin-ta's expression registered neither surprise nor anxiety when Henry indicated the advancing threat with a tilt of his chin. Sam came on deck, chewing on a mouthful of breakfast, and advised him to hold his course.

The sun dried up the mist and brought a small breeze. The watch hauled on the braces and cranked the yards round to make the most of it. The clipper began to stride out but the lumbering junks made no move to harden in their sails and head her off. Only when they converged on the clipper's wake, half a mile astern, did Henry realise the gun ports were fakes. Their only armament was half a dozen puny cannon that the leading junk fired in an erratic broadside toward a distant island, the grey smoke and muffled bangs characteristic of low-grade powder. 'Let's have some fun with them,' Sam suggested. 'Back your main and see what happens.'

'I know what will happen, the devils will board us.'

'I don't think so. Try it and see.'

The yards on the mainmast swung round to counter the wind's effort on the other two masts and the *Quiver* braked to a gentle halt. At once the pursuing junks let fly their sails to avoid catching up. Laughing, Henry got the ship sailing again and the war squadron soon dropped astern.

'As I thought, Fowqua is covering himself,' Sam explained. 'Those are probably his own junks and they rushed out to put up a fight to satisfy the mandarins ashore, just as our own escape from the anchorage was dressed up to look like an attack. I told you he was a cunning old bird.'

The last piece of the Chinese puzzle that had tortured Henry's confused brain through the long night at last dropped into place. With rebels hammering down the gates of Canton Fowqua had been forced to flee with his silver and his treasures. It was treason to smuggle undeclared objects out of the city, whatever their value, so he had avoided paying massive bribes by cooking up this enterprise using his chin-chin friend and the *Quiver*.

Half the coffins in Fowqua's baggage were filled with his most precious jade and porcelain pieces, the rest with 'sycee' silver. When Spanish silver dollars first landed in China they were smoothly minted and fit for circulation, but no merchant or accountant would exchange a dollar unless his own brand was upon it, so in every transaction it was stamped with an iron brand which quickly flattened it to such a degree that when half a dollar or less was required a piece was simply broken off. Because money deteriorated with use, commercial deals were settled by weight. When the money became too battered to handle it was melted into convenient ingots and adulterated with other metals. Called 'sycee' silver it was smuggled out of Canton for the purchase of opium from Outer Babarian merchants.

The sun warmed quickly as it climbed and Henry rolled back his sleeves. 'I'd like to see old Tidewater's face when he sees we've disappeared,' he said with relish. 'What will the rest of them do, Sam?'

'Sit it out, I expect, what else can they do?'

'Until hell freezes over or they die of old age? There's no tea in Canton.'

'Not exactly true, lad. There's always a bit here and there though it would fill only a ship or two and that's what they're hoping for. Or maybe the tea shipments from inland will start getting through, nobody knows.'

'Christ, why didn't Fowqua say so when you were asking him yesterday?'

'He wouldn't, would he, when he saw a way of getting himself out with all his valuables? We have to land him in a bay on an island near Lintin then he wants us to cross over to Hong Kong.'

'And what are we supposed to do there?'

'Just wait – and light joss sticks if you think it will help.'

'Ha!' Henry thrust his hands deeply into his pockets and took an angry turn round the deck. 'How would he expect to find us a tea cargo in Hong Kong, for God's sake? And we daren't show up in Whampoa. The Grand Hoppo would have our bollocks for mah-jong tiles even if the washee-washee girls didn't slit our throats – we didn't settle up with them.'

'You don't have to go back to Whampoa to get your throat cut,' Sam said, gazing warily at the junks dotted around the horizon. 'The Royal Navy's paid head money on pirates for years, twenty pounds a chop, but they keep on thriving and you can see why.'

The bare hummocky islands on every side offered a thousand inlets, bays and secret harbours where whole fleets could hide. Similar rugged terrain extended for hundreds of miles in both directions along the China coast.

Henry was confident the *Quiver* would out-run anything afloat as long as the wind held, but it wouldn't do to hit something. The navigation charts were sketchy to say the least. Henry gave orders to double the look-outs. Then, to the astonishment of Chin-ta's men who squatted on the coffins playing cards, he shouted for Big Tree, stripped off, and took his usual shower of sea-water.

For'ard, Will Lamshire supervised the cleaning out of the gig, then it was turned upside down and the farmers brought their

tools to replace a plank splintered in the press of boats at
Canton. Manfred Longhandle, the crumpled bowler hat filled
with sail-needles and heavy thread, patched an awning that
had been ripped in the haste of getting it down during the
night. Ruefully thinking of the uncollected emerald green
waistcoat he had ordered to match his red one, Martin Peake
had a party of men scrubbing the Whampoa mud off the
anchor; Flynn and Gabb nursed aching heads and averted their
faces from the nauseous gases emanating from the mud as they
worked. Aloft, two men on each mast threw the lashings off
the royals and the watch hoisted the yards. The *Quiver*
responded to the added power, her lean bow tossing up a
bouquet of spray.

Sam joyfully showed Henry the present Fowqua had
brought, a rampant dragon, twelve inches long, in jade as
green and translucent as a coral lagoon. 'Well, I hope he
remembers he owes the master of this ship a favour, too,'
Henry said sourly.

The harbour to which Chin-ta piloted the clipper was not
marked on the chart but was called Yat-moon. It lay on the
south-east shore of a deeply indented and high island twenty
miles short of Hong Kong and offered good shelter. Like the
harbour at Hong Kong, the anchorage was a channel only two
or three cables wide between a rocky crag and the crooked
shore of the larger island. The reason Fowqua had chosen it
was plain: the harbour offered two entrances, two escape
routes.

The high island was fringed with white sand and black
rocks. Its steep grassy slopes were dotted with white-painted
graves and mausoleums. A nine-storey pagoda with a neighbouring tile-roofed joss house occupied a dominating hilltop
at the end of a winding trail of bare clay. But Henry had no eyes
for the scenery as he conned the ship into the harbour. Young
China-tea, as Meadows dubbed Fowqua's son and captain,
might well be correct when he claimed there was plenty of
depth but you never could tell, and the clipper drew three or
four times more than any junk. Charlie Field sounded with the
lead as the ship crept in towards the land, only her topsails
spread to the brisk noon-day breeze.

After three-quarters of a mile a dense barricade of junks
blocking the passage came into view. Henry swept them
worriedly in the glass, seeing figures running and waving their
arms in alarm as the big ship glided in. 'No worry, all-o same

flend,' Chin-ta said and made an imperious gesture to one
of his men who removed his tunic and hung it in the fore-
rigging as a recognition signal.

'By the mark, six!' Field called, coiling the lead-line in his
hands ready for the next throw.

Thirty-six feet, little enough for a ship eighteen feet deep in
the water. 'Stand by!' Henry warned.

'And a half, four!' came the next report.

'Let go!' Lamshire flicked the toggle of the slip-rope. The
iron anchor dropped with a mighty splash, dragging fathoms
of thundering chain after it.

'Let fly your sheets! Clew up topsails! Down the jibs! Up and
furl, smartly now!'

As the ship rounded up to her anchor and the rippling sails
diminished into slender bundles lashed down on the spars, a
horde of sampans raced down on her. Chin-ta leapt on the rail
and silenced the jabbering occupants with a shrill command.
Reluctantly the sampans parted to let a larger craft approach.
Fowqua came on deck, stiff-backed and cool. On seeing Henry
he joined his hands and raised them to his brow. 'These all my
fleet, you like?' he asked.

'Number-one-chop fleet,' Henry agreed with a grin and
Fowqua inclined his head in the fractional way that was as
near as he ever came to an open smile.

The farewells seemed to take for ever. Henry, looking
distractedly at the pretty hillside bathed in sunshine, saw the
pagoda on the summit and wondered what the view would be
like from the top. His feet had not touched green grass since his
brief walk a lifetime ago across Greenwich Park to visit Mrs
Plunkett. Suddenly he itched to take some exercise. Sam was
handling the transfer of treasure-caskets with Chin-ta and
there was nothing for Henry to do. He beckoned a sampan and
was sculled ashore. Only when he had climbed the first couple
of hundred yards and paused to look back, his thigh and calf
muscles already protesting, did he see a second sampan touch
the beach where he had landed and Big Tree came ashore.

Henry did not wait but climbed steadily up the steep hill.
The path twisted between clusters of stone houses from which
startled people peered out and dogs barked. He passed the
tombs he had spotted from the sea, always placed in the most
beautiful spots, shaded by pines or junipers and neatly kept but
for the long, untidy strands of paper flapping round them.
Butterflies and insects fluttered round his head. The mellow

whirring of the crickets, the dusty smell of the grass and the fierce sun hitting the back of his neck reminded him of home in New South Wales.

As he climbed higher Henry had a bird's-eye view of Fowqua's fleet, at least a hundred strong. The *Quiver* with her green hull and white spars lay surrounded by the small craft like a grasshopper among beetles and had evidently already relinquished her valuable cargo. Henry plodded on, hearing Big Tree panting behind him.

After forty minutes Henry came up to the magnificent pagoda stretching tall above him, its nine levels of curling eaves fluting quietly in the wind. Thick creepers festooned its lower levels and when he pushed into the dim interior there was a quick rustle as snakes and lizards darted for cover beneath the dry leaves. Stamping heavily and watching his step, Henry walked to the centre of the floor and looked up. To his surprise the whole edifice was hollow: he could see through skeins of cobwebs all the way to the top where swifts and swallows jabbered in scores of tiny nests. Big Tree was waiting when Henry stepped blinking into the sunlight, sitting on the grass a few yards distant as if respecting his captain's privacy.

Henry said nothing but inspected the joss house, a small and low-roofed chapel where burnt-out candles, paper ashes and the remains of joss sticks lay on a hearth beneath a vividly coloured figure that looked to Henry more like a demon than a god. He followed the track over the crest of the ridge and overlooked a breathtaking view of the islands spread out on the ruffled satin of the sea like pieces of a jigsaw puzzle. Twenty miles off lay the distinctive peak of Hong Kong. Nearer, almost at his feet and on the same island, another fleet of junks milled in a wide bay. Henry blinked, at first not believing his own eyes.

The junks were swarming around a ship, a lofty vessel similar to *Quiver* but black with golden, white-capped masts and spars. Incredulously Henry saw a puff of smoke rise from a junk bearing down on her. Good God! It was the *Musket* at anchor in the remote bay, and Screech Gander was under attack.

Henry did not follow the zig-zag path but slithered and slid by the direct route. Big Tree, after a startled look at the Yankee ship, soon overtook him. Henry saw him reach the shore. The waiting sampan backed off in alarm at his wild approach but Big Tree leapt into the water and grabbed the sampan's bow which he held ready as Henry piled aboard, his legs torn raw by flints and brambles.

From a hundred yards away Henry waved his shirt and shouted to attract the *Quiver*'s attention. When he saw Sam gaping at him over the rail he yelled at him to get the anchor up.

Fowqua had left but Chin-ta was still on board with his men and Henry bundled him off without ceremony as the capstan clanked round and the chain inched inboard. The moment it was up and down he bellowed for the topsails to be let fall and sheeted home, jibs and staysails run up. The breeze was coming directly into the bay but Henry, handling his ship prettily, worked her clear.

It was well over an hour since he had started down from the peak, and he judged it would take at least as long again to sail around the island to where the *Musket* lay. There was no time to feel relief at locating his rival after weeks of uncertainty. His one aim was to help the Yankee drive off the pirates. Not a white man afloat, no matter how black his heart, deserved to wriggle on the end of a yellow devil's pike.

But the *Quiver* was no frigate. She did not have a cannon to her name. 'We've just two things on our side, boldness and surprise,' Henry told Sam and the mates at a hasty conference around the binnacle. 'Range on deck anything you can throw, fire, bang or spill. Arm the Macaroons with marline spikes and belaying pins. One pair of knuckles comes over the rail, smash it. The Murphies will stand by sheets and braces for some swift manoeuvring. We have to hope the *Musket* will hold 'em off until we get there.'

As the *Quiver* creamed round the point, furling her royals so she sailed under topsails and topgallants alone, Henry trained his glass on the *Musket* and stared till his eyes watered. The Yankee clipper was hemmed in by rafts of small junks and sampans. Knots of men were attempting to storm her decks but the crew seemed to be succeeding in holding them off, though for how much longer would be anybody's guess. Her anchor was off the bottom, its cable vertical, and with the boats massing round her she was slowly drifting seawards.

Henry trimmed his yards hard up and with a dangerously lifting luff — the ship on the point of being taken aback — drove into the bay as close to the wind as he dared. More cannon-fire was heard and smoke drifted over the *Musket* but the sound was more a series of pops than a roar. When the Yankee ship lay broad on the bow Henry ordered Adam Robinson to put the wheel over. The *Quiver* surged inshore of the *Musket* and drove directly for the sampans packing round her.

The farmers had stuffed into half a dozen casks the gunpowder left on board by their California-bound gold-diggers. On Henry's signal they lit the short fuses, hammered down the lids, and dropped them over the stern.

Big Tree ran to the for'ard end of the bowsprit and stood erect, pulling awful faces, beating his chest and hollering. The *patu* was shoved ready in the belt at his back.

At sight of the green ship bearing down like a gigantic, white-winged battle-axe, the sampans scattered. Not quickly enough. The first thumped into the bow and rolled over and over, tossing its screaming occupants into the sea. Another was smashed beneath the forefoot. The first of the small barrels exploded, followed by the others in succession, creating a satisfactory blast of smoke and noise which added to the mayhem but hurt nobody except a lot of fish that floated belly-up to the surface.

The splintered sampans dragging along the ship's side made her stagger and Henry took a suddenly fearful look at the masts but the Murphies were ready and at Lamshire's bark the sheets were eased to spill wind and relieve the strain. Nix Barlow, ready at the starboard fore-shrouds with an iron vat, dipped his beaker and tossed scalding water at any face that came near enough; the feathers of steam gave an impression of smoke.

In a few moments the *Quiver* broke free and gathered way. Robinson put the wheel hard over once more and the ship, turning sharply downwind with her yards hastily squared round, headed close across the *Musket*'s bow. Junks and sampans fled in all directions and not one was left at the black ship's side. Her men were running aloft to let fall the sails and the anchor was coming in. The display of bravado had done the job. Henry inspected the American narrowly as he swept by. He saw the tall figure of her captain at the poop rail, rapping out orders. Her main hatch was open. Sam pointed to wooden chests littering her deck. 'You know what that is, lad?'

'Doesn't look like tea, that's certain.'

'It's opium.'

Henry did not want to leave the *Musket* too quickly in case she was attacked again. If her cargo was opium the raiders might not give up so easily. The main was backed and the

Quiver hove to a cable distant. Big Tree's loud cry caught the farmers' attention. The Maori was pointing to something under the bowsprit. They ran to the fo'c's'le head and peered over the rail. A wounded white man clinging to a piece of timber lay in the water. Blood flowed from a wound in his chest, the lips were blue in a white face, and he was on the point of letting go. Big Tree jumped into the sea, grabbed the rope that Meadows lowered, and looped it under the man's shoulders. As soon as the Maori was on board the farmers carried the injured man aft. Henry recognised the crescent-shaped bite in his ear at once. 'That's Albert Evans, he must have fallen overboard when the chinks got him. Put him in the saloon where Withers can look after him.'

The two ships sailed slowly in company out of the bay. It seemed to Henry that few of the *Musket*'s men, if any, had been seriously hurt. The vessel herself was undamaged but for splintered rails and marks along the hull where sampans had rubbed, and her crew was busy tidying the disorder of her decks. As Gander looked across at him Henry jabbed a finger in the direction of Hong Kong. The rangy captain made a motion of touching the brim of an imaginary hat then nodded agreement. As the sun dropped behind monsoon clouds boiling low in the south-west, the tracks of the twin ships moved apart but continued on a generally parallel course into the grey twilight.

'How's our patient?' Henry asked when Sam came on deck with the look of a man wanting to sleep for a year. Seeing a ship through a hard night was part of a master's life but running from crazed rebels, being hunted by mysterious junks and doing battle with pirates was foreign even to Sam's long experience. His eyes were glazed with tension.

Sam shook his head numbly. 'I don't think he's long for this world, he's got it bad in the stomach.'

Henry, too, ached to the marrow as he stumbled down the companion-way. Evans was wrapped in a blanket beneath the swaying lamp in the saloon. For some reason Henry was surprised he did not still have his impressive black eye. In the six months since he had last seen the Liverpool seaman the reddish hair had greyed and the puffy face become thin and lined; had it not been for the ear, Henry doubted he would have recognised him. Evans gave a weak smile and spoke faintly. 'I should-a jumped when you did,' he said. 'Trouble is, I can't swim.'

'What happened, Bert? You were swimming well enough when we picked you up.'

'One o' them yellow bastards sent a monkey up the side. It had a bomb tied to its tail. Ran up the rigging right in front of me and blew my goots away . . . Hurts like bloody 'ell.'

Withers leaned over and gave him a sip of tea. 'Can you talk?' Henry asked gently. 'We'll have you in Hong Kong before dawn, don't worry, but I'd like to know what game our friend the Blue Nose thought he was playing.'

'Opium, of course,' Evans said. 'We went to Hong Kong first to pick up some American gent called Clark and he piloted us to the island where the bastards got us.'

'What was your next move going to be?' Henry pressed. 'There's no tea in Canton. What is Gander's plan?'

Evans coughed and Henry hated himself. 'The devil has found some, I can tell you. He's heading up to Foo-chow-foo. They're bringing it down the Min River for him. He'll load there and go off home.' Evans groaned and pressed his hands to his stomach. 'Christ, I'll be glad to see the back of him, the slave-driving, man-killing bastard.'

Henry went on deck. 'Ever hear of an American called Clark?'

'Certainly, one of the top men in Russell and Co, the American agency,' Sam replied. 'He's the one supposed to be sick from varnish fumes.'

As his eyes accustomed themselves to the darkness Henry automatically scanned the set of the sails, the horizon, and checked the course. 'Tell the watch to keep their peepers open for any unlit junk that might get under our bow, Mr Lamshire,' he called.

'Aye aye!'

Foo-chow-foo! Henry paced up and down the deck in the darkness, whistling softly. He knew it was one of the Treaty Ports, and it lay four or five hundred miles northward up the coast. Though opened ten years before it had never been developed as a gateway for commerce, like Shanghai, Amoy and the others.

The *Quiver* carried no charts of the approaches to the place; probably none existed. She had no contacts there and the Americans would be hostile. But worse still, the port lay down-wind. The ship could reach it in a couple of days but it would be a long and arduous struggle to get back, beating into the teeth of the monsoon.

Withers brought the dinner on deck because the saloon was occupied by the sick man. Henry sat on the seat that formed part of the skylight frame and ate stew and potatoes off his knees while gazing at the distant form of the *Musket*, now barely visible in the faintly luminous haze that veiled the dark sky.

He ate in silence, pondering. Then Withers brought coffee, and with it the news that Henry had not dared to let himself hope for. 'I'm afraid Evans has just died, Captain.'

Henry could have hugged him but he kept his face straight. 'That's a pity, get Longhandle to help you wrap him up.'

'Aye, Cap'n.'

As Withers went below Henry strode to the poop rail and bellowed for Meadows and Field. Sam and the mates joined him wonderingly at the binnacle. 'The ship's a mess, it's time we slapped some paint around,' he said.

Lamshire looked dumbfounded. 'Give us a chance,' he bleated but Henry cut him short.

'No criticism, Mister, just plain fact,' he said. 'I want her painted from stem to stern and you've got two days and two nights to do it, no more. You can get the watch started on it right away . . .'

Henry paused to squint at where he last saw the *Musket* but she was invisible in the dark. 'Now listen carefully. We're cutting away to the south. Brace up hard, kill the lights, and keep an eye on the sky because I don't want the moon leaping out from behind a cloud so Screech Gander sees us crossing his wake.'

Mystified, the mates acknowledged curtly but as they turned away Henry stopped them. 'One more thing. I want to change the colour of the hull. Let's see how she looks black, and we'll give her a red stripe.'

Two days and nights of balling off the knots, barrelling up the China coast with the south-west monsoon on the tail, were as good as a tonic. With the crew slapping it on, almost as much black paint as spray had flown through the air. The sea was too violent for men to hang over the side on platforms so a variety of long-handled paintbrushes had been contrived from brooms and oars. As a paint job it was far from satisfactory to the eagle eyes of the mates but it did the trick. The clipper was transformed.

The *Quiver*'s cherubic figurehead with his drawn bow and

arrow was stowed away and replaced by a carved eagle's head painted yellow. The American flag which the sailmaker made up from a red table cloth, a blue shirt and a white sheet, whipped from the gaff. 'And what about the masts and spars, don't tell me you're going to rub them down to the wood, it will take years?' Sam demanded. He was dubious about the adventure and wanted to wait in Hong Kong as Fowqua had advised.

'The Chinks won't know the difference,' Henry said. 'They're expecting a black ship called the *Musket* flying the stars and bars, and that's what they're going to see.'

'It's a hell of a risk, you don't know what you're getting into.'

'But I do,' Henry insisted. 'Screech Gander ran his opium into the island where he was attacked. Now he will finish his business in Hong Kong then run up to Foo-chow to collect his tea. We're going to do him a favour and save him the trouble, all simple and straight-forward.'

'What about the Russell men, you won't find the Yankees as easily gulled as the Chinese, unless . . . ?' Sam's troubled face clouded. 'Don't tell me you're planning to dress up in a buckskin jacket! Where will you find a dog?'

'Listen, you old fool, Screech Gander's got the agency men on board with him.' Sam had not been called a fool in forty years and Henry contritely hurried to head off an eruption for he knew he could ill afford to alienate the old man. 'Listen, you're missing the point, Sam. I know we're taking a hell of a risk but a long shot is better than no shot. What chance was there of picking up a freight swinging round our hook in Whampoa?'

But Henry felt rather less confident when dawn broke on their third morning at sea. Flying clouds sagged heavily over the reeling masts. The odd drop of rain flew in the wind and the wet decks gleamed blackly in the grey light. Boiling seas raced up astern and hurled the ship forward in a series of violent thrusts. Henry grabbed the binnacle for balance as the sea bunched its fist under the rudder and punched her down the steep slope. He blinked stinging salt out of his eyes and peered at the bulwark coast off to port, endless rounded hills shooting up to lofty coxcombs of bare and jagged rock. With every inlet and haphazard island a hiding place, every fisherman and trading junk a part-time pirate, this was no place to take a wrong turning. But according to the sketchy information on their pathetically inadequate chart the cut of the land at least looked right. 'What do you think, Sam?' Henry asked.

'You're the captain, my lad,' Sam answered unhelpfully. Then he took a grip on himself. He couldn't sulk for ever. 'Aye, if you turn in now, north by half-west, you might hit the White Dogs on the nose.'

The helm was put down, the yards squared, and the clipper ran fast through waves as grey and steep as the chops of the Channel straight for the unknown shore.

Somewhere beyond the thrusting bowsprit, cradled deep within the rain-hazed ridges and valleys far inland, lay the city of Foo-chow-foo, capital of Fukien Province. For centuries the major part of the Celestial Empire's tea crop had been cultivated on the terraced hills of the rugged Fukien interior. This season's first soft, spring buds of tea bushes would already have been plucked by tens of thousands of lightning fingers and suffered the long process of heating, fermenting and tatching. This 'pekoe' crop, most delicate and fragrant of the season's four pickings, was manufactured with unremitting manual labour. Every individual leaf of the millions upon countless millions of leaves was curled by the rubbing action of human palms, not once but many times as its flesh was crushed to release its tangy juices.

In the forcing climate of the Wu-ee hills (the name corrupted in English to Bohea), where a bamboo shoot would grow eighteen inches in a day, the tea bush recovered quickly from the first pick and sent out new shoots. These tender open buds had also been plucked and the 'souchong' tea was cured in a similar way. In ordinary years the chests of highly valued pekoe and souchong teas were transported over six hundred miles of tortuous mountain trails and rice-plain tracks to the Provincial City, Canton. There it was tasted by skilled expectorators, selected by Foreign Devil merchants, and packed in catties of one and a third pounds weight, one hundred catties to a chest. From the Canton godowns it was despatched by chop boats to the clippers and Indiamen waiting at Whampoa. But this was no ordinary year. The country was in ferment and the American merchants had cunningly contrived to bypass entirely the long trail to Canton and the squeegee of the countless mandarins.

They had found that the three rivers winding through the Bohea Hills merged above the city of Foo-chow-foo then spilled into a broad estuary affording a perfect anchorage for tea clippers. Instead of spending five weeks on the trail, the tea could be barged down in three days. It was a bold and breathtakingly simple plan that Henry and Sam had deduced after giving poor Evans a decent burial. There was only one overwhelming obstacle.

Where on this uncharted and pirate-infested rim of the infernal Celestial Kingdom was Foo-chow-foo?

Forecourse and main were already furled on their great yards but the ship's headlong dash towards the lee shore had to be slowed. 'Get the royals off her, Mr Peake,' Henry growled.

'Aye captain.'

Henry swept the shoreline with the glass and saw high surf smashing white on the rocks. 'We'll run off to the north-east, there's no river here deep enough to fill our boots,' he told Sam.

'Maybe round the next headland.'

'Let's hope.'

But no great dip in the skyline of eroded rock suggested the presence of an estuary when the clipper weathered an out-thrust sand-coloured rock and entered a wide bay. Martin Peake, stationed in the foretop to spot reefs or shoals ahead, reported a number of small islands standing out from the shore. 'With any luck those will be the so-called Dogs,' Sam said, squinting at the chart.

'We'll head in for a look-see,' Henry agreed.

The next hail from the foretop struck a chill in his heart. 'Captain . . . ! Fleet of small junks between the islands, fifty or a hundred of 'em.'

Sam took one look at the mass of junks lying athwart the wind. They bobbed over the waves like a flock of petrels after a feed. 'Let's get out of here, they're pirates for certain.'

Henry dismissed Sam's pleading glance with a curt order. 'Steady as she goes. If you ask me, this is the reception committee.'

In the lee of the headland the waves were calmer and the clipper ran on swiftly. Clearly not planning an attack the junks were spaced out in a ragged line that curved towards a lane of dark-coloured water. On either side of this channel the waves rolled in white smothers, but if it was indeed the outlet of a sizeable river, where was the break in the rugged skyline to indicate its track through the gaunt hills?

With the nearest junk barely half a mile away, a gang of blue-clad figures heaving on the sheets to trim its patched sail, Henry felt cold fingers of apprehension walk up his backbone.

He sensed the anxious glances of the crew gathered on the maindeck. Perhaps they were right and the ship was sailing straight into a trap. Then Henry recalled the signal Chin-ta had hoisted to indicate his friendly intentions towards Fowqua's junk fleet. He wriggled out of his jacket and tossed it over the poop rail to Flynn. 'Peg it in the fore-rigging where the Chinks can see it – quick!'

The men in the junk waved as the navy-blue serge coat fluttered in the wind. 'Heave to and get the topgallants off her, Mr Lamshire. Flake out some chain in case we need the anchor. Seems like we're going to have visitors.'

The first man to climb up the Jacob's ladder was tall for a Chinese but despite his youth looked every inch a man of decision and action. He wore a baggy suit of black, the silk cuffs and collar richly embossed with red, green and gold. His queue was tied with a leather thong and he carried on his wide gold belt, fixed with an ornate jade clasp, a dirk with a jewel-encrusted handle. The cool eyes which took in the deck and the curiously watching crew with a single glance did not slant up at the corners but down, and when he met the man's stare Henry was uncomfortably reminded of Nightingale. 'I bling gleeting, Captain Gander,' the man said and made a fractional bow which Henry returned in an equally perfunctory way. 'Pliss, makee sail die. We must wait for tide.'

The anchor splashed down and the watch sprang to furl topsails and lower the jibs. More Chinese clambered over the rail and half a dozen wooden crates were passed up from the junk and piled on deck. They were filled with plump black hens, a gift for the captain.

'Think quickly, Sam, we don't have a present to give in return,' Henry said out of the corner of his mouth.

But Sam, forewarned by the crates coming on board and familiar with the protocol, presented the mercury barometer that Henry had inherited from Captain Plunkett and which, through the voyage, had occupied a pride of place in his sleeping cabin. Henry peevishly concealed his anger which grew when he saw the visitor was not greatly impressed, though he knew what the instrument was. 'Velly fine plum-letter,' he muttered in a dissatisfied tone.

His name, the visitor explained grumpily, was A-tung, number one son of the most honourable Fowqua. He was glad to see the Flowery Flag ship arrive so quickly: they had only just moved into position to welcome her and were anticipating a wait of several days. All the necessary chops were arranged. As number-one-chop mandarin of the Min River, it was A-tung himself whose duty was to patrol the river and ensure compliance with the Imperial Viceroy's regulations, so there would be no difficulty with the formalities.

After a tense wait through the heat of the day the young mandarin at last indicated that the anchor could be weighed. The tide was on the turn and the ship could begin her approach to the coast. Henry had spent many minutes astride the fore-topgallant yard, scrutinising the route. Steep-sided islands clothed in scrub and creepers were surrounded by the pale and milky green of sands nearly uncovered by the tide. Like a river of dark jade, the deep channel snaked towards a wall of thousand-foot peaks with no evident opening.

Carrying the last of the sea breeze, the disguised *Quiver* cut cleanly through the bottle-green water, passing one black-hulled junk after another. There was consternation when Will Lamshire spotted a barrier blocking the fairway but it proved to be a line of rocks, every one under-cut by wave action to resemble a mushroom five or six feet high. It seemed there was no way through but A-tung blandly ignored Henry's protests. 'This is the reckoning, lad,' Sam said. 'We turn now or go all the way, you've got thirty seconds to make up your mind.'

Henry braced his shoulders and clamped his mouth shut. Charlie Meadows, standing in the bow and coiling the lead-line for another cast as the sandy bottom rose to meet the keel, cracked over his shoulder: 'Would all the lay-dies and gents please be up-standin' till we've passed the shallow bit . . .' All on board held their breaths as the ship sneaked through a gap with only yards to spare and the leadline measured a depth of barely a fathom and a half under her keel.

A gentle current carried the ship across a mirror-smooth pool and the flaring light of the setting sun revealed a narrow tongue twisting between steep rocky escarpments. From this gap, as if emerging from a cave, beetled a mass of small river craft rowed by six or eight oars apiece and covered amidships with a curved roof. They formed a ragged line ahead of the ship. A-tung told Henry, 'Pliss, make lopes for pull-pull.'

Startled because he had expected to anchor until daylight, Henry began to argue but his resistance soon collapsed. He had committed the ship to this madcap enterprise so there was no point in trying to do it by halves. He cast an anxious look at the wall of rock ahead. A small gunboat with a full head of steam might have poked her nose in, but a full-rigged sailing ship, and at night . . . !

Not one but five warps were passed over the bow to the waiting boats which arranged themselves in groups of four. Sails were furled. A-tung indicated with sign language that the yards should be braced sharp up to bring them nearly parallel with the ship's centre-line so they did not overhang the bulwarks. Could the river really be so narrow? Henry tugged at the scar tissue on the rim of his ear. Sam Handyside's accusing looks as he paced nervously across the deck were sending him mad. 'I've got a job to keep you busy, Sam,' he said. 'Will you take the farmers and a couple of lanterns and go ahead in the gig to make soundings? God knows what we're going to find around the corner.'

The smooth water was a tea-tray lacquered with reflections of the brooding rock-faces. At an order from A-tung the towing warps tautened. Shrill cries echoed from boat to boat as if a cliff-face of nesting seabirds were settling in for the night. Two hundred oars bit the shining water, every blade leaving a shimmering eddy. Then another. As interlocking ripples spread between the boats there was a weird sound, like the sighing of a great wind. Only when the ship had overcome her inertia and was gliding easily forward did Henry make sense of it. The noise was the concerted grunting of men hauling on their sweeps.

Henry climbed twenty feet up the starboard mizzen shrouds from where he could overlook the entire deck and see the towing boats for'ard, yet remain close to the poop. It was an eerie scene. First the white speck of the gig was swallowed between the buttresses of rock, then the towing boats. As the ship crept into the opening the illusion of narrowness was overwhelming. The pale twilight sky narrowed to a thin strip high above the royal yards. The rock walls shaving close along the bulwarks seemed near enough to touch in the darkness, though in reality the gap might have been measured in yards rather than feet. There was no sign of life, no sound but the water gulping along the shore and the grunts of the men slaving at the sweeps. From the gig's distant lantern a yellow worm lay on the river's slick surface, ridged and furrowed where large eddies were thrown up by water swirling over the rocky bottom.

After scarcely half a mile the gorge turned a right angle to the left which explained why it had been so completely concealed from seaward. Thereafter, it ran straight. In two places it narrowed to less than three cables – three-tenths of a mile – but in pitch darkness with sheer cliffs rising five hundred feet on either side, and a higher range of peaks beyond, the canyon seemed no wider than a mountain stream.

A-tung distrustfully eyed the eddies swirling in patterns like giant black cobblestones. 'Chow-chow water, vellee bad,' he said. After thirty minutes of strenuous efforts by the men on the sweeps the ship broke into a wider section of river where the current was less fierce and they made swifter progress. Lights glimmered along the banks and there were sounds of village life. Dogs barked, children laughed, people exclaimed at the silhouetted masts and spars of the lofty ship gliding across the starry sky.

Again the river narrowed but here the channel was speckled with rocks round which the current swirled. This was the end of the road, Henry thought. Not five hundred galleys could tow a large ship against such a torrent. Even Sam was in trouble. The lantern in the gig cast its glow over half a dozen bare-legged figures wading knee-deep in the shallows, pushing the boat ahead of them. But if they were unable to row against the current, why wasn't Sam dropping down the river to warn him off?

Unruffled, A-tung shouted his orders. Half the towing boats headed into the bank. Their warps were passed ashore to gangs of men who bent them to other ropes that divided into numerous bridles, each held by one man. To martial commands the men looped the bridles round their foreheads, bent forward with feet and hands locked on the ground, and took the strain. The rest of the boats passed their warps to the other bank where another regiment of coolies took up their bridles. At a single barked command two hundred pairs of feet stamped the bare earth of the towpaths cut like ledges into either bank. Dust lifted in the light of glowing lanterns and the ship moved slowly ahead. Though she made hardly half a knot over the ground the bow-wave creaming around her cut-water suggested a speed through the water of at least three knots.

Dawn revealed the ship under tow of the boats once more and creeping slowly up a wide stretch of river between bold hills clothed in small pines. To Sam, tracking back and forth in the gig with the sounding lead as he sketched rough maps, with grey mists rising off the river and wafting through the trees, the landscape bore a marked resemblance to the Clyde. In the ship, long strings of clear droplets adorned every strand of rigging and the gentlest touch brought a shower of chill diamonds. Moisture gathered in Henry's lank hair and in the stubble on his chin. He yawned and stretched his stiff legs. Worst thing about being a shipmaster, he had discovered, was the standing. All day and all night, for ever, the captain did nothing but stand on his poop and look important. But what a small penalty to pay for the sheer exhilaration of a morning like this, the morning sun drying up the mists as the ship glided into an anchorage of perfect beauty.

The expansive sound, surrounded by painted hills, was the meeting point of three arms of water. One was the spectacular Min River gorge, eleven miles long, up which the ship had laboured through the night. Twisting off to the west was another gorge, narrower and not navigable. The main channel of the river doubled back around a towering bluff, all of six hundred feet high, that jutted into the sound like the bow of a ship. At the foot of the bluff lay an island of rice paddies on which a white nine-storey pagoda rose from the summit of a conical hill. Out on the water a stone-walled temple with a green-tilted roof was perched on a knoll of rock; a gnarled tree, rooted deep in its foundations, was cantilevered above its own perfect reflection. Beyond, the river curved across a wide plain to the city of Foo-chow, its banks shallow, muddy and cluttered with fishing traps. Junks lay motionless on the broad stretch of water as if pinioned by their reflections. As the men rested on their oars and the ship glided on under her own momentum, slowly losing way, there was no sound but the plunk of a cormorant diving from a slender boat near the pagoda. A moment later it reappeared with a silver fish held cross-ways in its bill, which its master sternly confiscated as it returned to its perch.

All six cormorants abandoned the little craft at the splash of the *Quiver*'s anchor and the thunder of her chain, but returned while the ripples rolled on and on, as if to the edge of the world. The towing boats cast off the warps. The gig paddled alongside and Sam climbed tiredly aboard with a mass of figures and drawings crumpled under his jacket.

Hardly had the reflections steadied in the twinkling sunlight when they were shattered by a lesser splash, more a gulp, as Henry took a clean header from the taffrail. The water was only slightly salty and pleasantly warm. Watched by the incredulous young mandarin, Henry swam lazily round the ship. He noticed a lot of green patches in the black where the men had failed to reach with their long-handled paintbrushes. Big Tree lowered a rope and he hauled himself aboard. Feeling a new man, he asked A-tung when the tea cargo would come down the river. 'Maybe tomollow, maybe two days,' was the cautious reply.

'Look at this place, Sam,' Henry said happily. 'A landlocked harbour with none of that Whampoa filth, beautiful surroundings, a cargo of tea scooting down the river – doesn't it make you glad to be alive? Let's call it Sunday for all hands. We're all tired, especially you. Me, I'm going to sleep right here . . .'

Henry sank down on the warm deck, his bare back propped against the skylight and his hands behind his head. He closed his eyes and turned his face up to the sun, making none of his usual effort to fend off the sleep that stole upon him. When a shadow fell on his face he opened his eyes irritably. It was A-tung, scowling ferociously and pointing at a bunch of cargo lighters approaching down the river from the city. 'Chop boats come,' he said. 'We takee opium cargo now. Pliss, you fix.'

Henry blinked. His blood was suddenly ice in his veins. He got to his feet and scrutinised the oncoming boats. They swarmed with men. He looked anxiously at Sam who dropped his eyes and turned away. Playing for time Henry went slowly to the taffrail, his bare feet leaving wet footprints on the dry deck. Opium? The Chinese were coming to collect their opium!

Small wonder the conceited river mandarin had been disappointed at the gift of the barometer. No doubt he had expected to be given a couple of chests of opium for his own use, part of his cumshaw. The Chinese imagined the ship was filled with the stuff. The monumental scale of his simple error of deduction struck Henry with the force of a cannon-ball. His mind was blown to bits. The *Musket* had not imported a cargo of opium which she was discharging at the island near Hong Kong when raided by pirates. Quite the reverse. She had been *loading* opium.

Henry straightened up and met A-tung's suspicious scowl with a curt nod. 'Stand by port side, chop-boats coming alongside!' he ordered. He told Big Tree to bring his clothes and dressed hurriedly. Some Sunday this was going to be.

Sam was watching him curiously, his arms folded and

thunder on his brow. Henry forestalled any question. 'Just don't say a thing, Sam. We're going to play for time and hope for the best.'

'Do what you like lad. You've just signed our death warrants. We'll be butchered where we stand.'

Henry swallowed and put Sam out of his mind. He hurried forward and told Will Lamshire to open up the hatches. 'The Chinks are expecting chests of opium but we'll give 'em some Lancashire woollens to put in their pipes and see how it smokes,' he said.

Conscious of A-tung watching him from the poop, Henry beckoned Martin Peake and Charlie Meadows to come within hearing. 'They've got us in a clinch, I'm afraid,' he told them quickly. 'There's bound to be trouble but I don't want the men to fight. The British Vice-Consul at Foo-chow might be able to help but you mustn't do anything that will make it hard for him. Unless we're careful every man jack of us will fetch up with his head on a pole. Now swing the first of those bales up and we'll see how they take it.'

Henry strolled aft as if he did not have a care in the world and smiled confidently at A-tung who returned a stony look. The chop boats were made fast and prepared to receive cargo. Four tally clerks set up little tables at the hatchway and sat with pens poised. A gant-line was rigged with a sling, and the tail end was led through a block on deck. Slack was paid out as the sling was taken down to the lower hold. There was a long delay while the first bales of goods was levered out to free the others. The slings were attached. The squad of coolies tramped along the deck, hauling on the rope so the hessian-wrapped parcel rose spinning into the air.

The mandarin barked a sharp command, descended to the maindeck and slashed his jewel-encrusted dirk through the bales. An assortment of woolly vests and chemises spilled out. A-tung crumpled a garment in his hand and turned on Henry but his angry words were interrupted by a strange noise. It came like the call of an owl heard from afar on a still night, a wailing note that echoed among the hills.

Henry stared aft, shading his eyes, and saw it at once: a smudge of black against the pinewood slopes. It was a small steam vessel, working hard to judge by the smoke billowing from the thin funnel, and astern of her towed an all-too familiar trellis of golden masts and spars capped with white. The paddleboat crept nearer, hooting again when a junk crossed her path. The clatter of machinery was loud in the still air. 'A nice enough life for them that likes it,' Sam sniffed, staring at the uniformed figures whose gold braid twinkled in the sun. The White Ensign flying limply from her gaff was blackened by smoke, but distinctive enough for Henry and Sam to stare uncomprehendingly.

Thanks to the services of Her Britannic Majesty's gunboat *Pluto* the Yankee clipper *Musket*, with her holds stuffed with opium, had arrived safely at her anchorage in the Min River at Foo-chow-foo.

The cell was barred with bamboo so hard and impervious it might as well have been solid iron. On the other side of the bars lay a heap of dead bodies, half a dozen youthful Chinese killed in a riot by soldiers wielding bamboo pikes. Every morning and evening a wrinkle-faced coolie squeezed through the prisoners crowding the yard, carrying from a yoke across his shoulders two buckets of ice that he sprinkled over the corpses. The meltwater trickled under the bamboo bars into the tiny cell and made a puddle in which Henry and Sam had to sit, their legs manacled by iron chains to a heavy timber beam. By hauling on the chains with their hands they had been able to shift the beam a few inches so they could lean their backs against the wall. For three days they had not moved except to reach for the little bowl of gruel handed through the bars every evening and to swat at the glossy green flies that rose from the corpses to drink on their sweat.

With glazed eyes Henry watched the chirruping lizards chasing across the mouldy ceiling. Beside him, Sam's breath came in laboured grunts, as if he were snoring; his eyes were closed but he was not asleep. Their nostrils had long since become accustomed to the nauseous odours of the prison, their ears attuned to the grim moans of those lying in the dirt with fractured limbs shackled at deliberately agonising angles. Harder to put up with were the unblinking eyes that stared at them through the bars. It was better not to look at them, but when he closed his eyes Henry had nightmare visions of being trapped in a pit of snakes.

Their arrest had been accomplished within minutes of the *Musket* joining the *Quiver* in Pagoda Anchorage. The gunboat had cast off the towing warp and proceeded onward to Foo-chow, eleven miles further up the river. Henry and Sam had followed more slowly, trussed in the dark hold of A-tung's junk and guarded by a squad of yellow monkeys with drawn swords.

In darkness they had been landed at a city quay. Prodded with bamboos, they had stumbled the few yards to the gaol gates. The bodies had been pitched in soon afterwards, with the injured rioters.

Henry slapped at a mosquito. His face was already a pulpy mass of raw welts from their bites. Sam stirred with a low moan and opened his puffy eyelids. 'You don't have a semaphore in your pocket, lad?' he asked wanly.

'Ready to make a signal, sir.'

'Make the Heavenly Father's numbers, Mr Mate. Tell him we're holed beneath the waterline and making water fast . . .'

'Excuse me, Captain, don't you mean the Celestial Father?'

'I know what I mean.' Sam screwed up his eyes as pain wracked his numbed buttocks. 'Dear God, how long must we endure this . . . ?'

There was a flurry of movement in the crowded courtyard. Prisoners were elbowed aside by guards who formed two lines, facing inwards. The Englishman who approached between them covered his nose with a scented handkerchief. 'Her Majesty's Government takes a dim view of your deliberate, thoughtless and dangerous provocation of the civil authorities,' the visitor said at once, his voice muffled by the handkerchief. 'You have only yourselves to blame for this uncomfortable predicament and I can tell you it will be very difficult to extricate you. It may well take weeks.'

'As the answer to a prisoner's prayer you're not exactly bringing hope and cheer,' Henry said sourly. 'Who the hell might you be?'

The visitor folded his thin arms and leaned a bony shoulder against the bars, his ankles crossed. 'I am the Reverend Doctor Andrew Medhurst, Vice-Consul of Her Majesty's Government at the city of Foo-chow-foo. I take it you are Captain Ardent?'

'How do you do,' Henry said drily. 'May I present my friend and colleague, Captain Handyside. If you would be kind enough to ring the bell my servant will fetch the sherry.'

Medhurst was a tall, thin-faced man of middle age with iron grey hair and a complexion sallowed by fever. His contemptuous sniff betrayed, if not humour, at least a token appreciation of Henry's bravado. 'I must say, you do look exceedingly uncomfortable,' he observed.

'I trust Her Majesty's representative won't let his eyes deceive him.'

Medhurst smiled thinly. 'Now that I've located your where-abouts perhaps I might be prevailed upon to arrange a supply of decent food and water.'

'Can't you get us out of here?' Sam said.

'Eventually, perhaps. You were most indiscreet, bringing a whole shipload of opium into the port without even crossing a few palms with silver. Don't you know anything about how this God-forsaken empire works?'

Henry moaned aloud and hung his head in his hands. 'The opium was not landed by us, Doctor Medhurst. It was brought in the Yankee ship. All we've got in our hold is Lancashire textiles.'

Medhurst wrinkled his long nose and dabbed at it with the handkerchief. 'Textiles, opium, it's all the same. The Chinese consider all foreigners to be Outer Barbarians and you can see why. What do they need with machine-made textiles? Every second house has its own loom. They buy cotton grown from their neighbours and sell the garments they make to other neighbours. Bring in mass-produced goods from the mills in Britain and the entire way of life is distorted. Trade is poison-ing this country to the stomach. Already it's suffering paroxysms as a result of Western interference. We should leave it alone, we should . . .'

'Doctor Medhurst,' Henry interrupted tiredly. 'I think you missed the point. My ship did nothing illegal . . . '

'In a few days the magistrate who is governor of this establishment will hear your case. He will consider evidence that eight hundred chests of opium were removed from a black-painted three-piecey bamboo flying the Flowery Flag and named the *Musket*. Does the accused, who was arrested on board such a ship of which he was the master, have anything to tell the court?'

The long silence that answered the Vice-Consul's question was broken by Sam speaking softly through cracked lips. 'I'd be most grateful, Reverend Doctor, if you would bring sweet water on your next visit.'

'Of course, Captain,' Medhurst agreed, for the first time showing a spark of genuine sympathy. 'I'm afraid the rights and wrongs of your case will prove to be quite irrelevant. The only thing that counts is the way it looks, and it looks bad. You must understand the selfish and conceited attitude of the

Chinese. To them, the world is China and ten thousand regions. They have neither knowledge of world geography and political influence nor interest in it. They do not desire the manufactured goods we offer to trade for their tea, although this is changing. The Chinese are suspicious of us, and you can see why. Our gunboats come into their ports and at once half a dozen little boats are sent out, exploring and sounding and making maps. Nothing of that sort happens when, say, a Korean junk comes in to trade.'

Henry leaned back gingerly against the cold wall and stared at the lizards as the loquacious consul banged on. 'Take this place, Foo-chow, for example,' Medhurst continued. 'It's a great university city, an ancient capital of learning, and has no interest whatever in trade with foreigners. It has no need of anything we can offer. Life has been going on here in quite a civilised way, by their standards, for hundreds of years. When the *Pluto* brought us up the gorge three days ago with the Yankee ship in tow I felt in my heart it was the beginning of the end, and old Fowqua was saying the same only yesterday when he summoned me to his . . .'

'Fowqua . . . ?' Henry raised an eyebrow. 'He moves fast, that old bird. A few days back he was in Canton. What's he doing here?'

'Ha!' Medhurst let loose a withering guffaw. 'He's only Number One Lord round here, Prince of Fukien. Fowqua and his regiment of sons have the place in a stranglehold. Nobody sneezes without paying squeegee to Fowqua.'

Henry stirred Sam with a gentle elbow. 'Yes,' Sam mumbled blearily. 'I heard.'

'He owes us, does Fowqua.'

'Of course, but do we have a semaphore?'

Henry twisted his head to look up at Medhurst. 'His arms might be long enough.'

Sam opened his eyes and for the first time took a hard look at Her Majesty's representative, who dampened his white handkerchief with scented water from a flat-sided bottle carried in his waistcoat pocket. 'Couldn't you sprinkle some of that round, before you go,' he said limply.

Medhurst straightened up and said briskly, 'I'll bid you a comfortable sojourn, gentlemen. I will do what I can for you, of course. I expect your case will come up in a couple of weeks, so until then . . .' 'Two weeks!' Henry felt as if the bottom was dropping out of his stomach. 'What will they do with us?'

'Oh, there isn't much to worry about. I shouldn't think it's the cangue or the death of the thousand cuts. I shall prevail upon the authorities to run you out of the country. The Royal Navy will take you down to Hong Kong where you can meet up with your ship in due course.'

'Doctor Medhurst, won't you intercede with Fowqua on our behalf?' Henry said urgently. 'Captain Handyside and myself do have a connection with him. We had luncheon at his residence in Canton only ten days ago.'

'No, no. I couldn't possibly bring such a trifling matter – and, I must say, an embarrassment to Her Majesty's Government – before a figure of Fowqua's importance. Quite impossible. I'm afraid you'll just have to suffer the inconvenience and be thankful you can still waggle your heads on your shoulders.'

Sam painfully propped himself more upright and fixed Medhurst with a stern and baleful stare. 'You might be an old China hand, Doctor, but you are new to Foo-chow-foo. The success of your posting depends on Fowqua. He can make things easy for you, or break you. Am I right?' The Vice-Consul nodded reluctantly and Sam plunged on. 'I must tell you I have known Fowqua since you were sucking your thumb. I'm not blackmailing you, I'm not asking you officially, I'm *pleading* with you. Please tell Fowqua where we are.'

Sam sat back, exhausted. Though couched in soft language, the threat was implicit.

'Look here,' Henry said, fumbling under his shirt. 'It's not necessary to prejudice your position officially. You don't need to put anything in writing. Just get one of your messengers to give Fowqua this, and make sure he knows where to find us.' Henry drew the twine loop over his head, grimacing at the pain which the movement caused, and passed the *tiki* through the bars. 'Captain Handyside is not swinging the lead. He and Fowqua are old mates, he could help you a lot.'

The Reverend Doctor Medhurst put the green figure in his pocket. 'I'll have to give the matter some thought,' he said, and departed.

Having lit the fuse, Henry and Sam waited with aching anticipation for their charge to explode. And when it did go bang, after five hours that seemed like as many weeks, the effect was most satisfactory.

The guards did not merely run to unlock the cell for Chin-ta, they crawled in abject terror. Henry and Sam were helped on to covered litters. Reclining on silk cushions, they were borne at a trot through the streets and into a palatial building. Their agonisingly stiff limbs were swathed in hot, wet, scented towels and expertly massaged. They were shaved and manicured. Their clothes were taken away to be laundered, and replaced with comfortable warm gowns of silk and velvet. They were plied with countless beakers of pale amber tea and delectable morsels of sweetmeats, fruit, nuts and preserves. The mosquito bites that puffed their faces were soothed with cooling ointments. The raw wounds caused by the fetters were dressed and Henry smiled at the thought of finding himself back in the Artichoke Tavern, displaying at Screech Gander's bidding his shackle marks: now he had real shackle marks to be proud of, though they were intolerably sore. Not until next morning, when their bodies had again been bathed and treated, and their minds were refreshed by a long and dreamless sleep, were they conducted to the presence of the Prince of Fukien.

Fowqua greeted them courteously but coolly. In Canton, Henry realised, Fowqua had been keeping them sweet because he intended using the *Quiver* to escape with his treasures. Now the tables were turned and Fowqua's hospitality was tempered by natural caution. There was none of the customary hedging over who should accept the place of honour in the left-hand chair. Fowqua took it at once and demanded, 'Why you fly Hong Kong, I no savvy?'

Sam's long-winded explanation was cut short by Henry's blunt question. 'Fowqua, ol' flend – we talkee tea-pidgin, chop-chop. You have tea, you have no tea?'

'Maybe I have tea,' Fowqua answered carefully.

'Of course you have tea!' Henry plunged on determinedly, ignoring Sam's frown of warning. 'Fowqua's number-one big man. Fowqua brings tea by chop-boat to Flowery Flag ship. Fowqua makes plenty pidgin . . .' Henry emphasised the point by jabbing the palm of his hand with a finger. 'Fowqua makee plenty silver dollar, eh? You savvy me, ol' flend?'

It was impossible to read the thoughts behind the neutral expression of the skull-like face clothed in the black silk cap with its smooth gold button. The small black eyes were neither hostile, nor friendly, but guarded and a little curious. Henry played his one and only card. He put his hand on Sam's shoulder to show they were a team. 'We makee deal, more better Melican fashion . . .' Henry lifted Sam's hand and placed it lightly on the edge of Fowqua's robe. 'Muchee dollar for ol' flends together, special deal.' Henry drew a deep breath and concluded huskily, 'Can, no can?'

Fowqua regarded Henry's flushed face for long seconds then briefly touched the sleeve of Sam's coat and his stony eyes gleamed.

'Can,' he smiled solemnly, and offered on the flat of his hand the little green *tiki* for Henry to take back.

The deal took hours of wrangling and Henry's head reeled with the effort of calculating percentages and shares. Finally he begged paper and pen from Fowqua who looked upon Henry's scribbled figurings with a withering scorn.

When at last Chin-ta delivered Sam and himself to a smart little sampan propelled by six oars, which carried them down-river to the ship, Henry's churning mind reviewed the agreement with an excitement he found hard to conceal.

By despatching tea through Foo-chow instead of Canton, Fowqua was not only cutting the delivery time by at least a month but reaping a huge profit. He was saving on transport costs, taxes, port dues, the countless cumshaws demanded by petty mandarins and the thirty per cent profit added on by merchants. It was agreed he would immediately send down the river a shipment of 11,200 chests of tea, sufficient to fill the *Quiver*'s hold. This would be supplied at Canton prices and Fowqua himself would pocket the immense savings.

Once on board, the tea would become the property of a joint merchant venture between the Arrow Line, in the person of Captain Sam Handyside, and Fowqua. As the partnership had no funds of its own to invest, the cost of the tea would be advanced from Fowqua's coffers at an interest rate of twenty per cent per annum.

Only one problem remained: Mr Chamberlayne's chow-chow cargo of woollen goods. After much persuasion, Fowqua reluctantly agreed to take it off their hands but he would not pay cash. Instead, the interest on the borrowed sum would be reduced to twelve per cent.

Henry used this as a lever to introduce a condition of his own into the bargaining. Since the purchase of the tea was outside their partnership, the cost of freight should also be accounted separately. The *Quiver* would charge the partnership a freight of six pounds and fifteen shillings a ton for her voyage to London, with an added premium of one pound per ton to be shared among her captain and crew if she was first to land her cargo.

'How does it look?' Sam asked when he saw Henry's satisfied smile.

Henry struggled to keep the grin off his face. 'It looks good!'

'Tell me,' Sam demanded suspiciously.

'Fowqua's sending down 11,200 chests, just short of one and a half million pounds of raw tea. He will buy it in at sevenpence a pound from the growers and put it over the ship's rail for double that, so the Arrow-Fowqua merchant partnership will pay him £86,000. The ship will be paid £4,500 to run it to London plus a £666 bonus for the crew and ourselves for getting in ahead of other ships. The partnership will sell the tea in Mincing Lane for, say, two shillings and sixpence a pound then repay Fowqua's loan at twelve per cent.'

'What does that leave?'

'Around £86,000 – say $400,000 – to split between the partners.'

'Hmm.' Sam's glance was troubled as he looked ahead and saw the tall masts of the clippers anchored side by side near the mossy stone temple with its quaint tiled roof and over-leaning tree. 'Maybe we should stop and light a joss stick,' he said. 'You found us good cargo, my lad, and you sprang us out of prison. But there's one thing you haven't accounted in your calculations.'

Though Henry wracked his brains he could find no weak link in his reckoning and when the shadow of the *Musket's* bow fell over the racy junk he gave up the struggle. Nightingale put his paws on the rail and barked to warn them off. Smoke Lapierre hurried down the companion to pass news of their release to the captain.

Sam jutted his round chin at the Yankee ship, her black paint fresh and her rigging in tip-top order. 'What you are overlooking, lad, is the fact that the Blue Nose scoundrel, too, has done a deal with Fowqua.

'Your two-and-sixpence a pound will certainly bring a pretty profit but it all hangs on one thing. Mincing Lane will not pay such whacking premiums for new season's tea unless their tongues are hanging out for it. To get that price you have to sail up the Thames in a blaze of glory, ahead of every other ship. In this race there'll be no second place. If *Quiver* fails to beat *Musket* to London your tea will be lucky to make the standard price of around one-and-fourpence, which by my reckoning means your fancy partnership will be lucky to break even . . .'

With Sam's warning ringing in his ears, Henry climbed the rope ladder, vaulted the rail, and jumped lightly to the deck. Will Lamshire and Martin Peake shook his hand warmly and helped Sam to lower himself less athletically over the bulwarks. Some of the Murphies and Macaroons working nearby called out greetings. Big Tree hurried aft from the coops where he had been feeding the hens, a clutch of new-laid eggs heaped in his brown hands.

'Gawd Almighty, it's the Second Coming!' Meadows cracked with a beaming smile.

'You're wrong there Oatsy, I'm afraid it's not Jesus Christ, only me.' Henry lifted his voice to be heard among the men who clustered round, but not so loudly that it would carry to the neighbouring ship. 'Now listen, men! We've got miracles to perform. There's tea coming down the river for us. We have to make ready to load, and be ready to sail. And when I say sail I mean a passage to Gravesend that breaks all records and won't be equalled for a hundred years, least of all by the slaggy hulk yonder. Understand me?'

Work began at once and the days merged in a blur of frantic shipboard maintenance. Both the rival clippers swinging to their anchors within the cradle of hills prepared pell-mell for the testing voyage ahead. The perfect misty silence of the early dawns, when the only sounds were the plop of a mullet and the clash of feathers as Ancestor of Thunder and Unblemished Rectitude fought for wing-room on the perch of the cormorant fisherman's skiff, was shattered by the thunder of caulking mallets, the squeal of blocks as stages were lowered over-side for the painting gangs, and the chipping and sawing and banging of shipwrights' tools. Other gangs high aloft shouted orders from mast to mast as they end-for-ended the running rigging: every one of the hundreds of ropes were reversed to reduce the likelihood of their parting disastrously, while under strain, due to the wearing effects of chafe. The farmers completed repairs on the gig, replaced the ship's proper figurehead, and smoothed out the splinters which the Whampoa junks had gouged from the hull.

Through the mornings, as oily aromas of paint and turpentine overwhelmed the delicate fragrances of pine and meadowsweet drifting off the land, and the blue sky became dotted with puffy clouds that merged and grew into ominous thunderheads, the sampans sculling down the river did a brisk trade with both ships. They sold crisp green vegetables, onions, varnished duck, live hens, rice, trussed-up pigs, fresh water in barrels, *tung* oil with which to feed sun-cracked timbers and straight-grained poles that could serve for replacement spars. Henry chuckled at the sight of the hulking Charlie Field cooling himself in the noon-day torpor with lady-like flutters of a bamboo fan bought from a bumboat. Sitting on his bucket beneath a paper umbrella, Manfred Longhandle used every minute of daylight to renew the bolt-rope stitching of the three topsails which, as the ship's all-weather driving engines, were already showing signs of wear.

By early afternoon the grey clouds were too heavy to float and began to jettison cargo. Rain filled the deck, spouting in cataracts through the scuppers and hissing on the water. Stripped to the waist and skylarking, the men worked on with canvas and sand, rubbing down the brightwork. Then the sun broke through, the clouds dissolved, and the exotic landscape with its ivory pagodas and brilliant hills lay bathed in a soft afternoon light, a living willow-pattern washed clean.

In the brief glowing minutes after sunset, bringing a satisfying end to a hard day's toil, Henry sometimes gazed across at the *Musket* where the activity was equally intense. Once he saw Screech Gander throw a wooden pin for Nightingale, who bounded over the rail with a splash that brought a flutter among the ever-present cormorants, and swam proudly back to the lowered gangway with tail wagging above the surface.

Although he had suffered much in his prison ordeal Sam did not rest. Instead, he took a cruise. With Martin Peake and six men he set out – in the heavy longboat, because it was big enough to sleep in – with supplies, water and Henry's revolver. He aimed to fill in the gaps of his brief survey of the Min gorge, and sound the channels through the sandbars at the entrance.

While Sam was away Chin-ta came alongside with three chop-boats into which the bales of textiles were loaded. With no ballast in her hold the ship would be more than ever at the mercy of a gale because there was no longer any weight to counterbalance the lofty top-hamper. Henry kept his fingers crossed, knowing Screech Gander faced the same risks, but the Yankee ship's problem was soon solved. Early one morning half a dozen deeply laden barges drifted down on the tide and clustered around the black ship. Watching through the glass, Henry saw bag after bag of river shingle being hoisted aboard. The stones were emptied into the hold then smoothed to provide a foundation for the chests of tea, raising them above the level of the bilges so they would not be wetted by bilge-water slopping up the inside of the hull as the ship heeled. The weight also stiffened a ship against the leverage of the wind in her sails and helped her sail better.

Weary and numb after living for three nights in an open boat but refreshed by his adventure, Sam returned to find the ship's paintwork as good as new and her captain in a sweat of impatience. 'Why does Gander get his ballast and we don't?' Henry stormed. 'Fowqua promised on his honourable ances-tors' graves to send it down to us but where is it?'

Sam laid down his mapping pen with care so as not to smudge his work. 'Why don't you ask him?'

'I did,' Henry fumed. 'At least, I took the gig and intercepted Chin-ta as he headed up-river. He sat looking at me all inscrutable like one of your porcelain statues and said, 'Maybe tomollow!' Yesterday was tomollow, and today is the day after tomollow and can you see any ballast coming down the river . . . ?'

'No,' Sam agreed, 'but I saw tons of clean shingle on the beach near the nine-storey pagoda.'

If the Murphies and Macaroons considered they had given all they had in working to prepare the *Quiver* for sea, their opinions underwent a hasty revision moments after the cap-tain erupted from the companion-way and glared across the smooth water at the *Musket*. Screech Gander was reclining in a deck chair, boots propped comfortably on the rail of his poop, puffing a cheroot as he stared smugly at the British clipper. 'Mr Lamshire, Mr Peake!' Henry bawled. 'Meadows, Field, get your daisy beaters up here . . .'

The sailmaker was turned out of his hammock and put to sewing sacks from old canvas. Half a dozen shovels had been saved from the baggage of their 'Frisco passengers and these were dropped in the longboat. As Henry headed for the beach near the pagoda, the longboat crowded with men, the others launched the lifeboat. In the soft light cast by a pair of lanterns hung from oars stuck into the beach, Meadows lifted the first shovel of gravel into the sack which Flynn held open. ''Struth it's 'eavy, 'ow much o' this muck do we need?'

'At least a hundred tons, maybe more,' Henry said.

Six men wielded the shovels while others, in pairs, carried the filled sacks to the longboat and lifeboat which relayed them to the ship. The sacks were sweated aboard by gant-line and tipped into the hold. After working alongside his men until midnight Henry went aboard and was sobered by the diminutive size of the heap of stones won with so much labour. A couple of tons an hour was the best they could do, so the job would have to be accomplished more systematically.

One watch at a time worked on the ballasting while the other rested, fed, or did ship's work. Day and night, keeping to the regular watch-change routine, the monumental job progressed. Even Tom Withers was flushed from his cuddy to take a turn on the shovels, as did Henry and the mates. Sam did his stint in charge of the longboat. The one-handed Nix Barlow was no use on a shovel but muscle-power had to be fuelled and on the captain's orders he worked a double day, providing a hot meal at midnight as well as at noon. Only in the torrential rain of mid-afternoon did operations pause, because there was no point in loading wet gravel. While the rain drummed down a rough awning was rigged over the open hatch and in the stiffling hold the men smoothed the heaps to make a perfectly level bed.

On the third successive day of ballasting the bone-weary crew leant on their shovels and make-shift wooden rakes in the dim hold as Henry lay flat on the twenty-inch bed of gravel they had laid, sighting along its surface to spot humps and hollows. The glistening deck was deserted as the rainstorm eased. With screwed-up eyes, Sam worked over his chart in the saloon. Barlow decided to finish peeling the sweet potatoes he had bought from a sampan before bringing in the buckets he had positioned strategically to collect rain water. The only outward sign of life in the rain-hammered clipper was Big Tree. After his customary wash in the downpour he climbed down to the longboat and, as the rain eased, began bailing out the water that filled it to six inches over the floorboards. Working hard, the drumming of the rain and the splash of the bucket in his ears, he did not hear the hissed order that boated the oars of a ship's gig gliding towards him. The first he knew of it was a gentle lurch of the longboat as the gig touched, then he was grabbed from behind and doubled over with his arms wrenched up his back.

It all happened so quickly. The cherished *patu* was jerked from his waistband. The devil Yankee captain whispered his instructions so close to Big Tree's ear that the Maori felt the heat of the cheroot on his cheek. Then he was pushed sideways into the bottom of the boat and Screech Gander stepped over him to the rope ladder. With his long legs astride the rail he uttered a piercing whistle. Nightingale jumped from the gig into the longboat then bounded with scrabbling feet up the rope ladder. Gander grabbed the dog by the scruff and swung him inboard then dropped to the deck.

Hearing the drumbeat of rain begin to fade, Henry told the men only a few more boatloads of gravel were required to trim the level to his satisfaction and he mounted the ladder. He was greeted by a shrill squawk. With neck outstretched and clipped wings beating the air, one of his prized black hens streaked along the deck with Nightingale in hot pursuit.

Henry shouted but too late. The dog caught the hen in its jaws then crashed under its own momentum into the port-side poop steps. There was a whirlwind of feathers. The dog dropped the dead bird and, spitting fluff, fixed his yellow eyes on a clucking hen trying to disappear beneath the foremast fife-rail.

The hen fled for'ard as Henry jumped towards its hiding place and scooped off the deck a chunky piece of driftwood that Big Tree had brought aboard for whittling. He intercepted the dog as it gave chase. Nightingale slid to a halt, but his growl turned to a joyful bark as Henry jousted the driftwood under his snout. This was just the kind of game he liked, and when Henry tossed the stick over the rail the dog followed it.

The commotion had brought Sam to the poop and Barlow from his galley. Screech Gander, his hands thrust deeply in his pockets and the cheroot tilted upwards beneath the wide brim of his bleached-straw hat, languidly kicked the dead hen along the deck and told Barlow, 'Here's one for your stewpot.' He nodded casually at Henry, as if the two captains were passing in the street. 'Came aboard to drop a word of thanks for helping us: we had the little bastards on the retreat but your timely arrival clinched it. Where's Evans, didn't you get him out of the water?'

'Evans is dead and buried,' Henry answered shortly. 'Thank you for your thanks, but you still owe us, Screech. What are you going to do for us, besides ensuring A-tung throws us in choky and slaughtering my chickens?'

The deck was already drying in the hot sunlight. The *Musket*'s mates, having hauled Nightingale out of the water and left him in the gig, climbed over the rail. Ben Whipple took a bottle out of his jacket pocket and offered it to Henry. 'What's this for?' Henry asked suspiciously.

Screech Gander made a slight attempt at a smile. 'We're

mighty tired of sitting looking at you and thought it was time for a drink.'

'And about time too, come on up.' Sam's cheery answer from the poop diverted attention from Henry's indifferent shrug. The cane chairs bought at Whampoa were set round a small table. The steward set out glasses. Gander pulled the cork of the whisky bottle with his teeth, poured liberal portions, then he held his own glass high. 'Here's to Fowqua,' he toasted. 'May the Celestial Emperor decorate his hat with many a peacock feather.'

'Here's to trade,' Henry responded and sipped the fiery liquor. 'What's this rot-gut, Screech?'

'California red-eye, none better.'

While the *Quiver's* crew collected the last few bags of shingle from the beach, the masters and mates of the rival clipper ships caroused in the softening sunlight of late afternoon. By sundown they were on their second bottle, which Withers produced from the ship's store. Sam was bombastically proclaiming the merits of conventional topsails over the new-fangled arrangement of upper and lower topsails seen for the first time on a new ship at Whampoa, and his mind did not register that Screech Gander agreed with every word. The two young mates, Whipple and Peake, conversed in low tones on the dark subject of flower boats. Will Lamshire had spoken with Gander about the Nova Scotia timber ports he knew and now fell silent, his long nose glowing pinkly in the lingering ray's of the sunset. The rumpled and scrawny figure of Smoke Lapierre began to curl like a withering leaf as the liquor caught hold, and nobody paid him any attention when, staggering a little, he went below to the water closet.

Bemused by the unexpected social event, though he drank little, Henry watched the last boat-load of ballast creep across the water with the lanterns and spades from the beach. He saw Big Tree cross the poop once or twice and idly wondered what had given him a stomach ache because he looked tense and pale. Nightingale whined from the *Musket's* gig and took no notice of Gander's shouts to shut up. Will stumbled to the poop rail and told Robinson to light the riding light. A few minutes after the lantern was hoisted over the bow the American ship followed suit.

Henry had already passed the word to Withers and Barlow that the visitors would stay for dinner when Meadows reported a cluster of lights moving down on both ships. With visions of the Pearl River war junks still in his mind, Henry snatched up the glass. In the faint glow cast by the lanterns he could just make out a number of low, barge-like craft with curve-roofed huts amidships. They lumbered along slowly, propelled by long-handled sweeps that moved to the beat of clashing cymbals. Puzzled, Henry handed the glass to Gander. With one quick glance his hawk-like features split in triumphant grin. 'This is where the fun starts, my Botany Bay friend, I wish you luck,' he said, clapping a friendly hand on Henry's shoulder. 'Don't you see what's coming down the river? Fowqua has delivered. Here comes our tea!'

With ironical thanks for the hospitality, the Yankee ship's master and mates returned aboard. Minutes later, with loud splashing of sweeps and sing-song cries of the boatmen, the first of the river barges swung alongside the *Quiver*. The mates had fenders and lanterns ready, the hatch covers thrown back. Loading began at once. Stout ladders of thick bamboos were laid against the ship's sides. An army of coolies, naked but for loin-cloths and rags around their heads, carried the chests aboard by one ladder and descended by the other. From the hold came a thunder of hammering as every row of chests was wedged in place, forming a platform as smooth as a ballroom floor. Henry could hardly believe what was happening. The ship was actually loading tea for London. In a few hours they would be away down the river and setting sail with thousands of miles to run.

He looked across to the *Musket*. More than one barge lay alongside her, perhaps half a dozen in all, but others were coming down the river and no doubt most of them were intended for the *Quiver*. Delightedly, Henry slipped down the companion-way into the lighted saloon to fetch his pipe. Sam's ink and chart drawing instruments lay on the table where he had left them but there was no sign of the chart he had drawn. Smelling disaster in the air, Henry descended the ladder to the floor of the hold. His face running with sweat, Sam was helping the mates get the first layer of chests perfectly level. 'I want to look at your chart, Sam, did you stow it away?'

'The ink was wet.'

'So it's on the saloon table?'

'Of course.'

'Not any more, that Blue Nose bastard must have stuffed it under his shirt.'

'Ah.' Sam paused, frowning, then tapped his forehead. 'Well

236

don't fret, lad, it's all in here. Soon as we get this layer down the rest of the tea can be squared away in no time.'

But Henry did fret. If Screech Gander or one of his men had stolen Sam's chart what other tricks were they trying? He picked up a hammer and began to rain unscientific blows on the nearest tea-chest. The coolies stopped carrying and stowing at the sight of the ship's captain dementedly breaking open a chest. When a heap of small and fragile boxes tumbled out, Henry stood one on its corner and struck it a heavy blow. The cattie shattered and a dark brown dust spilled into his hand.

Henry held it under Sam's nose and poked the dust with a finger. 'Not tea, Mr Handyside,' he said grimly, 'Unless you think Mincing Lane will develop a new taste for sand and sawdust.'

Shaded by the sailmaker's paper umbrella, Captain Henry Ardent sat erect and motionless in an upright chair in the centre of the *Quiver*'s poop. The galley meat-knife was stuck point-first in the timber of the rail just in front of him, its blade glinting in the early sunlight. On either side of the knife two pairs of feet clad in black silk slippers stood on the tips of their toes. The owners of the feet, A-tung and Chin-ta, sweated profusely as they struggled to maintain their awkward and precarious positions. For each of Fowqua's sons was suspended by his pigtail from a tarry manilla line that disappeared high into the ship's rigging. The line was set so that strain came on the queue only when its owner dropped down on his heels.

A few hours before, his face smeared with galley grease and the knife in his teeth, Henry had swum silently across to the barges loading their tea into the *Musket*. Big Tree, heartened by the return of his *patu* which bulged familiarly under his waistband at the small of his back, paddled with him. Carefully the two men had drifted from boat to boat until they found Fowqua's speedy sampan. By good luck both A-tung and Chin-ta were aboard, conferring by lamplight over the tally of chests being put aboard.

At Henry's signal the wicked blade of Big Tree's jade club had laid out all six of the men dozing at their oars. Henry relieved the two young mandarins of broad swords and daggers before they could blink. At once the gig had glided out of the darkness. Meadows and Field and half a dozen men had streamed aboard, cast off the sampan, and towed it to the *Quiver*.

Manhandled roughly to the *Quiver*'s maindeck, the hostages had bowed courteously in the face of Henry's bitter and angry accusations. 'So sollee, no mistake. Tea for you come soon, maybe tomollow.'

'Horse feathers!' Henry snapped.

'Oh no,' Chin-ta argued with persistence. 'My honour-lable father is partner you, is partner Flowery Flag captain. No ploblem. Flowery Flag captain take Fowqua tea today, you take Fowqua tea maybe tomollow.'

Sick at heart, Henry was in no mood to be trifled with. He sent the sampan to Foo-chow with word to bring Fowqua, chop-chop. Just before sun-up he hoisted his hostages into position and settled into the chair. Dozens of junks and sampans stood off at a distance, agog to witness the outcome. When Chin-ta gave a moan, screwing up his eyes at the pain in his scalp as he flexed his trembling limbs, Sam tried to intervene but Henry told him to hold his tongue.

From the corner of his eye he watched the *Musket* prepare for sea. Hatches were closed and covered with heavy tarpaulins wedged tight with hammered wedges. Awnings were stowed, the last couple of sails swung aloft and bent to the yards, the anchor shortened up. When the last tea-barge crawled away the Yankee clipper was well down on her marks. The clanking pawl of the capstan carried clearly over the water, then Ben Whipple's cry of 'Anchor's aweigh!'

The stiff cotton topsails, so white compared with those of the *Quiver*, caught the breeze ruffling over the water. Coated with shining black mud, the anchor broke the surface. The helm was put down and the black clipper ghosted towards the mouth of the gorge where a line of towing boats was forming up. This was a blow, for Henry had supposed they would not be able to operate without A-tung to do the pilotage.

When Fowqua came aboard near noon the Yankee was far down the gorge and out of sight while his sons whimpered with the strain of their ordeal. Henry did not rise from his chair or alter his stiff posture. Nor did he give the visitor opportunity to speak. 'Chin-chin, ol' flend! You send velly find tea. I think maybe you send number-one-chop tea cargo velly soon, or . . .' Henry gripped his throat and let his tongue loll.

Fowqua's skeletal figure paused on the maindeck as Big Tree blocked his approach to the poop ladder and with a thunderous crash let a tea chest drop to the deck. Fowqua blenched when he saw the sand and sawdust that filled the catties. He questioned his sons and Henry signalled Meadows to slacken the ropes so they could answer. The language was indecipherable but A-tung's expression could be read like a book. Obviously it was he, the river mandarin, whom Screech Gander had bribed. And how close he had come to getting away with it, Henry thought, shuddering at what a fool he could have looked, sailing proudly up the Thames to discharge six hundred tons of oriental sand and sawdust.

Fowqua halted A-tung's fevered explanation with a word of withering scorn. Then he looked up at Henry and made a deep and apologetic kow-tow. 'So sollee, ol' flend, maybe make mistake. I bling tea for you, chop-chop.'

Though he was certain Fowqua would fulfil his bargain Henry shook his head firmly when the skeletal fingers beckoned his sons down from the rail. 'Bling tea, can, no can?' Henry demanded.

'Can,' Fowqua said, and returned to his sampan.

All through the noon-day heat and the routine afternoon rainstorm, Henry remained stern and immobile in his chair. The ropes were lowered to give his hostages support but they were not permitted to descend. The knife stayed in the rail.

It was half an hour before sunset when Charlie Meadows ran aft along the maindeck and threw himself full length at Henry's feet. 'Pardon me, yer Loyal 'Ighness!' he cried. 'Plentee boats bling tea down liver . . . !' The crew erupted into cheers.

'Wait and see,' Henry said, unmoving. 'I'll believe it when we're out of here and setting stunsails.'

The hold had already been emptied of the chests filled with dust. Now, as the tea came aboard and was wedged in smooth floors with bundles of split bamboos that would be sold later in London for making umbrellas and furniture, Henry walked woodenly down the companion and poured himself a stiff tot of rum. Through most of the day his mind had been occupied with an apparently insoluble problem.

Whether loaded or flying light made little difference, for the dash down the rushing waters of the Min River Gorge, eleven miles to the bar and the shoal-infested channels beyond, would be fraught with more dangers than all the rest of the voyage ahead. To negotiate the gorge under sail was out of the question, even with a following wind, for the ship would never pick up enough speed for steerage way. The chow-chow water would swirl her round in a second, flinging her into shards of rock that tumbled from the high slopes and edged the racing currents like teeth.

Henry was disinclined to put all his trust in A-tung, even if the river boats were available. There was no reason to hope for a timely visit from HMS *Pluto*, the second in two weeks. With neither a steam-paddle boat nor a score of Chinese towing boats and two hundred coolies at her beck and call, the British clipper was on her own. But Sam had a plan, and while Henry sipped his rum he explained it with sketches drawn up on the tablecloth with a knife handle.

A sweet perfume hung over the deck on the still, dawn air as the last few chests were hammered into place and the hatch boards lifted on. It was the fragrance of the elixir of immortality: eleven thousand and two hundred wooden chests of *pekoe* and *souchong* destined for the parlours and drawing rooms of the British Isles. The advertisements and testimonials claimed it would relieve fatigue, repair the eyesight, strengthen the will and delight the soul. Here in Pagoda Anchorage at Foo-chow-foo Henry was forced to confess his soul was anything but delighted, his fatigue far from relieved. After so many hours of intense and chaotic activity he was tired beyond belief. As the clipper lifted her anchor, let fall her topsails, and gathered way across the smooth misty water, her captain squared his shoulders and said, 'Take the con and line her up as you see fit, Sam.'

'Aye, thanks lad.'

'And God help us,' Henry muttered as he stepped back from the binnacle to make it clear that Sam had full authority. As the ship entered the throat of the gorge the current took a grip on her keel. The slender white pillar of the pagoda, a lighthouse with ruffled feathers, slid by rapidly. The ebb was just beginning, and the speed of the current would help rather than hinder, but if the ship did touch bottom the outgoing tide would strand her within minutes.

Every inch a rock of confidence, the breeze fluffing his whiskers and his blue eyes fixed on the rocky narrows towards which the ship was rushing, Sam boomed a succession of orders.

'Let fly your sheets and furl . . . !'

'Let go the anchor . . . !'

'Clew up there, smartly or we'll pay for it . . . !'

'Snub her now, hand . . . some . . . ly!'

Will Lamshire, in charge of the port watch on the fo'c's'le head, instructed his men to feed the hawser around the bitts as the iron flukes of the kedge anchor dug into the gravel riverbed. The heavy frame of timbers smoked as the entire momentum of the ship was slowed and stopped by the stiff and trembling hawser. The rope creaked, dripping water as it stretched under the strain. The men added figure-of-eight loops over the bitts. The ship swung round, all sail off her and the bowsprit pointing upstream, the way she had come.

The starboard watch tumbled into the lifeboat and longboat which towed alongside. Meadows took charge of one and Field the other. Towing warps were passed down from each quarter. Sam winked encouragingly at Henry. 'Here goes, lad, hold your hat.' Then he filled his lungs and bellowed, 'For'ard there, take a pawl!'

The Macaroons slotted capstan bars into the trundlehead and took the strain. Sweat poured in rivers down their backs as – click by click – the ship was hauled against the current and up to her anchor. Until suddenly the anchor started to lift. The pine-clad hills on either beam began to move, slowly at first then faster. The ship was borne stern-first down the gorge, braking her progress on the anchor dragging along the riverbed.

The vibration of the anchor dredging through the mud travelled up the hawser. Will Lamshire's fingers, blunt and calloused, tuned the strain of the great warp as delicately as any musician ever adjusted a fiddle. When the vibration faded and the shoreline gathered speed the anchor was too high and losing its grip so slack was paid out. When the hawser jerked and shuddered, causing the whole ship to stagger, the anchor was snagging and there was a risk of a fluke breaking off or the hawser itself parting: the men threw their muscles behind the capstan bars and the tension was relieved by hauling the anchor higher.

Astern, the two boats manoeuvred out from each quarter, ready to swing the stern one way or the other on Sam's command. The old mariner showed what skill and judgement lay behind that title, master. He was truly master of the ship, letting the loaded vessel down the gorge like a mountaineer inching down a cliff-face on the end of a rope, the two boats steadying her like a climber's out-thrust feet.

In the first narrows where the coolies had towed the ship against the current there was hardly a ship's length between the jags of rock covered with fern and moss. Sam lined up carefully but the riverbed was swept clean of silt and without warning the anchor began to skid over a smooth bottom. The ship shied like a frightened mare. There was no stopping her. An eddy threw the ship sideways. The rocks moved in with appalling speed. Sam trumpeted to Meadows, 'Pull, man! Pull thunderbolts!'

At the last second the anchor found a patch of soft mud and dug in, dragging the ship's head round so she straightened up with a jerk that sent the gear rattling aloft.

The second narrows were passed without incident and the ship drifted swiftly down to the mouth of the gorge where the current was more sluggish. The anchor was lifted off the bottom and with the two boats guiding her, the *Quiver* threaded the narrow gap between the mushrooms of rock. Her stern-first drift was checked by a brisk gust of breeze tangy with the smell of open ocean, clean and raw after their days amid the sweet scents of the land. For a brief moment Henry clasped Sam's shoulders warmly, then ordered the anchor to be dropped. The ship stopped and turned her bowsprit to seaward. The boats were recovered and inverted on the skids. Topsails were let fall, jibs hoisted, topgallants loosened, and with the anchor dangling from the cat-head but ready to be let go on the instant, her yards braced sharp-up, the *Quiver* cut from the shelter of the islands crowding the river-mouth.

It was only as she cleared the craggy outcrop of a small island that her weary and exultant crew sighted the *Musket*. The Yankee clipper rode to anchor a couple of miles from the shore, surrounded by the fleet of riverboats that had helped her down the gorge. The buzz of ribald comments was silenced by Sam's gruff comment. 'Be quiet, there's enough time for this ship to suffer the same fate.'

Henry turned the glass on the *Musket*. 'I reckon she came off the putty at the top of the tide after lightening ship during the night and now she's taking her cargo on board again.'

Sam closed his telescope with a decisive snap. 'You're right. He's got two kedges run out astern and the ship is obviously afloat. He's had a lucky escape.'

Henry climbed a few feet up the mizzen shrouds for a better look then descended again. 'I don't see any distress flag so we'll stand on unless he signals, but it's a funny place to fetch up, so far out of the channel . . .' Henry caught Sam's sheepish look and prodded him sharply in the belly. 'I do declare you're blushing, you devious old rogue. Come along, there are no secrets in my ship . . .'

Sam turned away with a shrug and said innocently, 'You know Screech Gander or one of his gang stole my chart. It wasn't my fault he lifted the wrong one, was it?'

'You mean you set a deliberate trap?' Henry demanded. 'You went to all the trouble of drawing up a dummy, but how did you know Gander would come on board . . . ?'

'I sent him an invitation,' Sam said.

The sky was quilted with bands of thick grey cloud between which the sun flared a threatening and angry yellow. Squall clouds like a mountain of cushions piled up in the south. Henry sniffed the weather. 'We're in for a slammer,' he said to himself, then more loudly he called along the deck. 'Mr Lamshire, set courses and royals. Mr Peake, get yourself to the foretop and keep me informed on the lie of the channel. And keep that lead going there, Mr Meadows . . . '

It was the first dogwatch on the eighth day of June, 1853.

FOUR:

Blackwall Reach   16,140 *miles*

DAWN FOUND THE *Quiver* clothed in rosy pink from truck to waterway and beating down the Formosa Strait into the teeth of a fierce monsoon. A sprinkle of morning stars faded like lingering sky rockets over the distant coast of China, her mountains visible from the topgallant yards as a murky mass, almost a cloud. The water, blackly blue, hissed in misty veils from the hurtling blade of the ship's bow. Beneath her tuck the foam swirling along her green and gold flanks converged in a wake pointing a crooked, scintillating finger at the sunrise.

The tilting cathedral of sail was soon washed in a saffron glow, as if lit from within by candles. The delicate pink was chased by a lurid yellow sun flaring briefly through a chink beneath a granite cliff of cloud. But there was nothing of the rigidity and permanence of stone and mortar about this soaring architecture of wind-punched canvas and straining rope. In some eyes the beautiful ship dancing close-hauled over hunched and battering seas might have been a testimony to the glory of God's gifts. But the red-rimmed eyes of Captain Henry Ardent were far from wonder struck.

In a raw fury he stamped his aching legs on the wet deck and flailed his arms to ease the cramp in his shoulders. His blond hair, stiff with salt, was twisted in damp and tangled strands. A golden stubble covered cheeks pinched with exhaustion. All night he had been on deck, conning the heavily pressed clipper through short, steep seas. With the change of watch at four o'clock Will Lamshire had taken charge. Hardly had Henry's weary head touched the pillow than his instincts registered a change in the wild rhythm of pitch and leap. He stumbled on deck to find the royals being taken in. 'What's going on here, Mr Lamshire?' he growled.

The mate was startled to see him suddenly reappear. 'Just shortening in, Captain,' he said, tipping his long nose at the mass of cloud gathering ominously in the paling sky.

'So I see, Mr Lamshire, and I'll have your guts for reef penants if the royals aren't set and drawing again in thirty seconds flat.'

'There's a ton of wind under that cloud Captain, I thought it was prudent . . . '

Henry bunched his fists and rounded fiercely on the mate. 'Let fall the royals, Mister, and if your skills of prudence need exercise in future I suggest you shorten sail only when I give the word.'

With a woolly cap pulled down to cover his ears and his jacket collar turned up, Sam Handyside stepped out of the shadows. 'Your mate's only doing his job, lad, and that's to look after the ship. There was no reason to seek permission for sensible seamanship.'

'Give me the truth of it, *Mr* Handyside,' Henry demanded, weighting the title with withering scorn. 'Was it your idea to pull the canvas off her?'

'Will's a good seaman, I wouldn't stop him doing what was right. You didn't say you wanted to tear the sticks out of her.'

The royals flogged out of the gaskets the moment the men aloft pulled the knots. A thunderous drumming of canvas drowned out the advancing roar of wind. As the yards were hoisted by men toiling at the halyards the squall struck. The ship staggered as if slapped in the face by a giant hand. Water creamed over the rail and sluiced along the maindeck, wetting the men to the waist. Sam grabbed the skylight as his feet slipped.

Balancing like a steeplejack, Henry made a leap for the wheel. 'Bring her up!' he grunted, and lent his weight to the palm-smoothed spokes. On the weather side of the wheel Charlie Field heaved the helm down with all his considerable strength. The rudder bit sharply, reining in the shying bows.

For an instant the *Quiver* lay trapped in a sea hollow, her spars bending under a deadweight of wind. Then a grey-black sea rolled under the bow and tossed it high. The ship slewed into the wind. Gasping with effort, Henry and Charlie Field whirled the spokes the opposite way. The sails shivered as the burden of wind spilled out of them. The masts swung towards the vertical and the deck levelled. The ship sprang ahead. Amidships, the men quickly cleated the halyards on the pins and darted nervous glances aft. To them, this technique of spilling wind from the sails, which their captain had learned from observing Screech Gander in the *Musket*, was a new and alarming way of handling a ship. Instead of turning away from the wind, taking the pressure off by scudding before it, the ship was shaving perilously near to the eye of the wind, cutting some of the power of it away along the lee side of the canvas.

Sweat of fear as well as exertion oozed into Henry's eyes. The slightest misjudgement now would prove old Handy-side right and be the end of them. If the wind came too much on the beam, with so much sail up the *Quiver* would be knocked flat, perhaps never to rise again. But if she came too close into the wind she would be thrown aback and the masts would go over the side.

But the *Quiver* handled like a thoroughbred, instantly obeying the touch of the helm, and after a few minutes Henry gained confidence. Amidships, the men crawled up to the weather deck out of reach of the seas swirling in the scuppers. Sam found his feet and looked on in grudging and uneasy admiration. Never had he seen a ship put so deliberately into danger but he had to admit it had worked, this time. They had lost no ground to leeward. In fact the reverse, for the ship had eaten up to windward and every mile was precious.

The spike in the wind soon blunted. After ten minutes of lashing fury the squall tapered away and Henry left the wheel. 'Box her off,' he told Field, who put the helm up to bear the ship away on her original course. Henry went to the poop rail and saw the mate standing at the pump. 'Put some jelly into the jib-staysail, Mr Lamshire, this is a sailing ship with a race to win not a Whampoa washee-washee boat.'

'Aye aye,' Lamshire acknowledged stiffly.

The dawn colours had long since been swallowed up by a forbidding greyness. Henry stared grimly at the toppling seas and spoke from the side of his mouth. 'Let's get something straight between us, Sam. There's only one way to beat the Yankee bastard to London and that's to pile on the muslin. You shorten sail behind my back again, I'll ram your jade dragon down your throat.'

Sam folded his big arms across his chest and his cheeks flushed all the colours of a sunrise. 'I have a responsibility, same as you, and that's to see this ship comes home safe, race or no race, and cramming on sail with a squall coming down is suicide.'

'There's only one master of this ship.'

'Then start acting like one.'

Henry stared into Sam's eyes which his anger had made as cold and grey as the sea. 'You saw how I handled her. I'm going to sail this ship every inch of the way to London if it kills me.'

'And it probably will, and me and everyone else along with you. I'll not let you take such risks.'

The seamen coiling up the halyards paused in their work as the angry voices carried on the wind. Four bells sounded, thin against the wild music of the morning. Henry turned his shoulder to a spat of spray then forced himself to smile. 'Breakfast, Sam. You'll feel better with something to fill that big belly of yours.'

Sam took the olive branch. 'Aren't you coming down?'

'I'll be feeding myself on deck.'

Sam gave the young captain a narrow look, noted the determined set of the jaw, and bit off a retort. It was only their first morning out and there were many miles to go. The lad would find out soon enough that no man can stay on deck for ever.

Henry watched Sam's rounded figure lurch along the wet deck and disappear down the companion-way. The old boy might have thousands of sea miles under his keel, Henry acknowledged, but he had a lot to learn about sailing for speed. The first secret of a fast passage was consistency and the second was endurance. He resolved that not until the mooring lines were ashore in the West India Dock would he sit down to a meal at the saloon table.

With relief Henry saw Big Tree emerge from the galley for'ard. Dancing with the pitch of the deck, the Maori came aft with a large mug of black coffee. As Henry gratefully cupped his hands round it there was a flutter of canvas aloft as the wind caught the lee side of the fore-topgallant. 'Watch her, can't you feel her griping!' Henry growled.

Charlie Field fed a couple of spokes through his big hands, letting the bows fall half a point off the wind so the sail filled again with a crack. Serve him right for letting his mind wander off to the flower boats again. It would be good to snatch a bit of real grumble and grunt down Limehouse Road. But Charlie wished the girls would pull harder on the bowlines. This battling to windward, zig-zagging back and forth against the wind while being set back by the current, was violent and exhausting. Adam Robinson, the tall negro who had been wounded in the knife fight with Dingle, came to relieve him at the wheel. 'Sarf-west by sarf,' Charlie muttered.

'South-west by south,' Adam acknowledged in his soft and rounded accent.

'Watch yerself, the old man's friendly as a scorpion dahn yer bed.'

Robinson nodded but said nothing, concentrating on getting the feel of the ship and testing her strength under his hands.

Charlie joined the queue of men at the galley door. A cock crowed shrilly from the poultry coops as the cook splashed coffee into his mug. 'First one fer the pot, eh Nix, wotcha fink?'

'He's only 'appy, ain't you?' the cook said.

'I'll be 'appy when I sees that noisy bastard in the stewpot,' Charlie muttered grumpily. The men had taken their coffee to sheltered spots on deck, but their respite was brief.

The captain's strident voice drove against the wind like a hurled spear. 'Mr Lamshire! While the men are sitting round the deck they might as well get their bodies up to windward where the weight will do some good . . .'

'Aye aye!'

'Five minutes, Mr Lamshire, there's much to do.'

The mate sourly surveyed the men. 'You heard, five minutes to fill yer boots, and get yourselves up to windward.' He paused, careful to keep his expression neutral, as the captain called again from the poop rail.

'A word with you, Mr Lamshire.'

'Aye Captain?'

Henry stood with legs wide on the wet deck, bending the weather knee to remain upright as the ship heeled. Beads of moisture collected in the pale straw of his eyebrows and dripped off the end of his nose. His blue eyes were redly rimmed but alert and relentlessly observant. His short oilskin jacket was open at the throat and the collar of his blue shirt was ink-dark with wetness. He turned up his collar. 'She's munching like an old cow with her head in the grass, eight inches down by the bow, I'd say,' he told the mate. 'We have to get some weight aft. Pass the Europe hawsers aft and coil them down in my cabin, and all the paint. The salt pork can come aft too, lash the casks down under a tarpaulin. And you can haul out the bower chains and pass 'em aft, there's room in the lazarette if Longhandle shifts some of his canvas into my day-room . . .'

Will Lamshire tugged at his nose, reflecting on the problems and knowing the captain's plan was sensible and coherent. The ship had too much weight for'ard which made her hard to steer. This meant the rudder was constantly dragging her back on course, acting like a brake. A ship would not sail well unless she was perfectly trimmed. 'Aye, and all them shackles and ironwork can go into the gig if we can turn it upright.'

'Yes I agree,' Henry said curtly. 'And chafing gear, we need it fast because she's cutting herself to pieces in this sea.' The mate was turning away to get started when Henry thought of something else. 'Better get another cover on the main hatch right away, wedge it home tight, and how's the well?'

'A couple of inches,' Will answered.

'All right, look alive. No good standing with your thumbs in your beckets and your mouth open catching flies. This is a winning ship, Mister . . .'

Sitting alone at the saloon table, the fiddles erected to prevent crockery from sliding to the floor, Sam chewed on a piece of bread and sighed. This bashing into the weather was unendurable. One part of his mind recognised it could not be avoided. To win her way west and south, the *Quiver* could only battle on and the ship would stand it longer than the crew. But it was against the laws of nature to treat a ship like this. Ships were made to use the winds, not fight them. In six or eight weeks the monsoon would reverse itself. A ship bound to the south-west, as the *Quiver* was, would have the wind aft and she would bowl along before it, serene and comfortable.

Sam grabbed for a handhold as the ship flicked over a crest, leaving him momentarily hanging in space. His bread roll jumped off his plate and skidded across the saloon. Sam saved his coffee and cursed under his breath.

There was a loud thud over his head then the sound of many feet. Half a dozen Macaroons came down the companion-way bringing the end of a heavy hawser which they started to coil down, as it was passed from hand to hand the length of the ship, in the captain's day-room. Martin Peake came down and saw the heavy tarred rope would leave little space. ''Vast coiling,' he ordered and went on deck.

Sam heard him tell Henry the door to his cabin could not be opened if the hawser was stowed there. 'Who needs doors? Take 'em off the hinges,' Henry told him. Then he added more loudly, 'And there's room for a couple of ton of chain in Mr Handyside's berth, I'd say . . .'

Hardly had he got the words out than Sam was on deck,

scowling ferociously. 'Belay that, Mr Peake! I may be a poop
ornament in this ship but you stow so much as an end of
spunyarn in my berth I'll have you wishing you still had your
hands in the tar barrel, my oath I will . . .'

Sam's tirade tailed off when he saw Henry laughing at him.
'Just stay on the poop, Sam, and the ballast will be where it's
needed,' Henry said, patting Sam's belly. 'It's gone seven bells,
I think we should tack.'

'Are you asking me or telling me?' Sam demanded.

'You're the navigator, Sam. I'm telling you I want your
advice.'

Sam scanned the murky horizon with troubled eyes. Visibility was little more than a mile at best. It would be wise to make
short tacks and try to stay in the centre of the strait. 'Eight
hours on each board, is that what you're thinking?' Without
waiting for an answer he nodded. 'Yes, it's a good plan. But
you won't tack in this steep head sea, you'll have to wear
round.'

Henry shook his head determinedly then bawled for'ard.
'Ready about! All clear for stays?'

Sam swallowed the protest that rose automatically to his lips
and moved to the leeward side of the poop with the resentful
air of a dog that has had its nose slapped once too often for
stealing from the table. Sam had spent his entire career in
comparatively heavy, slab-sided ships. They were too sluggish
to turn through the eye of the wind in anything but a smooth
sea and a pretty breeze. The first heavy pitch into a heavy sea
would stop such a ship dead in the water then, unable to turn
one way or the other, she would be caught in irons. The rudder
could go. Even the masts. To avoid this kind of disaster the
wind was brought from one side of the ship to the other by
turning the ship away from it. The yards were trimmed round
as the wind came over the stern. The disadvantage of wearing
ship was that in making a big circle down wind she lost a lot of
hard-won ground, perhaps miles. But that was the price you
paid. For Sam it had been the habit of a professional lifetime
and he viewed any other option as madness. Grim faced, he
watched the men run to their stations. 'Lash down your back
teeth, m'boys,' said the red-headed Irish seaman called Flynn.
'This side will be t'other side directly.'

Henry stood beside Adam Robinson at the wheel giving
instructions in a low voice. The bows came off the wind a little
and the ship heeled sharply as she gathered speed, flinging

spray high enough to wet the reefed main and fore course. 'Ready, Mr Lamshire?' Henry shouted.

Standing at the break of the fo'c's'le and staring aft, the mate checked the deck. 'Aye aye, all ready for'ard!'

'Helm's a-lee!'

Robinson heaved the wheel over. The rudder flung the ship into the wind. Lamshire hooked his thumb at the four Murphies awaiting his signal at the foremast. The fore-topmast-staysail rattled down, whipping like a demon. The bowsprit dipped into a grey swell and the air was blurred with stinging spray. The ship was within a point of the wind – barely ten degrees – and the captain's bellow was heard all over the ship. 'Mainsail haul!'

There was frenzied activity. Martin Peake jerked the pins to which the braces of all the yards on mainmast and crossjack were made up. Bowlines were let go, main tack raised. Then a dozen men on the maindeck, led by Meadows and Field, grabbed the lee braces and lustily hauled hand over hand.

The ship arrowed directly into the wind's eye, plunging heavily into a trough that opened like a chasm beneath her forefoot. The oncoming wave smashed into the concave cheeks of her bow. The ship quivered from stem to stern then a dense cloud of spray smoked the length of her maindeck with a hissing roar. Oblivious to the drenching water the men hauled. High above them on the after two masts the great yards swivelled. They bucked and whipped under the weight of shaking canvas.

With a peel of thunder the sails on the foremast came aback, every curve reversing itself. Because the fore yards were not yet trimmed round, the action of the wind deflecting off the canvas helped to push the bows round. Also, it made a lee so the yards on the other two masts could be braced round more easily. The jibs and staysails shook dementedly. Tripping over wildly whipping ropes, ducking beneath blocks that swung violently to and fro with skull-crushing force, the men on the fo'c's'le fed the sheets round the stays and made them clear to run.

For an anxious moment the ship hung in balance. Would she miss stays and fall back on her previous tack? Henry was on the point of telling Robinson to reverse the helm when he saw Sam heaving on the spanker sheet. Two men jumped to help him. The big sail was dragged across the poop until it back-winded. Sam got a turn on the pin a split second before the sail filled. The extra leverage was just enough to kick the stern round. With increasing speed the bowsprit swept across the tumbling horizon.

'Let go and haul!'

Now the yards on the foremast had to be braced round, and quickly. Staysails and foresails were sheeted home. With a succession of explosions the sails clapped full of wind. The clipper seemed to hunch under the impact, dipping her rail as she put her shoulder to it, then she soared up and over the next sea.

All over the ship the orientation of life was altered. One side of the tilting world had suddenly become the other. Every slope reversed itself and for a few minutes there was confusion as the clipper's people adjusted to the new slant.

The change of tack brought a clatter of pans from the galley. A lid slithered from the iron pot in which the day's dumplings were simmering but the pots on the cooking range were held fast by cross-bars slotted into a surrounding frame. Soup slopped on the red-hot iron and danced with a smell of burning. As the dipping bulwarks filled the scuppers Nix Barlow swung round on the low box he used as a stool and squirted a jet of tobacco juice into the swirling foam.

In the sail locker Manfred Longhandle, too, swivelled on his upturned tub as he heard the rattle of gear aloft and felt the deck sway through the horizontal. At the same time every shadow turned as the lantern hanging from the bulkhead shifted its angle of lean by ninety degrees. The sailmaker moved the bowler hat filled with needles, palms and threads to a more convenient position and cursed bad-temperedly until he located the knife that had slipped between folds of the sail he was stitching.

In his little pantry off the saloon Tom Withers was plucking the now silent rooster when he heard the warning cry of 'Helm's a-lee!' He did not waste time cursing. The pastry for the pie was rolled out on the bench and all the ingredients were lodged safely against the bulkhead on the low side of the slope. In a moment it would become the high side. The bloody lot would shoot into his lap if he didn't move fast.

He flipped the pastry into folds and hung it like a napkin on the door handle. As the deckhead thundered with the stamp of feet and the bench tilted towards the horizontal he threw out both arms.

Stone jars of flour, sugar and salt, plus rolling pin, spoon, carving knife, the bag of currants . . . all avalanched into his embrace. For a moment he waited, knowing what was coming. The sails filled. The whole pantry seemed to turn on end. Everything slid across the cupboards. Tom's feet slipped on the tilting floor. Then the helmsman caught her, the angle lessened.

Wedging the flour drum beneath his chin and taking a chance with the sugar, he transferred his armload, item by item, to the other end of the bench. Then, humming quietly, he settled the fowl in his lap and continued ripping the glossy feathers from its breast. Behind him, the pastry slowly sagged to the floor.

At the other end of the ship Neptunia slithered across the wet floor of her pen with a loud squeal. Big Tree heard the splintering crack of a mahogany bar and vaulted over the windlass. The pink pig, now grown to considerable dimensions, scrabbled on the deck for a foothold as it dropped away beneath her. Then the deck came up to meet her again and she fell on her chin with a grunt. At the same moment the Maori fell sprawling on top of her and the two of them skidded with elbows and trotters flailing into the open door of the port-side water closet.

The whole manoeuvre had taken barely a minute. As the ship steadied on her course, cutting back towards the China coast, Will Lamshire checked her trim. The fore-topmast-staysail was hoisted again and sheeted home then the four triangular foresails were adjusted in tight parallel curves. The squaresails were harder to get right.

The braces controlling the angle of the yards led aft to the poop where a gang of men stood by to heave or slack away as the mate ordered. The trick was to get the huge lower yard in sharp then to free the topsail yard by half a point and the topgallant yard by another half point and so on, each mast by turn. 'T'gallant yard a small pull!' Will shouted.

The men threw the fore-topgallant brace off its pin, took the strain, and sweated it in a couple of feet until they heard, 'Well the t'gallant yard . . . Heave in the royal!'

Meanwhile Martin Peake put other men to coiling up the tails of the sheets and hanging them on their pins. He ran up the poop ladder. 'Tobacco and slop chest, captain?'

Henry nodded. It was the second mate's job to dispense tobacco to the men, marking the cost of each purchase against the wages to be paid on arrival. The ship also carried a small stock of clothing and boots for men to buy. 'Five minutes, not a second longer, Mr Peake,' Henry growled.

Peake took a carton of tobacco from the stores and hurried for'ard to remove himself as far as possible from the captain's gaze. 'Baccy up!' he shouted.

Under the break of the fo'c's'le he made himself comfortable on the windlass and was opening the box on his knees when he glimpsed Big Tree's face. The Maori's tattooed cheeks had a grey pallor and he was staring aghast at the tobacco. Neptunia took advantage of the moment to free herself from his clutches. Charlie Meadows headed her off and with two Macaroons steered her back into her pen. 'I never made an 'ammock for a pig but that's what she needs,' Meadows said, watching Neptunia scrabbling painfully on the plunging deck.

'The sooner I see that hog in the oven the happier I'll be,' Peake said, offering a handful of plug to Big Tree who had recovered his composure. 'How many you want, you cannibal?'

The hard-edged seas racing up in endless procession were not the smooth hills and vales of mid-ocean but were chopped up in cliffs and canyons. Henry was reminded of the endless vista of slate rooftops and terraced brick houses he had viewed from the masthead on his first morning in London. The ship plunged and reared from street to street with a violent see-saw motion that unsettled even the toughest of cast-iron stomachs. Toiling from handhold to handhold, leaping for the lifelines stretched across the deck when a knee-high wave spilled across the deck, the men staggered aft with burden after burden of ironware, paint and heavy casks which were transferred from the fo'c's'le to the aft cabins to bring her stern deeper.

As noon approached Sam Handyside loitered hopefully on the poop with the sextant under his coat but there was no chance of catching a sight of the sun in the low grey scud of cloud. The navigation chart was a sight to chill any mariner to the bones. Only the outlines of the coasts – China, the Indies, Borneo – were clearly defined. The space between was blankly white but for the words printed large: NUMEROUS REEFS AND SHOALS. 'The China Sea is more reefs than water, no place for cracking on,' Sam warned Henry worriedly.

'I'm not taking sail off her,' Henry snapped. His clothes whipped in the wind and his hair was plastered wetly across his forehead. He was stiff with cold and exhaustion and in no mood for further argument.

'Whips of luck to you, lad, but you've got to take into account we're sailing blind. I don't know where we are.'

'That makes two of us,' Henry replied. 'You don't think that Yankee bastard will heave to and wait for the sun to come out, do you?'

Drizzle engulfed the ship but so thick was the flying spray that the rain could be distinguished only by taste. Sam hunched his neck deeper into his coat and turned his shoulder into the wind. 'Perhaps not, but I daresay the *Musket* is cautious enough to sail through this muck with look-outs posted.'

The barb found its mark and Henry knew he had been caught out. He cupped his hands and called, 'Mr Lamshire, a sharp pair of eyes in the foretop.'

A rogue wave towered high along the lee side then its tumbling crest spilled on board. It caught the ship on the wrong foot. A wall of water nearly waist high surfed across the deck. It spurted over the storm sill into the crew's quarters. There was a furious cry from the galley and a cloud of steam as the fire was put out. 'Christ, there goes dinner,' Peake muttered.

Meadows let out a long moan. 'Gawd, Barley, why didn't we buy the bleedin' farm?'

Rolling his eyes despairingly to heaven, Field momentarily froze then roughly pushed Meadows and Peake into the lee of the deckhouse. He had spotted the luckless Bunce, sent to do look-out duty in the wildly swinging foretop, vomiting into space. But there had been no need to worry about being in the firing line for the string of orange slime was bent in the airflow round the sails, and it blew away to leeward.

Peake sniffed contemptuously but his moustache had filled out in recent months and he found himself with a nostril full of salt water that made him sneeze. 'How much more of this do we have to take?' he gasped.

'Abaht an 'undred days,' Meadows said bleakly. Then his eye caught the haggard face of the captain. 'Look at the ol' man, poor sod. Barley, we gotta fink o' somefink for 'im.'

Even with a score of heavy casks lashed under the break of the poop and several tons of weight stowed aft, the *Quiver* was not handling as sweetly as Henry desired. She ought to be stiffer, standing up to the wind instead of heeling so tenderly and increasing her leeway. Perhaps he had not loaded enough ballast, Henry thought, as he hunched his body against the wet wind and tried to apply a mind numbed by two days and nights without rest.

His eyes blinked open. With a start he realised he had been asleep on his feet. Hearing a thump behind him, he peered round blearily. Meadows was helping Big Tree lash a chair to the skylight. It was one of Sam's rattan deckchairs, with a sloping back, wide arms, and a fold-out footrest. Then Withers came up with a couple of pillows and a blanket which Meadows told him to put in place. Henry was suddenly engulfed by weariness and he flopped down with a small smile of thanks. He was asleep before Big Tree returned with a square of tarpaulin that he tucked round the captain's legs.

At every bell Henry woke briefly, squinted at the set of sails of which he had a direct view without the necessity of lifting his head, and slept again. Every hour the new man on the helm learnt to his cost that he could not relax just because his captain was asleep. The luff of the fore-topgallant only had to lift with the promise of a shiver for Henry to snap awake with a warning growl. At eight bells the ship was tacked and headed off again towards the south-west having made only about twenty miles in a forward direction through the long day.

It was pea soup and bread for supper which Henry ate from his knees on deck. 'She's too tender, you can feel it in the gusts,' he told Sam, running his fingers wearily through his knotted hair. 'It's my fault for not loading more ballast. We've got to get some weight up to windward.'

'Like what, lad? Hoist the anchor to the windward end of the mainyard? It might work.'

'Don't be stupid. Any weight we hang out to windward will be to leeward on the next tack.'

'I know,' Sam said with a scowl.

'Pardon Cap'n . . . ?' Will Lamshire, who had the watch, pulled his long nose reflectively as he interrupted. 'I couldn't help hearing what you were saying. You can move a couple o' ton every time we tack, no problem.'

'You mean have the men sitting on the windward rail all night with shackles in their pockets?'

Lamshire smiled shyly. 'Not at all, Cap'n. But you could put the shackles and weights in a box and trim it athwartships on a tackle.'

'Good thinking,' Henry said at once, wiping his plate with a crust. 'Tell the farmers I want a coffin wide enough for six men and if it isn't ready by dawn they'll be the first residents.'

For ten days the *Quiver* battled south-westwards, chewing into constant headwinds and contrary currents as she drove deeper into the narrowing funnel of the South China Sea.

At every tack the trimming box which Meadows and Field had made, mounted on skids and filled with two tons of galley coal and ironware, was hauled across the maindeck to add weight to windward. The benefit was hard to gauge but it did seem to Henry that the ship carried herself a little more stiffly. And if it made a difference of only a quarter of a degree on every tack it might shorten their misery by half an hour overall. At ten knots, half an hour might put her five miles ahead of the *Musket*, more than enough to put the Yankee hull-down over the horizon.

Snatching thirty-minute naps in the deckchair and getting at most four or five hours rest in every twenty-four, Henry lived on the poop. He was tireless in his will to drive the ship on, as if his own shoulders lifted her bows over every wave. When a squall came down, Henry was instantly at the helmsman's side to con her through the blast. When the wind relented a little he was invariably first to become conscious of it and order the reef to be shaken out of the main.

Twice the look-out hailed to report feathers of spray rising from breakers spilling over a distant reef. Each time, to Henry's unspoken question, Sam answered with a helpless shrug. With no sights of the sun possible in the overcast, the constant tacking, and unmeasured currents playing ducks and drakes with his dead reckoning, Sam had to admit he was lost. Not that accurate navigation would have helped greatly, because few of these deadly reefs were charted.

While Henry adapted quickly to the hard life he had made for himself, constantly exposed to the wind and relaxing for only a few minutes at a time, Sam grew gaunt with anxiety. Henry knew it would be prudent to shorten sail at night when the killer reefs lurked invisibly in the darkness. But his only option was to press on and take the risk. Talking about it only made him angry. It was his decision as master and if Sam didn't like it he could stew. But Henry felt a certain sympathy for the older man. Every nerve must be shrieking. No wonder he looked as if he had been socked in both eyes.

The relentless hammering into the weather was equally hard on the crew. The deckhouse ran with water, swilling sea chests back and forth between the bunks. Blankets and straw mattresses were damp and mouldy and smelled like a stable. There was no lulling to sleep. In the violent pitching, sleep was a battle. Manfred Longhandle made himself a hammock which he slung in the sail locker. Big Tree crawled among the bolts of canvas where he made himself a nest like a rat in a wardrobe. Most of the men had raw skin on their wrist-bones and elbows from the need to brace their bodies in their bunks but this was nothing to the bumps and bruises from being flung about on deck as seas crashed aboard, nor the aching weariness from clinging to the wildly arcing spars when it was necessary to go aloft.

Until suddenly, one miraculous evening, the long slog ended. At sunset there was a diamond-bright flare in the west. The sun gleamed through a slot of clear sky just above the horizon, like a light showing beneath a door. For a few minutes it bathed the dark wet stains on the canvas in a warm light. Henry's new beard took on a reddish tone and Lamshire's nose became a cheerful pink as he smiled in the sunlight.

It did not last long. Almost at once the sun dropped into the sea. During the night the wind fell away. In the morning, eleven days out of the Min River, everything was different.

'Easy all!'

The gig lost way and swung round as Henry heaved on the tiller to get a direct view of his ship rolling gently on the calm blue sea. With a faint bow wave crinkling the glossy water, and bright reflections of the figurehead smearing the shadows under the high arch of her bow, the *Quiver* ghosted along with bare steerage way. Sitting tensely in the sternsheets, his sleeves rolled up to his armpits and his faded blue shirt open at the front, Henry critically weighed the trim of the dark green hull as a larger swell lifted the ship towards the blue sky. 'Down by the stern, an inch or two,' he said to himself.

The ship dropped into a trough and the hull vanished from view as the swell trundled towards the men resting on their oars, low in the boat. For a few moments only her sails jutted above the smooth ridge of the wave, the dark tan of the canvas mottled with pale patches as they dried. Then ship and gig lifted together and Henry again had a perfect view of her profile.

Cheerful noises carried over the water. The rhythmic scratch-scratch of holystones honing a silky smoothness into the deckboards. The clank of the pump and slosh of water. A

snatch of whistling abruptly cut off as a jet from the hosepipe
found its mark. A loud clatter and a splash as the cook scraped
a pot over the side. A jabble of excited clucking as Big Tree
threw the hens a handful of rice grains for their breakfast.

The sounds grew fainter as the clipper slipped away, showing the gold scroll-work of her escutcheon to the gig's crew
who began to shoot alarmed glances at their captain gazing
dreamily at his disappearing ship. The boundless immensity of
the ocean seemed never so great as from an open boat. Only
now was the ship that was their whole world seen in true
perspective, small and frail amid such vastness.

The ship was half a mile off, water bubbling under her tuck
as a lipper of wind sighed through her sails. Adam Robinson
rattled his oar significantly in its pins and said, 'Ah, Cap'n, sah,
she's gonna be a long pull . . .'

'All right, give way,' Henry ordered. It was fifteen minutes'
hard row up the *Quiver*'s wake to catch her, then the puff of
breeze faded and she was left rocking again. Henry clambered
up the channels, vaulted the rail and gave rapid instructions to
the mate for adjusting the trim.

Within the hour the ship had every appearance of a real
washee-washee boat. Wet clothes and mattresses festooned
the lower rigging. Spare sails were dragged from Longhandle's
locker and hoisted high by their corners where they flapped
and rumbled like giant laundry. Ropes and hawsers that had
been stowed wet were flaked back and forth across the deck so
the couple of tons of moisture they contained would be blotted
up by the dazzling sun. The spanker outhaul was hung with
Withers' table cloths and dishcloths, then he washed and
pegged out Henry's clothes to rid them of mildew while the
mates did the same with their own gear.

The heavy awnings that had not seen fresh air since the
pagoda anchorage were spread to dry. The crew's quarters in
the deckhouse were scrubbed out and whitewashed. Even
Neptunia was given a run, her pink flanks steaming as she was
chased away from the heaps of drying clothes in which she
tried to make a nest. 'Lock her up, she'll get sunburned,' Will
Lamshire told Big Tree.

'Eh, what you say?' the Maori asked.

'Pig go pig-pen, savvy?' Meadows translated, pinching his
skin and pointing at the sun.

Big Tree smiled. 'Maybe black pig more better than *pakeha*,'
he said.

'Gawd, ain't we got enuff of 'em,' Meadows grumbled, eyeing the men, half of them black and the other half rapidly changing from white to pink, who were taking advantage of the holiday mood and giving every appearance of being hard at work without raising a sweat.

Martin Peake thumbed the blade of his knife and licked his lips as Big Tree steered Neptunia for'ard. 'A bit of sun on that crackling won't do any harm,' he said. 'When is the old man going to do for her, after Anjer when we hit the trades? If he leaves it any longer she'll get old and scrawny.'

'I reckon the ol' man's gone soft on the old sow,' Meadows said.

'I hope not!' Martin exclaimed.

'Sure, the pig's 'is good-luck charm, I reckon. Don't you remember who gave it to him?'

Martin folded his knife. 'Bloody hell, I never thought of that.'

Work on the gently steaming decks was interrupted every few minutes by orders from the poop to brace round the great yards to make the most of every puff of wind pawing lightly over the sea. The wind baffled through all points of the compass, stretching her tense captain to a high pitch of frustration.

Withers unscrewed the mirror from the bulkhead in the captain's store-filled cabin then took it on deck with a mug of hot water and held it steady while Henry shaved his inch of new beard. Then Henry sat on the corner of the skylight with a towel round his shoulders while the pale steward hacked at his hair with blunt scissors, cutting it especially short over the neck behind each ear. These bare areas became Henry's secret weapon for detecting the faintest breaths of wind. He thought of them as his wind patches. Prowling the deck and turning his head this way and that, the sensitive skin behind his ears would suddenly feel a coolness. Long before any hint of a changing breeze was visible on the surface of the sea, the crew were driven protestingly to the braces. Then it would come, tickling over the oily surface, and the sails were ready trimmed for it.

Day after day the ship hop-scotched through the baffling airs, turning this way and that to make the most of every puff and determinedly working her way west and south. Every few hours a squall rolled over the horizon. Some glided by, filling half the sky with snowy alpine peaks and trailing grey curtains of rain. At least one squall a day crashed over the ship, driving her forward in a lash of wind and stinging rain then leaving her, steaming wetly and lurching in the lop.

Only when the *Quiver* wore a hat full of wind did her restless captain entrust her to his mates and sink into his chair. As the ship drove on he snatched a few winks. Then a sail flapped, a block rattled, and he was prowling the poop again, tenaciously hunting for a breeze.

With a sun sight giving him a position line every morning, then a noon fix, Sam Handyside was content. His tiny pencilled crosses that marked the ship's position on the chart at every noon made a wriggling line pointing the way to the bottleneck of narrow straits and uncharted hazards where the trailing land-shapes of the Malays tangled with the lofty island peaks of the Dutch East Indies. The maze of islands set in a milky way of coral reefs stretched across the path of every vessel routed between the Orient and the Cape of Good Hope. In later years the tough breed of sailormen racing cargoes of wool across the Southern Ocean and round Cape Horn would scoff at the easy life of the flying fish sailors, as the tea men were known. But the shellbacks balling off the knots in the roaring forties could hardly begin to imagine the perils of the Java Sea and its approaches, and the heights of nautical skill and cunning required to catch what fickle winds there were to emerge unscathed in the friendly tradewinds of the Indian Ocean.

Nineteen days out, Sam was woken suddenly. His ears had long become accustomed to the magnified noises of a sailing ship heard below deck. To sailors, silence was not an absence of noise but the gulp of water streaming along the planks, the creak of knees and beams as the hull worked and twisted, the steady scrape of oilskins and clothing swaying from the pegs on which it hung, and a multitude of other sounds so familiar that they were not heard. But a faint cry from the look-out straddling the fore-topgallant yard was enough to jerk Sam abruptly from a deep sleep.

'Land ho!'

His cotton nightshirt flapping against his thick white calves, Sam stood on the poop and screwed his eyes against the glare. No doubt about it. The distinct shadow on the horizon ahead – paler than the sea but darker than the sky – was the outlying corner of Borneo.

Beaming contentedly, Sam went below and spread out the chart though he knew it as familiarly as the back of his hand. But his smile became a scowl of concentration. Before she entered the Sunda Strait between Sumatra and Java, and tasted the freedom of the Indian Ocean, the *Quiver* faced six hundred miles of sea congested with uncharted reefs and numerous islands. One great mass of dots on the chart, each denoting the presence of a killer reef, was marked simply, Thousand Islands. Over large areas the navigation hazards were established by a single word printed large, UNEXPLORED.

All day the ship ran south, five or six miles off the Borneo coast: densely jungled headlands separated by wide delta marshes where a careful scrutiny with the glass from the royal yard revealed mangrove swamps creeping out to meet the mud-coloured sea. Native *proas*, long and slender craft with sails shaped like broad, curved dagger blades – dainty and speedy compared with the lumbering and boxy Chinese junks – sheered off as the ship approached, her tiers of canvas spread to the brisk sea breeze off the beam.

At sunset a long stretch of steep shoreline lay ahead and the breeze died. Sam tapped the chart with the blunt end of his pencil as Henry looked over his shoulder. 'A bad place to be in the dark, lad. They're head-hunters on this coast and if we give 'em half a chance we'll be grinning at each other while hanging by our hair in the rafters of a long-house. Best stand off, I say.'

Henry patted Sam's bald pate. 'No risk, Sam, they will have to use you for a doorstop.' He went on deck and told the helmsman to put up the helm. Sam threw his pencil across the saloon. They were not turning away from the coast but heading in.

As a sea breeze had carried through the day, Henry decided it was a fair bet a land breeze would come up during the night. The closer he could work the ship in with the land the sooner he would fill her sails. He kept the bowsprit pointing straight for the murky shore until Charlie Meadows found fifteen fathoms with the leadline, then turned parallel. Under full sail the *Quiver* gentled through the black water so calm and soft that bright stars danced on its surface. At four bells – ten o'clock in the evening – Henry's wind patch detected the first whisper of the land breeze. It brought all the strange and pungent fragrances of the jungle: moss, mud, mangrove roots; cinnamon, cloves, flowers; tree bark, rotting leaves, matted creepers . . .

Henry felt a surge of nostalgia for the earthy fragrances of New South Wales with its red dust and aromatic gum trees. His mouth twisted in a private ironical smile as he wished his father could see him now, conning his tea clipper home from China. A blood-curdling scream startled him out of his reverie then he laughed as he realised he had been frightened by the squawk of a parrot. It was followed by a distant jabbering of monkeys. They might have been exclaiming at the sight of the full-rigged ship cutting fast across the track of the moon.

The watch changed at midnight but most men were content to stretch out on deck and be lulled to sleep by the strange sounds and smells of the jungle. The lead was kept going in shifts, sounding the way ahead. When the depth came less than fifteen fathoms Henry altered course to seaward, feeling his way along the contour of the seabed.

When the watch changed again at four the moon dropped behind the high rise of land and the breeze began to die. Within twenty minutes the *Quiver* was becalmed in a blackness made luminous by stars.

Henry patrolled the poop, his wind patches finding no hint of a breeze. There was a sound of feet running fast on the maindeck then Big Tree bounded up the ladder and pointed ahead, his eyes as large and round as balls of ivory. It took a few moments to make sense of what he was trying to say. 'I hear dog!' he gasped, and made a loud noise in his throat that was half growl, half bark.

'Pass the word for'ard, silence in the ship!' Henry snapped to Martin Peake.

There was no point in trying to verify what the Maori's keen hearing had picked up. If Big Tree thought he heard a dog that sounded like Nightingale then it was reliable enough to act upon instantly. It was not at all unlikely that the *Musket* could be a little way ahead, perhaps ghosting along the coast as the *Quiver* was, or lying at anchor waiting for daylight. Henry gave quick orders in a low voice.

The watch below was roused. One by one the boats were dropped over the side and manned. Hardly a word was spoken and the only sound was the clatter of an oar being dropped, a muttered oath, the squeal of a block. Then towing warps were passed to the three boats and they began to heave ahead, slewing the clipper round and laboriously hauling her off the coast.

The dawn was heralded by a sky of palest rosy pink, promising a warm day to come, but the shadows of the land revealed no sign of another ship. As the light brightened Henry saw a mauve-grey mist skirling along the shore, now two or three miles distant. It was more than enough to conceal a ship.

In the three boats strung ahead of the bow there was no let-up. Towing a fully laden ship with oars alone made hot and heavy work. Flynn's orange hair flamed in the low sunlight and his face was crimson with effort. 'If me mudder could see her poor boy a-spoilin' his hands with blisters and blood . . . ' he complained.

'Shut up and pull, yer bog orange,' Meadows grunted, squinting up at the sails which hung as limply as washing in a thunderstorm.

Even when the sun burned up the skeins of mist spilling down the valleys and rolling over the glinting sea, the *Quiver*'s searching telescopes found nothing that any eye could distinguish for certain as a ship rather than a clump of palm trees.

At last a dark line became visible on the surface to seaward. The ribbon of ruffled blue grew broader as the sea breeze crept towards the warming land. Blistered and weary, the pullers groaned with relief as Henry gave the order to swing in the boats. The sails filled and the ship gathered way, heeling more as the wind strengthened.

Four bells sounded, signalling ten in the morning, as the last of the boats was chocked down. 'Ten minutes for breakfast then work as usual, there's a lot to do, Mister,' Henry said, and the hands were too dead to raise a grouse.

'Excuse me, Captain, was it really the *Musket* under the shore?'

'Shall we put back and check, Mr Peake?' Henry replied unkindly. 'It might be a good experience for you to see how Screech Gander runs a ship.'

'Who cares?' Sam interrupted. 'If it was really Gander we heard back there he must be sitting on the spot scratching his arse and whistling for a wind.'

But Henry did care. If indeed it had been Nightingale barking on the rival ship's deck as she lay close in with the shore then the *Musket* must have passed the *Quiver* during the long slog down the China Sea. If she could overhaul so easily and without being seen, she could do it again. And there was another problem.

With no land at her back and no mist to hide her, the *Quiver* would have made a clear silhouette on the seaward horizon. Gander would not have failed to see her and he would lose no time giving chase.

Unconscious of his tuneless whistling that skirled like a cold wind through a castle ruin, Henry was wearing a furrow up and down the weather side of the poop when Sam asked him to come below and look at the chart.

The saloon was dim and easy on the eye after the dazzling sea and sky. The sun glowed through the white duck shades laced across the glass panels and the mahogany returned a ruddy reflection. Sam sat in an upholstered chair with his charts spread out on the table and Henry did not have to ask what he wanted. The tap of Sam's blunt finger on the paper was enough.

Clear across the *Quiver*'s southward track, stretching three hundred miles between Borneo and Sumatra, lay a barrier of reefs and islands. For large ships whose navigators had spent anything less than a lifetime in these waters, there were only two safe passages. The wisest choice, the one Sam knew of old, was the Banca Strait. Like a broad river estuary it twisted for more than 150 miles between the large island of that name and the mainland coast of Sumatra. The shores of the strait were gently sloping and muddy. If a ship ran ashore the crew could heave her off with a kedge as long as the *proas*, carrying hordes of native pirates, did not get to her first.

The more direct route was also more exposed: the ill-famed Macclesfield Channel in the Gaspar Strait, where Captain Enright of the *Chrysolite* had so misled the American clipper *Memnon*. Here the reefs rose sheer, like underwater cliffs, from great depths. Any ship that hit one could count herself finished. The ship-hungry coral would chew her to bits even if the breakers did not splinter her to smithereens in the first few seconds. But in most conditions the breakers served as signposts; the reefs were easy enough to avoid as long as you could see them.

'You'll be taking the Banca Strait, lad. I've marked off the courses, and . . .'

Henry took a chair opposite Sam and shook his head firmly but with an apologetic smile. 'I'm sorry, Sam, we'll lose two days that way and you know it.'

Sam pushed his fingers through his whiskers and pulled at his jowls. 'Yes, I rather fancied you would take the Macclesfield,' he said resignedly. 'It's not too difficult. I have done it myself once or twice. There's a horse-shoe of reefs at the northern end where you can drop the hook in smooth water and the holding's good.'

Henry took a deep breath. 'Why do you want to anchor, Sam?'

The old man's shaggy white eyebrows arched in surprise. 'The channel's only a couple of hours away and dark's coming on, it's no place to loiter unless you can see where you're going.'

'I'm not proposing to linger, Sam, we're sailing right on through and I'm not shortening down by so much as a single royal.'

Sam was dumbfounded. He knuckled his eyes then looked at Henry as if he were seeing an apparition. 'The Macclesfield in the dark? You're out of your mind! Don't you remember the *Memnon* . . . ?'

'If that was the *Musket* we heard off the coast she'll come right up on us if we sit around waiting,' Henry said. 'I don't want to see that Yankee bastard's topsails on the horizon when the sun comes up. Do you?'

'The Macclesfield in the dark is suicide!'

'Not necessarily.' Henry paused and waved the angry old man down into his seat then continued in a quiet and even voice. 'Listen, the surf on the reefs will show up in the moonlight like the white cliffs of Dover laid flat. We can con her from the masthead. And you're right, maybe I ought to take the royals off her, more if the wind freshens, but I don't think I will.'

'That is exactly your problem,' Sam interrupted stiffly. 'No wind means no surf. If the wind drops any more you won't see the reefs before the current carries you into them. I think you're mad.'

Henry knew well enough from his sailing in the South Pacific that reefs were often at their most dangerous in a flat calm, especially when they lay up-sun in a hazy light. And moonlight, he grudgingly admitted, would have much the same effect because it would be impossible for the look-outs to distinguish the changing colours indicating shallow water.

Sam mistook Henry's hesitation for agreement and he pushed back his chair. 'I'll tell old Lampshades to rouse out the cable.'

'Sit down, Sam, we're not anchoring.'

Scarlet with fury, Sam thumped the table with a bunched fist and glared at Henry. 'I'll stop this madness if it's the last thing I do. You're a reckless young fool who doesn't know what he's doing. I forbid it, and Mr Winkworth gave me the authority to do so, as you well know.'

'That's all right, Sam, you can report to the owner when we reach London,' Henry said calmly, and went on deck.

'If we reach London, which we won't,' Sam shouted at his retreating back.

Unhappily Henry returned to his beat on the poop. The ship sluiced along at a comfortable five knots. The sun lay fist-high above a hazy horizon and a skim of filmy clouds promised a calm, quiet night. Perhaps too calm, Henry worried, but it couldn't be helped. Henry was turning to tell the mate double up on bow and foretop lookouts when Sam came out of the companion-way and blocked his path. 'Listen to an experienced old mariner, lad. I know you're not going to change your mind because you're a stubborn and crazy young idiot. But if you have to take the Macclesfield in the dark why not send a boat ahead, to scout . . . ?'

Whistling like a paddleboat with steam up, Henry marched rapidly to the taffrail then back again, turning it over in his mind. What Sam said made perfect sense. 'I think you're right,' he said. 'Six picked men at the oars, the lead-line trailing over the stern at a fixed depth – say ten fathoms – and a couple of lanterns to signal with.'

'You will have to shorten sail but the longboat will do four or five knots under sail, and she pulls well.'

'Yes, I'll take Meadows and Field. And the cannibal, he'll have a nose for reefs.'

'You?' Sam cried. 'You're not proposing to go in the longboat yourself, send young Peake or I'll go myself.'

'No, I want you to take the *Quiver* because that puts every man in the job he can do best,' Henry told him. 'I'll go in the longboat to scout ahead. You can handle the ship under reduced sail. That leaves Mr Peake who has the best eyes to watch for our lights from the fore-topgallant yard and Lampshades to run the deck.'

Sam had objection written over every inch of his stocky frame but after a few moments' thought he grudgingly acquiesced and the mates were summoned to hear what was in store for them through the long night to come.

In the last of the rapidly fading twilight the longboat was put over the side and stocked with water, provisions and lanterns. The wind feathered out of the north-east, puffing the ship along in gentle spurts. A distant island trailed a cap of cloud from its lofty summit which caught the last orange glow of the sun, then it was dissolved in the smoky dusk.

Henry went through it all one last time as his men scrambled into the boat. 'I'll crack on as hard as I dare, trailing the lead-line. When it touches, or we see a reef ahead, I'll hoist a second lantern and cut off to port or starboard at ninety degrees. All you have to do is follow my lights. When I'm in safe water again and back on course I'll revert to one lantern.'

'I'll leave you plenty of sea room, at least seven or eight cables,' Sam confirmed.

Henry signalled to the men and the longboat dropped into the water. In a few minutes the mast was rigged, the lugsail hoisted, and the thirty-two-foot open boat, a single lantern burning brightly from a jigger mast guyed upright in the stern, started to draw away.

'What about a signal for extreme danger?' Sam called.

'No lights at all,' Henry said. 'If you don't see any lights do something fast.'

'Aye aye, good luck lad.'

The longboat heeled to the breeze and moved ahead into the purpling darkness. High aloft, the warm air fanning his cheeks, Martin Peake saw the unwinking light grow gradually smaller. When he judged it to be about three-quarters of a mile distant he hailed the deck. Sam ordered the braces hardened in and the clipper, sailing under topsails and topgallants alone, moved slowly along the longboat's wake.

For three hours there was no change. The lantern glowed steadily like a low evening star. Suddenly the one light became two. 'Deck there, two lights showing!' Martin shouted.

'Which way is he going?'

One above the other, the two lights shifted off to the north-west and the ship followed. In the faint luminosity of the veiled moonlight the second mate saw a line of heaving ripples where the small waves peaked over a reef. Soon the two lights became one again and the little convoy resumed its course, making a similar jink to the eastward around midnight.

The squall came out of nowhere.

One moment the longboat bubbled quietly over the low waves, next she was fighting for her life. Henry had been staring at the compass and concentrating on the chart spread out on his knees. His eyes had lost their night vision because the glow of the lantern reflected brightly on the white paper. Like a massive figurehead Big Tree stood erect in the bow with his arms folded and his eyes screwed up against the faint light that stole into the corners.

Henry felt a chill breath on the back of his neck and the chart fluttered wildly. He looked up into a wall of blackness. A gust of wind slapped his face with a ferocity that made him fling up an arm. The sail bowed taut, the leech drumming like a mad thing. Meadows eased the mainsheet to spill some wind as the lee gunwale dipped and the men who sprawled lazily in the bottom boards scrambled hastily up to windward. Heaving the tiller in the crook of his elbow to keep her from flying up into the wind, Henry crammed the chart down the front of his coat then cringed as the rain struck like an ambush of spears and arrows. To steer any predetermined course was imposs-ible. Henry could not even see the compass. They could only free sheets and scud along with the fury of the squall at their backs. The lantern blew out. 'Quick as you like, Oatsy, get the bloody lamp burning!' Henry snapped.

Sheltering the lamp with their bodies, Meadows and Field struck match after match. The darkness was absolute. Nothing was visible but the faintest glow of the wake spouting like a rooster tail from the rudder. Big Tree was no longer keeping look-out but had dropped into the bottom of the boat. Henry was surprised but had no time to wonder why the experienced harpooner should lose his nerve so contemptibly. Instead, he worried whether the longboat would at any moment shoot off the edge of the world, so fast was she sailing.

The boat lurched precariously as Big Tree suddenly stood up, clinging to the forestay, and pointed ahead. Henry under-stood. Big Tree had not been hiding from the squall but had cupped his ear to the planks. He could not see the reef ahead, but through the boards of the longboat he had heard it.

'Stand by to tack!' Henry yelled.

The men turned startled faces towards him. Carrying too much sail the longboat was a runaway. It would be like trying to turn a bolting horse.

With perfect judgement and skill Henry threw the boat round. The sail flogged almost to pieces then filled with a thunderclap that heeled the boat until water gushed over the lee rail and threatened to swamp her. Henry caught the leeward dip of the bow with a deft wrench of the tiller but the lurch caused the lantern to slip from Meadows' grip. It crashed down to the lee side with a tinkle of broken glass. At the same moment the rain eased and the wind lessened. The squall was passing over. In half an hour the sky would be clear. Then Charlie Field pointed aft. The *Quiver* was racing out of the darkness, her crumpled topsails flogging and a white bone in her teeth.

'Oh no!'

'We better think o' somefink brilliant, Cap'n,' Meadows said.

'How many matches, Oatsy?'

'Just two is all.'

In the *Quiver*, Sam had seen the onrushing squall and the ship was prepared. Sheets were let fly but even under bare poles and flogging canvas the fine-lined hull sailed fast. When a faint cry was heard above the scream of the wind, as the second mate reported no sign of the light, Sam assumed it was a danger signal. But what if the longboat had capsized in the squall? In an agony of indecision, Sam shielded his eyes and blinked into the rain. Nothing. Give it two minutes, he decided. Then he would heave to as best he could and wait until daylight.

A stab of light caught his eye. First it was a tiny spark, like a cheroot glowing in the dark, then it grew into flames. They lit a circle of white faces and waving arms then fragments of flame peeled away and sparked into the darkness.

There was no mistaking the meaning. The longboat was cutting away to the west. 'Hard up the helm!' Sam thundered. 'Mind your braces, Mr Lamshire, and get your topsails drawing.'

The ship canted heavily under the sudden press of canvas as she bore up and Sam shuddered as he caught a brief glimpse of surf boiling over a reef not two cables to leeward: another quarter of a mile would have done for her. When the reef lay at a safe distance astern he gave orders to back the yards on the main and hove to.

Stars winked from behind the retreating squall as the longboat rounded up under the clipper's counter, rising and falling in the slop of the seas. New lanterns and matches were sent down. Every time the longboat lifted over a crest and the ship's counter dipped, bringing Henry and Sam almost face to face across ten feet of water, they snatched a few words. 'What the hell happened?'

'Smashed the bloody lantern,' Henry told him. 'Bundled up my trousers, soaked them in lamp oil and got them burning with the last match . . .'

'Find me another pair of trousers, we might need 'em again, and throw us a bottle of rum. I reckon we've got something to celebrate, eh Sam?'

'Celebrate?' Sam growled. 'You ought to be keel-hauled, you larrikin. Get going, you can put your trousers on in London.'

'For God's sake, Sam!' Henry bleated. Hiding his smile the old man turned away and gave orders to get the sails drawing. Henry shook his fist then cursed under his breath and reconciled himself to spending the rest of the night trouserless in an open boat. In a few minutes the longboat was casting ahead of the slowly moving clipper, her single lantern burning brightly from the jigger.

The azure sky was dappled with puffy clouds. Steady on the starboard beam, the breeze was strong enough to raise white horses and stream a man's hair as he worked aloft. Flying fish whirring low on silver wings darted from the blade of the bow axing through waves of deep and lovely indigo. This was the life for which men returned again and again to sea. The south-east trades, fanning across five thousand miles of open ocean between the East Indies and the Cape of Good Hope, were simply God's gift to the perfection of sail.

Spooning over the bright slopes, the *Quiver* had piled on her muslin. Studding sails were carried when the wind freed off a point, the long thin booms extending from the yards whipping like fishing rods as their large square sails snapped full of wind. A ringtail was laced to the leech of the spanker. The Jamie Green was set under the bowsprit. Skysails were carried above the royals and Henry would have set moonsails if the masts had been ten feet taller.

Teetering beneath a vast cumulus of canvas the stately and melodic gait of the ship became a wild helter skelter. It felt like walking a tightrope in a gale. The captain, his face and limbs deeply tanned by day and night exposure to sun, wind and rain, hovered at the binnacle to keep a hawk-like eye on the helm. Under such a mountain of sail any lapse of concentration at the wheel would spell disaster. Studding booms cracked under the strain. The auxiliary sails of light, fine-weather canvas split at the seams. Longhandle recruited Pat Flynn to assist him in the endless task of patch and make good as sail after sail was dumped at his feet for repairs.

When the wind headed the ship by a point the auxiliary sails had to be handed fast and were lashed in bundles aloft on the mast, ready for setting the instant Henry's wind patches told him the wind was freeing again. When the wind roused up and the ship pitched so much that the cushioning pressure was shaken out of her sails, the crossjack was furled and occasionally the main fore courses were reefed. But even when sprawled in the deckchair, napping in the shade of Sam's large black umbrella, Henry could sense the slightest change. The instant the wind strength diminished he snapped awake and rattled orders.

'Let fall the crossjack, Mr Peake . . .'

'Shake out those reefs . . . !'

'Stunsails, Mr Mate, do you think you're sailing a Thames marmalade boat?'

Every day, soon after the first bell of the afternoon watch sounded its solitary note in the hot sunlight and the hands formed a ragged line at the galley door, Henry looked over Sam's shoulder as he pencilled a little cross on the chart to make the ship's noon position. The crosses no longer fell almost on top of each other, as they had for so many days in the China Seas, but stepped out briskly across the broad sheet of the chart, pointing a finger at the mighty buttress of Africa jutting towards the south.

With the brass dividers Sam pricked off the distance between the new cross and the last one, then measured the gap against the scale of latitude on the side of the chart. Slogging through fickle winds and dangerous waters towards the Sunda Strait, her distance run had often been only double figures. Now Sam was logging mileage figures he had never expected to see in his life. Distance run 327 miles . . . Distance run 342 miles . . . Distance run 386 miles . . .

The *Quiver* had broken out of the Macclesfield Channel and cut down the Java Sea at a good clip then sighted the cloud-wrapped volcanic spines of Java and Sumatra and shaped her course for Anjer. Though spoken of in the same breath as other great nautical mileposts of world trade routes – like Gibraltar, Cape Horn, Ushant and Cape Cod – Anjer was a disappointing sprawl of houses with red-tiled roofs and white balconies surrounded by native huts. A barque, two ships and a number of schooners were anchored off the town and Henry had scrutinised them carefully as the *Quiver* slipped along a shoreline wooded with palms and banyan trees.

A dozen canoes had skimmed over the velvet water to greet her, natives racing to sell bundles of coconuts, heaps of yams, sweet potatoes, corn and other fresh vegetables. Hens and ducks were trussed in bindings of twine. Wicker baskets were filled with eggs, cowrie shells and dry provisions. The hawkers were even selling little monkeys with cheeky faces, and brilliant parrots perched in cages of fine rattan.

A florid Dutchman in a crumpled suit of bleached linen came alongside in a gig pulled by six Malays and climbed stiffly up the gangway. He introduced himself as pilot and harbourmaster but did not seem surprised when Henry announced he had no plans to stop but was sailing on.

'It is dangerous in the dark, you have pirates, you have reefs, it is not so good . . .'

Though he dreaded the reply, Henry forced himself to ask the question that burnt a hole in his brain. 'What news of the *Musket*, the Yankee clipper?'

The official broke the deathly hush with a loud laugh. 'The big race, eh? We have heard of it, even here in Anjer. Everyone is looking for you.' He accepted a glass of rum that Withers offered on a tray and drained it at a gulp. 'Oh yes, the *Musket*,' he said, as if suddenly remembering. 'A fine ship, very fine ship. Must be half way to the Cape now . . .'

'That's a belch of claptrap!' Henry snapped, before realising the Dutchman was teasing and his anger became a throttled laugh.

'No, I must tell you the American has not yet passed Anjer. Unless of course she came also in the dark, like you . . .'

The official had left with cordial expressions of good luck. The *prahu* fleet was cast off. With the distant cones of Krakatoa silhouetted by the setting sun, the *Quiver* had braced up and angled out from the shore. During a long night lit by lightning flickering weirdly through the cloud piled over the cones and ridges of the high land on either side of the twelve-mile strait, the ship worked forward on a spineless breeze that did not blow from the same direction for more than thirty minutes. Tirelessly Henry had patrolled the poop, sniffing the air and reaching out to the elements through the wind patches behind his ears. Never before, neither in storm nor calm, had the crew been worked to such a pitch of exhaustion. The wind boxed the compass and at every change the heavy yards draped with sagging canvas were braced round. When dawn revealed Krakatoa abeam and the broad horizon of the Indian Ocean sprawling ahead of the eager bowsprit, men and mates alike were glassy-eyed and spent.

Only the captain, gaunt with strain and his eyes fever bright with concentration, had a spring in his stride. It was the restless tension of a caged lion. When daylight brought no sign of a wind he had the boats lowered. For eight back-breaking hours the clipper was towed out from the land until at last the haze crystallised in a sharp horizon. The boats came inboard as a stiff breeze slammed the canvas into hard curves. Day after day they had balled off the knots, bowling free across a seemingly limitless ocean.

The fine weather, when the ship could sail for hours at a time without a hand being laid on any of her thirty-six separate sails, provided no excuse for soldiering. The mates were as determined as her captain that the *Quiver* would arrive in the Thames looking as pretty as a picture. The Murphies and Macaroons were kept hard at it from dawn till dusk and Will Lamshire's energy, and his capacity to find endless tasks for the men, was at least as great as the captain's tenacious driving of the ship. Between the two, the men hardly had time to draw breath.

The anchor chains were heaved out, scraped down, chipped free of rust then oiled and restowed. The coal hole was cleaned and painted. The pump, boat skids, davits, channels and other ironwork were rubbed down and given coats of pine oil. Brasswork was painted with a light coat to save time wasted in polishing; later, it would be cleaned off and the metal polished for arrival. Aloft, the masts were oiled and the rigging slushed down with grease. The iron trusses on which the yards swivelled were oiled. Lower and topmast shrouds were stripped then tarred, served and parcelled.

In any sailing ship the constant enemy was chafe. Where any two ropes crossed one could saw through the other until it parted. Any rope that rubbed on canvas would soon fray a hole. With five tiers of sail on three masts, all stitched together by eight miles of criss-crossing ropes and stays, the battle against chafe might never be won but it had to be fought. It drove the mates half mad with frustration.

Yet these were the nautical tasks in which seamen took pleasure and pride. In their calloused fingers stiff strands of hemp and manilla were as soft and pliable as threads of silk, and their splices and servings were as artistic as embroidery. The Macaroons crooned at their work. Quick flashes of gleaming white teeth in black faces betrayed their satisfaction. The Murphies, half a brilliant shade of sunburned pink and the rest tanned a golden brown, whistled and hummed contentedly as they worked.

The unlikely mix of crew had been together a long time now, more than half a year, and they were unified by the common purpose of getting the ship home ahead of their rival. Though the *Quiver* was a happy ship this was nearly her undoing, for the old tensions lurking never far beneath the surface were brought to a head not by the deadly rivalry that burned as strongly as ever between the watches but by high spirits.

It started ten days out of Anjer, when it was beginning to seem to all on board that they had never lived any life but this full-tilt gallop under a press of sail. The Macaroons had shaved twenty seconds off the record time for setting stunsails and Henry rewarded the watch with a special plum duff for their dinner.

All mighty well for the old man, Nix Barlow grumbled as he rummaged in the storeroom with his one arm for extra currants, but who had to cook it? If he smelt the curry powder that had been introduced to his mixture during his absence from the galley he gave no sign. But this was not the reaction of the Macaroons when they scented the steam wafting from their portions of hot pudding and put the first spoonfuls of their treat to their lips.

In a red rage, with tears streaming down their cheeks, the Negroes swarmed out of their quarters and chased every Irishman in sight into the rigging. No blood was spilled and even the victims laughed, in the end, and secretly laid their plans.

Two days later during a rare spell of humid calm the Irishmen chewed contentedly on a new and tasty dish: spicy meatballs swimming in gravy. 'Haven't you tasted that blood puddin' over in Liverpool, it's the same 'an all,' said John Gabb, dipping his spoon into the kid for another helping.

Only then, through the open door, did he catch sight of a couple of Macaroons holding their sides with laughter. Suddenly suspicious he sniffed the delicacy that he was about to fork into his mouth.

'Holy Mother of God we're eating pig shit!' he cried, and flung the kid against the bulkhead. The Irishmen reeled on deck spitting their dinner to the four winds.

The gleeful black men made themselves scarce but the

Murphies had murder in their hearts. Bunce was grabbed as he tried to escape into the rigging and dragged down, half a dozen men pounding and kicking him. His watchmates dropped from aloft to rush to his aid. Within seconds a full riot was raging.

Martin Peake, who had the watch while Henry and Sam conferred over the chart, lifted his arms helplessly as they rushed on deck and saw the crew milling back and forth across the waist of the ship, locked in battle.

At that moment the grey cloud that had been gathering overhead through most of the forenoon seemed to split apart with a crack that stopped every fist and boot in mid-air. The heavens opened. The rain came down like a rock fall, every drop a slammer. So great was the noise that Henry had to cup his hand round Martin's ear to make himself heard. 'Block the scuppers . . . Give the men a bath . . . Cool 'em down a bit.'

With the lee scuppers bolted shut and tons of fresh water cascading like mountain streams from the limp sails, the maindeck filled. Waves surfed from end to end as the ship pitched. Whooping shrilly, the men tore off their clothes and played like babies in the bubbling water, the sharp raindrops pricking their bare skin. The water filled with suds as the men scrubbed themselves with soap then attacked their sun-bleached clothes.

When the ship sailed out into the sunlight half an hour later the plugs were pulled and the soapy water spilled away down her sides. The riot was forgotten as her rigging was strewn with clothes hanging out to dry and Henry declared the rest of the day an unofficial Sunday, with a tot of rum for every hand. A pig he had bought from the canoe at Anjer was butchered, leaving Neptunia alone again in her pen, and at sundown an impromptu foo-foo band started up on the capstan for'ard.

Henry leant contentedly on the poop rail in the twilight and listened to the singing. Only the Maori was not joining in but sitting apart, his normally cheerful face stiff and sulky. 'What's up with the cannibal?' Henry asked Meadows when he came to relieve the wheel.

'Eating 'is 'eart out abaht somefink since we saw the last of China, dunno why.'

'Well he's not getting any nearer home, is he?'

'Poor sod,' Meadows muttered.

Seventeen days out of Anjer the first Cape pigeon was sighted, a petrel that was sure sign of colder weather and the edge of the southern winter not far ahead. But disaster did not wait that long to strike.

The morning began well. Henry brimmed with confidence and bounce. He had napped four hours in his deckchair during the night. The wind was holding up. The *Quiver* made twelve knots, snoring smoothly over the large and evenly spaced swells.

Henry stripped off and stood in the lee scuppers as Big Tree drew a bucket of sea water and dashed it in his face. Towelling himself vigorously he went below and changed into a clean shirt then dragged a brush through his ragged mop of hair and returned to the deck where he saw Martin Peake and Sam waiting for him with long faces.

'Cap'n, I've just been to draw tobacco for the men,' Martin reported, offering a carton for Henry to see.

'I'll take the usual half dozen cakes for my pipe,' Henry told him.

'Look in the box, Sir.'

Henry tugged open the lid and found it was filled with a tangle of yarns and small stuff unpicked from old rope, the sort of things mates kept in sacks for a multitude of different uses around the ship. 'What's this?'

'We had four boxes of tobacco and it's all been nicked, replaced by this rubbish,' Martin explained. 'We're cleaned out.'

The news raced through the ship like flames in a tar barrel.

By any standard a sailor's lot was physically hard. His bed was thin straw, usually damp if not saturated. His diet would turn a landsman's stomach. From the moment he stepped on board he was committed for the duration of the voyage ahead to the life of a slave. He had no decision to make because all freedoms were surrendered to the demands of the ship. But he could be happy. A man could find contentment enough, given a sea-kindly ship, a decent run of weather, a mate and master who knew their business – and a plug of tobacco.

Now even that small essential was to be denied the crew of the *Quiver*. It was not ordinary gloom and despondency that Sam heard, as he listened with an acute ear to the alarm spreading through the ship. He doubted sailors would have shed much of a tear had the female breed been removed from the face of the earth at one stroke, or if all supplies of alcohol had magically evaporated. But tobacco was different. A life at sea without a chaw or a smoke was catastrophe.

Henry did not see it that way. 'The men will have to get used to doing without it,' he told Sam curtly when the old man remonstrated during the evening. 'I'm sorry for them, and I would certainly give them tobacco if I had it, but the stuff doesn't drift around the ocean like seaweed. I have to give up smoking, too, so make sure they know it.'

Next morning brought a ship's topgallants visible on the horizon, the first vessel seen for many days. All eyes turned on the captain as he snapped his glass closed. 'Wishful thinking will do you no good,' he told Sam firmly. 'I'm not putting the helm up for a few pounds of tobacco and that's final.'

Crestfallen, the men turned half-heartedly back to their jobs. Though he was not himself a smoker, Sam took up their case vigorously. 'There is something you can do and all the men know it,' he said. 'If you don't speak a ship you will have to run up to Cape Town. It's only a couple of days off our track at most.'

Henry forced a derisive hoot of laughter. 'What we can do, Sam, is simply take the sail off her and when the *Musket* cruises up astern we can ask that two ends and a bight of a Yankee scoundrel to pass a few pounds of Virginia over the bulwarks. Is that what you and the boys want?'

The zest went out of the ship and, as if to match the despondency, the skies turned grey and the sea became greenly black and chill. When the jib clew blew out in a gust the men stared listlessly at the thrashing sail until Will Lamshire harried them for'ard and chased them out on the plunging bowsprit. The sail was finally tamed and lashed down but only after the mate was driven to the peak of frustration by men who acted like zombies. Even the little sailmaker, though he knew well enough his services were required to sew new reinforcing canvas into the clew of the damaged sail, did not move until the mate stormed aft to rouse him out. Dull-eyed, the men stood around watching and did not hoist the sail until ordered, or coil up the halyard until told to do so.

With the men behaving with sullen sluggishness, the spring vanished from the *Quiver*'s eager stride. She dragged her heels, sailing like a bag of bones.

'When are we buyin' the farm, Barley?' Meadows asked glumly.

'Gawd, I wish we bought it yesterday,' Field replied gnawing his thumbnail.

Worse than the listlessness plaguing the ship was the distrust and suspicion generated by the question that became the sole topic of conversation. Who stole the tobacco?

The distraught second mate was accused so often of making a mistake in his reckoning that he half believed it was all his fault. The Murphies accused the Macaroons and the Macaroons lashed out at the Murphies. Will Lamshire equipped himself with a knotted starter which he laid across the men's backs to break up the fights and Martin Peake followed suit.

It was Sam, sensing the pulse of the ship and her disintegrating spirit, who was first to realise Big Tree had not shown his face on deck since the loss of the tobacco had been discovered. Thinking back, he remembered how tense and withdrawn the Maori had become during their forty-five days of voyaging from China. In darkness Sam went for'ard to seek him out.

Big Tree did not sleep in the deckhouse with the two watches but in a cuddy under the fo'c's'le head, near the poultry coops and pig pen, where he had slung a hammock. Sam wasted no time on preliminaries. He dug his knee sharply into the lowest part of the sagging hammock and when a startled tattooed face peered out at him Sam grabbed it by both ears. 'What have you done with the tobacco, you cannibal?'

The ashamed droop of the Maori's eyelids told its own story. Sam tipped him out of the hammock, knelt on his chest with all his considerable weight, and held the Maori with such a fierce eye that Big Tree did not dare to resist. As the story haltingly came out, however, Sam slowly released the pressure.

Later, Sam chose a place where he could not be overheard by the helmsman and told Henry what he had discovered. 'Screech Gander made Big Tree steal the tobacco when he came on board at the anchorage. I thought it was only my chart he was after. Apparently he snatched the cannibal's jade club as he came on board and blackmailed him into stealing the tobacco. That's why the poor fellow has been so hangdog these past weeks. He was practically crying on my shoulder when he told me about it.'

'Bastard!' Henry breathed feelingly.

'You're not hanging it on the native, it wasn't his fault.'

'No, I mean Gander. The crew will kill the cannibal if they hear of this. Better tip off Meadows to look after him. See what you can do to cheer him up.'

'The one thing that would really cheer him up,' Sam grumbled, 'is a wad of tobacco in his cheek.'

On latitude 36 degrees south, seven weeks and 7,340 miles

out of the Min River, the *Quiver* swung her bows to the north-west. Amid confused, uncomfortable seas well south of the Cape of Good Hope, she began to pound out of winter into spring.

It was one of the most significant mileposts of the voyage yet nobody found much cause for celebration. More vessels were sighted but Henry adamantly refused to speak any of them. Table Mountain was glimpsed far to the north, a shadow between turbulent ranges of cloud. At noon next day, by Sam's calculation, the African coast and the nearest tobacco shop lay 188 miles astern. He was quite alone when he marked off the day's run. Not even the mates were interested. The voyage had become a treadmill in a limbo of wind and wave. With no joy to lighten the load, every job took twice as long and seemed three times harder.

Day by day, Sam kept his own counsel as he watched the pig-headed young captain dig a grave for himself. Henry no longer took bracing showerbaths of sea water. His beard grew into an untidy stubble that failed to conceal the deep hollows of mental and physical fatigue in his cheeks. No sooner did he throw himself into a chair and squeeze shut his eyes, unsuccessfully willing sleep to release him from his frustration, than he was jumping up and on the prowl again, ready to find fault with anything and everything that caught his eye.

All the way down from the mates to the cook, the rest of the crew lived on their nerves. There was no singing round the capstan now, not even when the *Quiver* ran into the mild weather of the south-east trades and stepped out for the line.

The climax came with dramatic suddenness.

Like the rig, every muscle and nerve fibre in Henry's being seemed to be in a state of chafe. From the innermost recesses of his brain to his feet he was red raw with fatigue and strain. Yet he was determined not to give Sam Handyside or anybody else the satisfaction of seeing him give in. With arms folded he stood at the poop rail and glowered along the deck where the men went half-heartedly about their jobs. At any moment they were expecting the order to stow their tools and rush to shorten sail before the oncoming squall wrapped round their ears.

Henry jutted his jaw and refused to give the order. The ship would stand up to the squall and the men would stick at their work, by God! He would show them who was master around here.

The ship sailed headlong into the wall of weather and staggered as if she had hit a reef. The wind threw her violently on her beam ends. Two royals and two jibs blew out with double bangs. The men grabbed for their paintpots as the deck tilted steeply and green water creamed over the lee rail. The fore-topsail yard snapped with a jolt felt in every part of the ship and the broken piece flailed wildly, starting a tear in the fore-course which opened like a crevasse before their eyes.

Meadows took one look at the damage and raced up the shrouds, Field close at his heels. They tamed the flogging sail and threw a noose around the broken spar which was hauled up tight to prevent further damage.

Henry scrambled up the steep deck and gave swift orders to Bunce who was on the wheel. The ship answered her rudder reluctantly. There was wild thundering as the wind spilled then she came more upright.

When the worst was over and the squall tailed away, leaving the mates and crew staring gloomily at the damaged rigging to be made good, Henry rounded on Martin Peake. 'Call yourself a mate!' he raged. 'You're not fit to clean the cook's boots! Why didn't you reef down? Didn't you see the weight in the squall, you dunderhead!'

The young mate paled as the captain shook a bunched fist under his nose but Sam Handyside stepped between them and firmly pushed Henry to the taffrail. 'It wasn't Martin's fault and you know it,' Sam rasped in a fierce, forceful tone that compelled Henry to listen. 'Do you know why the crew won't work? Because they haven't got a smoke. Do you know why they are glaring at you now? Because you disappointed them, lad. You failed. You made a big mistake. You lost concentration and blamed somebody else for your own shortcoming. You need a smoke as much as they do. Stick that pipe back in your mouth and maybe you'll think straight again . . .'

Henry tore his arm from Sam's strong grip and stalked to his post at the poop rail. His tired brain grappled with the realisation that Sam must be right. But what could he do about it?

Next day found most of the damage repaired and the ship lurching on a steely grey sea with little wind, her canvas thundering in the scend.

'Sail . . . No, *steamer* ho!'

Martin Peake, coming up the poop ladder, saw it first, a feather of smoke on the horizon aft which grew rapidly into a tall smokestack and beneath it a lean steamship, the sails of her low and spare rig tightly furled.

Sam fixed her in the glass and read the name aloud. '*Countess of Shrewsbury* . . . Burns her weight in coal every voyage I'll be bound, and look at the water she's pushing.'

The crew eyed the steamer with blank faces. Henry beckoned Martin who had the watch. 'Hoist a signal, Mister, and we'll see if a fancy steamship can spare a poor old windbag a puff of smoke.'

Grinning broadly, Martin sorted out the flags and with Meadows' help ran them up to the gaff. The men happily clapped each other on the back when they saw what the captain intended. The message pleaded its case in limp bunting but the Marryat Code of Signals was universal and could not be misunderstood, least of all between two ships flying the Red Ensign. The three flags spelled out, WE ARE IN NEED OF PROVISIONS.

Trailing smoke, the steamer came abeam less than half a mile off. Officers on the bridgeway between her high sponsons could be seen reading the flags. Passengers leant over her rail waving their handkerchiefs and hats. But the steady beat of her paddles never faltered. Sam could hardly believe it. 'There's a steam kettle for you,' he sniffed, contempt in every syllable.

Henry maintained an eloquent silence except to order the yards to be trimmed round to meet a breeze creeping up on the starboard quarter. The steamer tramped away out of sight, cursed every foot of the way.

But the dawn brought a steady breeze and a welcome sight on the port beam. She was a barque flying the Stars and Stripes and Henry ordered the helm put down to approach more closely. Not a man remained below as the clipper ran up on the smaller, sturdier vessel. She was the *Light Horse*, of Salem, and when the signal flags fluttered at the *Quiver*'s gaff for the second time in as many days the answer was a ready affirmative.

The ships hove to a couple of cables apart. Sam went across in the gig with Martin Peake, taking two chests of best tea from the cargo as a present.

'I met old Josh Nicholls in the Artichoke a couple of years back,' Sam reported when he returned aboard. 'He knew all about the race and says it's the talk of the waterfront in Salem, and Bombay too.'

'Didn't he throw you over the side, being a Yankee?' Henry asked between giving orders for squaring away the yards.

Sam's blue eyes twinkled. 'I've an idea he doesn't care too much for King O'Cain.'

The wooden case Sam had brought from the Salem barque was broken open on deck and with all eyes upon him, Martin Peake drew out a carton stencilled with the words,

OLD BRUIN
Dark Virginia Plug

Henry took his plug as eagerly as the rest, shaved it into the palm of his hand and filled his pipe. With a knowing smile, Sam watched him light up.

The barque dropped quickly from sight and with every sail punched full of wind the *Quiver* danced across the blue billows as if she had magically shed half her deadweight. Henry dozed fitfully in his chair through part of the night and the crew slopped the water round the deck with abandon when they turned out soon after dawn.

'Sail ho!' Again it was not a sailing ship but a side-wheeler, corkscrewing uncomfortably in the quartering sea and choking greasily in her smoke. Two squaresails were set on her single mast but even in the stiff wind they were constantly backwinded by her violent motion. It was a few minutes before the steamer was recognised as the same one that had ignored their signals two days before.

'I fancy we should pass her close, just to show the *Countess* what we think of her, eh?'

The mates grinned their ready approval of the captain's suggestion but Sam was taken aback. 'What, and make a dog-leg for the sake of your pride! You might lose five minutes . . .'

'Damn right,' Henry said fervently.

Chewing or smoking contentedly, the men gathered along the starboard bulwarks and a few clambered out on the mainyard. Henry steered a close course. The green-hulled clipper with bone-white masts and canvas drumming tautly from every spar tore up on the labouring steamer. 'Make a signal, Mr Peake,' Henry ordered.

Moments later the crew broke into contemptuous cheers and waved ropes' ends as the code flags climbed up to the gaff and streamed away in the wind. Meadows grinned from ear to ear and slapped Big Tree joyfully on the back as Field waved his hat like a big black bucket and Sam did a jig of joy.

Pat Flynn grabbed Meadows' arm. 'What does it mean, Oatsy?' he demanded.

'We're asking if he needs assistance,' Meadows told him. For a moment he contemplated the gaunt and wrung-out young captain who was standing in his familiar position at the poop rail, shading his eyes as he stared across at the steamer.

The signal flags posed a question that Meadows would shrewdly liked to have put to the captain himself. ''Ow long's it gonna be, Captain h'Ardent, before you cracks like that fore-topgallant yard? Two days? Ten days?'

In the choke of the Atlantic where the elbow of Brazil juts towards the armpit of Africa, the clipper ran into the doldrums. The mates seized on the calm weather to brighten up the topsides faded by brilliant tropic suns. The crew hummed and crooned as they slapped on paint while hanging over the rail on planks. Will Lamshire passed word that whistling was banned. The captain might be desperate for a breeze but his own job was to get the ship painted. It could blow as much as it liked but not until the last patch of new green was on.

Swinging in a bosun's chair beneath the bowsprit, Charlie Field touched up the figurehead of Eros, giving him scarlet lips, china blue eyes and liverishly pink cheeks. Later, while gilding the scroll-work on the trailboard and carefully painting the large letters which spelt out the ship's name, Field leaned down and with a dab of the brush gave a touch of gold to the figurehead's manly equipment.

Eleven weeks out, the *Quiver* broke free of the belt of calms on the equator and spooled across the north-east trades, swinging wide into the Atlantic to be sure of catching the westerlies that would drive her to England. Spindrift flashed over the knight-heads like handfuls of diamonds. The reef points drummed invigoratingly. With her acres of canvas, miles of rope and tons of timber in perfect harmony, it sometimes seemed the vessel had what many an old sailor claimed for sailing ships: a heart – and a will – all of her own.

The *Quiver* had a will to win. The urge to crack on, to crowd on sail and drive the ship like no ship had ever been driven before, was no longer the passion of one individual but a collective compulsion. The captain did not have to hound the mates. The mates had no need to haze the crew.

It was the men who put the twist on each other. In both watches they became obsessed with speed. The race with the

Musket was forgotten in the heated competition to rack up more miles in four hours than the previous watch; Sam Handyside was called in to read the patent log streaming over the stern and pronounce an official verdict on the distance run through the water.

The Murphies' record of seventy-four miles remained unbroken for three days then the Macaroons smashed it with a run of seventy-seven miles, an average of nearly twenty knots. In the next watch the Murphies improved on it by half a mile and hazed the disappointed black men unmercifully. But the next day the Macaroons broke the eighty-mile barrier.

The men did not doze while on watch but waited at the sheets, poised to adjust the trim, often before the mate of the watch gave the word. Any helmsman who steered less than a perfect course was given stick from every part of ship. Every morning at dawn, the cook limped round the deck collecting the flying fish – called night sluggers – which had glided over the rail during the night. The men ate them fried, with their fingers, when they had their coffee.

In all his years at sea Sam Handyside had never seen such a tight and efficient body of seamen outside the Royal Navy, but a man-o'-war carried twelve or even fifteen men for every one in a merchant ship. He could find no fault with the beautiful clipper which gleamed from jibboom to escutcheon with new paint, gilt and oil. It was as if the ship herself reflected the buoyant and fighting mood of her men. Somehow, the greyhound of the ocean was not only stretching out with all her power and showing off her beauty; she was joyfully wagging her tail.

It was getting on for eighty days since the captain had last slept in a bunk or spent more than a few minutes at a time below deck. His lean and darkly burnt figure was never still except for the brief intervals when, despite himself, he lapsed into a restless doze in his chair. His ragged hair, bleached paper-white by the sun, stuck up like tail feathers. His eyes were bright and deep, all but invisible through constant squinting at the dazzling sea and the sunlight reflecting on brilliant sails. He ate on the run, shoving half meals down his throat with hasty fingers as he paced the poop. Since the *Countess of Shrewsbury* had been lost over the stern, Henry had exchanged hardly a word of conversation but he found plenty to say.

'The main royal's baggy as a whore's drawers, Mr Lamshire, take up on the sheets . . . '

The mate cocked an eye at the perfectly set and wrinkleless royal and said patiently, 'The clews are well down on the topgallant yard, Cap'n, they won't come any tighter.'

Henry charged along the deck, cast the main royal sheet off the starboard pin rail and beckoned half a dozen men to tail on. 'Now heave!' he shouted. 'Pull thunderbolts you fairies! Now every inch o' that! Make her up!'

As the men warily made the sheet up on the pin in exactly the same position as before, Henry stamped back to the poop. 'Do I have to do your job on top of everything else, Mr Lamshire?'

Even a job as routine as holystoning the deck incurred the captain's muddling interference. Shaking their heads with vexation, Lamshire and Peake stepped away as Henry personally directed the places on deck where water was to be thrown.

'Mr Lamshire, are we a steam kettle? Tell the cook to make less smoke. And what's happening for'ard, why is the inner jib furled? I didn't give orders to shorten sail?'

'Replacing the clump-block, Cap'n, the strop is working loose.'

'I don't want excuses, I want the sail up and working.'

'Aye aye, Cap'n,' the mate agreed. But the captain did not notice the delay while the men finished replacing the block before the sail was run up the stay.

Sam Handyside's generation of master mariners, and every generation before them, had been raised in an art of voyaging that depended upon imperturbable tenacity. If the wind blew too hard you shortened sail, if too soft you whistled, and when it blew from ahead you marked time until it changed. The fierce and single-minded driving of the ship had been contrary to all Sam's instincts. In the early days of the voyage he had feared for the ship herself, believing the eager young captain would simply overburden her with canvas until the masts went over the side or she drove into a wave and sailed right under.

Although the ship's perfect pitch of tuning had been achieved through the unrelenting concentration and heroic persistence of one man, and Sam grudgingly acknowledged that Henry Ardent had proved him wrong, it took him a long while to realise that in fact the ship was a lot stronger than the man.

Sam had voyaged with strange shipmates often enough. The sea got men in funny ways. Once, long ago, the cook in Sam's ship calmly hung up his ladle, climbed on the rail, called 'See you in Madagascar, boys!' then jumped over the side.

Now Sam's fears were clinched on a day when he waited at the weather rail, holding the brass sextant beneath his jacket to protect it from any spray that might jump aboard. The sun was hidden by a small cloud and Sam could already see the trailing edge of its shadow racing towards him. As the whitecaps came flashing into the sunlight beyond, it seemed the dark patch was being chased by a pack of hounds. Henry's rasping voice broke into Sam's thoughts. 'Is it going to take you all day to get your sight, Mr Handyside?'

'No lad, just waiting for the cloud.'

'Christ, why don't you have a game of shuffleboard while you're waiting?'

Sam restrained an impulse to put the sextant into the captain's hands and tell him to do his own navigating. At that moment the cloud tore away and he lifted the sextant to his eye, fixing the sharp horizon in the telescope then swinging the arm to bring the reflection of the sun down to touch it in the horizontal mirror.

At just the right moment he clamped the arm and began counting the seconds so when he read the time on the chronometer in its baize-lined box clamped to the sideboard in the saloon he could calculate the precise time at which he had measured the angle of the sun above the horizon. But his counting went awry when he passed Charlie Meadows, who was on the wheel. Sam heard him mutter from the side of his mouth, 'Useless as a cut snake.'

'Eh, what do you mean?'

Meadows glanced at the captain's stiff back to ensure he was out of hearing. 'We gotta do somefink, Mr 'Andyside, the ol' man's losin 'is nuts.'

Sam took the sight again and went below to complete his figuring and rule a position line on the chart. But he worked at the tables and calculations out of habit, his mind turning over what Meadows had said. There was no doubt about it. Henry Ardent had created the sailing machine in which they were storming across the ocean but his own performance and skill were being left behind. The men could feel it and were resentful. The mates knew it but could do or say nothing unless Henry took a walk to Madagascar or was confined to his berth in a strait jacket.

Sam deliberated, tapping the chart with the dividers. Unless deserted completely by the fates, the *Quiver* would make a triumphant passage, one for the record books. But landfall was still two weeks off at the very least. It seemed they were involved in yet another race, to raise the Lizard before the captain cracked up.

It mustn't be allowed to happen. Sam stowed his instruments, climbed blinking to the deck. Standing close to the wheel he told Meadows in a low tone what must be done.

Sam took his second sun sight at noon, pencilled the cross on the chart, and as usual Henry came below to look at it. As the captain pored over the chart, measuring distances with the span of his fingers, Sam filled a tumbler with rum from a bottle wedged for safety among the settee cushions and sipped it noisily. 'Want a drink, lad?'

Henry shot him a look of faint surprise then shook his head. 'No.'

Sam slumped over the table, spilling a little rum which he tried to blot up with shaking fingers. 'God, I envy you,' he mumbled, sipping again.

'What?'

Sam sighed and drank again. 'Sit down a minute, lad.'

Sam swiftly grabbed Henry's wrist as he made to leave. He pulled him into a chair then pushed a glass into his hand which he filled to the brim. 'Have a drink with an old has-been. You don't know how lucky you are. A fine ship. All your life ahead of you. If only I had your luck to . . .'

Henry cast around for somewhere to put the over-filled glass then reduced it with a little sip. 'What's the matter with you all of a sudden? I've got work to do.'

'Do me a favour, lad, and have a drink with me. You've got to. It's my birthday. Sixty-three today and no prospects but a life sitting at home looking at jade statues.' Sam shook his head in a maudlin way then lifted his glass. Henry had to drink. Sam topped up Henry's glass and sat back with a sigh. 'Aye, it's good to talk with friends, especially men you admire. You've done well, lad. Let's drink to you. Come on, knock it back . . .'

Henry smiled tightly and lifted his glass. 'Happy birthday, Sam.' He drank then put down his glass which Sam promptly filled. Henry started to get up but sank down again and stared helplessly at the darkly golden rum.

Sam realised the plot was beginning to bear fruit. It helped him force a beaming smile. 'And what about the *Quiver*, eh? A beautiful ship, and you've done us proud. Drink to your ship, lad. Here's to her!'

Sam pretended to drink thirstily but the level in his glass fell by hardly a spit while Henry's emptied by half.

Peeping through a crack in the pantry door, Tom Withers watched in silent wonder as the old mariner skilfully persuaded the stiff and reluctant captain to lift his elbow. Sam's instructions to serve no lunch today and keep out of the light had mystified Tom, but now he understood. The mates, too, had been told to grab a bite from the galley and stay on deck. According to plan, Meadows and Field came down the companion-way at two bells. Sam welcomed them heartily and bade them take a seat then pushed tumblers of rum into their horny hands. The level of the bottle was already well down and he opened another. The new visitors gave him the excuse to begin the toasts all over again: his birthday, the captain, the crew, their lovely ship . . .

The captain's resistance quickly faltered and soon he was drinking with abandon. Nor did Meadows and Field hold back. The saloon filled with smoke as all but Sam fired up their pipes. Gusts of laughter swept up the companion-way to mystify the man at the wheel and the crew who wondered at the strange disappearance of the captain from the poop for the first time in weeks. Will Lamshire took the con, and tugged at his nose in a satisfied way, smiling as a burst of cockney singing came up through the skylight.

It was getting on for six bells when Henry's chin sank to his chest. He shook his head blearily and drained his glass which Meadows at once refilled. Henry sniggered, hiccupped, and drank the entire contents of the tumbler. Then he passed out.

'My oath what a bender!' Meadows sighed contentedly, counting the necks of four empty bottles jutting from behind the cushion. 'How many of 'em did the ol' man put away?'

'At least two,' Sam told him.

'He'll be ashore for a good while then, won't 'e, the cap'n I mean?'

Sam's face was the sickly pink that Field had painted the figurehead and his head felt like a rock. 'You don't want to be around when he wakes up,' he said.

'No chance,' Field grunted. 'Where shall we put 'im?'

'Leave him be,' Sam said. They made the unconscious captain comfortable on the leeward side of the settee and left him snoring deeply then staggered on deck. Sam dropped in the captain's deckchair and soon his snores, too, were adding their music to the creak and squeal of the ship as she ploughed her furrow towards the North Atlantic.

It was soon after midnight when the captain, looking pale and ragged, clumped on deck. He glared groggily at the sails gleaming like porcelain platters in the moonlight then flopped into his chair which Sam had vacated and soon was sleeping again like a baby. The whole ship worked through the night on tiptoes. The bell was not sounded to mark the intervals of time. Orders were given in whispers.

'How's he goin', Oatsy?' the watch asked when Meadows roused them out with hisses and kicks at four o'clock.

'All serene,' Meadows confided, grinning broadly.

Henry snapped awake as the sun rose over the horizon and shone across the calm sea to strike him full in the eyes. He blinked, held his head, then swayed to his feet and with his hands thrust deeply in his pockets walked grumpily for'ard along the maindeck. His crew watched stonily as the captain took a long look at Neptunia snoring in her pen, checked the tension of some of the sheets and halyards, and glanced over the rail. Then he went aft again. 'Good morning, Will, the copper's dragging a green beard a fathom long,' he said. 'Muster the swimmers and give 'em scrubbers, we'll give the old girl a rub down.'

The weed growing on the underwater body of the hull was barely two inches long, but more than enough to knock half a knot off her speed.

'Six swimmers is all we have, Cap'n, including Mr Peake and the cannibal.'

'Seven,' said Henry, peeling off his shirt. He caught sight of Sam watching warily from the poop. Though Henry's head ached abominably he felt better than he had for days but he wasn't going to let the old man off lightly. He took a long-handled scrubber and attacked Sam's belly, rubbing vigorously. 'What we have to do is dive down and scrub the weed off her, like this, see? Use some elbow grease. Get those scrubbers really moving, see?'

Twisting and turning to escape Henry's rough and painful tickling, bellowing with rage, Sam hoisted himself up the mizzen rigging and the men fell about with laughter. Henry shook his brush defiantly at Sam as he climbed out of reach. 'While you're up there, you can look out for sharks,' Henry told him. 'When you see one, shout like hell!'

Henry clambered up a few rungs of the ratlines as if giving

chase, causing Sam to climb even higher, then he tossed his brush into the sea and followed it with a head-first dive.

The tiny rudder fish scattered as six more splashes followed but with no purchase while swimming it was difficult for the men to make any progress with the long-handled scrubbing brushes. After twenty minutes Henry gave up, called in his helpers, and climbed to the deck with his chest heaving.

'If it was so easy every shipmaster would be doing it,' Sam teased him.

'Don't worry, I haven't finished,' Henry panted. When he recovered his breath he superintended the construction of an underwater scrubbing mat. It was a six-by-four pad of bristly coir hawser, a rope fixed to each corner. The mat was worked under the hull then sawed back and forth by teams of men hauling on the ropes.

Will clapped his hand to his forehead as he saw the new paint flaked away by the rubbing of the ropes, but clean copper glinted amid the cloud of green slime and silky weed floating to the surface.

'Sure, the old girl's enjoyin' a bit o' slap an' tickle,' Flynn said as he hauled on the rope, sweat pouring off his sunburned brow.

'What would you know about it, yer whore-bangin' sod?'

'The old bitch likes having her stomach rubbed, I reckon.'

'Thundersides oughta scam the old man more often if it makes him this easy going.'

The trades gave up the ghost. For seven days the *Quiver* made a noon to noon run of no better than 114 miles. On two days the distance run was a miserable thirty-three and thirty-seven miles. The men cast many an anxious glance aft as Henry stalked up and down the poop, always that hollow whistle as he racked his brains for ways of making his ship go faster, but he found no inspiration in the greasy swells unfolding from a horizon of filmy rain. The drinking bout followed by a long sleep had spilled some of the wind out of his sails and, like the ship herself, he cut along better with his sheets freed. On Sam's insistence he started taking proper meals at the saloon table and drank half a glass of rum every evening to help himself relax; he slept better and his judgement improved. The captain was no longer half a step behind his mates and their men but several steps in front.

Then came an abrupt sea change. It happened in the middle of the dog watches after a day of fretful breezes. Mourning their slow progress, Henry happened to glance down from the rail. He noticed the rudder fish that had accompanied the ship through so many miles of ocean were no longer in attendance. In the same instant his wind patches registered a chill shiver. The sails sighed as the weave of the flax bent to take the strain. The watch needed no bidding to trim the yards. The new wind had the long arm of the northern climate behind its punch, and it came out of the west. Two hours later, the change of the watch brought the Murphies out on deck togged in Cape Horn gear.

Not only was it colder, with a threatening bite in the wind, but the colour of the sea changed from the clear and holy blue of great oceanic depths to a cloudier hue transformed by the overcast into a sinister grey. The seabed beneath the keel was no longer two or three miles down, but only a hundred fathoms. The *Quiver* was on soundings.

It brought a change in the rhythm, the swells shorter and steeper. It brought more birds, for the microscopic plant and animal life clouding the water provided grazing for fish which in turn were preyed upon by birds wheeling stiff-winged in the sky. And with the sea lanes of the Western Ocean converging on Great Britain and Europe, it brought more ships. After the empty vastness of middle latitudes, the constant sighting of other sails on the horizon screwed up the tension. It brought a realisation that the *Quiver* was in the last phase of her long voyage. But it was more than a mere homecoming that she approached: it was a reckoning.

Repeatedly the *Quiver* overhauled inbound vessels, storming past them under a mountain of canvas. Other sailors watched her smoking through the grey seas with admiration and awe. But the clipper's officers and crew knew nothing of this. Henry resisted the temptation to put up the helm and speak an outward bounder. He did not want to know whether the *Musket* was ahead. The suspense was itself a driving force and he concentrated his mind on squeezing his ship for her last drop of power and speed.

Sam faced a different crisis. Until a headland or lighthouse was sighted, and the ship's position pinpointed, he would get no rest. His track of pencilled crosses marched up the chart and pointed directly between the out-thrust fingers of Cornwall and Brittany, each a sinister maze of rocks forming pillars of dread on either side of the entrance to the English Channel. But his calculations and careful plotting were only as good as the longitude and this depended on the exact accuracy of the two chronometers whose cogs and springs might easily have been affected by tropical temperatures or been nudged by some leap of the ship during her pasting in the China Sea. The accuracy of the timepieces was easy to check by speaking an outward-bounder whose chronometers would have been set only a few days before. Henry flatly refused.

On the ninety-seventh day of the voyage, Sam ruminated over his latest position fix and checked the distance run, 212 miles in twenty-four hours. He slapped his pencil down and swept the murky horizon with worried eyes. There was a restlessness in the ship as if she, too, could smell the land. A barque ran hull-down to starboard. A cluster of fishing boats jilled over the waves to port, Mounts Bay drifters out of Mousehole and Newlyn; Sam knew their habit was to remain within a day's fetch of the shore.

No land was sighted before sundown. Henry ordered a white lantern hoisted, as the British navigation regulations required. Near midnight the air turned clammy. Beads of moisture collected on every rope. Henry and Sam, incapable of sleep, both paced the deck. The helmsman smiled when the two frequently came near to collision.

Sam's beard was a mass of tangled damp strands which made him look as haggard as he felt. 'I don't like it, we can't see a thing, we don't know where we are, and you're cracking on like a mad man,' he protested.

'Most nights at sea you don't see a thing because there is nothing to be seen,' Henry argued. 'In fact we're fanning along just nicely. I was thinking of hoisting out the skysail gear because the wind's dropping off, if anything.'

Sam greeted Henry's comment with a shudder. 'Look round you for God's sake. I'm not talking about seeing land. Soon you won't be seeing the bowsprit. We're sailing into fog, blind as bats, and you're talking of shaking out more sail!'

'What do you suggest?' Henry asked guardedly.

Sam's nerves were as taut as a back-stay. He sniffed the dank air, tasted it, and ran his tongue nervously along his lips. 'Heave to, lad, else we'll pile-up ashore. The Scillies or Land's End are right in our lee.'

Henry shook his head and summoned Will Lamshire who had been hovering within hearing. 'Double the look-outs, Mister, and have the watch stand by at sheets and braces so we can manoeuvre instantly if we must.'

Soon there was no doubt of it. What Sam had feared was happening. A dense blanket of moisture sighed into every crevice and sent a shivery promise of rheumatism through many an aching joint. They were in fog.

The ship made six or seven knots in a large quartering sea. The thud and rattle of gear being shaken aloft by the violent motion was muffled by the white cloud enveloping her. The fog was invisible but for a pearly arc around the lantern, but Henry could smell it and taste it and feel it on his cheek.

The wind died some more and the rolling increased. The noise aloft grew louder. Men moved quietly around the deck, their voices muffled by the blanketing fog. Every head was cocked, alert for the sound of crashing breakers or the threshing of an oncoming steamer. It was the only warning they would get of catastrophe.

Imperceptibly, dawn stole upon the ship. The outlines of spars and silhouettes of motionless listening figures grew out of the dark. It was a long time before the inching dawn made enough light for individual features to be distinguished, but the men on the clipper's silent poop had worked so closely as a team, and for so long, that they could detect each other almost by instinct: Sam Handyside, barrel chested and sloping shouldered, his chubby cheeks cut by ravines of anxiety; Will Lamshire, his nose jutting like a bowsprit as he sniffed the air; Martin Peake, aping the captain's calm, idly twirling the bushy moustache with which he planned to caress many a blushing cheek before too many days.

Henry himself did not pace wildly, as before, but remained as still as a rock, every nerve strained. His blood tingled with a sense of anticipation, as if he were towelling himself down after a cold swim.

It was hardly to be believed that the coast of England could be so close. What sort of welcome awaited him? At least he had a cargo of tea, that much was certain. And he had made a creditable passage, though he knew he had made mistakes. But was he faster or slower than the *Musket*?

Henry pushed the burning question to the back of his mind with a shiver of apprehension. How good it would be to be outward bound, leaving all this uncertainty astern. Staring sightlessly into the chill fog, the English coast somewhere in his lee, he didn't feel much like a hero, was frightened by the alternative, and dreaded finding out the truth.

Tugging at the scar on the rim of his ear and feeling the

wetness in his hair, Henry blinked tiredly. His eye fell on Big Tree moving wraithlike along the deck, bringing coffee. The Maori mounted the starboard ladder, balancing the tray carefully, then paused and looked over the bow. His keen hearing had detected a strange sound. Henry reached for the coffee pot. 'What is it?'

Then Martin Peake heard it. As he pointed over the starboard bow Henry's own ears caught it too: the creak and rumble of a ship rocking over the waves with her gear banging, as the *Quiver*'s was. 'Rattle that bell for your life, there's a ship on the bow!' Henry ordered.

The strident clamour of the bell was swallowed up by the fog. Like an echo, an answering ring carried faintly from the opaque void and with it came the frenzied barking of a dog. A broad and manic grin – glee, relief, and shock all at once – lit Henry's face as he looked round at Sam and the mates. 'Nightingale never did like that bell,' he said.

Running blind, the *Quiver* tore through the white wet wool. Every wave tossed up her stern, punched her forward and left her lurching in the smother. The creak and gurgle of the other ship running parallel was loud, and the crew stood along the rail bursting their eyes to see the first shadow of her in the fog.

With a safety rope under his arms in case he was swept away when a dip of the ship wetted him to the waist, Charlie Meadows hung outboard in the lee rigging for'ard and heaved the lead. Twenty fathoms of line snaked through his fingers before it touched the bottom. The tallow arming the hollow in the bottom of the lead brought up a grey muddy shingle. Sam rubbed it between his fingers and sniffed it. 'Might be English, might be French,' he ruminated. 'Might even be Irish, for all that; only a fisherman would know.'

Henry ran his finger through his lank hair, sending out a spray of moisture. His eyebrows, like every strand of rope and wire in the rigging, were beaded with little droplets. It seemed the whole ship was in a cold sweat of agonising tension. 'We're pressing on,' Henry said. 'If we come a gutser now it can't be helped.'

'Look at how the waves are peaking, you can tell we're in with the land even if you can't smell it.'

Henry silenced Sam with a look as, faint but distinct, a familiar voice came out of the fog. 'Hoy there! What ship?'

Sam made a trumpet with his hands, 'Ho-ho, what cheer?'

This last came out as an abbreviated grunt, wotcha. In an undertone he asked, 'What name shall we give ourselves?'

'Lady Godiva?' Martin Peake suggested.

Sam shrugged then boomed the name into the fog, adding London as her home port. Back came the reply, '*Musket . . .* Boston . . . China for London . . . Where are you bound?'

'Liverpool!' Sam replied unhesitatingly, then explained to Henry and the mates. 'That's a cough lozenge for him. He will be wondering whether he is on the north or the south side of Cornwall.'

'And which side is he on?' Will Lamshire inquired in a gently mocking voice.

'Don't ask,' Henry told him feelingly. According to Sam's dead reckoning since the last fix at noon yesterday, which might have been wildly inaccurate, they would have passed the Scilly Isles during the night and now the killer coast of Cornwall was somewhere off the port beam, though just how far off was anybody's guess. It might be thirty miles, or thirty yards.

There was only one thing to be done, Henry decided. 'The wind's freshening,' he told the mates. 'Hoist everything we've got – every sail, every blanket, you can knot your shirts in the ratlines if you think it will help.'

Henry stared helplessly at the wall of fog, bracing himself on the binnacle as the ship hurtled forward on a hissing whitecap as if she were a spear thrown by a muscular arm. 'Ditch all the deadweight you can,' he went on. 'Pump ship, jettison the fresh water, get the galley coal over. But do it quietly. The Yankees still don't know who we are.'

The mates dropped swiftly to the maindeck, calling out in low voices for their watches. So dense was the fog that the men running up the shrouds to set the skysails – small scraps of canvas on stick-thin yards above the royals – were swallowed from the view of those on deck. Clinging grimly to the scything topgallant masts arcing through the murk, they were treated to an astonishing spectacle. The fog was lighter 150 feet above the sea, almost blue, and through a break in the streamers of mist they snatched a glimpse of ghostly grey sails, the royals and topgallants of their neighbour.

With coffee warming and relaxing the tight cramp in his stomach, Henry wondered at the strange turn of fate that had brought both ships in with each other after so many thousands of miles. The ocean, he knew, was a broad place. A thousand ships could sail the same route home from China and hardly see each other. But the English Channel was barely one hundred miles broad at its threshold and it grew narrower. Also, every master approaching from the south or west wanted to make his landfall on The Lizard. He could signal his number there, so the ship's arrival would be reported to London, and it put him right for the run along the coast. Once in the Channel it was reassuring to sail from lighthouse to lighthouse, as if being passed from the custody of one friendly and protective pair of hands to the next, but first the coast had to be located so the navigator could get his bearings. The granite headland of The Lizard, with its patchwork fields and little fishing villages nestling in the rocky coves, made a small enough target for a sailing vessel weeks at sea with no sight of land and no confirmation of the navigator's reckoning.

Sam let a moan of exasperation escape his pressed lips and Henry tried to cheer him up. 'With this sea running we'll hear the surf before we hit.'

'Just in time to say your prayers, if we're lucky.'

'Can you swim?'

'Shut your trap and listen, for God's sake.'

It was hard to hear anything above the sea noise and the sounds of feverish activity. Studding booms were run out like long pointed fingers from the tips of every yard and the stunsails spread to the wind. The *Quiver* was tramping. The high wall of water tumbling away from her hollow cheeks began to sparkle as the light changed from grey to silver.

The fresh-water tank was emptied of all but the last few gallons. The last chunks of coal were tossed over the side and whole hogsheads of salt beef were left turning over and over in the ship's broad wake.

The bitter rivalry between watches was history. Murphies and Macaroons heaved heartily on the same ropes, worked shoulder to shoulder at the pump, grinned as they danced along the slender foot-ropes high aloft, eyes eager for the first sight of the *Musket*.

Henry's glance fell on the twelve fire buckets in the rack under poop rail. The men had toiled for hours to bring a golden shine to the heavy brass hoops and Meadows and Field had made every bucket a fancy ropework handle. One by one they splashed into the sea, making a wavering line stretching far astern. Suddenly the visibility improved. The fog peeled away.

Every sail ablaze in a bright glow, the *Quiver* burst into soft sunshine.

Far off the port bow, indistinct behind shifting trails of mist, lay a proud knuckle of land. Low hills made a hazy wall off the port beam. 'My God, that's Start Point ahead and we're miles inside The Lizard!' Sam cried, his cheeks pink with unbounded relief. His flush of happines went unobserved for every eye was turned to starboard, where the *Musket* creamed out of the fogbank less than half a mile away. The consternation on board the black-hulled Yankee clipper as her captain and crew clapped eyes on their rival was revealed in a flurry of action. Henry wished he were a seagull soaring over the *Musket*'s poop so he could read the bumsquabbled features of her captain.

Sam turned his own telescope on the coastline to the north and picked out the clear silhouette of a slender pillar of masonry standing out against the distant shore. 'There's the Eddystone, five miles abeam!' he crowed triumphantly. 'Right on the knocker! How's that for navigation, Captain Ardent?'

Henry clapped him on the shoulder but his gaze was on the Yankee. 'I wonder if he really thought we were bound for Liverpool?' he pondered.

'Who cares?' Sam declared. 'The bucko bastard will be screeching now, and no mistake.'

The rising south-westerly whisked away all traces of fog. Peaking crests spilled, dotting the sea with whitecaps. Clouds marched across the sun. It was a brisk autumn day, none too warm after the balmy tropics, but no sailor could have desired a finer breeze for stretching his ship up the Channel.

Wing to wing, the two ships thrashed across the bluff nose of Prawle Point; beyond, the headland of the Start made a razorback of rocks sloping into a tiderace of white water. The *Quiver* hoisted her numbers, the flags rippling boldly in the wind, and the *Musket* did the same. As they skirted the broken water Henry trained his glass on the white cross of the signal yard standing out against the dark green of the cliffs and saw its flag dip in acknowledgement. While the two ships cut parallel tracks across Lyme Bay, the news was sparked from the signal station to Lloyds of London. Within the hour messengers were dashing through the streets broadcasting the news. By noon it was the talk of the City.

'Monkey Winkworth's flyer is reported at the Start . . .'

'Neck and neck with the Yankee . . .'

'Less than half a mile in it, they say . . .'

In the offices of Mincing Lane tea merchants, the news had the effect of a bomb explosion. The new season's teas were in the Channel!

The wind streamed the smokes of London low over the spires and rooftops. Down Channel it was racking up into a handy bit of breeze. From afar the two clipper ships made a sight that none who saw them smoking through the seas would ever forget. The *Musket*'s gilded figurehead soared like a hunting hawk over a shadowy country of grey-green hills and valleys. Her sails, white as a swan and as plump and smooth, made her velvet hull seem all the blacker. Her masts and spars were whipping canes of gleaming amber. The Stars and Stripes streamed from her gaff and the curtains of spray flowering from her bow and driving across her dripping deck were slashed with rainbows.

Glory for glory, the *Quiver* was her perfect equal. More tender than the Yankee, she rolled harder. The bright washed metal of her copper lifted above the white-laced sea streaming along her topsides, then dipped deeply until it seemed the tips of her bone-white yards would spear into the depths. The green hull set off her golden scroll-work and sheer-stripe, and was complemented by the tawnier brown of her canvas. In her mountain of sail every stitch-hole was an elongated slot through which splinters of weak sunlight glanced, keyholes to the heavens. Every spar, shroud and sheet was a juddering bar, every knot and splice a trembling fingerhold on the cliff-edge of catastrophe.

Whistling dementedly, Henry watched his overburdened spars bend and whip. With every nerve and muscle that was his to command he willed the gear to hold. The mates were stationed along the maindeck, Lamshire for'ard and Peake amidships, ready to deal with any emergency. Four men clung to the tops in each of the reeling masts, ready to throw themselves out on any yard where urgent action was demanded. Manfred Longhandle dragged an assortment of spare sails from the locker and laid them ready for instant use. Nix Barlow made a duff with a triple ration of currants and jam, but the men were so absorbed they hardly ate.

'Wotcha fink, Barley, still gonna buy the farm?'

'Wot, and miss a day like this? You mad or somefink?'

'Ask me, the ol' man's gone stark raving, he's carryin' on too 'ard, she'll dive under an' never come up.'

'Christ, 'ow long can you 'old yer breff?'

There was a wild flutter in the *Musket*'s rig as her main royal blew out at the boltropes. 'That will cure his cold,' Sam said happily. He ought not to have gloated.

A violent shock trembled through the *Quiver* and there was an instantaneous pandemonium of thrashing canvas as the mizzen topgallant split from top to bottom like a melon hacked with a cutlass. A moment later the lee studding sail burst and flogged away to leeward, shaking the mast. Adam Robinson's hands and feet seemed hardly to touch the yard as he threw himself along the foot-ropes and cut the stunsail away. Spinning in the wind it flew ahead of the ship and flopped into the water.

The instant the yard was lowered eight men were lying out on it, twice the usual number, helping Adam Robinson to fold the thrashing canvas under his belly and make a tight sausage of it. With John Gabb and Bunce inboard to take the bunt, the sail was quickly tamed, cut from the yard, and lowered on a gant-line. The farmers and Longhandle had the replacement laid out ready and it was swayed aloft at once. Clew and reef tackle were transferred, then the bunt-lines. In a few minutes the new sail was full and drawing.

The chalk cliffs of Dorset slid along the lee while the bulging forehead of the Isle of Wight grew more distinct on the bow. Inward-bound ships and schooners, and two coastal steamers, were overhauled by the flyers as if becalmed. Fishing boats loomed fleetingly nearby then vanished. Vessels heading down the Channel had only a brief glimpse of the clippers before they were gone.

When Sam took a reading of the dial on the patent log streaming astern he could not believe what he saw. He took bearings on landmarks as they passed to confirm it. Both ships were making twenty-two knots – nearly twenty-five land miles every hour – through the water. Sam knew it to be a breathtaking performance which he would never live to see again. He did not linger over his charts in the deserted cabin but returned to the deck where he stood with legs planted wide against the roll and his jaw clamped shut.

The sun dipped into a clear magnolia sky astern and with evening the spike in the wind grew blunt. At St Catherine's, the signal station on the southern point of the Isle of Wight, the Lloyds lookouts trained their powerful spyglasses on the twin towers of sail. On the shoreline below them the lighthouse was already shootings its sparks of comfort into the twilight. The news was flashed along the telegraph wires to London. The *Musket* and *Quiver* has passed St Catherine's Point together at 6.33pm precisely. Wind: south-west. Strength: strong breeze, diminishing. Weather: fair.

All over London, from the boardrooms of the great shipping houses to the meanest tap houses behind the Commercial Road, thousands staked their bets on the outcome. The return of the clippers generated more excitement than the Derby. It seemed only yesterday the challenge between the two ships had raised such speculation, the rakish bucko from America and the greenhorn from the colonies. But young Captain Ardent could not be as green as he was cabbage looking to have got so far, and if he was that good he could beat the breeches off the Yankee yet. Queues for places in the steamers, departing at dawn to meet the ships down-river, started forming while the evening was still young. At sea it was a long and wearisome night.

As the *Quiver* fanned along the coast her men slept where and when they could. The change of the watches was a mere formality because every man was on deck. The *Musket* was lost in the darkness to seaward and not even a light was seen. Possibly she was not burning one. Henry composed himself in the deck chair but could not sleep. Nix Barlow kept the galley stove fired up and at midnight, with Beachy Head light abeam, served a pot of soup. Henry was draining his mug with relish when he heard a cry of alarm from the dark water beyond the bulwarks. He jumped to the rail as an open fishing boat spun helplessly along the length of the ship, inches from catastrophe. Three frightened faces peered up at the tower of sail as they whirled by. In an instant the fishing boat was gone, bouncing in the wake.

Henry shook his fist forward. 'The look-out's asleep – by God, I'll kill him!'

'Not his fault, lad, the fisherman had no light,' Sam reminded him. 'Look, Dungeness is on the bow. We'll signal a pilot.'

'Will Screech Gander take a pilot?'

'He's a damned fool if he doesn't, and so are you. These are tricky waters. The tides push and pull you all ways. You've got the Goodwins to think of, and the channels in the estuary are a real mystery.'

'All right, Sam, we'll take a pilot – but we're not going to stop and wait.'

A wedge of shingle jutting into the sea with a lighthouse at its tip, Dungeness was the gateway to the Dover straits. The cutters normally found cruising in its lee competed for the business offered by inbound ships. Tonight a flare lit on the poop to attract the attention of the pilot cutters cast a ghostly light over the deck and the wafting sails, and left fiery images in the backs of the eyes, but prompted no answering signal. Henry saw no similar signal from the *Musket*, assuming she was near enough for it to have been seen. 'We're standing on, pilot or no pilot.'

Sam was long past arguing. 'I thought as much,' he sighed.

'Mr Lamshire,' Henry called. 'You can give all hands a tot to warm their blood. Whether we beat the Yankee home or not, I'm proud of 'em.'

The men raised a thin cheer and clustered round the mate to collect their nips of rum. Henry beat his usual track up and down the windward side of the poop and prayed for daylight to hasten. So much would rest on the next few hours but the waiting was torture. Six bells were sounded. Three more hours to daylight.

Sam Handyside sprawled with aching limbs on the skylight seat but he could not bear to go below. Dully his eye followed the young captain. Henry's hair streamed in the gentle breeze, his shirt collar flapped against his neck, his jacket open at the front. He was tense, certainly, but there was no comparison between the mature shipmaster Sam saw before him now and the unconfident young colonial he had greeted in mid-ocean a year ago. They had had their differences, God knows, but Sam was unstinting in his admiration.

In New York the lad had collected a crew when all the cards were stacked against him, and made up for his embarrassing episode there with a neat bit of roguery in 'Frisco. In China he had been quick enough to grab half a chance, though Sam continued to suffer pangs of numbness from his uncomfortable stint in the Foo-chow cell. Then Henry had driven his ship home in a way that Sam had never imagined was possible. 'It's been a good voyage all round, lad,' Sam called out. 'Your reputation's made, as long as you keep off the mud between here and Blackwall.'

'Ha, I wish I had your confidence,' Henry said. 'Who's to say we won't get up to Blackwall and find old John Tidewater and the rest laughing themselves to death in the Artichoke?'

Dawn on the sixteenth of September, 1853, found the

British clipper *Quiver* one hundred days out from China and standing in towards the little harbour town of Folkestone which lay three miles ahead, fine on the port bow.

And the Yankee clipper *Musket* lay fine on the starboard bow, one mile ahead.

The wind had backed round to the north-west during the night but there was hardly enough to fill the sails. It was the tide rather than the breeze that bore both ships steadily towards the bulwark cliffs of Dover. In the grey dawn the cliffs looked no whiter than when Henry had seen them for the first time, nearly a year before. Now he paced the deck in an agony of dejection. From the first moment when the paling sky revealed the outline of a lofty ship well ahead there had been a painful silence all round him. How the Yankee had crept ahead during the night he did not know. It must have been some trick of the tide further out, or one last puff of breeze could have done it.

Sam worked out his frustration by ranting at the lack of wind. He eyed the feathery clouds high in the sky. 'We're in for a nose-ender before long, I can feel it in my water . . .'

He was interrupted by an excited report from Martin Peake. 'Steam-kettle rounding the corner from Dover, Cap'n, looks like a tug.'

'The *Musket* will scoop him up,' Henry asserted gloomily. 'Screech Gander won't be inclined to haggle towage rates, not today.'

'Don't bank on it, Cap'n,' the young mate said after a while. 'The tug is shaping for us, not the Yankee.'

Henry snatched the glass. It was true. The tug presented the head-on profile of a bulldog: her sponsons like flopped-over ears and her stubby black nose set in a snarl of white. A mile astern of her a second tug was sheering off towards the other ship. 'Flake out the best towing hawser, Mr Lamshire,' Henry ordered. 'I fancy we'll be needing it inside ten minutes.'

The tug *Vesuvius* was all bulldog from stem to stern. As she rounded alongside, the tugmaster waved his gold-badged cap and shouted, 'Heave over your messenger, Cap'n!'

Henry was puzzled. He needed a tow as badly as he needed water to float in, but would not fall into the old trap of passing his warp to a stranger without fixing a price. 'What are you asking, Mister?' he growled.

It was not the tug master who answered but Monkton Winkworth. Wrapped in a blanket and wearing a tall silk hat, the lord and master of the Arrow Line came suddenly into view as Skitter pushed his wheelchair out on the tug's spray-wetted foredeck. 'The price is agreed, Captain Ardent,' he piped in a reedy voice. 'You're wasting time and we have none to spare.' The old man removed a gloved hand from beneath the blanket he clutched at his throat and clenched it angrily. 'Why don't you get on with it, are you asleep?'

Charlie Meadows coiled the light heaving line expertly, swung the monkey knot until it hummed, then let it fall neatly across the tug's stern where three hands grabbed it and began to haul. The heavy warp came aboard and was looped over the iron hook. A jet of black smoke spurted from the twin funnels, then a swirl of white from the paddles. The warp lifted as the strain came on and the clipper fell obediently into line astern.

'Let fly and furl, Mr Lamshire!' Henry ordered. 'You can put the canvas to bed.'

'Send down from aloft, Captain?'

The mate waited while Henry tugged at his scarred ear. To lower the sails and running gear from aloft while under tow would save a lot of time later, and please the owner who would otherwise have to employ a special gang of men to do it while the vessel was unloading. But some instinct made him pause. He shook his head firmly. The *Quiver* would stay in sea-going trim until she nudged the quay.

Henry knuckled the weariness from his eyes and gazed unhappily at the town of Dover nestling beneath the cliffs. For nearly twelve months he had lived for this day when the *Quiver* should lead the *Musket* up the Thames River to London. Instead, the positions were reversed. The tugs appeared to be evenly matched. He did not doubt that in each one the boiler safety valves were firmly jammed shut, and if it was mechanically or humanly possible for the *Vesuvius* to steam faster, old Monkey Winkworth would be certain to arrange it.

'One hundred days, it's a creditable passage under any flag,' Sam observed.

'Not really,' Henry replied gloomily. 'Last voyage, Screech Gander came home in ninety-eight days, remember?'

'But that was from Whampoa, five hundred miles up-wind of Foo-chow.'

'What does that prove?'

'Only that a British clipper is at least as good as any Yankee.'

Henry turned away to hide the depth of his bitter disappointment. 'No, not as good – not quite.'

The South Foreland slipped close along the beam. The convoy of tugs and wing-furled clippers filtered through the crowded Downs. Sunshine slashed through the skim of cloud, flooding over the town of Deal with its stone-walled castle and shingle beach cluttered with longshoremen's boats and watch towers. On the other beam, the sun dried the brown sands of the Goodwins, uncovered by the ebb. A gust of wind brought a slap and rattle of gear aloft, like the sound of applause. Sam cast an eye at the sky, now as clear as a bottle. 'Told you we'd get a nose-ender.'

'We won't be the only ship headed,' Will Lamshire pointed out.

'And when we get round the corner it will be a tail-ender,' Martin Peake added.

Henry frowned at Sam. 'Can you guarantee it?' he asked. Sam glanced at the sky again, and the ruffles on the brilliant green water, then he nodded.

As the wind piped up the tugs began to fling gobs of spray over their bows. The ship didn't like dead-pegging on the end of a warp. Her furled sails tried to break away, loose corners of canvas fluttering like wild birds behind a glass pane. The yellow cliffs of Pegwell Bay slipped under the lee, then the spires and slate roofs of Ramsgate and Broadstairs. Henry's excitement grew with the temper of the wind. Oblivious of the spray speckling the air and the sharp movement of the deck, he fixed the *Musket* in his glass. Screech Gander was just near enough to be distinguished, his hair and buck-skin tassles streaming. The crew of the black clipper were aloft, unbending forecourse and maincourse from the yards and sending them down to make ready for the stevedores who would lift from her holds the tea all England was thirsty for.

Sam saw the tension in Henry's stiff figure and heard his tuneless whistle. The lad was up to something. What madness this time?

Henry dropped the glass into its rack. The low bulwark of the North Foreland, the corner of Kent, crept slowly along the port rail until the squat granite tower of its lighthouse was abeam. The tug began slowly to edge to the west, crabbing into the estuary of the Thames. Taking the short, steep seas broad on the bow she rolled as much as she pitched, showing the whirling red blades of her paddles. The wind snatching vigorously at her rigging, the clipper skewed sharply out of her wake.

His heart pounding like the tug's piston, Henry made his decision. He summoned the mates to the poop. 'This is a nor-easter getting stoked up and it will blow straight up the river,' he told them. 'What speed will we make with a strong breeze on the stern and no swell, no sea? Four knots under bare poles, easily. We'll have a job holding her back because the tug's not doing four. But if we hoist some sail, everything we've got . . .'

Will Lamshire caught his drift immediately. 'What about the warp?'

'Chop it.'

'We can't sail up the river, we don't have a pilot,' Sam expostulated.

'That's where you're wrong,' Henry said, tapping Sam firmly in the chest. 'We've got one of the best. No, there's no time for argument. Station your men. Wait for the bell then move like lightning. I want all plain sail full and drawing in one strike – like a broadside!'

As the grinning mates turned to go for'ard, Henry added, 'If we do it right we'll be up and over the *Musket*'s taffrail before Screech Gander has time to clench his arse.'

The broad expanse of the Thames Estuary opened out to the west. Its murky grey water, speckled with white horses, was busy with all kinds of craft. Oyster smacks dredged off Whitstable. Well smacks hastened up to Barking Creek with live cod swilling in their holds. Collier brigs with coal from Newcastle and Durham spilled wind so as not to arrive too early in the river. Steamers flinging sheets of spray over themselves plugged out for the ports of near Europe. Marmalade boats stirred their noisome cargo as they beat out on the ebb to feed London sewage to the fishes. The horizon was dotted with the black and brown sails of spritsail barges carrying all kinds of cargo from the shires up to the capital: bricks, hay, timber, potatoes, corn, clay and straw. Henry took it all in at a glance.

The *Musket* was a good mile in front. A mile was not much after sailing 16,140 miles from the mouth of the Min River on the China coast. But it was a dismally long way when both ships were charging pell-mell into a constricting channel with only fifty miles to run.

Henry reached inside his shirt and touched the greenstone *tiki*. Then he filled his lungs and beat the bell half to death. 'Hoist and let fall, smartly now!'

With a cheer like a battle cry men swarmed out on the yards to let go the gaskets. Others leapt for the falls of the halyards. Thick rolls of canvas dropped from the spars. The yards ran up on the lifts. Jibs and staysails chased each other up the stays. The sudden resistance of an acre of canvas thundering wildly in the wind caused the ship to lurch. The men ran to the braces. The shuddering yards were hauled round. Sheets and down-hauls tamed the chaos, settling the canvas into harness.

The thundering gave way to a tensely fluting hum. The *Quiver* dipped her lee scuppers and accelerated. As she drew level, the floundering tug came in deadly peril. The towing warp, curving between the two vessels like the blade of a giant sickle, threatened to swing the tug by the stern and drag her under. The astounded tug-master saw an axe flash on the clipper's fo'c's'le head. A moment later the warp dropped dead in the water, cut through.

Sheltering behind a tarpaulin with his wheelchair lashed to a stanchion, Monkton Winkworth heard the tug-master's cry and looked up to see sail flowering from every yard of his beautiful ship. She gathered speed with every dip of her bows. What was the young fool of a captain doing? He had no pilot. There was no tug to meet him up-river. The tide was ebbing, pouring out of the Thames.

Miserably bedraggled and wet, the shipowner shook off his coverings and Skitter rushed to prop him up as he stood erect on spindly legs. Winkworth punched the air with a little fist, his face alight. 'Bravo!' he gasped into the wind. 'Crack on, boy, crack on!'

Mariners of the river clung to their violently pitching decks and stared in awe and wonder at the two ocean greyhounds speeding up the channel. Bargees, oystermen, colliermen, lightermen, cabin boys and certified masters in steam, they watched the clippers howling up the river estuary – knot for knot, spar for spar – and knew they were witnessing a spectacle they would describe to their grandchildren.

There was mystery, too, for the two magnificent ships were racing headlong into a river that was rapidly emptying. Obviously they would have to anchor and wait at Gravesend, but if that was the case, why were the lunatic captains engaged in this desperate duel?

Henry Ardent was stiff with disappointment. He had hoped to surprise Screech Gander before the *Musket* could crowd on

sail but he had failed by no more than half a minute. The
Yankee's crew had needed no bucko hazing to drive them out
on the yards, no rope starters, whips or pistol shots to make
them work. Caught up in the excitement of the race, they
slaved like demons. Snowy canvas was spread to the wind. The
towing warp was cut. The *Musket* sprang ahead with the
Quiver storming to within two lengths of her starboard quarter.

'Can't we cut some corners through these channels, Sam?'
Henry demanded.

'Don't bother me with fancy schemes, it will be a miracle
enough if we don't run up on the mud as it is,' Sam said. He
was systematically plotting the ship's position on the chart,
taking bearings on suitable church spires and navigation
marks when they presented themselves. But the mathematics
were irrefutable. The ebb running at a couple of knots would
slow both ships a little but if the wind held, and they kept up
this mad rate of progress, they would sail into Blackwall Reach
two hours before the lock gates opened. How would it all end?

Port and starboard anchors were cock-billed from the bow
and chain was flaked out on deck ready for instant release.
Meadows and Field squatted on the rusty chain-links, staring
at the dainty elliptical stern of the ship ahead. 'Ain't yer got a
cannon in yer pocket, Oatsy, we could ding the bugger a nice
'un from 'ere?'

'Nah, if I 'ad a Chink stinkpot I'd chuck it.'

'Well 'e did orl right, the ol' man, whatever you say.'

'Wot's it gonna be ternight, meat pie and onion gravy dahn
Lime'ouse?'

'This rate, the ol' man's gonna sail right up Commercial
Road.'

The bullet made a faint whirring sound and pinged off a
yard. Meadows swore and threw himself flat, pulling Field
down on the deck. An instant later came the distant report of a
revolver. 'Tryin' to plug a shroud, the bastard,' Meadows
growled as he peered cautiously over the bow.

The dog springing and leaping excitedly at his side, Screech
Gander emptied his revolver at the *Quiver* but scored no lucky
hit. With an overarm throw, he hurled the gun at the British
ship but it splashed into the water in front of her bow.
Nightingale cowered, shivering, as Gander kicked him.

The sun broke out and the murky water became a milky
green flecked with white feathers, like a seascape painted by a
Dutch old master. The wind-punched curves of canvas

gleamed like porcelain. For the ocean-weary men in both ships it was strange to sail so fast in smooth water; the fussy breaking waves that gave small craft a rough time of it had no effect on the large vessels. They cut through the water as smoothly as carriages on rails, rolling a little but with none of the violent jolts and surges that had been part of their lives for one hundred days.

Calmly, firmly, Henry passed a stream of orders to the men waiting alertly in the waist. 'Check the sheet of your outer jib, Mr Peake, only an inch or two . . .'

'Move the men to windward, Mr Lamshire, every little helps . . .'

'See if you can't sweat some flat into the fore-topgallant, she's losing wind under the leeward clew . . .'

'Give the spanker some sheet there . . .'

'Steer small, damn you, she's jacketing all over the river . . .'

Imperceptibly the shore on both sides converged, vague grey lines resolving into mudflats, twisting creeks, fields of marshy sedgegrass, flocks of swooping estuary birds. Imperceptively the *Quiver* stole up on the *Musket*. As the windward vessel she carried a cleaner wind and in these waters her finer lines were a small advantage, but Henry knew it was unlikely he would be able to overhaul the other ship even if he stole the Yankee's wind. Whatever the risk, Screech Gander would baulk him.

After midday the stream of ships and small craft spilling down the river on the last of the ebb began to tail away. The second phase in the daily life of the great waterway began to assert itself. The barges and coasting vessels which had anchored to ride out the ebb, and await the inward flow of the tide, now began to get under way. In a mass they winched up their anchors, hoisted sail and crabbed out into the channel.

Sam glared at the glimmering mud less than a mile away on either beam and threw his pencil and chart down the companion-way. 'What's the use, we're all mad. Keep her in the middle until you get there, lad, that's the best I can tell you. And remember, it's deeper on the outside of the bends but the current will tend to throw you into the far bank.'

'How much water?' Henry asked.

Sam lifted his shoulders in a resigned shrug. 'Plenty in the middle and dry at the edges, what else do you want to know?'

Henry bit his lip and stared ahead. A procession of sails varying in hue from red to black signposted the curve of the river. Four miles beyond, a forest of tall masts and spars lifting over the marshy riverbank indicated Gravesend. Henry remembered how busy the tideway had been when he came through in the *Partridge* and Monkey Winkworth had been swung aboard in his wheelchair. Henry had no steam tug to take his hawser now, no Mr Brown to relieve him of the responsibility of conning the ship through the traffic and the shoals to reach the docks. Henry wondered what the taciturn mud pilot would have thought of this tearing up the reach under full sail.

Henry snatched a glance aft but there was no sign of the *Vesuvius*, she had been left far astern. Screech Gander was looking over his shoulder, too. From his station on the *Musket*'s poop it must seem the jibboom spearing sixty feet ahead of the *Quiver*'s bow would at any moment burst through his spanker and wipe his mizzen over the side.

In the course of a couple of miles the river swung south, turning through ninety degrees. Then it headed west again, turning more tightly, and narrowed through Gravesend. Conning every inch of the way, signalling Lamshire and his men at the braces with one hand, the helmsman with the other, Henry conducted his ship around the bend. The yards wore round as the *Quiver* gradually altered her course, following the trend in the river. A length ahead, the *Musket* did the same but the *Quiver* trapped her wind. Neck and neck, hardly a ship's length apart, the two ships charged on.

At Gravesend there was astonishment and consternation as the two clippers tore full-tilt around the bend. With the inside station as they turned their bowsprits westward, the snowy-canvassed black ship edged half a length in front and with a clean wind once more held her lead.

The sight was unexpected, frightening and magnificent. Lightermen, who would not get out of the way of a tidal wave if their dignity were at stake, threw knotted muscles behind their sweeps and manoeuvred as best they could to clear the fairway. A barque moving into the channel in tow of a tug managed to swing away. On the ships moored at buoys in the reach crews raced into the rigging to catch a view of the clippers racing by. Little boats scattered like flying fish from the cutting stems of the two ships. Passengers on the steamer piers shouted and pointed in surprise, their cries taken up along the shore. Shoppers and businessmen and cabbies and drinkers and thieves all came running. Though word of the homecoming tea-racers had been on everyone's lips since the night before, none had bargained for thrills on such a scale.

Henry saw it all from the corner of his eye and absorbed the yells and cheers to remember later on. His whole attention was concentrated on steering through the maze. The *Quiver* handled like a dream. A spoke of the helm this way, a spoke that way, she responded immediately to the lightest touch of her rudder.

He knew it was madness, this glorious dash up the river under full sail, but his mind was no more concerned with prudent seamanship than it was with getting a good price for Fowqua's tea. All that was another world. Henry was locked in a battle of wills with an enemy he scorned, despised, and with a little part of him which he dared not admit, respected. Henry was hunting Screech Gander with the same ferocious determination and physical strength with which he had chased him through the rigging. Too bad if they arrived early for the lock gates. Too bad if there were no tugs standing by. These problems were a hundred years in the future.

The Yankee ship surging just off the *Quiver*'s starboard bow blocked the view ahead, making it hard for Henry to anticipate the *Musket*'s intentions. He saw Screech Gander take the wheel into his own hands, Smoke Lapierre with a speaking trumpet. Nightingale stood his front paws on the rail and barked while Meadows and Field, out on the bowsprit, fired potatoes at Yankee's poop.

'I'm going aloft, Sam, stand by the wheel,' Henry said, and ran for'ard. Moments later he threw a leg over the fore-topsail yard and was momentarily surprised to find a familiar face grinning at him across a hundred feet of open space. It was the seasick farm boy, Tom, sitting casually astride the *Musket*'s mizzen royal yard.

From this lofty perch eighty feet above the deck, Henry saw the river stretching ahead like a muddy road. It made two sharp turns before running straight towards the smokes of London, first to the left then to the right. Lamshire and his team trimmed the braces as the ship charged up the mile-long reach. To Henry, sitting on the yard, it seemed he remained at the same angle athwart the wind while the entire ship twisted beneath him.

As the zig-zag bends approached Henry saw it was going to be tight, requiring some precise manoeuvring. A pair of paddlers with high funnels and chequer-board stripes along their low topsides raced into view. Their decks were crowded with sightseers who had queued most of the night to meet the clippers down the estuary. Suddenly they were here, head on. The steamers split away to either bank. The racing tea clippers cut between them to a storm of cheering and waving hats. With much backing and filling and clouds of smoke, the steamers turned in the river and set off in pursuit but even with full heads of steam they could not catch up.

The first sharp bend came up with breathtaking suddenness. The *Quiver* was on the inside of the curve. The *Musket* turned early, trying to crowd her into shallow water, but she would lose her wind completely if Screech Gander came close enough to be blanketed. If this happened, it might give the *Quiver* the chance to surge past.

Sam and the helmsmen were obscured by the sails. Henry passed his orders with furious hand signals and shouts to Martin Peake who relayed them aft. Over the mudbanks inside the turn Henry saw a large tanned sail. It was a spritsail barge, a long and slender vessel with water bubbling around her snub nose and the deck piled to a height of twelve feet with hay for London's horses.

On top of this sailing haystack, his legs planted firmly apart and his bowler pulled hard down over his ears, the master stared resolutely forward and gave steering orders to the boy who could see nothing but a wall of hay as he heaved at the heavy tiller. The barge hogged the dead centre of the channel, her man and boy blissfully unaware of the two mighty vessels powering up their wake.

'Spring the royals, Mr Peake, and stand by on sheets!' Henry shouted. Above his head the fore-royal thudded heavily as men on deck jumped to let go the sheets and spill wind.

On the *Musket*'s poop, Screech Gander waved his fist at the obstructing barge and did a dance of fury on the deck. The barge came out of the crook of the bend two hundred feet ahead of the Yankee's jibboom. Her master on top of the haystack extended an arm ahead. The boy pulled with all his might on the carved beam of a tiller and the barge began to straighten up. Only then did the bargee notice from the corner of his eye that something unusual was coming out of the bend behind him.

Henry saw his jaw drop. The man visibly staggered as if his foot had found a hole in the hay. He waved an arm and shouted frantically at his boy who swung the tiller to leeward.

314

Then he changed his mind, pointed his other arm, and the boy dragged the helm down.

The disaster unfolded at Henry's feet.

As the barge began to move to the left bank Screech Gander shifted his helm to pass outside it while Smoke Lapierre screamed orders through the brass trumpet, bracing the yards round in anticipation of the new course.

Then the barge wove across the *Musket*'s path. Gander's curse fell back in his wake as he reversed his helm.

The *Musket* yawed wildly and the *Quiver* ran up on her.

'Put your helm up, go to port!' Henry yelled in desperation. His instruction was intercepted by the second mate but Sam, on the poop, had needed no telling. There was no time to speak. He shouldered the helmsman aside and put the wheel over with his own hands. The ship heeled sharply as her rudder bit. She swung inside the *Musket* which bore up sharply while her yards were being braced the wrong way. She stalled, every sail a-shiver.

Henry and Sam simultaneously cried 'Let fly all!' As the belaying pins were pulled to let the sheets run out, Henry slid down a halyard so fast he hit the deck with seared palms. He did not notice the pain. The black bow was swinging into the stern. The two ships were nearly parallel so the blow was a glancing one, a jarring thud just aft of the mizzen shrouds which shook both vessels from end to end. But that was not the worst of it. The great fluke of the *Musket*'s anchor catted over her bow hooked into the *Quiver*'s rail. The stanchions ripped out by the roots. Timber splintered in a series of frightening bangs and tortured squeals. The ironwork twisted as if it were string.

For an instant Sam stood in deadly peril. The clew of the *Musket*'s forecourse trailed its sheet over the *Quiver*'s poop. It was around Sam's knees before he knew it, dragging him towards the gaping hole in the bulwarks where the anchor momentarily locked the two ships together.

It was Big Tree who saved him. The Maori threw himself along the deck and heaved the encircling rope over Sam's bulky shoulders. Nightingale, half over the rail and barking with his paws on the stock of the anchor, saw the big brown man spring towards him as if mounting a single-handed attack on the *Musket*. Teeth bared in a furious snarl, the dog launched himself across the narrow gap between the two ships. The sun gleamed briefly on the broad flank of the greenstone

patu as Big Tree brought it down hard on Nightingale's head.
The dog jerked backwards and yelped as the club missed its
aim and glanced off his skull. Big Tree lashed out with a heavy
foot, caught the dog full in the chest, and pushed him overboard through the splintered hole in the bulwarks.

The strain of the *Quiver*'s momentum dragging the *Musket*
along was too much for the anchor tackle which parted. The
huge iron anchor plummeted into the river on top of the dog,
dragging fathom after fathom of chain with it.

The *Musket*'s jibboom raked the after end of the *Quiver*'s
poop as she twisted clear. There was an ominous crash aloft.
The spanker gaff, ripped from the gooseneck, drooped like a
broken wing. The mainbraces were snagged but slithered
clear. As a last insult, the tip of the jibboom tangled the flag
halyards and the Red Ensign was carried away, trailing upside
down beneath the Yankee's bowsprit.

As Henry reached the poop Sam put the helm over. The ship
still carried momentum enough to straighten up. The wind in
the shaking and thundering sails was sufficient to drive her
hard ahead. Henry sent the men racing aloft to stow everything
but the topsails.

Close astern, he saw the *Musket* gripe into the wind as the
heavy anchor and chain dragged in the mud of the river bed. In
the far distance the steamers filled with sightseers tore round
the bend just in time to see her golden foremast fold in the
middle. The fore-topmast tilted outboard at a crazy angle then
crashed over her rail. It was not every day you saw a full-rigged
sailing ship dismasted in the Thames.

As the *Quiver* slipped swiftly up the river on the tide it
seemed to Henry that the wild beating of his heart had hardly
begun to settle before the Royal Navy arsenal at Woolwich
was on his port hand and Blackwall Reach opened up ahead.
From every craft on the river and along the shore men gaped at
the spectacle of a full-rigged ship sailing blithely up the river.
And when they saw what ship it was they threw their hats in
the air. Steamers hooted. A frigate at a buoy gave her three
cheers. Even the Dutch galiots and eel-boats waved, as did
the timber-droghers in from Quebec, the billiboys down from
the Goole and the mudlarks fossicking for treasures in the
mud.

The monkey's clipper was in with the tea, ahead of the
Yankee. But Henry knew the race was not yet won. The winner
was the ship that unloaded fifty chests of tea at the West India

Dock, and it would be two hours yet before the tide was high enough for the Blackwall Basin to open up.

Intently Henry gazed up the river, gauging distances. He made out the knuckle at the entrance to the lock, and the blue flag hoisted to indicate the tide was on the flood. Nearby was the white façade of the Artichoke. The old salts lifting their elbows behind its windows would see something today, Henry thought wryly.

With the tide under her keel the ship seemed unstoppable. The jetties and warehouses along both banks moved by at an alarming rate and there was not a tug in sight. The mates and crew watched their captain anxiously then he rattled out a string of orders. 'Ease sheets, lower and furl topsails, smartly does it! Lower the jibs! Stand by the anchor!'

Way came off the ship as the sails were taken in leaving her yards bare, but she still seemed to hurtle along at a frightening speed. Henry dropped his arm. On the fo'c's'le head Will Lamshire tugged the lanyard. The anchor dropped, raising a cloud of rust as the chain snaked through the hawsehole. At the same moment the helm went over and the *Quiver* shivered protestingly. The anchor dredged through the mud and dragged her head round. With no sails drawing she suffered no damage and in a few minutes was riding quietly in the fairway, her bows pointing the way she had come. It was unbelievable. Damaged but undaunted, the *Quiver* lay at anchor in Blackwall Reach. But still the outcome of the race was wide open.

'Run up another ensign, Mr Lamshire,' Henry ordered, and clapped his eye to the glass. There was no sign of a tug upstream but three or four were apparently stuck in the lock for he could see jets of smoke and steam rising from their funnels. Downstream he saw the three yellow masts, one of them broken, jutting above a smudge of smoke. The *Musket* had untangled her mess and found a tug. She was still a couple of miles down the reach but advancing steadily. Something else caught Henry's eye. The fool of a bargee whose sailing haystack had caused all the trouble was bowling up the river as determined as before to hog the middle.

Had he not noticed the *Quiver* anchored in the fairway, her bowsprit cocked straight at him like a lance waiting to spear a hole in his stiff brown sail?

Henry focussed on the figure of the bargee who stood on top of his hay with the nonchalance of a peasant farmer on a donkey cart. The barge was coming on strongly, her cap full of wind. The man must be blind.

Then he saw the bargee stoop. A puff of smoke spurted from between his hands and was torn away in the wind. The man disappeared from sight, climbing down the back of the hay-pile. Streaming smoke, the barge drove straight at the *Quiver*.

'Sam! Will! Jesus Christ . . . !' Henry rang the bell and spouted orders thick and fast. 'Hard over the helm . . . ! Slack away the chain . . . ! Hoist a jib . . . !

The mates looked at their captain as if all the strain had finally proved too much and he had lost his marbles. Then they saw the haystack, well alight with the breeze behind it, intent on impaling itself on the *Quiver*'s bow.

Henry vaulted the rail and sprinted for'ard. Flames a fathom high were leaping from the hay. A plume of acrid smoke rolling ahead on the wind enveloped the anchored clipper. Standing horrified in the eyes of his ship, Henry saw the sturdy bluff bows of the barge appear in the smoke and felt on his face the heat of the crackling flames. But the aim was so good that the barge struck the anchor chain which deflected her. In the same moment the ship's own rudder went hard over and the current canted her across the river.

Henry slashed his knife through the stoppers on the anchor cable and Meadows and Field jumped to assist. The chain began to run out, letting the bows fall away. 'Outer jib, hoist away!' Henry rapped. Mercifully the outer jib had not been stowed so no one had to venture into the flames now leaping high around the bowsprit to cut the gaskets. The sail climbed rapidly out of the flames and smoke and snapped full of wind, helping to push the bows round faster. The chain spewed out of the hawsepipe. Meadows threw himself down the hatch to the chain locker. Protecting his head with his arms as the chain flogged from side to side, he loosened the shackle at the bitter end before strain came on it. The chain ran out and the end plunked over the side leaving a shrieking silence.

The *Quiver* was athwart the stream, smoke and flame boiling away on the beam but clearing from her deck. Smuts of burning hay floated in the air and caught in the men's clothes. The barge broke away from beneath the bowsprit, leaving paint well alight around the clipper's bows.

Blinking his stinging eyes, Henry glimpsed a small boat sculling furiously for the shore. He would recognise that rat-faced figure anywhere. Smoke Lapierre had hijacked the barge and driven it up on the *Quiver*. Now he was making his escape.

'Starboard anchor, let go!' Henry yelled. The second anchor dropped over the side but fell only a few feet before the run of the chain was checked. In the same moment there was a shiver underfoot. Henry stared around and was amazed to see how far the ship had drifted in what had seemed such a short interval. She had been carried almost to the lock gates and was close to the north bank, directly beneath the windows of the Artichoke where she ran gently but firmly aground.

A crowd fought for space on the wall. Never had such drama been seen at Blackwall since the last pirates were hanged, but that was a grandfather's memory. The beautiful green clipper that had been the talk of London for so long now lay less than a ship's length off the bank, her bows smoking as seamen beat at the burning paint with their shirts. Her topsides were splintered along her starboard quarter. A chunk of bulwarks was missing. Her spanker gaff drooped limply. The young captain was seen running aft, his weather-tanned face black with soot and his tousled blond hair thick with ashes.

Henry knew the ship was in no danger. The anchor was holding and the flood tide would simply bump her higher and higher up the steep muddy slope until she touched the wall. But the *Musket* was coming on, too fast for comfort.

There was a clatter of hooves and wheels ashore. Angry shouts cleared the way. Henry heard, 'Ho there, *Quiver*! What in God's name are you waiting for?'

It was George Chamberlayne, his grizzled face a beacon of excitement as he jumped from his coach while it was still moving, waving with one hand and elbowing the crowd back with the other. 'Send over a rope!' he bawled as soon as he had the *Quiver*'s attention. 'Fifty chests is all we need, don't stand there gawping!'

The distance between the ship and the wall was less than a hundred feet, for the glistening mudbanks sloping between the bottom of the slime-covered wall and the water's edge were narrow and steep. But it was just too far to throw a rope. Charlie Meadows took the heaving line to the top of the mainyard and flung it with all his might but it fell short by twenty feet. They would have to wait until the tide came in some more.

At last a tug came down river and swung alongside but Henry waved it off. It was too small to help, and in lining up for the lock gates when they opened it would be too easy for the *Musket* to nip in front.

Henry glared at the ooze. Gingery brown, streaked with blue and black, it promised to be bottomless and stank worse than the Pearl River. No man could walk on it: the mud would swallow him to the neck.

Martin Peake touched Henry's arm. 'There is one thing we could try,' he said.

Neptunia's frightened pink eyes rolled horribly as she was dragged along the deck on a halter. Instead of a long blade slicing into her throat, as she might have expected, a light cord was tied to her back leg. She was unceremoniously hoisted into the air and dumped over the side.

The sightseers cheered and laughed as the pink pig struck out for the shore but Chamberlayne flailed his arms for silence. 'Shhh, don't frighten her!' He gave swift orders to the young man who had come with him. The assistant disappeared at the run.

Neptunia's toes sank into the mud and she rested. On shore and on board there were groans of dismay. Gazing pleadingly at the people lining the wall, the pig made an effort to sledge her plump body through the mud but gave up with a sigh. There was a splash as Big Tree lowered himself into the water on a rope and with a knife in his teeth paddled up behind the pig. Lying flat in the water he reached out with the knife and prodded Neptunia in the backside. She responded with a squeal and drove forward. Spreadeagled, Big Tree slithered across the mud and prodded her again, his tattooed cheeks becoming spattered with mud as she scrabbled away from him.

In an agony of frustration Henry glanced down stream. The *Musket* was less than a mile away. The lock master was standing on the dummy looking at the tide which had only half an hour to run before the gates could be opened. Inch by inch, the floundering Maori prodded the pig up to the wall. Chamberlayne offered a silver sixpence to the sport who brought the line ashore. An urchin risked a mud-bath to reach out from the bottom rung of a rickety ladder and grab the line from the pig's leg. In a minute George Chamberlayne had it in his grasp. Spattering his frock coat and eager face with mud, he hauled over a heavier line, then a warp. The assistant arrived with a dozen stevedores. A pair of drays pulled by heavy horses rumbled to the edge of the wall.

Meanwhile the Murphies and Macaroons in the *Quiver* had

knocked the wedges from the tarpaulins and boards covering the main hatch. A rich fragrance of sweet smelling tea rose in the fetid marsh air. The chests were so firmly hammered down it was like trying to lever a cobblestone out of a roadway with bare fingers. Finally Meadows smashed one with a marline spike so it could be levered upwards, then the remainder came loose.

Charlie Field sprang aloft, rove a gant-line from the main-royal-yard and used it to lower himself swiftly down to the deck. Manfred Longhandle spread his hammock out on deck as a sling. Four tea chests were laid upon it. The two ends were lifted and the hammock strings bent to the gant-line. The tail of the gant-line was led through a block on the bulwarks.

'Ready men?' Henry called. 'Walk away now!'

A dozen hands tramped along the deck, hauling the line. The sling rose high in the air, trailing two ropes. One dropped to the deck and the other dipped across to the wall. 'Vast hauling there! Give some slack now. Hand-some-ly!'

As the seamen retraced their steps, keeping tension on the line but lowering it steadily, Chamberlayne's gang of steve-dores hauled it over the gap.

Henry glanced quickly down the river. The *Musket* was close now, her crew piling tea chests along her bulwarks to toss them ashore as she entered the lock.

With a loud 'Hurrah!' from the crowd, the first of the *Quiver*'s cargo dropped none too gently on the cobbles and were humped on to the dray. The next four chests followed in less than a minute. The first dray clattered away with twenty chests.

George Chamberlayne paused in his supervising long enough to clench both hands and raise them above his head in a gesture of joy. The pig was rescued from the shore and Big Tree swam back to the ship, washing the slime off his body. Meadows threw him a rope. 'Come on, yer cannibal, and get a blanket round yer shoulders before you croak.'

Grinning broadly, Sam pumped Henry's hand. The cap-tain's face was splattered with equal quantities of mud, em-bers, salt, weariness, joy and relief.

As the fiftieth chest was swung over the side the tide lifted the ship higher on the mud and she shivered as if she, too, was capable of swelling with pride.

The first of the new season's China teas were landed.